JOHN D. ROCKEFELLER'S

SECRET WEAPON

Books by Albert Z. Carr

JUGGERNAUT: THE PATH OF DICTATORSHIP

MEN OF POWER

AMERICA'S LAST CHANCE

NAPOLEON SPEAKS

TRUMAN, STALIN AND PEACE

THE COMING OF WAR

JOHN D. ROCKEFELLER'S SECRET WEAPON

"We never deceived ourselves"

JOHN D. ROCKEFELLER

NEW YORK   TORONTO   LONDON

JOHN D. ROCKEFELLER'S SECRET WEAPON

By ALBERT Z. CARR

 McGraw-Hill Book Company, Inc.

CONTENTS

FOREWORD   vii

PART ONE: INSTRUMENT OF POWER
(1859–1891)

1. Background for Trouble   3
2. Free-enterprise Heaven   16
3. The Shape of Success   24
4. Challenge to Mortal Combat   37
5. The Geat Tank Car Squeeze   45
6. Nimble on Their Feet   62
7. "Perfectly Truthful"   80

PART TWO: ONE STEP AHEAD OF THE
GOVERNMENT (1892–1911)

1. Old Wine in New Bottles   91
2. Page Stands Fast   106
3. "No Turpitude Whatever"   123
4. Deep Water   139
5. "Well, Gentlemen, Shall We Proceed?"   148

PART THREE: HANDLED WITH CARE (1912–1929)

1. Orphan—With Big Brothers   163
2. The Great Decision   178
3. Executive Suite   192
4. "A Hell of a Lot of Nerve"   202
5. The Old School Tie   211

PART FOUR: THE TWISTING LINE OF FATE (1930–1952)

1. The Art of Cashmanship   227
2. "We Did Not Cut Back"   233
3. The Big Test   240
4. A Reminder from the Government   255
5. With a Little Bit of Luck   263
6. Chemical Reaction   275

PART FIVE: YEARS OF ASTONISHMENT (1953–1961)

1. "The Old Order Changeth . . ."   285
2. Nothing Sacred   295
3. Point of No Return   304
4. No Letup   312

APPENDIX   327

BIBLIOGRAPHY   361

INDEX   369

FOREWORD

Some years ago I became convinced that the inside story of how John D. Rockefeller made a billion dollars had not been fully told, and that even after two generations it was a story of peculiar import for businessmen and for those interested in American history in general. To be sure, most of the ground had already been covered in masterful fashion by Ida Tarbell in her *History of the Standard Oil Company*, and by Allan Nevins in his biography of Rockefeller, *A Study in Power;* and there were other good books on the subject. Nevertheless it seemed to me that the precise means and methods used by Rockefeller in his extraordinary achievement were yet to be described.

It was obvious that to bring this story to fruition as a book information would be needed of a kind not available except in the files of companies founded by Rockefeller and which are very much alive in our time. One of these in particular, the Union Tank Car Company, held the essential facts, for its life story was part and parcel of Rockefeller's success and ran through the colorful decades in which he startled the world. The question arose: could Union and other companies be persuaded to cooperate to the extent of giving me the freedom of their archives?

This question linked itself with another. Was it possible to write the true story of a living corporation without falling into either of the two obvious traps: without protecting or defending on the one hand and without seeking to "expose" on the other? From this line of thought the conception of the present book emerged. It was to describe John D. Rockefeller's adroit manipulation of his "secret weapon," the tank car—the first and crucial element of his ascendancy in the oil industry, and one of which the public was largely unaware. The book would go on to bring the account up to date through the story of the company that Rockefeller established to operate his tank cars. It would report the unvarnished facts and try to understand them. Its spirit would be that not of formal history, but rather of modern biography—stressing the inner life of the company—bringing out its problems and fears, its pressures and tensions, and the psychological effects of big business on the men who run it.

In first discussing the matter with officials of the Union Tank Car Company I put a good deal of emphasis on the informal character of the book—a point which turned out to be of considerable interest for them. As I later discovered, they had already considered the preparation of a history, and had determined that if they ever proceeded in this field, they would aim to interest as well as to record. Consequently they understood my wish to use a broad canvas and the full spectrum of colors, excluding only whitewash. After due reflection, they assured me of all the information I needed to produce a book such as I had described, a book deeply concerned with their company, and the text of which they could not control or alter.* Perhaps they concluded that American corporate enterprise has entered an era of heightened awareness, in which a company gains strength through candor.

During the period in which the book was written developments occurred within the company that could not have been anticipated by anyone outside its top management, and perhaps not even by them. When our talks began early in 1957, Union Tank Car, in terms of gross income, was fairly typical of the 1,500 American corporations whose securities were listed on the New York Stock Exchange. By the time the manuscript was in its later stages the company had lifted itself into the select group of the country's 400 largest concerns. I had thought of the book as a

* The company reserved the right to insert footnotes, questioning or amplifying statements which in its judgment are misleading or inadequate. It has availed itself of this right at several points in the book. Footnotes headed UTC NOTE are of this character. In some instances, I have replied to them.

A.Z.C.

study of an old and quiescent if remarkable business the chief interest of which lay largely in the past. It turned at the end into the story of a renascence. The final chapters had to be written hot on the heels of events of the utmost importance to the company's future.

Cooperation from the company in facilitating research for the book was unstinted. At the direction of its president, every record that I considered relevant was made available for my use. Executives took time to recall for me the precise circumstances surrounding policy decisions and company actions, responding frankly to questioning which in several instances lasted for days at a time. I am especially indebted to Mr. B. Clifford Graves, former president and chairman (retired); to Mr. E. A. Locke, Jr., president; to Mr. J. W. Van Gorkom, executive vice-president; to Mr. W. B. Browder, secretary and general counsel; to Mr. A. E. Gebhardt and Mr. D. C. Graves, vice-presidents; to Mr. Ray M. Smith, former vice-president (retired); to Mr. Clyde Folmsbee, former chief engineer (retired); to Mr. Russell Eustice and Mr. J. W. Garretson, former treasurers (retired); and to Mr. F. Baird-Smith, president of Refiners Transport and Terminal Corporation, a subsidiary of Union Tank Car.

Other companies, too, with which Union Tank Car once had corporate ties generously allowed me access to their archives, notably the Standard Oil Company of New Jersey and the Standard Oil Company of Ohio. The cooperation of the American Petroleum Institute and the Association of American Railroads was also exceedingly useful. Mr. E. N. Goodwin and Mr. A. Turney Savage, of the New York law firm of Goodwin, Danforth, Savage, and Whitehead, provided important information. Mr. Robert E. Wilson, former chairman of the Standard Oil Company of Indiana, and a member of the Atomic Energy Commission, was kind enough to review certain points, as was Mr. R. A. Williams, president of Stanray Corporation. And I cannot speak warmly enough of the librarians at the Widener and Baker libraries of Harvard University, the New York Public Library, and Library of Congress, whose intelligent and willing efforts greatly speeded the exploration of old public documents, newspapers, and books now almost forgotten. In this work I was ably assisted by Mrs. Joan E. Clark, of Wellfleet, Massachusetts.

It hardly needs to be added that responsibility for all statements made in the book is mine alone. Much of the factual material in the earlier part is based on testimony given before investigating groups set up by state and Federal governments between 1874 and 1907.

The absence of documentary footnotes was a deliberate decision on my part to eliminate the typographic clutter which a huge number of references, of little interest to most readers, would otherwise have produced.

Albert Z. Carr

Truro, Massachusetts

PART ONE:

INSTRUMENT OF POWER

1859-1891

"Whether the law [of competition] be benign or not, we must say of it ... it is here; we cannot evade it." ANDREW CARNEGIE

ONE

BACKGROUND FOR TROUBLE

"Great events sometimes take their rise from small circumstances," wrote Benjamin Franklin. It was a small circumstance that in the summer of 1859 a twenty-year-old Cleveland bookkeeper named John D. Rockefeller resigned from his fifty-dollar-a-month job with a firm of commission merchants, and in partnership with another young man founded a similar business. None of the few people who were then aware of Rockefeller's existence could have guessed that his action would vividly color America's future economic history. The crucial fact was that his resignation coincided with another unmistakably important event. From Titusville in northwestern Pennsylvania came proof that much-wanted petroleum could be pumped out of the ground in commercial quantities. The profound influence of chance on individual and corporate destiny is well illustrated by the link between the clerk's decision and the Pennsylvania oil strike.

There is a poignant story by Stephen Vincent Benét, in which he makes the point that if Napoleon Bonaparte had been born twenty years too soon he might have wound up as a frustrated army major on half pay. The possibility that John D. Rockefeller, born a few years too late, might have been merely a successful merchant and produce shipper offers a tempting speculation. But his star was in the ascendant. The capital accumulated in the three years following the establishment of his new enterprise would enable him to go into the blossoming oil industry in 1863, at the precise moment when the opportunity for profit was at its peak. One can understand the feeling behind his famous remark of later years: "God gave me my money."

3

The drilling of the first oil well, a day's journey by train and horse from Cleveland, made the city buzz. During subsequent months newspapers reported that the successful prospector, Edwin L. Drake, was backed by New England financiers; that he had used a salt-mine drilling rig; that scores of such rigs were being ordered by Pennsylvania farmers delirious with anticipation of wealth; that the scene was reminiscent of the California gold rush of ten years earlier. But Rockefeller and his partner, Maurice Clark, were too preoccupied with the cares of their new business to spend much time in envying the lucky well drillers of Pennsylvania. Some who found oil, in fact, were not so lucky; Drake himself drifted into poverty. In any event, reports from the oil regions were soon pushed out of prominence by graver and more dramatic news. In that autumn of 1859, John Brown raided into Kansas and Virginia, President Buchanan made futile efforts to end the African slave trade, Jefferson Davis incited Southern extremists with stirring speeches, and a radical from Illinois, Abe Lincoln, emerged as a possible presidential candidate of the Republican party.

The looming shadow of war made every businessman, North and South, ponder his future. In the North, where most people believed that victory could be quickly achieved, the prospect of war was not generally unwelcome to men who lived by trade. War, after all, meant government orders for arms, munitions, uniforms, foodstuffs, supplies of all kinds; it meant high prices and large profit margins; it would be a useful stimulant to almost every kind of business. Rockefeller and Clark apparently took just such a practical view. Neither had any romantic notions about joining the Army and seeking military glory if war came.

Black Gold?

Rockefeller at that time thought of petroleum primarily as a commodity on which a good profit could be made when he and Clark managed to get hold of a few barrels of it. The stuff was always in demand, selling at prices upward of a dollar a gallon. Prior to 1859 farmers in the oil country, using primitive methods, had skimmed small amounts of oil off the surface of ponds and sold it for use in medicinal preparations or as a lubricant for steam engines. Some even quarried oil shale, out of which petroleum was pressed. The refining industry had also been putting down roots. A Canadian geologist, Abraham Gesner, had shown that crude oil, properly distilled, would yield a thin and nearly colorless substance which he called kerosene, and which was a practical illuminant and fuel. Its possibilities as a substitute for high-priced whale oil and cumbersome coal were obvious, and kerosene lamps and stoves were not long in appearing on the market. Since the distillation and refining process was not complicated and almost any iron foundry could build the necessary equipment for the early refineries, only the shortage of crude oil prevented kerosene from being widely used in the 1850s. Now as the decade ended the oil boom was irresistibly on its way.

Tooth-and-claw competition in the oil fields soon reached a point of frenzy. To men who were gambling for millions with an acre of land and a drilling rig, even the battles of Cold Harbor and Gettysburg seemed pale and unimportant. The demand for petroleum was so great, the price so high, that any man who could bring it in quantity to a refinery was sure of growing rich. Fortunes were made and lost overnight as Pennsylvania farms turned into oil fields and as explosive speculation in the shares of wildcat companies drove men crazy with greed. A farm that sold for $30,000 in 1859—considered a great price—was resold for a million in 1863. The selling price of one piece of pasture jumped from $25,000 to $1,600,000 in three months. Many farms in the oil country were broken up into quarter-acre lots, for which speculators paid $10,000 each. Villages mushroomed into cities as new wells were brought in, and dwindled swiftly into ghost towns when the wells gave out. In May, 1865, the "town" of Pithole consisted of two buildings. Three months later 15,000 people had found shelter there. Hotels and theaters were built, a railroad and pipe line brought in. A few years later the Pithole wells were exhausted, and the town was deserted. A luxury hotel which had cost $65,000 was sold for taxes, and brought $50. But in most places the boom lasted longer. Thousands of would-be millionaires flocked to the regions north of Pittsburgh, to find that every conceivable land claim had been staked out and the only opportunity open to them was as the hired hands of more fortunate men.

To cooler heads it soon became evident that the name of

"black gold" popularly given to Pennsylvania crude oil was highly misleading. In one respect especially—transportation— the problem of the early oil producers differed essentially from that of California's gold miners. Placer gold could be carried in small sacks, and after smelters and railroads were built the movement of gold ore from the mines presented no difficulties. Liquid petroleum was another matter. Its handling posed major technical problems. Producers soon discovered that there was little use in pumping up the inflammable, pervasive stuff unless it could be safely contained and moved. A well owner of the period, writing some years later in a Pennsylvania newspaper, recalled that in the winter of 1861–1862 he was able to market only about half of the oil which he brought out of the ground. The rest was wasted, and "all the tar and naphtha, which are now worth as much as refined oil, was then run into the creek or burned up."

Ways and Means

Most of the early wells lay in a narrow ten-mile strip bordering a twisting stream known as Oil Creek which ran southward from its source in the northwest corner of Pennsylvania to feed into the Allegheny River. It was by means of this uneasy waterway that the first producers started their oil on the way to market. At the point where creek and river met, a boom town sprang up—Oil City—which in 1860 became a major distribution point for petroleum.

The well owners had scows and flatboats towed by horses from the river to loading points on the creek, and since barrels were then scarce in the region, the crude oil for the most part was simply poured "in bulk" into the bottom of the boats. These perilous containers, lying deep in the water under their heavy, sloshing cargoes, were then poled down the narrow creek to nearby Oil City to await barreling for further shipment.

With nothing between the well owners and wealth except transportation, ingenuity in finding ways to speed up the movement of oil was heavily rewarded. When it was found that the water in the creek was often too low for the loaded boats, a scheme to overcome the difficulty was promptly worked out with owners of lumber mills upstream. The mills had built crude dams for their own operations, and by working in tandem could release enough water to create a small artificial flood, a so-called pond freshet, which would float the oil boats and send them on their way to the river. Once the millowners discovered their unexpected power over oil transport, they quickly formed a company to put the system on a sound business basis. At selected times agents of the company would appear at the wells to announce an imminent freshet and to collect a fee from every shipper who expected to make use of the creek as it rose. This toll was based on the capacity of the shipper's boats and usually ranged from two to four cents a barrel, a barrel being taken as equivalent to 45 gallons.

As oil production increased, the company provided two freshets a week, each moving hundreds of boats which among them carried perhaps 30,000 barrels of bulk oil. Packed together in a tight jam and trying to work free into the rising waters, these boats faced formidable hazards of capsizing, wreck, and fire. Since no insurance was available to the shippers, they had to put their trust in the creek pilots, who, if they had good reputations, could command up to two hundred dollars for a trip of a few hours.

But even more troublesome than the low waters of Oil Creek was the serious bottleneck that existed at the Oil City wharves. There the bulk oil had to be pumped from small open boats into barrels before it could be sent on its way in railroad freight cars, or put on coal barges for river travel to Pittsburgh, where several refineries had been built. Among men who had bulk oil on their hands and no place to store it, the demand for barrels was often hysterical. The soaring output of the wells had hopelessly overtaxed lumber mills and cooperage works in the vicinity, so that empty barrels had to be brought at considerable expense from Pittsburgh and other large towns. The wastefulness of this operation was the greater because many of the barrels were damaged in transit and handling, or had been carelessly put together in the first place, or were weakened by exposure to rough weather.

Barreled oil, moreover, was a standing invitation to thieves. It was estimated that 10 per cent or even 20 per cent of oil awaiting shipment at Oil City was lost by theft and leakage. Watchmen assigned to wharves and railroad sidings to guard loaded barrels were frequently overpowered by desperate men bent on getting into the oil business in one way or another.

There was an alternative to barreling at Oil City—to send the creekside scows and flatboats on the hazardous river trip all the way to Pittsburgh, where refineries on the banks of the Allegheny could pump the oil directly into their plants. The refined oil was then barreled and shipped by rail to Philadelphia, New York, or other markets. Although small craft seldom risked the currents of the river and the vagaries of weather all the way to Pittsburgh, a few shippers who had got hold of sizable boats were able to avoid the Oil City bottleneck.

Late in 1861, a Pittsburgh steamboat owner, "Captain" Jacob Jay Vandergrift, was hired to tow barges carrying 4,000 empty barrels to Oil City. In the course of the trip he observed one of the bulk boats being arduously poled down the Allegheny; and he conceived an idea which was to make him rich more quickly than if he had struck oil. He could, he believed, build large barges designed to carry bulk oil efficiently and by towing them with his steamer, the *Red Fox*, greatly accelerate the movement of oil to the Pittsburgh refineries.

A short time later he had a dozen such barges in service, each carrying 400 barrels of bulk oil in tin-lined compartments. The barges were loaded at creekside, floated by pond freshet, poled to the river, tied to the *Red Fox* and towed rapidly to Pittsburgh. Now the tedious and expensive transfer of bulk oil to barrels at Oil City became outmoded, and so did the slow poling of scows down the treacherous river. Since prices offered by refineries for crude oil frequently depended on speed of delivery, the steamboat tow to Pittsburgh, saving precious hours, could make a large difference to a shipper.

Well owners and oil buyers, finding that Captain Vandergrift offered their best hope of profit, competed for his services, and he became almost a feudal overlord of the region, able to exact a toll on a sizable proportion of the petroleum produced. Fortunately for the producers he was not a gouger; but neither was he Santa Claus, whom he somewhat resembled in appearance. When the market price of oil was high, barrels scarce, and shippers desperate, he charged as much as a thousand dollars for towing a single bargeful of "crude" from Oil City to Pittsburgh, a distance of about 130 river miles. It was also easy for him to buy substantial quantities of oil for his own account with assured priority in delivery, and to acquire an interest in refineries dependent on his services. Each trip of the *Red Fox* from Oil City to Pittsburgh, pulling a long string of barges, yielded him a profit greater than any well owner of the time could make on a day's production of oil.

The Railroads Reach for Oil

While Vandergrift coped with river traffic in oil, another serious transportation problem was developing. Wells had been brought in too far from Oil Creek to make bulk shipment by water feasible, and their owners had no recourse but to rely on barrels. These were carried empty from Oil City to the wells by wagon, and after being filled, had to be hoisted again on to the wagons, and hauled by horses back to Oil City, or, in some instances, to the nearest railroad line 40 miles to the north. Often the rickety wagons, each carrying four or five heavy barrels with an aggregate weight of a ton or more, had to be pulled axle deep for miles through the thick muck of the oil field before they could hit a passable road. Exhausted horses, completely denuded of hair by the chemical action of petroleum on their skins, and left to die where they fell, were a familiar sight. The well owner could only hope that his oil would reach Oil City before the wretched animals dropped between the shafts, or the whip-wielding, hard-drinking, swaggering driver got himself pulverized in a fist fight, or decided to steal a few barrels of oil for himself.

By 1862, railroad men, recognizing that fortunes were being made in oil transportation, had moved actively to organize the direct shipment of petroleum from well to freight car. The Atlantic and Great Western road, owned by British capital and reaching from New York to Cleveland, pioneered the way. Its tracks roughly paralleled the southern boundary of New York State, within striking distance of the oil country. A group of Pennsylvania oil men were encouraged to finance and construct a single-track, narrow-gauge line, known as the Oil Creek Railroad, from the heart of the petroleum country to the A&GW tracks.

This undertaking was an immediate and immense success.

The Oil Creek Railroad promptly proceeded to get rid of its waterway competition by buying out the creekside lumber mills and putting an end to the freshet system. With water-borne traffic badly hampered, the producers increasingly turned to the railroad, depending on horses, wagons, and teamsters to reach the nearest depot. Inevitably, the meager facilities of the railroad were soon swamped. Countless barrels of oil stayed for days at a time on sidings along the tracks, while production at the wells had to be shut down. But although producers swore, the little railroad throve. Carrying 30,000 empty barrels a month to the wells and bringing them away full, it paid a 25 per cent dividend to its stockholders in its first year and a 53 per cent dividend in its second.

The big A&GW road likewise profited mightily on its oil freight. Soon its success excited the envy of the notorious Jim Fisk and Jay Gould, who controlled the competing Erie line, running from New York to Erie, Pennsylvania. Since A&GW was then getting more oil freight than it could handle, the Erie management found it easy to make a deal under which the two roads shared the haulage from the oil fields, while keeping freight charges at a very high level. Using their joint capital, they thrust another spur into the oil country, this time a broad-gauge, double-track known as the Oil City line. This carried barreled petroleum to both of the big trunk roads, whose revenues soared as dozens of new refineries sprang up in New York and Cleveland.

Cleveland was turning out to be a major refining center. Its site on Lake Erie, its considerable heavy industry, its expanding population, its rail connections with Chicago, St. Louis, and Cincinnati, and above all its proximity to the Pennsylvania wells, made it the natural oil capital of the Midwest. The increasing amounts of crude oil pouring into the Cleveland refineries and the profits they were making impressed the observant Rockefeller. Whatever money he and Clark could earn on oil as merchants was insignificant as compared with the revenue of even a small refiner. They were accumulating a substantial surplus in their produce business; the only major obstacle standing between them and the building of their own refinery was lack of the requisite technical knowledge. In 1863 another energetic young man, Samuel Andrews, who had technical flair and experience in petroleum distillation, crossed Rockefeller's path. This was the moment of decision. Scraping together their own capital and borrowing from others, they built a modest refinery on a three-acre tract just outside the city. Andrews ran the plant, Clark looked after the buying and some of the selling, and Rockefeller had charge of administration and sales.

Almost from the first the venture was profitable, but Rockefeller now revealed a restless urge to expand that compelled the firm to increase its indebtedness, until in 1865 it owed $100,000. When Clark, a cautious man, became alarmed, Rockefeller unhesitatingly bought him out, meanwhile divesting himself of all connection with the produce business. Thus, as the Civil War came to its end, he found himself in control of a highly profitable refinery in a strategic location. The qualities which were later to make him a living legend of American business—the independence of mind, the need for power, the driving energy, the economy of speech, the austerity of manner, the intense religiosity, the aversion to publicity—were already firmly fixed in his character.

Defenders of the Barrel

His experience as a produce shipper had sensitized young Rockefeller to problems of transportation. He recognized that the use of barrels, while playing into the hands of the railroads, sharply limited the profits of producers and refiners. Barrels were constantly in short supply, high priced, hard to handle, leaky, and easily damaged. He watched eagerly as major technical steps were taken in the Pennsylvania fields to displace the barrel as the standard container for oil. The year 1865 saw the opening, by a producer named Samuel Van Syckel, of the first pipe line. Made of two-inch iron pipe, and running five miles from well to railroad, it functioned successfully. But Van Syckel had not allowed for the reaction of the uninhibited workers of the oil country. The picturesque, highly-paid teamsters who transported barreled oil from well to rail depot realized that their jobs were about to be eliminated by the newfangled pipe line. Night after night gangs of teamsters descended on the line and broke it, and even smashed the pumps at Van Syckel's well, until he despairingly abandoned the project.

Immediately afterward, however, a second line was constructed, capable of carrying more than a thousand barrels a day from its intake at the wells to the railroad loading point. Its owner, Henry Harley, a railroad executive, also built large storage tanks to hold reserve oil near the wells. More resourceful than Van Syckel, he hired Pinkerton detectives to defend his line and protect his life, which had been threatened by disgruntled teamsters. The detectives, posing as teamsters, were able to identify the ringleaders of the attacks on the line. Thereafter court convictions and long jail sentences quickly broke the spirit of the revolt. Four hundred teamsters left the region to find jobs elsewhere, and construction of other pipe lines soon got under way. The new era had arrived.

Less dramatic, but equally as significant as the pipe line, was the construction of a novel kind of railroad car to carry oil. Prior to 1865, with barreled oil exposed on open flatcars for long, jolting journeys, loss due to breakage, leakage, and theft had plagued the shippers. It was not unusual for a typical carload of oil, comprising 55 or 60 barrels, to arrive at its destination with 10 or more barrels half empty. A demand arose for enclosed cars which would provide greater safety, and some old boxcars were finally put into the oil service; but in general the railroads, which provided most of the flatcars, felt that they were doing well as matters stood and saw no reason to sink capital in new equipment.

The New Tyranny

The first attempt to design a car which would carry oil in relative safety and large quantities was an imitation of Vandergrift's bulk boats. A model of an ordinary freight car, its interior fitted with a number of tin-lined compartments, was exhibited in 1863, and for a time was seriously considered by producers and railroads. But while it promised to eliminate leakage, it created other technical problems even more serious, notably in loading and unloading. Two more years passed before a practical oil car appeared. The inventor was a well owner named Amos Densmore, who persuaded the A&GW Railroad to let him use one of their flatcars to try out his idea. Building a pair of large, cylindrical wooden tubs, he mounted them securely to minimize the effects of jolting. The tubs were made of clear pine planking with closely fitted covers, and could carry more oil than the typical flatcar or boxcar. The mere report that such a car was under construction was enough to set the oil men agog, as for the first time they saw a hope of eliminating the heavy cost of barrels and of their handling. The Densmore car also afforded considerable protection against theft and leakage. News of its first trial run in September, 1865, from Oil City to New York, was tensely awaited. As messages were telegraphed to Oil City from stops along the route, triumphantly announcing that the loaded tubs showed no sign of leakage, men cheered in the streets.

From this moment the tank car, as it quickly came to be called, was established as a successful traveling container for oil. Attempts were made to improve on Densmore's model. An enclosed car containing similar tubs was built, and an open car with three tubs, but both were found to be harder to load and unload and less sturdy than the original two-tub flatcar. With some associates Densmore formed a car-building and oil-shipping company which quickly became a major force, for their tank cars gave them important advantages in getting oil to the refineries. A string of Densmore's cars would be run under the outlet nozzle of Harley's pipe line, the tubs would be filled, and the cars would be on their way in a fraction of the time that it took other producers to barrel the oil and load the barrels on flatcars. It transpired, however, that the swift success of Densmore's company was based on more than his economic contribution. He had allowed it to be assumed that the tubs on his cars held about 30 barrels each, so that his loaded tank cars had been shipped at the conventional carload rate for 60-barrel cars. After many months it occurred to the manager of the Oil City Railroad to calculate the capacity of the tubs from their exterior dimensions. Their actual load, he discovered, was 45 barrels per tub. Densmore had been paying freight on 60 barrels per car and shipping 90. It was not surprising that his company rolled up handsome profits.

As dozens, scores, and then hundreds of tank cars were built to Densmore's model, many producers of crude oil who had gleefully turned to the new device gradually discovered that their enthusiasm had in one respect been premature. The shipper had been freed from his old servitude to the barrel, but only to find himself at the mercy of new masters. Use of the tank car required prior use of the pipe line, and once barreling at the well had been given up, oil could not be shipped until the pipe line and tank cars were ready to receive it.

Previously the producer had been compelled to beg coopers to take his orders and teamsters to work for him. But whatever their differences, they, at least, had shared his desire for maximum production at the wells. No such common purpose linked him to the railroads. For them heavy oil production did not necessarily mean higher revenues. On the contrary, it could produce costly irregularities in the demand for cars, locomotives, and yard space. They much preferred a steady, high-level movement of oil from the fields. But production was then in an anarchic state. New wells were being put into operation without regard to existing supply and demand. Old wells were petering out. Alarming excess one week would be followed by shortage the next, with the result that prices fluctuated outrageously, ranging in a few months from a few cents to more than five dollars per barrel. Under these conditions the railroads realized that their profits from oil freight depended less on the producers than on the refineries which bought the oil, established its price, and could regulate the volume of its traffic. A steady and high freight volume in oil could be assured only if the larger refiners consented to spread their purchases of crude to conform to the railroads' needs. In return for consistent, large-volume oil freight the roads were ready to concede reductions in freight rates and other advantages to the refiners.

Working alliances promptly followed between railroads and refineries, and Harley's pipe line, with its storage tanks, joined forces with these powers. The producers, to their dismay, found themselves almost wholly dependent for storage and shipment of their output on men whose interests were in fundamental ways opposed to their own, who did not mind seeing a vast surplus of oil accumulate at the wells, or even a shutdown, so long as the pipe line was full and the tank cars continued to run. The oil shipper had been able to cope with the cooperage firms and teamsters' groups, but against the vastly greater power of the railroads and refineries he could do little. If he antagonized them he might find the pipe line strangely dilatory in pumping his oil to the railroad and tank cars remarkably scarce when wanted. Under these conditions it was inevitable that prices of crude at the well should increasingly be dictated by the buyers and carriers. In self-defense the producers in 1866 formed an association in an effort to present a common front to the other segments of the industry, but this availed them little.

TWO

FREE-ENTERPRISE HEAVEN

The economic tyranny exerted by special interests in the Pennsylvania oil fields was merely one example of a condition then prevailing all over the country. The 1860s saw the adolescence of American industry, and an irresponsible adolescence it was, verging on delinquency. As usual during and after a major war there were shortages of many kinds of manufactured goods, of housing, transportation, and fuel. Recently printed greenbacks, although depressed in value, were plentiful, and people were in a mood to spend freely. These factors, together with high wartime tariffs still in force, pushed wholesale and retail prices sharply upward. By comparison, however, manufacturing costs remained low. Labor was cheap, owing to a flood of recent immigrants from Ireland and Germany and the return of soldiers to civilian life; and improved steam engines and newly-invented machines and equipment were expanding low-cost production in many lines.

Shrewd businessmen could see a field day ahead. Taxes, by twentieth-century standards, were insignificant. Costs of many raw materials were held in check by increasing domestic production of minerals and commercial lumber. Factory owners and distributors from Chicago to Boston found themselves in a beautiful world of inflated prices and large-profit margins. The remark made by John Jacob Astor to Julia Ward Howe was quoted widely and with appreciation: "A man who has a million dollars is as well off as if he were rich." In spite of the collapse of the wartime speculative boom, there were many new American fortunes seeking investment opportunities; and British and French financiers, sensing that business in the victorious North would grow fast, were also eager to participate in large-scale ventures —railroad construction, cable and telegraph lines, mining, and steel manufacture.

Anything Goes

Enterprises of a monopolistic or semimonopolistic character, such as railroads, were especially popular with investors. There was little in the law to restrict monopoly. The Federal government's interest in commerce and industry was confined largely to its tax revenues from tariffs and excise. It was a generation away from even the mildest attempts to regulate business. As for state governments, they offered no problem to any businessman with enough cash to hire clever lawyers and seek out venal legislators. Old Cornelius Vanderbilt summed up the attitude of his fellow tycoons when he said, "What do I care about the law? Haven't I got the power?"

It was inevitable that such conditions should spawn a host of corporate enterprises that felt no compunctions about doing anything that served their interests, and that a few of them, the more vigorous and able, should make their owners immensely wealthy. The years 1865–1870 saw the American multimillionaire at his most arrogant. Jay Cooke was dominant in the nation's finance, while Vanderbilt, with his $90,000,000, stood astride American shipping, and competed in railroading and stock deals with buccaneers like Jay Gould, Daniel Drew, and James Fisk. Gould had begun the watering of Erie Railroad's stock which in five years caused the road's capital to jump from $17,000,000 to $78,000,000, largely on fictional grounds. For such men nothing was too audacious. The only risks they ran were in private financial wars with other money masters of the time. The stock market was at the mercy of their combinations, and their bond issues often were nothing more than traps for the unwary. This was the period when an embittered stockbroker, looking at side-by-side portraits of Fisk and Gould, remarked, "Yes, I see the thieves, but where is Christ?"

The Darwinian doctrine of the "survival of the fittest," in distorted form, had already in the 1860s begun to permeate the business communities of England and America. The man who made millions, it was assumed, had proved himself the "fittest," regardless of how he made them. No one bothered to ask, "Fittest for what?" To interfere with the businessman was to fly in the face of nature's own law. To be sure, outstanding rascality in finance or industry was persistently attacked by high-minded clergymen and political radicals, but such gadfly insolence was shrugged aside. The world of business was a jungle, and the spirit of the times was on the side of the tiger. When in 1869 Gould and Fisk came within a hairsbreadth of cornering the nation's gold market and precipitated the financial panic known as Black Friday, they were denounced in pulpits and pamphlets, they were investigated by a congressional committee, but what laws, after all, had they broken?

Whisky into Oil

It was against this background that John D. Rockefeller, at the age of twenty-seven, reached out for a larger share of the oil business. In 1866, his Cleveland refinery had begun to expand with almost explosive force. To help him carry the administrative load he brought an energetic new partner, Henry M. Flagler, into the company, which thereafter was known as Rockefeller, Andrews, and Flagler—or, in the abbreviation of the trade, RAF. "The ability to deal with people," wrote Rockefeller in later years, "is as purchasable a commodity as sugar or coffee, and I pay more for that ability than for any other under the sun." Flagler knew how to deal with people. He and Rockefeller were kindred spirits, spare in physique, quiet of speech, abstemious. Both had a passion for efficiency and the ability to achieve it, and Flagler soon became Rockefeller's closest friend and most intimate adviser. Experience in the salt and grain trade had given him a considerable knowledge of the railroad freight problem. Rockefeller showed his faith in his new partner's capacity by assigning to him the key task of reorganizing the company's oil traffic to eliminate waste.

At the same time, with his first refinery operating at capacity, Rockefeller unhesitatingly launched a second. Here he ran into a money problem. Land values and construction costs were rising in Cleveland, and refinery equipment had become far more elaborate and expensive than it had been a few years earlier. The second plant involved expenditure on a scale that might well have daunted anyone less venturesome and confident than Rockefeller. Needing capital and unwilling to borrow from lip-pursing bankers, he followed a suggestion from Flagler. The latter's wife had an uncle, H. V. Harkness, who had grown rich in whisky distilling, and knew a good proposition when he saw one. It took but little persuasion to bring Harkness's money into the firm, for he sensed that these sagacious, hard-working young men were on their way to fortune and power. But how much fortune and how much power neither Harkness nor anyone else could guess.

A man of strong family feeling, Rockefeller entrusted the management of the new refinery to his younger brother, William, who was almost as energetic and keen as himself. Getting business was not a problem. Kerosene lamps and stoves were now to be found everywhere, and petroleum was becoming the established lubricant for heavy machinery. John D. was content to let others do the manufacturing, buying, and selling, while he concentrated on finances and costs.

Tom Scott Steps In

The monopoly of rail freight into Cleveland from the East, then exercised by the Atlantic and Great Western, had always concerned him. Working in harmony with Erie, A&GW controlled shipments of crude oil to the Cleveland refineries, which had no choice but to pay whatever freight rates were demanded. This was a sore spot with Rockefeller. It was not in his nature to let his interests be dominated by any other man or corporation. No time was to be lost, as he saw it, in persuading other Eastern roads to extend their tracks to Cleveland and offer competition to A&GW. Flagler played a leading part in organizing sentiment among Cleveland shippers to this end. Promises of substantial freight shipments were given to other East–West railroads if they would extend their tracks to Cleveland.

The first road to take action was the Pennsylvania, which dominated traffic between Pittsburgh and Philadelphia, and which until 1866 had somewhat neglected the possibilities of the oil business. During the Civil War the road's guiding genius, Thomas A. Scott, known to the nation as Tom Scott, had spent most of his time in Washington as the War Department's chief adviser on transportation. His return to the railroad signaled a dramatic change in its policy.

He was a vital, able, strong-willed, and intensely ambitious man. The Pennsylvania, he saw at once, would benefit greatly from oil-freight revenues if Philadelphia's position as an oil center could be strengthened. The need was for control of track running directly from the oil regions to Philadelphia, and this the Pennsylvania lacked. However, there existed a minor independent line, the Philadelphia and Erie, which would serve the purpose. Scott leased the P&E road, and found himself accordingly with a terminal at Erie, only 100 miles from Cleveland. Why not share in the profitable Cleveland oil traffic? To extend his lines to the West and break the A&GW monopoly in Cleveland was a logical step for Scott. Another was to buy control of the old Oil Creek single-track railroad, modernize it, and link it to the P&E.

He had no wish, however, to antagonize such powerful roads as A&GW and Gould's Erie. In a characteristically bold approach he convinced them that there was plenty of oil business for all, and that they would be well advised to work together. The first result of this new harmony was their joint purchase of a controlling interest in Harley's pipe line. With this acquisition the three railroads, A&GW, Erie, and Pennsylvania, held the oil producers even more tightly in their grasp.

And Joe Potts

The entry of the Pennsylvania and a little later of the Lake Shore into Cleveland benefited all of the refiners of the city, including Rockefeller. With freight rates falling as a result of competition among the roads, the main need was to find an adequate and assured supply of rolling stock. It became Flagler's problem to persuade the roads to put more tank cars at Rockefeller's disposal. According to testimony later given before a New York State Senate investigating committee, his first success was a deal with the Erie under which all of the oil cars in the road's service were assigned to RAF. As a result Rockefeller could obtain petroleum shipments in tank cars when other Cleveland refiners still had to depend largely on barrels, with all the accompanying handicaps.

A further easing in oil transport came with the appearance

of several "fast-freight" lines to serve the oil regions. The large number of short, independent, interconnecting railroads which then existed created aggravating problems for shippers and consignees. For example, the Philadelphia and Erie, which the Pennsylvania had leased, connected with about ten other roads in its east–west movements. Shippers using this route were compelled to make separate arrangements with each of the connecting roads—a costly nuisance.

The way to overcome this problem was found when a capable Pennsylvanian named Joseph Potts devised a new service, which he called the Empire Transportation Company. With the backing of the Pennsylvania Railroad, he announced that Empire would handle the routing of oil for them over the entire Pennsylvania system and the roads connecting with it. The service was soon afterward extended to include the Erie. At the same time, new pipe line and tank car facilities were put into construction by Potts.

Here was good news for harassed shippers and barrel-plagued refiners. They were glad to pay Empire's charges in order to be relieved of routing problems. Furthermore, Empire's new tank cars, when they appeared, were found to be the best seen up to that time. Cylindrical iron tanks, painted bright green, were used in place of Densmore's wooden tubs. A new kind of valve, which could be opened only by a special wrench, gave greater safety from leakage, fire, and theft. Many hundreds of the new cars came into use within the next few years. From the first the Empire was a success.

Rockefeller Makes a Note

Captain Vandergrift, whose waterway transport business had been blighted by the railroads, promptly organized a fast freight line to compete with Empire. His company, the Star Tank Line, built a pipe line and a short new railroad to carry oil to the big east–west trunk lines from the then-gushing Pithole field. Star rapidly became an important force in the oil country, second only to Empire in the volume of freight handled. Its pipe line and railroad fell into disuse some years later, when the Pithole wells gave out, but the Star Tank Line continued in existence and prospered.

Rockefeller took advantage of the competition between Empire and Star to persuade the latter to devote a high proportion of its new cars to RAF's exclusive use. In those days he carried a pocket notebook in which he entered memoranda and observations. One page of this notebook, which is still preserved in the Rockefeller documents, carried a handwritten note showing the significance that he attributed to his control of shipping facilities. "Tank cars in use Sept. 1, 1869–Doan Westlake 50 Payne 42 Shurmer 15 Scofield 30 Hanna 12 Critchely 12 Hussy 15 ... 216 (total) RAF 74, added say Sept. 20th 4."

RAF were not yet the largest refiners in the Cleveland area, but already they were far ahead of their best-equipped competitor in the number of tank cars in service. This fact, perhaps more than any other, suggests the direction of Rockefeller's outlook on the oil business. Control of transportation facilities meant efficiency, efficiency meant power, and power meant profit. A generation later, testifying before a government investigatory commission, he recalled his thinking of those earlier days. "We soon discovered, as the business grew, that the primary method of transporting oil in barrels could not last. The package often cost more than the contents, and the forests of the country were not sufficient to supply the necessary material for an extended length of time. Hence we devoted attention to other methods of transportation ... and found capital for pipe line construction equal to the necessities of the business. ... The pipe line system required other improvements, such as tank cars upon railways. ... Capital had to be furnished for them [pipe lines and tank cars] and corporations created to own and operate them." The logic of the oil business—and he was nothing if not logical—put transportation at the core of his operation. In the early days, before long pipe lines became a commonplace, the railroads especially were the focus of his interest. At a time when the only other available means of "rapid" overland freight movement was the horse-drawn express wagon, the railroads had an importance in business calculations that it is difficult for the mid-twentieth-century mind to conceive. To the burgeoning oil refineries of the 1860s movement of their products by rail was the basis of survival. It was Rockefeller's clear perception that the advantage in rail transportation, more than any other factor, was the key to success in oil that gave him his great head start over competitors, opening up a gap that they were never thereafter able to close.

Already by the late 1860s the lines of future battle were visible. On one side were the Rockefellers working in collaboration with Tom Scott of the Pennsylvania Railroad, Gould of the Erie, and with the masters of the fast freight lines, Potts of Empire and Vandergrift of Star. And on the other were unorganized hundreds of small refineries and uncommitted railroads, following the path of least resistance, working from day to day without cohesion or long-range planning. On the principle that power tends toward those who seek it, the advantage was all with Rockefeller and his associates. The American economy was asking to be exploited.

THREE

THE SHAPE OF SUCCESS

For the oil refiners of Cleveland, including Rockefeller, the decade of the 1870s began inauspiciously. Following the wild expansion of the 1860s depression blanketed the country, and the oil industry was hard hit. Hit by too much production and a falling off of consumption, prices of oil and oil-products dropped disastrously, by 25 per cent, by 50 per cent. Although the refiners could and did squeeze the Pennsylvania producers to the point of desperation, they, in turn, were squeezed by the railroads. The roads serving Cleveland by informal agreement among themselves kept their freight rates at a level which drained all profit from the refiners' greatly reduced sales.

Rockefeller was not caught by the wave of pessimism then engulfing the business community. In his youth he had experienced the crushing crisis of 1857, and all his life he had an intuition of the shape of the business cycle. That the new depression would soon run its course and the national economy resume its upward trend he had no doubt. The salvation of his company, it was clear to him, lay not in contraction but in further expansion. He perceived, as others did not, that for an oil refiner size alone could make the difference between failure and success. The chance of profit a great part of the time hinged on the freight rates paid to the railroads. High freight charges could keep a refiner forever struggling on the narrow edge of disaster, dependent on the whims of the Vanderbilts, Goulds, and Scotts, who were making more money than anyone else out of oil. Only a refiner controlling a large quantity of freight could hope to

24

make an advantageous deal with the roads. Such deals generally took the form of a rebate from the road's published tariffs. While these rebates were secret, in the sense that neither the shipper nor the railroad admitted to them, everyone connected with rail transportation knew of their existence. Their effect was, of course, to give the large shipper a powerful advantage over his smaller competitors. That in failing to provide equal treatment for shippers the roads violated state laws under which their charters had been issued was manifest. But since the state administrations had no evidence on which to act and no disposition to make trouble for the roads, there seemed little to fear from this quarter. From the railroad's point of view the payment of rebates was simple common sense. Why not give a special inducement to a shipper whose large volume of freight meant not only substantial revenue but also important economies? The more barrels or tank cars put on the tracks by a single shipper at one time, the lower the railroad's cost per barrel in handling the shipment.

"Them As Has, Gits"

Rockefeller saw that so long as RAF was only one of the pack its bargaining power with the railroads was bound to be very limited and its rebates small. Largely because of frugal management his company was feeling the pangs of the depression less than others, and thanks to Harkness's money RAF had the advantage of substantial capital resources.

Late in 1870, Rockefeller felt ready to force the issue with the railroads. Cleveland newspapers carried a brief report to the effect that a new corporation had been formed, the Standard Oil Company of Ohio. Its capitalization was only $1,000,000. Rockefeller always believed in presenting a modest financial front to the public. But almost at once the business began to expand. Many small refining concerns were pinched and uneasy, and could be bought out cheaply; and Standard was in the satisfying position of being able to buy when others were eager to sell. "Them as has," as Artemus Ward remarked, "gits." Quietly Rockefeller acquired several competitive refineries of the Cleveland area, integrating their properties and operations with his own.

Soon Standard's purchases of crude oil were calculated to be as much as 4 per cent of the total production of the oil fields. This was enough to open the mind of any railroad freight manager to reason and to rebates. Some refiners in New York, Philadelphia, and Pittsburgh were larger, but Standard was unmistakably a rising contender.

In later years Samuel C. T. Dodd, Rockefeller's able attorney, stated that the main motive behind the formation of the Standard Oil Company was "to cheapen transportation." The chief ways by which this was done, Dodd said, were "by perfecting and extending the pipe line system," and "by constructing and supplying cars by which oil might be shipped in bulk at less cost than packages." Nothing could be more succinct and explicit. With every refinery acquired Rockefeller increased the number of tank cars at his disposal, until by 1871 he counted them in the hundreds. Now he was on his way, riding the tank car to unparalleled fortune.

With each month the shrewdness of his strategy became more plain. As one railroad after another bid for his freight business his transportation costs fell drastically. The consequent savings made it possible for him to sell oil profitably at prices which his remaining Cleveland competitors could not meet without loss. Under this form of pressure one refinery after another was driven to the wall where Rockefeller waited calmly to pick up the pieces. Then, with the volume of his business ever growing, he called on the railroads to pay Standard still higher rebates, which were used to put yet more pressure on competitors.

The cycle was beautiful in its simplicity, irresistible in its momentum. In 1871, Standard's freight rates were as low as those of Pittsburgh's great refineries, its share of the market had doubled, and additional concerns, not only in Cleveland but in other cities as well, were falling into Rockefeller's lap like ripe apples from a tree in an autumn wind. And freight rates were not his only weapon for belaboring rivals. A competitor seeking to transport his oil would discover that the railroads on which he depended had no tank cars for him, that Standard had leased every available car owned by the railroads and fast freight companies, and car builders were tied up by large advance orders. Desperately the rival refiner would turn to barrels, only to find that Standard had preempted all staves, barrels, and barrel-making equipment in the area. When this happened, as it did more than once, the competitor either sold out on Rockefeller's terms or went under on his own.

"We Were Willing..."

With depression still rampant and total freight-car loadings still falling through 1871, the heads of the railroads serving the oil industry began to seek better solutions to their own problems. It was no longer possible for them to dictate to the larger refiners, but should they let the refiners dictate to them? Should the roads cut each other's throats by constantly lowering freight charges under coercion? Why not rather pool the total freight, divide it proportionally among themselves, and by mutual agreement maintain freight rates at a profitable level? A few of the largest refiners might be brought into the scheme and given special advantages so as to assure their support.

A specific plan to this purpose first took shape in the fertile mind of Tom Scott of the Pennsylvania. Other overlords of transport, Vanderbilt of the New York Central, Gould of the Erie, and McClellan of Atlantic and Great Western, gave their approval. There were certain restrictive laws in Pennsylvania and other states which would need to be circumvented, but such incidental problems were easily disposed of. Scott had some time before persuaded the notoriously venal Pennsylvania State Legislature to grant a remarkable charter for a corporation known as the South Improvement Company. The charter embraced rights so broad and so vaguely defined as to permit the company's owners to carry on virtually any business of their choosing and in virtually any way they chose. This document Scott now brought to light, and South Improvement became the vehicle for the new combination of railroads and refiners. Legislatures of other states also stood to attention at the behest of Scott and his associates, and meekly modified old laws or passed new ones to serve the aims of the tycoons.

Late in 1871 Scott approached Rockefeller: would Standard, as the leading Cleveland oil company, join with prominent refiners in New York, Philadelphia, and Pittsburgh under the aegis of the South Improvement Company? Working in association, the refiners would then act as "eveners," to assure each railroad its prearranged share of tank car freight. For the selected refiners there would be great rewards. Secret rebates so large as to assure the extinction of any competitor who dared raise his head would go to them. Tank car assignments and movements would be controlled by the roads in their interest. Pipe lines would cooperate. The selected refiners would be assured of dictatorial power over the Pennsylvania producers and the prices of crude oil. What more could they wish?

Rockefeller could have wished for much more. He was less than charmed by Scott's plan. It tended to confine Standard's marketing operations to the Cleveland area and the West. Other refiners were placed on a par with Standard—a conception, it is safe to say, which was far from Rockefeller's own. Nor was he pleased to see Standard deprived of the power to knock down freight rates from time to time by putting pressure on individual railroads.

Nevertheless, he recognized that it would be dangerous to reject the idea out of hand. Suppose the railroads and other large refiners went ahead without Standard? If there was to be a harvest, why let them reap it alone? The specific offer made by Scott was unquestionably tempting. Published freight rates for tank-car loads of oil would go up sharply, yes. But with secret rebates as high as 50 per cent Standard's rail costs would rise very little, while those of local competitors would be nearly doubled. And the refiners in the South Improvement ring would receive rebates not only on their own freight but even on the oil shipped by companies outside the group. Under Scott's plan every tank car of oil shipped from Cleveland by a rival refiner would bring about forty dollars into Standard's coffers!

In effect, the South Improvement Company planned to guarantee large profits for the railroads by turning the oil business of the country over to a cartel of a few large refiners, who could at their will extinguish all competition. The profits of the refiners would come, in the end, from the raising of prices of oil products to consumers—a purpose entirely agreeable to the prevailing theory of business at the time. The noted minister, Russell Conwell, summed up that theory in the much-quoted lecture, "Acres of Diamonds," which brought him a fortune of millions: "The number of poor who are to be sympathized with is very small. To sympathize with a man whom God has punished for his sins . . . is to do wrong, no doubt about it. . . . To secure wealth is an honorable ambition, and is one great test of a person's usefulness to others. . . . I say, get rich, get rich!"

In agreeing to the South Improvement scheme Rockefeller apparently regarded it in the light of a temporary expedient. From the first he doubted the ability of either the railroads or the refiners to remain long in harmonious association. "We were willing to go with them," he explained in later years, "as far as the plan could be used; so that when it failed, we would be in a position to say, 'Now try our plan.' Then we would be in a better position to get their cooperation than if we had said 'No' from the start." By "our plan," it would appear, Rockefeller meant the system of operation which, after South Improvement collapsed, was to make Standard by 1880 the producer of 95 per cent of the refined oil used in the United States.

"I Shall Never Cease to Regret..."

Reservations notwithstanding, once Rockefeller was committed to South Improvement he and Flagler threw themselves into the task of making the new combine effective. Here, for the first time, they felt the power of an outraged public opinion. The press of the oil regions got wind of the scheme and exposed it before it could be fairly launched. A wild explosion of rage followed. With poverty stalking the land such a display of greed on the part of big business was salt in the nation's economic wounds. Too many men were unemployed, too many families were hungry to permit the public to shrug. Newspapers throughout the country ran angry editorials, producers held mass meetings in protest, independent refiners stormed the Pennsylvania Legislature, workers in the oil fields blocked the movement of trains of tank cars loaded with oil for the South Improvement refineries. With each day the fat blazed hotter in the fire. Americans were then far more suspicious than they have since become of those whom Theodore Roosevelt labeled "malefactors of great wealth." For several years past great financial scandals had been rocking the nation—Gould's attempt to corner gold with the aid of high officials of the Grant administration; the appalling Crédit Mobilier failure, in which the connivance of railroad magnates and congressmen ruined thousands of small stockholders; the exposure of new depths of corruption in New York City, where the alliance of Jay Gould with the infamous Boss Tweed had been demonstrated. Rockefeller must have winced to find his respectable name coupled in print with those of some of the most notorious scoundrels of the period.

For a time, it appears, he and his associates failed to recognize the range and force of the country's passionate reaction. They thought the storm would pass quickly. But it stayed over their heads for many weeks, and scarred their reputations forever. The Pennsylvania Legislature in a panic withdrew the charter of the ill-begotten South Improvement Company; indictments were sought against its sponsors; and a congressional committee prepared to investigate.

Hastily, to avert worse troubles, the railroads canceled all contracts made with refiners under Scott's plan and piously sought to convince the public that the oil men alone were the villains of the piece. Triumphant independent producers in the oil regions now felt a surge of power. The arbitrary lowering of crude-oil prices by the large refiners had in the past cost most of them dear. Here was a chance for revenge. Suddenly the producers' association announced that its members would no longer sell to the refiners who had been part of the South Improvement gang.

The boycott hit Standard a telling blow. Work at the Cleveland refineries came to a standstill. Nine out of every ten employees had to be let go, until in March, 1872, only a skeleton force of 70 were on the Standard payroll. But Rockefeller remained coldly indifferent, refusing to kowtow to the producers or to make any apology or explanation to the clamorous newspapers and the angry public. Half a century later, after he had finally engaged a public relations adviser, the celebrated Ivy Lee, he recognized the seriousness of the error into which his native self-righteousness and reticence had led him in those early months of 1872. "I shall never cease to regret," he said ... "that at that time we never called in the reporters."

Divide and Conquer

Rockefeller was so far from being dismayed by the producers' boycott that even while it continued he was placing orders for new tank cars—tightening his grip on oil transportation in spite of the fact that he had no oil to ship. None to ship from Cleveland, that is to say. By paying a handsome price he managed to acquire at this period the New York firm of J. A. Bostwick and Company, the largest buyer of crude oil and refined products in its area, and the owner of a major oil-freight terminal in the Hudson River. Although the Bostwick firm was also a member of the South Improvement Company, it had been able to evade the worst effects of the producers' boycott through a hidden subsidiary. Standard's acquisition of Bostwick was kept secret, and through this channel Rockefeller was able to continue to buy oil in quantity, refining it in New York and shipping it to Standard's regular markets. Among the important assets gained by Standard in this transaction were the services of Bostwick himself and of his young partner, Wesley Hunt Tilford, who became an outstanding member of the high-powered operating team in Cleveland.

It was Rockefeller's conviction, and one justified by events, that the solid front of the boycotting producers would soon crack. There was bound to be "a weak sister" among them. It took only one breach in the wall to reduce a fortress, and every man had his price. Armed with this philosophy and a great deal of money, his agents quietly circulated through western Pennsylvania, looking for a producer who wanted to sell oil more than he wanted to hurt Standard. They had not long to search. The producers were discovering that the independent refiners alone simply could not absorb the output of the wells. Moreover, Standard and other boycotted refiners had withdrawn their rolling stock from the railroads. Even when sales of crude oil were made to independents it could not readily be shipped. Huge stocks of petroleum were piling up in storage tanks at the wells. Under these conditions the boycotters were vulnerable. The sophisticated were not surprised when one of the largest Oil City companies agreed to sell Standard 25,000 barrels, another 5,000. Screams went up from their betrayed fellows, more mass meetings were held, there were more stoppages of tank cars by mobs, but as one producer after another succumbed to Rockefeller's tempting prices the boycott collapsed. The producers' association solaced itself publicly with the statement that it had, after all, smashed the South Improvement ring and crushed monopoly. Rockefeller said nothing.

The Railroads Make a Fateful Decision

Standard emerged from the South Improvement fiasco tarnished perhaps in reputation but in economic terms stronger than ever. Now there was no more nonsense about voluntary associations, with their "live and let live" attitude. Instead, "dog eat dog" was the refrain. And Standard, if not yet top dog, was rising fast. Rockefeller's concentration on the tank car was showing positive results. Standard now had many tank cars of its own; it had exclusive use of all of Erie's cars, and it had leased others owned by the fast freight companies. Remaining rivals in Cleveland were finding that no tank cars could be had for money, and certainly not for love. With oil production increasing faster than new cars could be built many refiners had to depend almost entirely on the outmoded and expensive barrel, and their ability to withstand Rockefeller's pressure steadily deteriorated.

Even those rival Cleveland concerns which owned tank cars were generally at a disadvantage as compared with Standard, for the new cars which Rockefeller was putting into operation were much more efficient and economical to operate than those of the past. The year 1869 had seen the construction of a car in which the familiar upright tanks were replaced by a single horizontal boiler made of heavy iron, and which had a capacity as great as that of the two-tub car. In the older cars, expansion of oil in transit regularly produced leakage through manholes or valves, and invited fire and explosion. In the new car, however, a cupola, or dome mounted on the tank, allowed for expansion and gas formation. Leakage was reduced, safety promoted; and with only one tank to fill and empty, loading and unloading took less time.

The first few of these cars were manufactured in Milton, Pennsylvania, for the Empire Transportation Company. Immediately thereafter shops throughout the region began to turn out

cars on the same model. Empire and Star took most of this output, and Standard was the only Cleveland refiner to whom the
new cars were leased.

Unknown to themselves, the railroads were now at a crossroads of decision. Shippers still expected them to provide rolling
stock for their freight, but the roads, seeing the rapid obsolescence of the old Densmore-style tank cars in their possession,
were more reluctant than ever to invest in the so-called dome
cars. To provide the thousands of cars demanded would require
an outlay of millions. And who knew how long the oil fields of
Pennsylvania would last, how soon the bubble of oil refining
would burst? At that time, while there were vague rumors of oil
in Ohio and elsewhere, the future of the industry seemed highly
uncertain. Why, the railroad magnates reasoned, should they
tie up in specialized rolling stock with a dubious future capital
which could be used more profitably in other ways? Rather let
the fast freight lines and the shippers whose business depended
on the tank cars put up the money for new equipment. The railroads would make their tracks available, supply locomotives for
the haul, and allow the cars to be brought into their shops for
elementary repairs, for which they charged the car owner. As
they saw it, their freight charges were earned by these services;
it was unnecessary for them to provide tank cars in addition.

Since the privately-owned tank cars were used to produce
freight revenue, the owners of the cars had a reasonable claim
for compensation from the benefiting railroads. As early as 1867
the New York Central and Erie railroads had already agreed with
shipper-owners of cars on a method of payment for such compensation. Freight contracts of the time specified that for every
mile that loaded shipper-owned tank cars traveled over the railroad's tracks the railroad would pay $1\frac{1}{2}$ cents. With volume
of loadings and freight rates high, these payments were hardly
noticed by the roads, and the practice soon became widespread.

A little later the question of payment to the railroads for the
haulage of empty tank cars came to the fore. At first they insisted that the owner or user of the car pay a charge for having
it hauled back empty to his loading point. But as the competition for freight became sharper Standard and other important
shippers compelled the roads to drop this charge.

In turning their backs on the tank car the railroads had surrendered an instrument of great power. It was not long before they realized it.

Rockefeller Takes Every Trick—Almost

Most of the trump cards were now in Rockefeller's hands and he played them like a master. A few months after the collapse of the South Improvement Company he showed his strength. Sending Tilford to deal with the New York Central, he offered to guarantee an unprecedented amount of oil freight over Central's tracks at the prevailing freight rates. In return he asked for and got secret rebates of unparalleled size. Thereafter it was comparatively easy for Standard to drive the competitive Lake Shore road into a similar agreement. The terms imposed on the Erie were even stiffer. Gould's iniquities were catching up with him, and the road was in serious trouble. Standard took the moment to compel Erie not only to pay huge rebates but actually to confine its deliveries of Eastern oil freight exclusively to Standard's terminal on the Hudson River. In connection with this extraordinary agreement there is a suggestive fact buried in the old records. At about the time that Erie capitulated in 1872, its president, Peter Watson, became a stockholder of the Standard Oil Company.

Another new name appears on the list of stockholders in 1873— that of J. J. Vandergrift, the former steamboat captain, and the founder of the Star Tank Line and Pipeline. From the beginning Standard had been Star's largest customer. To purchase Vandergrift's properties in return for stock was a natural evolutionary step. With Star went a small affiliated fast freight company known as the Union Tank Line, which Vandergrift had founded to handle oil freight into Chicago. He himself became a member of Standard's board of directors, and soon afterward was placed at the head of the company's growing pipe line system. Among his many achievements was the building of the first natural gas pipe line near Pittsburgh, running directly from well to factory.

Only at one point was Rockefeller checked. Expansion of the company had produced a shortage of tank cars so acute as to be critical. Wanting every dollar of available cash for the purchase of refineries, and holding the provision of tank cars to be the railroad's responsibility, he was unwilling to buy cars on a large scale. To expect anything from the Erie was hopeless; the road was financially desperate, its credit ruined; no car manufacturer would accept its orders. The old Atlantic and Great Western was in similar straits, and the Lake Shore had been taken over by New York Central. The Pennsylvania's tank car service was in the hands of Empire Transportation, which could not be dictated to. It was only William Vanderbilt of the Central, with his imperial fortune, who could solve the tank car problem for Standard. Early in 1875 Rockefeller approached him. Vanderbilt, however, curtly declined to hear any discussion of the subject. Apparently he did not envisage the consequences of his refusal. A few days later Standard abruptly withdrew all of its business from the Central, in favor of the Erie and the Pennsylvania. Although the Central's freight revenues dropped with startling velocity and Vanderbilt's own aides urged him to reconsider, he was stubborn enough and rich enough to hold for a while to his position. The tank car shortage continued to plague Rockefeller; his only consolation was that it plagued competitors even more.

Standard's properties and holdings by now aggregated scores of millions in worth, but its capitalization was still $1,000,000. In 1874, Rockefeller thought it advisable to recapitalize at $3,500,-000. Although even this figure did not begin to reflect the growth of the company or its latent power, it commanded respect at a time when "a million dollars" was a phrase to conjure with. Partly the recapitalization was designed to increase the amount of stock available for new acquisitions. But Rockefeller had another reason as well.

The time had come for Standard to reveal itself as the largest and strongest refiner in the country. For Rockefeller had decided on a dramatic move—nothing less than the establishment of a new nationwide alliance of refineries, which he called the Central Refiners' Association, and the presidency of which he himself assumed. The announced purpose of Central Refiners was to benefit all members through economies in the purchase and transportation of crude oil. In effect, Rockefeller was offering his competitors a chance to share Standard's great advantages in buying oil and in freight rebates. In return Standard was given authority to buy and allocate crude-oil supplies, to allocate sales, and to make transportation agreements for all members. It took no special gift to perceive that the Central Association was a device by which Rockefeller could dominate independent refineries until such time as he wished to absorb them. Nevertheless, not many could resist the bait which he held out with one hand and the club which he carried in the other. The price of efficiency was dictatorship. Most of the refiners, not only in Cleveland but in the oil regions, Pittsburgh, Philadelphia, and New York as well, found it advisable to join the association.

In evaluating the reasons for the success of the association, Rockefeller's willingness to let other men get rich must have a high place. He was always ready to spend freely in order to buy power. While firmly in control of Standard and the association he saw to it that men who served him well shared the rewards. Around him, in addition to brother William and friend Flagler, he had by now gathered a large group of hard-driving, capable lieutenants, most of them out of companies absorbed by Standard. All of them owned Standard stock, and it did not take many shares to make them millionaires in their own right. Stocks of companies known to be affiliated with Standard through the association were similarly booming. Newspapers reported that when shares in such a company were offered for sale in staid Boston, eager investors queued up outside brokers' offices before opening time to be sure of "getting in on it."

To the public Rockefeller and Standard Oil were almost synonymous, and with reason. Although technically he was only the head of a combine of oil men he provided its essential spirit. The others had authority to act in many matters without consulting him, and did, but wherever the issue was of large consequence it was John D. who made the decision and who took the responsibility.

FOUR

CHALLENGE TO MORTAL COMBAT

Among those who observed Standard's growth with alarm was Joseph Potts, president of the Empire Company and master of 1,500 tank cars, by far the largest fleet then in existence. But Empire's bright green cars were only part of Potts' resources. In the few years of the company's existence its expansion had been comparable to that of Standard. Thirty-five hundred other railroad cars; twenty large freighters on the Great Lakes; more than 500 miles of newly constructed pipe line; numberless storage tanks; a large refinery—all this and more was in Potts' domain. And as he saw it he was only beginning. The Pennsylvania Railroad, with its far-reaching influence, stood solidly behind him. A contract signed by Tom Scott assured Empire of rebates comparable to those of Standard, while Potts, in turn, agreed to give the Pennsylvania all the oil traffic at his command.

Standard's purchase of the Star properties and steady accumulation of additional pipe lines were recognized by Potts as moves threatening Empire's supremacy in the field of oil transport. Rockefeller was a major customer of Potts' services, but in this very fact lay danger, for if he should suddenly withdraw his business Empire could be seriously hurt. Similar considerations worried Scott. The Pennsylvania had benefited from the quarrel between Standard and the New York Central, but it was intolerable that a single refiner should be able at his will to penalize any railroad which failed to meet his demands. And the rate at which Rockefeller's power was increasing boded trouble. Independent refiners continued to link themselves with his Central Association. The Pennsylvania would never be out from under Standard's shadow until it was linked by common interest to a refining combine other than Rockefeller's, and strong enough to compete with him in every major market.

A plan to this end, involving Empire, seems to have taken shape in Scott's mind soon after the failure of South Improvement. When Potts acquired his first refinery the move was seen by both men as a prelude to larger action. Empire was to become a serious competitor to Standard and a bulwark for the Pennsylvania against Rockefeller's pressure.

As long as Empire had only a single refinery Rockefeller ignored its intrusion into his own field. Nevertheless, by 1875 it was clear that two separate and formidable alliances were taking shape—mighty Standard and the compliant Erie on one side, and on the other Pottscott, as newspaper reporters of the period facetiously dubbed the powerful Pennsylvania team. For a time the two camps preserved the outward appearance of co-operation. But in 1876 an unexpected development forced the issue. Explorations at Bradford, Pennsylvania, almost on the border of New York State, resulted in a new oil strike of such scope as to change the entire outlook for the Pennsylvania oil regions. As one rich well after another was brought in, producing at a rate never before seen, it was evident that a fierce struggle would soon be under way to control transportation out of the Bradford fields. The prize reaped by the successful railroad and the refineries which it served would be counted in many millions. The Pennsylvania system, with tracks close by, and Empire, with its pipe line construction facilities and comparative abundance of tank cars, were in an ideal position. The Bradford well owners were ready to pay almost anything to get their oil to market. Without delay Potts began construction of a pipe line out of Bradford and diverted hundreds of tank cars to the area from other regions.

"We Determined to Make the Issue"

Thus far Rockefeller saw no cause for concern. His agents were among the first in Bradford, buying crude oil in great quantities. So long as he could use Empire's tank cars and route them over the Pennsylvania to Standard's refineries he had everything to gain from Potts' efforts. But in the first days of 1877 he was startled to learn that Potts and Scott had no intention of sharing their Bradford transportation facilities with Standard on an equal basis. Instead, Empire and the Pennsylvania had, to all intents, declared war. Huge new refineries at Philadelphia, it was announced, were under construction for Empire, to refine and market Bradford oil; while a new agreement with the Pennsylvania would bring Empire's freight rates down to Standard's level and below.

Here was a new kind of industrial consolidation, in which for the first time a large refiner, a great railroad, and all the other means of oil transport were brought together under single direction, to dispose of the output of a major oil field. On hearing the news the competitive railroads to the north instantly recognized that the gauntlet had been thrown down not only to Standard but to themselves. Even Vanderbilt, no friend to Rockefeller, saw that he could not permit the Pennsylvania to acquire a monopoly of Bradford oil. An officer of the Erie not long afterward described the situation as his road had seen it. Speaking to the New York State legislative investigators known as the Hepburn Committee, he said of the Pennsylvania–Empire combine: "Unless checked, the result would be a diversion largely of transportation of oil from our own roads. The New York Central and our own road were determined that we ought not to stand by.... We determined, therefore, to make the issue with the Pennsylvania R.R. Company." The making of the issue, as it turned out, involved nothing less than a national crisis.

Price War

For a few days Rockefeller gave no sign that he had heard of the Pennsylvania–Empire deal. Then mildly he ordered that all Standard units cease shipping over the Pennsylvania lines, and that all Standard tank cars on those lines be routed to other roads. With the tank cars safe in friendly territory, Standard informed Scott that they were canceling their freight contracts with the Pennsylvania. If, Scott was told, the Pennsylvania wished to retain Standard Oil as a customer Empire would have to withdraw from the refining business. When this suggestion was ignored, the Standard refinery at Pittsburgh, which was almost wholly dependent on the Pennsylvania's tracks, was abruptly closed and its working force dismissed.

Simultaneously Rockefeller took steps to meet the tank car shortage on the so-called northern lines, caused by the restriction of Empire's cars to the Pennsylvania. Construction of 400 new dome tank cars was rushed by Standard. Flagler then met privately with Vanderbilt in a Saratoga Springs hotel and persuaded him that the emergency justified a reversal of his earlier position. At the end of their talk the New York Central agreed to put up the capital for 600 tank cars, under a contract which bound Standard to use them continuously. Rockefeller, hearing this news, felt the relief which comes with assurance of victory. "We thought it a godsend," he said afterward.

With his own communications safeguarded, he was ready for the attack. It was at Empire's most vulnerable spots that he struck—its supply of oil and its market for refined-oil products. Standard's buyers swarmed through the oil fields outbidding Empire's men for crude oil in huge quantities. And as the price of crude rose, Rockefeller suddenly slashed his prices for refined oil and kerosene in every city where Empire was doing business. These moves were aided by large reductions in freight rates by Erie and New York Central.

Confronted by the imminent collapse of Empire's sales, Potts frantically reduced his own prices to meet Standard's, only to find that Rockefeller had undercut him once again. Whatever the cost, Potts had no choice but to follow suit. In the fierce competition between them Standard suffered, but Empire suffered far more. Standard's production of refined products was at least three times greater and its over-all costs of production materially lower than Empire's. When Rockefeller paid sky-high prices for crude, when he swamped a city with unprecedented bargains in oil, he might take a loss, but with the knowledge that Potts would have to take a much larger loss to stand against him.

Scott came to the aid of the desperate Potts by reducing the Pennsylvania's freight rates for oil to the lowest levels ever seen, and finally to nothing. But even without freight charges to pay, Potts had to take heavy losses to meet Standard's prices along the Atlantic coast. The mighty Pennsylvania was under similar strain.

Oil represented a far higher proportion of its total freight than of New York Central's or Erie's, so that it suffered more from every reduction in oil tariff rates. Within a month after the price war started it was estimated that the Pennsylvania was losing nearly eight dollars every time a tank car traveled over its tracks from Bradford to New York or Philadelphia with a load of crude oil. The operating deficit for the road's oil traffic in the spring of 1877 was later found to have been a million dollars. When Scott tried to retaliate by reducing tariffs on other commodities and on passenger fares, the magnates of the northern lines grimly fought him, rate slash for rate slash, in the same way that Rockefeller was fighting Potts.

Explosion from Below

By early summer Scott and Potts had had enough and were seeking a compromise. But events now rapidly moved far beyond their power to control. The outcome of the struggle was dictated less by the tycoons than by the forgotten men of the time, the railroad workers. All of the great roads, in their effort to reduce losses from the rate war, had cut costs at the expense of their employees, letting many go and forcing wage reductions on the rest. The discharged men did not confine themselves to words. Violence, which began in freight yards of the Baltimore and Ohio, soon spread to the Pennsylvania. Scott had been particularly hard-fisted, firing hundreds and cutting by 20 per cent the wages of men who were supporting families on ten dollars or less per week. Thereafter, ignoring vehement protests, he ordered his employees to double the number of freight cars per train—a measure which if put into effect meant further dismissals. The layoffs had been especially numerous and provocative in Pittsburgh, and on July 20, 1877, a riot of extraordinary ferocity broke out there. Supported by laborers from other affected industries and by small tradesmen whose interests were linked to theirs, the railroad men raided the Pennsylvania's machine shops for axes, hammers, and crowbars, seized its stations, demolished freight cars, tore up tracks.

When telegrams came to Scott in Philadelphia, saying that the Pittsburgh police were helpless to stop the destruction, he demanded military protection from the Governor of Pennsylvania.

Companies of the state militia were promptly ordered out to stop the rioting. But the mob, by then numbering thousands, refused to disperse. The militia had been instructed to use its rifles if necessary, and an officer gave the command to fire. The first volley killed 20 men and wounded a hundred. Contrary to expectation, the rioters were not cowed. Instead, they rushed to the attack with their crude weapons. Some of the troops were sickened by what they had done and loth to continue the massacre; others, frankly frightened, turned and ran. As night fell most of the militia force was crammed into a nearby roundhouse, while the telegraph wires to the east hummed with further appeals for help.

Rage and triumph were a heady mixture for the workers. Scores of men rushed off to break into gun shops for arms and ammunition, and when they returned fired a stream of bullets through the roundhouse windows. Others lighted torches and descended on the freight yards, where they set fire to hundreds of cars loaded with coal, oil, and merchandise, and fought off firemen who tried to extinguish the blaze. Cars full of flaming coke were pushed down the tracks to the roundhouse and sent crashing against its walls. The combination of incessant rifle fire and suffocating coke fumes was at last too much for the militiamen. Firing wildly to hold back the mob, they burst out and ran for a nearby bridge across the Allegheny River.

To Cleveland on Bended Knee

Desperately Scott appealed to President Rutherford B. Hayes in Washington, and Federal troops were promptly sent to restore order. By then most of the steam was out of the kettle; the rioters were surfeited with destruction, and the trouble subsided as suddenly as it had begun.

When Scott took stock of his losses he was appalled. Similar riots on other railroads at about the same time had resulted in costly damage, but nothing to compare with the Pennsylvania's. At Pittsburgh 500 tank cars and 1,000 other freight cars, many of them loaded, had been destroyed, together with 120 locomotives. Twenty-seven buildings had been gutted by fire. The total loss, not much of which was covered by insurance, ran into millions. The financial consequences for the railroad, coming on top of earlier losses owing to the price war, were catastrophic. Dividends had to be passed and huge loans made at high rates of interest, while Pennsylvania stock collapsed on the New York exchange. But more painful for Scott even than the financial losses was the necessity of surrendering to Standard Oil.

In September, 1877, an emissary went to Cleveland to learn Rockefeller's terms. They were very simple—the very terms, in fact, which he had stated at the outset of the contest. Empire had to withdraw from the refining business. Scott felt that he was getting off cheaply, but Potts balked. With Standard dictating to the Pennsylvania, Empire could no longer hope to function profitably as a fast freight concern. Its great transportation facilities had become mere pawns in the game. Potts' refineries were now his chief asset, and when Scott pushed him to compliance he demanded to be bought out entirely. A complicated negotiation ensued, at the end of which Standard had acquired all of Empire's refineries, storage tanks, pipe lines, tugs, barges, and oil terminals. For this the total price paid was only $2,500,000.

Soon afterward Rockefeller put up $900,000 more, in the form of a loan to the Pennsylvania, which used the money to buy Empire's rolling stock. So considerable had been the recent drain of Standard's capital by its expansion program that part of this money had to be borrowed from banks. In return for the loan Scott gave Rockefeller a mortgage, at an attractive rate of interest, on the 1,500 tank cars of Empire's Green Line. It was agreed that since Standard shipped 90 per cent of the crude oil of the region, it would have the right to requisition up to that percentage of the Pennsylvania's tank cars. A similar clause was written into contracts with other railroads.

But this was only the shell of the egg. The yolk was solid gold. In its new arrangements with the roads, Standard fulfilled Rockefeller's private plan of five years earlier. The resulting agreement was similar in essence to the old South Improvement deal, except that now Standard alone was delegated as "evener" to apportion the oil traffic among the railroads. The Pennsylvania was to get approximately 47 per cent of the eastbound freight, New York Central and Erie 21 per cent each, and the Baltimore and Ohio about 12 per cent. For its services Standard would be compensated by large uniform rebates paid by all the railroads, while the Pennsylvania was compelled to pay an additional 10 per cent, in the form of a commission, on all of Standard's freight shipments over its tracks. Beyond this the United Pipeline Company and the American Transfer Company, embracing Standard's and Empire's pipe lines, were granted a higher percentage of the railroads' freight charges than they had received before. When these benefits were lumped together Standard could ship oil by rail so cheaply as to put the remaining independent refiners at a hopeless disadvantage.

With the railroads compelled to his service, all the major overland oil transportation facilities of the country were now under Rockefeller's control, except one—a sizable independent pipeline system known as Columbia Conduit Company, which served the Baltimore and Ohio road. Such an exception was a flaw in Rockefeller's grand design and not to be tolerated. By diverting tank cars elsewhere and supplying oil to the B. and O. from other sources he was able to choke off Columbia's flow of crude oil, until the hapless owners of the pipe line were glad to sell out. Within the next two years 26 other smaller pipe lines followed their example.

Monopoly was just around the corner. There were still a number of independent refineries, it was true—five in Cleveland alone. But almost all the pipe lines were in Rockefeller's network, or subject to his policies. Nine-tenths of the tank cars on the Pennsylvania, the Erie, and the New York Central were either owned by him or leased to him. No one could ship oil in quantity anywhere in America without the approval of Standard Oil.

FIVE

THE GREAT TANK CAR SQUEEZE

Always the same question recurred—where to find more tank cars? By 1878, production of oil at the Bradford wells alone had soared to 22,000 barrels a day. There were simply not enough cars to go around, not enough storage tanks to hold the unshipped surplus. Standard's subsidiary, United Pipeline Company, which had taken over Empire's services at Bradford, made an extraordinary effort to provide adequate storage, but finally had to admit that it could not keep pace with the flow from the wells. The glut of oil, it announced, had to be checked at the source. A new policy was promulgated. United would accept in its storage tanks no more than one quarter of the daily production of any well. In order to ship the remainder tank cars would have to be immediately available, and the provision of these cars was the shipper's affair.

Standard officials regarded this policy, or so they said, as a measure to discourage wasteful overproduction and to encourage the building of tank cars and storage tanks by others. But in the eyes of the producers and small independent refiners served by United the underlying motive seemed very different. With producers desperate to ship, the price of crude oil fell almost to the giveaway point. Buyers at the wells had a field day, and most of them represented units of the Standard combine.

A new wave of resentment rose and crested in the oil regions. The Producers' Union called a meeting at which outraged well owners demanded action. Few of them were willing to be identified as leaders of the opposition to Standard—to do so might mean that they could never ship another drop of oil. But collectively they had the courage to protest. Word went out that there was to be a march on Standard's pipe line at Bradford. A thousand men gathered at a secret rendezvous, donned sheets and pillowcases, in the tradition of the Ku Klux Klan, and without saying a word paraded to the doors of the pipe line company. There they stood in grim silence until the implied threat had been driven home, after which, still saying nothing, they dispersed. By that time the pipe line's storage problem had somewhat eased, and it was able to announce an increase in the amount of oil that it would ship—just enough to take the steam out of the protest movement. But the concession was hardly a benefit to the producers, for the tank cars needed to move the oil to market remained as scarce as before, and meanwhile there were storage charges to be paid.

Runaround in Harrisburg

The anguished producers then turned to the state legislature with the cry, "Make them give us cars!" A number of witnesses, made brave by desperation, testified at Harrisburg that Standard was using its near-monopoly of tank cars to fix production and prices of oil for its profit, regardless of the interests of everyone else. What had become, they demanded, of the green tank cars which, when Empire owned them, had served Pennsylvania's producers and refiners? Suddenly they were hard to find—most of them seemed to have gone into the service of Standard's wide-flung marketing companies in other states.

The Pennsylvania legislature was full of men who preferred their bread buttered on both sides. Intimidated by rising popular resentment, it went so far as to consider a bill that aimed to provide, with public funds, a large new pipe line from the oil regions all the way to the Atlantic seaboard, and which would give Pennsylvania's producers an alternative to the tank car and the Standard-dominated railroads. The Producers' Union believed that this threat might be sufficient to force Standard to concede a higher proportion of pipe line flow and tank cars to independent refiners. They were doomed to disappointment.

Agents of Standard and the Pennsylvania Railroad promptly circulated among the legislators. The result was a remarkable

inability on the part of the responsible committee to bring a
bill to a vote. A little later one of the producers testified about
this abortive effort before a congressional committee in Washington. He was asked:

"Did you have an idea that you could, by legislative enactment,
get these gentlemen to agree to let your product be pumped?"

"Yes, sir, we did," the witness answered.

"In the state of Pennsylvania?"

"Yes, sir, we were suckers enough to think that."

The committee reporter at this point inserted the words "Great
laughter." The saying that "politicians act as though they thought
the will of the people is a document bequeathing them something" was fully borne out in Harrisburg.

Defeated in the legislature, the producers appealed to the
Governor of Pennsylvania, who felt impelled or compelled to
appoint a special state commission to investigate the troubled
industry. Its chief accomplishment was to bring to the surface
evidence of the "90 per cent deal" on tank cars between Standard
and the railroads. Independents contended that the arrangement
was manifestly unfair. Since Standard owned several hundred
tank cars of its own, and received the use of at least nine-tenths
of those belonging to the roads, its share of the total number of
tank cars in service was well over 90 per cent. In any event, said
the independents, 10 per cent of the railroads' cars was not
enough to meet the needs of the rest of the refining industry.

"It Seems to Be the Lord's Will"

For many people the evidence revealed at this time was the
first intimation that not the railroads, but Standard, controlled
the oil transportation of the country. One producer stated to the
investigators that even when he had obtained an order from the
Erie Railroad permitting him to use 100 tank cars belonging to
the road, and which were standing temporarily empty near his
well, the Standard official in charge of the Bradford pipe line
had refused to load the cars without authorization from Cleveland. Thereafter even the legislature of Pennsylvania could not
resist the tide of public opinion. Although not without much
argument, it authorized the construction of the first trunk pipe
line, the Tidewater, which would be a common carrier from the
oil regions to Philadelphia, in the interest of independent pro-

ducers and refiners. This was not all. The courts of the state
showed a new interest in the situation, granting indictments
against a number of Standard's top executives, including Rockefeller, for conspiracy to violate statutes of the state governing the
common carriers.

The defense plainly required the strongest available legal
counsel. It struck Rockefeller that no one could be better for his
purpose than a young Pennsylvania attorney, S. C. T. Dodd, who
had represented several members of the Producers' Union in
their hard fight against Standard, and whose appearances in
court had revealed unusual qualities of mind and personality.
Without delay Rockefeller set about to win Dodd over. It took a
little time, but in 1879 he managed to overcome the lawyer's
scruples and bring him into the Standard fold. Said Dodd,
when reproached by his former clients, "Well, as the ministers
say when they get a call to a higher salary, it seems to be the
Lord's will." It is an arresting fact that in his long connection with
Standard he never consented to become a director of the company, a post which for others was a short cut to riches. To the
end he remained a salaried employee. In his appearances before
courts and legislative bodies he was always able to speak as a
legal technician carrying out policies which were made by others.

The essence of Standard's defense against the Pennsylvania attack was that it did not own many tank cars, and that if the railroads which did own them chose to lease them to Standard on a
sound business basis, that was their right. Although skillful legal
tactics averted serious consequences from the investigation, the
collateral lawsuits and indictments were an irritant to Rockefeller. It was becoming clear that Standard could no longer avoid
an adjustment of its practices to the changing temper of the times.
Not that Rockefeller intended to yield. Far from it. What he
sought, specifically, was a way to bring more tank cars into the
company's use and yet relieve the railroads from blame for not
providing cars for others.

"The Simple Object of It Is..."

While the war with the Pennsylvania was at its height Rockefeller himself met with the new president of the Erie, Hugh
Jewett, who had been appointed receiver for the bankrupt road,

and described a plan designed to solve the tank-car problem. Hundreds of additional tank cars were to be provided for Standard—Erie's faltering freight revenues were to be bolstered —and without requiring either party to make any substantial cash outlay! The essence of the plan was a way to evade the laws governing corporations and persons by setting up an "Oil Tank Car Trust." This was a precursor of the great Standard Oil Trust established a few years afterward. Under the laws of the period the status of trusts was extremely vague. In most states they were exempted from restrictions imposed on ordinary corporations. The methods and contracts of a trust could be shrouded in a dark legalistic secrecy which even court orders could not penetrate.

According to testimony later given before a New York State legislative committee, Jewett saw no reason to demur to Rockefeller's proposal, and the Tank Car Trust was established in 1878. Shares in the trust at $1,000 each were authorized to the number of 3,000, but very little money was actually paid in. Control was put in the hands of a few trustees, unimportant in themselves, who were chosen primarily for their close mouths from the ranks of the railroad and of Standard's subsidiaries.

In this way an ostensibly independent enterprise was created with strong credit based on the obvious fact that Standard stood behind it. The trust had no operative organization. Its total administrative payroll was only $3,000 a year, used for the salaries of a clerk and a few car inspectors. It was never intended to make a profit. As one of the trustees told legislative investigators, "The simple object of it is . . . to secure to the car builder . . . a lien upon the cars until they are paid for."

The form of this lien was an "equipment certificate," issued by the trustees, and bearing interest rates somewhat higher than those prevailing in banks. Requesting bids for the construction of tank cars in unprecedented quantities, the trustees offered these certificates as advance payment in full to the car builder. The latter, eager for business on such a scale, took little risk. His own capital was not put under strain. He could reimburse the suppliers of materials with some of the certificates which he received, and the rest could be used as collateral for bank loans with which to pay for labor. In fact, the scheme was so popular with car builders that the trust was soon able to beat down their prices through competitive bidding, from $750 to $700, and finally to $650 per car.

As the cars were built, they were leased to the Erie, which in turn leased them to Standard. The Erie not only gained by having additional rolling stock on its tracks but was relieved of substantial maintenance costs. By this time the major Standard refineries had their own car shops, to which the Trust's tank cars were routed for all major repairs. Under a new contract with Erie, Standard continued to receive large secret rebates on freight charges, while the Car Trust was compensated for the use of its cars through a mileage allowance, calculated at three-fourths of a cent per "loaded mile." The Car Trust's income from the allowance proved more than ample to meet interest requirements on the trust's equipment certificates. Soon the Trust had a surplus which, as it accumulated, was used to buy in the equipment certificates from the holders.

Within a year, hundreds of new tank cars, of the latest model, were put into Standard's exclusive service, without involving the company or the railroad directly in the transaction with builders. Thereafter similar negotiations were worked out with other roads. The Pennsylvania Railroad turned over to the Trust the Green Line cars which it had just purchased from Empire, and agreed to pay the same mileage allowance as the Erie. No cash was necessary to complete this acquisition. As payment, Rockefeller merely canceled the mortgage which he held on the Green Line.

The New York Central, like most of the other railroads, was eager to get out of the troublesome tank car business. A secret agreement was worked out under which Vanderbilt consented to assign to the Trust about 1,000 tank cars owned by New York Central and to pay the mileage allowance and maintain rebates in return for substantial freight revenue guaranties by Standard.

By 1879, the Trust had acquired nearly 3,000 tank cars, and had placed orders for about 500 more—all without capital. It was estimated that only 200 tank cars, owned for the most part by the smaller railroads, still were available to independent refiners.

Barrels for the Others

The tank car stringency left many independent refiners with no recourse other than the barrel. By this time the oil barrel had been greatly improved. Made of heavy wood with closely fitted staves, tightly hooped, and coated with glues which enabled it to carry even kerosene without much leakage, it was a great advance over its ancestor of the 1860s. But with its technical superiority as a container went a far higher cost of manufacture and a much greater weight. The oil barrel of 1860 weighed when empty about 75 pounds, which represented about 20 per cent of the weight when full. The refiner who had to pay both the cost of the barrel and the railroad's charge for carrying it, empty or loaded, was at a hopeless disadvantage. To be sure, most of Standard's refineries customarily used barrels to supplement tank car shipments. But this was very different from being compelled, as many independents were, to use the barrel for the bulk of a refinery's output. Nevertheless, small refiners grimly put up with this heavy burden. Boxcars designed especially for barreled shipments were in heavy demand. Rockefeller encouraged this trend. In a letter to Jewett in 1879 he stated that he was about to add 500 of these "rack cars" to his fleet. This decision was undoubtedly motivated in part by a desire to facilitate barrel shipments by Standard's refineries, pending the construction of more tank cars; but it also served another purpose. If the road felt it necessary to comfort an agitated independent refiner with more rolling stock it could put rack cars at his disposal, reserving the more efficient tank cars for Standard.

The independent was thus thrown back to the shipping practices of the early days of the industry, while Standard's methods were progressively advancing. A Standard tank car could run at low shipping rates from the refinery to almost any railroad stop in the United States, carrying its load of kerosene, naphtha, or refined oil. There its load would be pumped at the railroad siding into tank wagons owned by Standard's marketing companies, and the tank wagon would carry it to the cans or barrels of the retail establishments which sold to the consumer. It was a system that held transportation costs at a minimum. Not so with the independent. Forced for the most part to ship in barrels from the refinery, he was subject to high freight charges on both oil and barrel, and he also created problems for the independent distributors to whom he sold. The barrels had to be transferred from the railroad siding onto a wagon, and then unloaded, barrel by barrel, at the doors of retailers. The cost of the extra labor involved had to come out of the middleman's profit, or be reflected in higher prices to the consumer.

"They Disgust Me"

With its unmatchable advantage in transportation Standard, selling a barrel of refined oil at the same wholesale price as that of a typical independent, could make twice or three times the profit. If it chose to drive a small rival out of business, it could, without itself feeling the pinch, lower prices to the point where competition could not survive. The independent refiner consequently took a long chance if he dared reach out for additional business. At the first sign of such aggressiveness the Standard Oil representative in his area would telegraph Cleveland. If Standard chose to retaliate, its prices in the affected marketing area might be cut below anything that was possible for the independent. Middlemen to whom he had been selling his output would thus be tempted to desert him; and he might find himself left only with those few customers whose resentment of Standard's practices was greater than the magnetic pull of low prices.

As long as the railroads owned most of the tank cars the independent had some chance. The roads' legal status as common carriers made them vulnerable to annoying court actions and legislative investigations if they, too, summarily dismissed his cry for tank car service. Recognizing the independent's potential nuisance value, if not his rights, the railroads, if not afraid of Standard's reprisals, would have been willing to release tank cars for the use of the independent. Certainly, they had no love for Standard. Many a railroad executive echoed the sentiment of William Vanderbilt when he said, apropos of Standard's hard-driven bargains, "They disgust me." The fact remains that Vanderbilt, like other railroad magnates, continued to toe Standard's line.

If the independent had felt frustrated while the railroads

owned the tank cars, his frustration was painfully compounded when the cars were transferred to the Car Trust. Whatever efforts the roads had made to preserve the fiction of their status as common carriers now dwindled fast. Even the most desperate and frantic offers could not make a railroad provide a tank car that it did not own. At the same time, they did not wish to admit that they no longer owned the cars. Instead, they multiplied excuses for not providing them. Independent refineries, they continued to assert, had as good a chance as anyone to get cars. But somehow, whenever a specific request was made by an independent, he was always too late; all the cars were in use.

That the Car Trust was deeply involved in the car shortage was of course strongly suspected by those who knew of its existence. But suspicion was one thing, evidence another. The trustees who ran the mysterious organization, and in whose hands all the stock had been placed, were nobodies; and their business was nobody's business. The independent refiner simply had no way to get at the Car Trust, no place to take hold of the problem which it created for him.

The Humor of It All

The state legislatures, for the most part, played Standard's game. When a Standard official wrote Rockefeller from Annapolis that he had arranged "to kill the two bills in the Maryland legislature at comparatively small expense," he was only putting on paper what everyone knew. Even in Pennsylvania, the center of agitation against Standard, every punitive bill had been blocked. But this record of defeat did not prevent the spirit of reform from arising every now and then, to try once more.

There was at that time in the New York State legislature a keen young assemblyman named Alonzo Barton Hepburn, who had a strong feeling both for underdogs and for the psychology of voters. The revelations of the Pennsylvania investigation into unfair railroad practices struck him as opening a fertile field. Since the tracks of both the Erie and the New York Central ran largely through New York State, a legislative probe in Albany was plainly indicated. Who knew what dramatic revelations might not be forthcoming if officials of these roads and the Standard Oil Company could be made to testify? And there were other possibilities. The great Chicago meat-packing houses had begun to use refrigerated boxcars in much the same way that Rockefeller had used the tank car—to obtain rebates from railroads, stifle competition, and compel consumers to pay high prices. The Assembly agreed with Hepburn as to the possibility of a juicy investigation, and a committee, with himself as chairman, went into action.

Testimony before the Hepburn Committee in 1879 revealed all that he could have expected and more about the rebate situation. Independent refiners and producers on the witness stand left little doubt that Standard Oil benefited from large secret rebates and other special favors granted by the railroads. Hepburn, who had been trained in finance and commercial practices, was an effective crusader. He knew the right questions to ask. But when he tried to extract admissions as to the exact nature of the arrangements between Standard and the roads he ran into a wall of silence.

Presently he managed to bring to Albany no less a figure than John D. Archbold, who had become one of Rockefeller's chief executives and a Standard director. Archbold began his testimony by lightheartedly assuring Hepburn that he was merely an officer of the Acme Oil Company, a Standard subsidiary. "I have nothing to do with the active administration of the Standard Oil Company at all." He knew nothing, he said, about Standard's transportation methods.

Pressed harder, he admitted that he was a stockholder of Standard. "I am a clamorer for dividends. That is the only function I have in connection with the Standard Oil Company." (Laughter.)

Everyone had heard rumors of huge annual dividend payments, some said as high as 40 per cent, to Standard Oil stockholders, and Hepburn asked the natural question: How large were the dividends? "I have no trouble," Archbold assured the committee ... "transporting my share ... That is the only transportation there is about it." (Laughter.)

Questioned on the railroad rates of his own company, Acme, he declined to answer. "You consider the rates that you get ... a secret between yourself and the railways?" said a committee member.

"Most assuredly," Archbold replied.

Hepburn then bade him return for further questioning. "I have given today to this matter," Archbold said politely. "It will be impossible for me to be with you again."

Who Owns What?

Jabez Bostwick of Standard accepted an invitation to appear before the committee. Who, Hepburn demanded, actually owned the tank cars run on the New York Central tracks—Standard Oil or the railroad? "I decline to answer," said Bostwick, and stonily repeated the phrase for a whole day, in answer to even the most elementary questions. The committee then turned to high officials of the Erie and New York Central roads. There, for a time, they seemed to find richer ore. Little by little facts began to emerge about the Car Trust. Hepburn, fascinated by this trail, followed it hotly. He learned something about the structure of the Trust and its operations. One of the trustees, Blanchard, who was also an officer of the Erie, described the operation of the Trust and its equipment certificates. He admitted that the method of its compensation, through the mileage allowance, "more than pays bank rates of interest on the investment" in tank cars. The Erie, he said, had 400 or 500 cars which it had leased from the Trust and also hauled about 400 cars which he thought were owned by Standard. He explained that the typical construction cost of a tank car of 100-barrel capacity was $800 and that the Trust had managed, by careful negotiation with builders, to bring this figure down to $750. But when it came to the scope of the Trust, the names of its stockholders and its contractual relations with the railroads, he became vague, uncertain, and uncommunicative. The Erie, he and other officers of the railroad insisted, had nearly 300 tank cars "of its own" available to all shippers; it had complied with its obligations, and could not be held responsible for anything done by the Car Trust. Hepburn was skeptical about those 300 cars. Did they really belong to the Erie? The legends on their tanks said so; and how could he prove otherwise?

Similar testimony was offered, if reluctantly, by the master of the New York Central, William Vanderbilt. "If we had the facilities," he told the committee, "the right of shipping oil over

New York Central's tracks is open to everybody." But had he the
facilities? Who actually owned the tank cars which the Central
had built? He was not sure—this was a detail handled by others.
The whole affair, he conveyed, was a regrettable nuisance; the
Standard Oil people had taken advantage of him. "The competition was so great between the roads that . . . the business
was hardly worth having."

The Virtues of Complexity

One of Standards' great advantages in resisting the investigators was the difficulty that most people had in comprehending
the technical details of railroad freight service. It was in these
details that the key to Standard's advantage lay, but few outside
of the industry cared to struggle through the labyrinth of tariffs,
rebates, and mileage allowances, of manifests, bills of lading,
and car-control records, of methods of determining charges, collecting from shippers, and distributing payments among railroads. The complexity and tedium of the subject held off the
probers and the newspapers like an invisible shield. They could
call Standard names, and the public would respond with suitable
growlings, but when it came to revealing just how Rockefeller's
alleged monopoly operated they were baffled. Even Hepburn
found it difficult to follow Standard's tortuous economic paths.
Again and again witnesses talked themselves and their legislative
audience into confusion which could not be cleared up. The
result was that Hepburn closed his investigation without having
discovered precisely who owned which tank cars.

When his report was published it pointed an accusing finger
at the shadowy Car Trust, as an instrument of Standard's monopolistic ambitions. No action was taken by the New York
legislature, but the report worked as a ferment in newspaper and
governmental circles and had a large part in crystallizing popular
indignation against Standard Oil.

Rockefeller, with his blind spot where publicity was concerned, seems to have regarded the Hepburn probe as a minor
nuisance. He was more interested in a suit brought about the
same time against some of the big railroads by his largest Cleveland competitor, Scofield, Shurmer, and Teagle. The fact that
brother Frank Rockefeller had married Scofield's daughter did

not prevent outbursts of hostility between Standard and the smaller concern, which was seeking to put an end to the use of rebates. It was a relief to John D. when a smiling Dodd brought him the verdict of the court. The law had spoken; the rebate system—for the time being, at least—was justified. The court found that Standard, by providing tank cars, tank stations, and terminal facilities, by reducing the railroads' fire hazard through the use of tank cars, and by guaranteeing very large freight shipments, had entitled itself to preferential arrangements by the roads. The tongue of justice may well have been in its cheek when part of the verdict was written: "Said arrangements are not exclusive, but are at all times open to others shipping a like quantity and furnishing like devices and facilities." Standard was then shipping 90 per cent or more of all oil products out of Cleveland.

"Prompt and Vigorous Action. . . "

Nevertheless, Rockefeller's problems were by no means ended. Competition kept rearing its ugly head. When the independent Tidewater pipe line was opened in 1879 and began pumping oil from the wells 200 miles over the mountains to Philadelphia, it immediately made deep inroads on the freight revenues of the larger railroads. The Pennsylvania and the Erie were especially shaken. Not only did most of their crude-oil traffic suddenly fall away, but they had to stand by while smaller railroads came forward with tank cars for the service of independent refiners in the Philadelphia area. The Pennsylvania was especially exercised by the Philadelphia and Reading road, which owned stock in the pipe line, and which immediately built 200 new tank cars for the refineries along its tracks.

Jewett, Scott, and Vanderbilt decided to stand together in trying to tempt independent shippers away from the pipe line and back to their routes. This could be done, they thought, by drastic cuts in tariffs. Rockefeller, however, recognized that the Tidewater line signaled the coming of a new era in crude-oil transportation. It was inevitable that there would be a sharp reduction in the use of tank cars for hauling petroleum from the wells to the metropolitan centers of the East. For a time he cooperated with the friendly roads by releasing some tank cars with which they could encourage refiners to make crude-oil shipments over their tracks. But this strategy, as he had foreseen, was ineffective.

It was soon unmistakable that the new pipe line was giving Rockefeller's competitors, for the first time, a transportation advantage over Standard. The Tidewater line was a success, stimulating the expansion of independent refineries, and making Philadelphia a center rivaling New York for the exportation of crude oil. Warning Jewett and the others of "the necessity of taking prompt and vigorous action in this matter at the earliest moment possible," Rockefeller prepared to meet the new challenge.

His first step was to demand that Jewett yield parts of Erie's right of way to aid Standard in the construction of a trunk pipe line, running from the oil regions to Cleveland. Jewett was taken aback—this was asking the Erie to cut its own throat. But Rockefeller reassured him. The move, he said, was not being made "with the expectation of withdrawing business from your road." When he agreed to give the Erie a percentage of the earnings of the new pipe line, Jewett capitulated. The line began pumping oil in March, 1880, and quickly brought Cleveland's crude-oil freight charges down below the level of Philadelphia's. Having protected Erie's revenue with a share in the pipe line, Rockefeller evidently felt justified in cutting down the road's tank car business after all, for now he gave orders to his staff to "discontinue shipping to Cleveland in cars. . . . Have cars sent East. We desire to use them on the Pennsylvania."

He then repeated the process with the Pennsylvania, building pipe lines along its tracks, using part of its right of way, and compensating the railroad by a share of the pipe lines' revenue to offset the loss of crude-oil rail freight. The New York Central, similarly involved, was given an interest in part of Standard's pipe line network to New York. Soon crude oil was being pumped via pipe line to Standard's refineries in Pittsburgh, Buffalo, New York, and Baltimore, and at transportation costs lower than those of competitors. As tank cars were released from Standard's crude-oil hauls, they were cleaned and put into the freightage of refined products, but still exclusively for Standard's use.

No Detail too Small

With the pipe line situation well in hand, Rockefeller concentrated on maintaining his advantages in rail freight. Any development in this area was sure of his eye and thought. Some of the roads, hard hit by the loss of crude-oil haulage, proposed to attract independent traffic in refined products by removing the freight surcharge for barrels. At once Rockefeller objected. Was the refiner who shipped in bulk, using the tank car, to be penalized for his efficiency? Standard let it be known that any road which did not make an additional charge for the weight of the barrels ran the risk of losing tank car shipments.

This was enough to block the move. But the desperate roads soon tried again. The president of the bankrupt A&GW, Devereux, was deeply disturbed by the discovery that more and more independent refiners were shipping via water routes, such as the Erie Canal and Great Lakes, during the ice-free seasons. He sounded out the Erie and New York Central on the possibility of collective action to meet the situation, even at the risk of resistance to Rockefeller. Specifically, he proposed that the three lines uniformly and sharply reduce tariffs on refined oil products east of Cleveland. In this way Standard's advantage in rail rebates would be partly offset, and independent refiners might be brought back to the railroads.

As soon as Rockefeller heard of the potential mutiny by the railroads, he moved to quell it. An emphatic letter went off to Oliver Payne, one of his Cleveland lieutenants. Its essence was that, if the railroads persisted in cutting rates in the East, Standard, which had a monopoly in the shipment of refined products west of Cleveland, would take reprisals. "State to Devereux... that the reduction... will compel a reduction on rates from Cleveland to the West... whereas if they hold firm... then we, as practically the only parties supplying refined oil, will not be pressing for a reduction of westbound rates. We must not allow the rate to Cleveland to go below 50 cents... I believe if we are firm with the railroads they will not yield this point." He was right. The roads, for a time at least, hastily fell back into Standard's line of march.

No detail, if it affected transportation, was too small for Rockefeller's personal attention. When the Lake Shore sought more business from him, he assented, but on condition that the railroad cease to charge Standard for switching its tank cars to other lines at junction points. The Lake Shore agreed, and thereafter received most of Standard's shipments in Michigan. A small com-

petitive railroad in Michigan found itself hurt by this development, and offered Standard "very cheap rates," in an effort to
recapture some of the lost business. Rockefeller wrote back
to refuse the offer. Free switching was of considerable value
to Standard, and he never ceased trying to get other roads to
make the same concession.

A number of tank cars used exclusively by Standard of Ohio
were causing some confusion among railroads because of varying
identification. Some still had Erie and New York Central marks;
others were labeled with the names or code letters of small tank
car lines which Standard had acquired by purchase—Star, Union,
Consolidated, Empire, etc. The green paint of the numerous
Empire cars separated them from the others, but there was need
for a single grouping to embrace all the rest, which, for the
most part, were painted railroad red. There is a tradition that
Rockefeller personally selected the name "Union Tank Line" as
appropriate for this purpose, and that on his order, the restencil-
ing of new insignia on all of Standard's cars was begun. The
order certainly showed his characteristic regard for economy.
The work was not allowed to interfere with traffic; it was done
only gradually as individual cars went into shops for necessary
cleaning or repairs, and it took several years to accomplish.

By the early 1880's, Standard of Ohio's red cars, bearing the
legend UTLX, followed by a serial number, were a familiar sight
on railroads throughout the land. Now the way was paved for
another useful step. Rockefeller personally authorized the preparation of a catalogue of all of the Union and Green Line cars,
with their identifying numbers and capacities, for circular distribution to railroads. This was primarily a service to the roads,
simplifying their routing of cars and record keeping. But it also
served another purpose. From time to time independents had
complained that the stated capacities of Standard's tank cars
as shown by their stenciled figures were not to be relied on—
that the railroads were letting Standard ship 120-barrel tank
cars at the 110-barrel rate, merely because the latter figure appeared on the cars. No one wanted to undertake the gigantic
task of calibrating the tanks, but the rumor was unpleasant and
some form of reassurance was needed. The distribution of the
complete listing of the cars gave the railroads a black-and-white

answer to skeptics. Standard's name did not appear as sponsor of the circular as printed. It bore the imprints of agents of the railroad associations of the period.[1] On the theory that there is always an aura of conviction about figures issued by outside authority, this move should have allayed suspicion, and it did, for a while; but only for a while.

[1] Frequently revised, the list was later expanded to include tank cars belonging to others besides Standard, and in time became a regular and respected feature of railroad operation.

SIX

NIMBLE ON THEIR FEET

By the early 1880s, hardly more than ten years after Standard Oil of Ohio came into existence, the company's power was so great that even Rockefeller must have been dazzled. Its share of the nation's total oil business, crude and refined, was estimated at about 85 per cent. This meant 85 per cent of a business which by 1883 was taking the output of 20,000 wells, embraced 4,000 miles of pipe line, used 5,000 tank cars, employed 100,000 people, and exported to Europe alone an average of 50,000 barrels per day. Fears that early exhaustion of the Pennsylvania wells might destroy this industry had been dissipated by the discovery of oil in Ohio, and by reports of great new fields waiting to be tapped in California and Texas.[1] One of Standard's rising young executives, Wesley H. Tilford, was sent to California by Rockefeller in 1878. When he returned, he had not only organized the western market for Standard but had laid long-range plans for the production and refining of California oil.

The markets of the industry were expanding as fast as, or faster, than its resources. To be sure, few if any could foresee the future of the "gasoline carriage," which had been patented a few years earlier. But the construction of great railroads in the West called for enormous quantities of lubricating oils; as did also Thomas Edison's applications of electricity to machinery, and the new power plants which were springing up in the nation's cities.

---

[1] Development of California oil had begun on a small scale as early as 1870. Oil had been found in Texas in the 1860s, but exploitation did not begin until the 1890s.

Appliance factories owned by Standard had brought out improved models of stoves, lamps, and wicks, and were selling their output below cost in order to expand the market for kerosene throughout the world. European refiners were affiliating themselves with the Rockefeller interests in order to be assured of a steady supply of American crude oil, carried in Standard's growing tanker fleet. Not since the days of royal monopoly had a business enterprise become prosperous on such a scale, and so quickly.

More Rage in Pennsylvania

Although Rockefeller's executive team was expending a great deal of capital and organizational talent in enlarging and improving refineries, developing better products and new products, exploring for additional oil fields and building pipe lines and tank cars, these economic contributions did not appreciably alter the public view of his enterprise. Standard's efficiency was recognized everywhere, but it was portrayed as the efficiency of the tiger. That the company had fattened at the expense of the railroads and the independent producers and refiners of oil was a charge difficult to evade. Rebates paid Standard by the Pennsylvania Railroad alone were estimated by government investigators to amount in a ten-year period to fifty or sixty million dollars. But it was not so much Standard's wealth as the poverty of the rest of the industry which agitated the righteous. By forcing down crude prices at the wells while raising fees for the use of its storage tanks and pipe lines, Standard had cut away the producer's margin of profit to the vanishing point. By monopolizing tank cars and compelling other refiners to use barrels, and insisting that the railroads charge freightage on the weight of the barrels, Rockefeller had burdened his rivals almost beyond endurance. They could survive only by picking up crumbs of business from Standard's feast. The old days when the Empire Line had served them seemed to the independents like Paradise lost. It was common among them in the 1880s to date their time of troubles from the surrender of Potts and Scott to Rockefeller.

Even the pioneering Tidewater pipe line, on which small refiners had for a time based high hopes, succumbed to Standard's pressure. When the independents whom it served, unable to com-

pete with Standard in the market, dwindled in number and
crude-oil purchasing power, the pipe line's business fell away.
Its owners in self-preservation then sold one-third of their stock
to Standard. Technically, this was not enough to give Standard
control, but in practice it served Rockefeller's needs. At once
Tidewater's rates for pumping oil rose, and within a year another
score of weak independent refineries in the East had given up
the struggle.

Once more storms of emotion played over the Pennsylvania
oil regions. Impassioned speakers addressing agitated audiences
pointed out that the natural resources of their state were being
depleted for the benefit of millionaires in Ohio and New York.
The facts bore out this view. In the 1860s Pennsylvania concerns
had refined 97 per cent of the oil produced in the state. By the
middle of the 1880s they refined only 14 per cent. Philadelphia,
which had once shipped 42 per cent of the nation's crude-oil
exports, had seen the figure dwindle to 17 per cent as the business was diverted to New York. More than 80 Pennsylvania refineries, it was estimated, had been "bankrupted, squeezed out,
bought up, leased, or dismantled" by the Standard Oil Company,
58 in the Pittsburgh area alone.

The disaster of the oil producers was as great as that of the
refiners. There was something intolerably frustrating in the
spectacle of men owning pools of "black gold" in a period of large
demand and yet going slowly broke. How did this happen? If
the producers themselves had a share of the responsibility, if
uncontrolled production had something to do with their problem,
the fact was ignored. All blame for the situation was assigned
to Standard's domination of pipe lines and tank cars.

Necessity Invents the Standard Trust

The producers' legal efforts of the late 1870s had failed, their
attorney, Dodd, had gone over to the enemy, the indictments
obtained against Standard officials had proved futile, but all hope
was not yet lost. A new and comparatively strong governor had
been elected in Pennsylvania, and he had found the state's finances gravely unbalanced. This was no time to permit outside
interests to profit at Pennsylvania's expense. The key to the problem was taxation. Standard of Ohio paid taxes on its physical

properties within the borders of Pennsylvania, but this was a comparatively trivial sum. At the Governor's urging the courts of Pennsylvania reinterpreted an old tax law which stood on the statute books. Under the new ruling the state was empowered to levy taxes on the entire capital stock and dividends of any company which transacted business within the state, regardless of its location. The assessment against Standard of Ohio, including penalties, was fixed at $3,200,000, and the state auditor was instructed to bring suit for this amount.

It was a complicated case, full of legal uncertainties, and would be dragged out for years before being settled for a small fraction of the sum asked. But the danger that other states might follow Pennsylvania's lead gave Rockefeller pause. Here was a kettle in which even big fish could be cooked, if they were not wary.

At that time there were 40 companies in the combine, controlled by policies set by Standard of Ohio, but technically separate. Many of these 40 companies owned property in more than one state, and so might be vulnerable to court actions like that of Pennsylvania. It was this situation that Rockefeller felt had to be corrected. Conferring with Flagler and Dodd, he decided on a characteristically direct procedure.

Each of the 40 companies was to divest itself of all holdings outside of its own state. Properties in each state would then be recombined into one or more separate corporations, subject to the tax laws of that one state only.

Two major questions immediately arose. How could the shares of the companies in the combine be properly reapportioned among their individual owners after the shuffling of properties? And where should control of the combine be centered? For a time Rockefeller considered making one of the new companies, Standard of New York, a holding corporation for all of the others. But the difficulty of obtaining a suitable charter from New York State, or from any state at that time, stood in the way.

In solving this problem Rockefeller agreed to a novel and ingenious strategy, the result of which was the formation of the Standard Oil Trust. Like all of his most successful moves, it was not an innovation which he imposed upon the business in the expectation of profit. Rather, it was an imaginative adaptation to necessity, a purely defensive move. The simple and fundamental principle on which he had built Standard's success—to control the market for oil by controlling its transportation—never changed. All of his famous financial manipulations, such as the Trust, were merely peripheral to his central plan of action.

The idea of the Trust in this particular connection seems to have originated with Dodd. Rockefeller had already successfully experimented with the trust principle in gaining control of the railroads' tank cars. He knew the agreeable vagueness of laws governing the fiduciary status in most states. He knew the trust's values of secrecy, of ambiguity, and of freedom of action. To put control of every unit of the vast combine in the hands of a small board of trustees, with himself at its head—to operate on a national scale, without serious responsibility to any state government, or to the federal government—was obviously desirable. Financially the thing was feasible. Effective stock control of the 40 Standard companies was held by only 40 investors, aside from himself, all of whom were either executives of the combine, or were otherwise responsive to his wishes, and whose power as stockholders was exercised by him. These men owned all of the shares of 14 of the companies and controlling interests in the other 26. Let them turn their shares in the various companies over to the board of trustees. The total value of the companies had been carried on their books at the exceedingly conservative figure of $55,000,000. The trustees would issue certificates based on the value of the Trust as a whole, in the more realistic but still conservative amount of $70,000,000, and would distribute these certificates on a pro-rata basis among the 41 key investors.

It was a beautifully simple plan. At one stroke the threat from the state tax laws was blocked, the operations of the combine were shrouded in an impenetrable legal mist, and a higher level of managerial efficiency was made possible.

The trustees under the new system could much more readily coordinate national operations. They could bring new disciplines and economies into every division of the vast enterprise. Control of oil transportation, on which the entire structure had been erected, could be centrally administered to plug loopholes and tighten contractual relationships with railroads. Making their headquarters in New York City, functioning in a secrecy denied to conventional corporations, the trustees, a handful of men, would rule the nation's oil industry.

"That Is Harmony ..."

The formation of the Trust blunted the spearhead of the states' legal attacks, but it only increased public suspicion. Demands for legislative action to break Rockefeller's monopoly continued loud, and they became louder as another thorny business depression gripped the country. The remaining independent refiners thronged the legislative halls of the Eastern states, urging action to save them by depriving Standard of its rail rebates and its tank-car monopoly. A parade of such witnesses appeared in 1885 before an investigating committee of the New York State Senate, and brought the report of the earlier Hepburn Committee up to date. Newspapers printed their testimony with gusto. Said one refiner, "If the books of ... Erie ... were examined, it would be found that only 10 cars of crude had been shipped to New York by any shipper outside the Standard ... within over a year." Another pointed out that the results of Standard's arrangements with the railroads had been to drive out of business or absorb all but five of New York's independent refiners.

Resolutions were passed and indictments on conspiracy charges were presently obtained against prominent officials of Standard Oil of New York. Among them was the immensely rich and mighty Henry H. Rogers. The state had obtained possession of documents linking his name to certain suspect activities of the company. Rogers, who was to become a friend of Mark Twain, had the light touch. Brought into court, he was required to testify as to the alleged aggressions of Standard Oil against other refiners. His blithe reply was that 95 per cent of the refiners of the country were "living in harmony." What, the prosecutor wanted to know, did he mean by "harmony"?

... "Just what harmony implies; I live in harmony with my wife."

The audience was amused; no one, in those days of Victorian propriety, dared to ask whether Standard was forcibly exercising a husband's rights on the reluctant independent refiners, but the thought was in many minds. Rogers was exonerated. Although two of his subordinates were found guilty of conspiracy, the attitude of the court is suggested by the amount of their fines —$250 each.

Always the weakness of Rockefeller's operation at this time, and the only weakness, was in its relation to the public. In this department he did not serve himself well, nor was he well served by others. The men who exercised power in his name sometimes grew careless in their confidence, and tried too hard to achieve too little. It was generally characteristic of Rockefeller's tactics, even at their most arrogant, that they made for efficiency, and that they kept roughly within the framework of the existing law. When he came a cropper, as in the South Improvement debacle, it was on a grand scale and in connection with a major issue. Not so with many of his subordinates and allies. Their heavy-handed actions, while limited in scope, frequently stirred up as much unpleasant dust as if they involved millions.

One notorious case was that of Standard's capable and aggressive pipe line manager, Daniel O'Day, who was to become a major executive of the combine. Operating in the new Ohio fields, O'Day engaged in a running feud with a small-scale independent refiner, George Rice. Rice was an articulate and often noisy critic of Standard's methods and a thorn in O'Day's flesh. There is evidence that Rice's antagonism stemmed in part, at least, from earlier refusal by Rockefeller to buy him out at a price which Rice considered fair, but he had plenty of other reasons for resentment. O'Day at the first opportunity struck recklessly at the jugular vein of Rice's business. The small railroad which served the oil field was bankrupt, and its receiver was under O'Day's muscular thumb. Suddenly the road, which was collecting 10 cents a barrel from Standard for short-haul freight, raised its rates for independents to 35 cents a barrel—and at the same time secretly agreed to pay the extra 25 cents to Standard's pipe line company, National Transit. It was the kind of error in judgment which is likely to occur when passions are in command. O'Day had exposed Standard to the embarrassment of a revelation. When Rice brought evidence of the illegal arrangement to court, O'Day had to retreat, refunding the tribute collected by National Transit on Rice's oil. The amount was only $340, but the effect on public opinion was incalculable.

"Please Turn Another Screw"

Rockefeller and his early intimates were noted for their economy in words and for their elaborate devices to insure secrecy. Some of the newer men, however, did not realize the extent of the precautions needed to prevent written communications embodying company policy from getting into the hands of outsiders. The head and former owner of Standard's refinery at Louisville, Kentucky, F. D. Carley, was guilty of a major slip of this kind. A single phrase of his in a letter to a railroad was destined to become copy for editorial writers throughout the country. Rice, the same independent refiner who had been hit by O'Day's low blow, had shipped seventy barrels of kerosene to a Louisville merchant. It was characteristic of Standard's remarkable system of intelligence that even so small a transaction by a competitor did not escape notice. The fact went on record that Rice had paid an unusually low rate for freight on this shipment. One of Carley's men promptly drafted a letter of rebuke to the railroad's general freight agent and Carley signed it. The car, he pointed out, had "slipped through" and should have been charged with an additional $16. Then was added the line, "Please turn another screw." These words haunted Standard executives for the next generation. Elaborate efforts were made to explain them away. They merely meant, a Standard official told investigators, "that the machinery of the railroad office was loose," and should be tightened up. But the public remained convinced that Standard was putting the screws on the independents.

Even friendly railroads by overzealousness or indiscretion sometimes made trouble for Standard. An independent refiner testified that a Midwestern railroad had declined to provide box cars for his barreled oil on the ground that cars so used became permeated with the smell of oil and had to be cleaned and aired for weeks before they were fit to carry ordinary merchandise. Yet it was shown that the same railroad unhesitatingly supplied box cars for Standard's use when tank car shipments needed to be supplemented. On one occasion the Pennsylvania Railroad, eager to cooperate with Standard, created an incident which was promptly aired in legislative halls. The comparatively small

Philadelphia and Reading line had received some requests for its tank cars from independent refiners located at points served by the Pennsylvania. When asked how much it would charge to run a few P&R cars over its tracks to the refineries and back, the Pennsylvania would make a quotation for the cars only when loaded. It refused to move them at any price while they were empty. The president of the P&R exploded with rage and sarcasm. "They will carry the oil . . . Oh, yes, they will make a proper charge for it, which is only three or four times higher than they charge the Standard, but they will not permit the empty cars to come over the road in order to get the oil. . . . They must be taken on a wheelbarrow, or by canal or balloon!" Episodes like these were repeatedly construed as proof of conspiracy between the railroads and Standard to do away with competition in oil refining.

There were accusations, too, that crude oil sent to independent refineries from storage tanks controlled by Standard was often of inferior quality. In some cases the allegation was that, when petroleum had been in the tanks too long and had deteriorated, it was earmarked for distribution to independents. In other cases the oil was shipped in tank cars which had not been cleaned for a long while and were full of sediment. Given Standard's enormous business, an occasional incident of this kind was to be expected and might, under ordinary conditions, be attributed to the negligence of individual employees. But the atmosphere of the time did not permit excuses. Where Standard was concerned each such episode was taken by the public to be proof of malicious intent.

"Our Full Share of the Business"

The roots of the public bitterness against Standard went much deeper, of course, than such scattered instances of injustice. They were nourished by the profound changes then taking place in the American economy. Everywhere there was uncontrolled activity and jostling growth. As the cities grew, as new businesses started up, as resources were exploited, as population and production soared together, an increasing need was felt to resist the tendency of the resulting wealth to flow into the hands of a few corporations. Oil was not the only industry threatened by monopoly. Similar dangers were recognized in the production of other basic commodities, such as lumber, steel, copper, and meat. Suspicion of the leading companies in these and other industries became fixed in the public mind. Labor was especially restive. Men were less willing than before to work twelve hours a day for subsistence wages, and with their jobs in peril from day to day, while their employers piled up millions.

Depression years had made matters worse. Strikes of long duration, marked with violence and bloodshed, were increasing in number. Idealistic advocates of socialism were to be found in cities throughout the country. In rural areas, too, populist movements, such as the Grangers, achieved considerable power, with the result that in 1884, for the first time in twenty-four years, a Democratic president, Grover Cleveland, was elected. Although considered by many even in his own party to be dangerously radical, Cleveland actually tried to restrain popular agitation against "the capitalists." Nevertheless, hatred of monopoly mushroomed rapidly into a major popular cause, and Standard Oil, as the most formidable single business in the country, became the chief target of attack by reformers.

Rockefeller seemed not to notice the buzzing around his ears. He continued to concentrate on the dollar-and-cents realities of the business. When independent refiners in a frantic effort to hold on to their markets began cutting their prices to the bone, he first gave orders to reduce Standard's prices "sufficient to hold on to the trade" and then a little later authorized another cut, this time "to secure our *full* share of the business." He had no disposition at this stage to temper the wind to the shorn lamb. For a time he even discussed with his top aides the reduction of Standard's prices to cost in order to drive the remaining independents into a still tighter corner and capture their markets for Standard. However, he finally came to agree with one of his executives, Benjamin Brewster, who counseled that "a safer and more profitable course ... is to make prices at which the outside interests may perhaps keep moving but not derive sufficient comfort to induce increased consumption. ... If we make the fight too sharp, the result is retaliatory measures."

Only such self-restraint, exercised in the spirit of self-protection, prevented Standard's percentage of the total oil business of the nation from rising to an absolute 100 per cent. Its economic advantages over competitors continued to grow. Its purchasing agency at the wells could buy oil in larger quantities and cheaper than any other buyer. Its pipe line network, efficiently managed by Daniel O'Day, controlled storage facilities for 40,000,000 barrels of oil, a gathering system from all parts of the oil region, and by 1885 more than 1,300 miles of trunk pipe lines. The Union Tank Line and the Green Line together comprised nine-tenths of the nation's tank cars. Standard's freight costs were far lower than those of any other oil shipper. Its near-monopoly of the manufacture of high-grade railroad lubricating oil compelled almost every American road to depend for shipments of this essential product on the Galena Signal Oil Company, a Standard subsidiary. This was a weapon which Rockefeller was careful not to brandish; resistance to high rebates by railroads was dealt with when possible by less aggressive measures; but it was part of the unwritten code of the railroads that any freight manager who dared to offer serious opposition to Standard's pressure could, by mere delay in the road's lubricating-oil shipments from Galena, be quickly broken to the wheel.

What Could Be Fairer?

By 1886, Rockefeller recognized that legislative attacks on the freight rebate might soon compel Standard to yield up this advantage. A bill which would enable the federal government to regulate interstate commerce and provide assurance of uniform treatment of shippers by all railroads was under consideration in the United States Congress. In the climate of the time it seemed certain that this bill would become law. After the development of the trunk pipe lines Standard had gradually ceased to demand rebates from railroads for crude-oil shipments, but rebates on refined products had remained in force. Now these, too, were imperiled.

The question arose: What could be put in place of the rebate to assure Standard a continuing advantage in freight rates? W. H. Tilford, one of the trustees and head of the company's powerful Domestic Trade Committee, concentrated on this all-important matter. Just before Congress passed the Interstate Commerce Act in 1887 he set in motion a gigantic effort to rewrite

Standard's contracts with the 166 railroads carrying its freight (out of a total of 196 lines operating in the United States). In the forefront of the negotiation he placed a formidable executive, Howard Page, then connected with Standard's refinery at Louisville, Kentucky. Page, noted for his forceful, outspoken style, and capable of beating a brow or two if the occasion called for it, had made a reputation as a hard bargainer for rebates, and had extracted concessions from railroads exceeding any previously known in Standard Oil history. As he later said modestly in testifying before a government body, "It was a man's business to get as low rates as he could."

Page met with the heads of the chief Midwestern railroads with a view to replacing the old arrangement. He quickly showed that the confidence reposed in him by Tilford was fully warranted. From his talks emerged new elements of advantage for Standard, far more subtle than the secret rebates of the past, and just as effective. These advantages lay primarily in determinations made by the railroads of the weight of oil products as transported in tank cars and as transported in barrels. The growing variety of oil products made it highly impractical for the railroads to try to fix a tariff separtely for each tank car or barrel transported. Instead, an average figure was arrived at and applied to all tank cars and barrels carrying oil in any form. This average figure was based on the average weight of such products in the quantities normally transported.

It was an intricate calculation which few were competent to make and still fewer competent to criticize. Under Page's guidance the roads agreed that the weight of the various oil products carried in tank cars averaged out at 6.3 pounds per gallon; but the actual weight, it was subsequently shown by the government, was closer to 7 pounds. When it came to barreled oil, however, his pressure on the railroads was all in the other direction. It was decided that the average weight of oil contained in a barrel was 315 pounds. In fact, it was about 300 pounds. Freight would continue to be charged on the barrels themselves, and the average barrel was assumed to weigh 85 pounds—10 pounds higher than the reality.

Page also insisted that tank car loads of oil were subject to loss due to evaporation or leakage in the amount on the average of 42 gallons per tank car, which consequently ought to be deducted from the railroad's freight charge. Probably every railroad man present knew that the average loss due to these causes was about 10 gallons, but none was in a position to contest the point, and the 42-gallon figure was allowed, with Standard as its beneficiary.

It would take nearly five years before the fledgling Interstate Commerce Commission was able to correct these inequities. Meanwhile, taken together, the weight determination for which Page was largely responsible gave the user of tank cars—which is to say, Standard—approximately a 25 per cent freight advantage over refiners using the barrel. Yet on the face of it these decisions on weight seemed nondiscriminatory and aboveboard; they could be published for the uninitiated to read as evidencing uniform treatment by the railroads for all shippers.

Page Wins Another Argument

This was not all. Page also demanded and got agreement to alter the established mileage allowance paid by the railroads to shippers who provided their own tank cars. For several years it had been the custom of the roads to pay three-fourths of a cent per "loaded mile"; now it was stipulated that they would pay the same amount whether the tank cars that ran over their tracks were loaded or empty.

The "empty mileage" allowance was not established without argument. Some of the roads protested that, far from paying such an allowance, they ought to charge for hauling Standard's empty tank cars, as had been done in the early days of the industry. Page would have none of this, and he had cogent arguments. Not only were the empty back hauls necessary to provide the loads which meant revenue to the railroads; was there not wear and tear on the cars empty or loaded? Did not Standard have to defray maintenance costs and provide replacements when the cars wore out? Since the railroads did not provide the tank cars from which they profited, it was only justice, Page contended, that the owners of the cars be compensated for all mileage, loaded and empty, except perhaps when the empty hauls were excessively long.

The midwestern railroads were deeply concerned by the

fact that tank cars were traveling a far higher proportion of empty miles over their tracks, relative to loaded miles, than before. This was especially true of cars delivering refined petroleum products to Southern cities. The railroads urged that Standard let its tank cars be used to carry turpentine and cottonseed oil on their return trips, and this was done in some instances, but the practice was frowned upon by Page, for it involved expensive cleaning of cars between hauls.

The fact was that the allowance for empty mileage was recognized by the roads as a partial substitute for the rebate system, in the sense that it was another increment of advantage to Standard over its competitors. Together with the weight determination agreed upon with Page it left Standard better off than under the rebate system. The freight rates on various oil products charged by the roads under the new arrangement averaged about .7 of a cent per ton per mile, for oil in general. A cargo of 100 barrels carried in bulk was calculated as representing 15 tons. Standard was thus obligated to pay the railroad about 10 cents per mile to haul a tank car of 100 barrels' capacity to its destination, but the loaded and empty mileage allowance reduced this charge to about 8½ cents per mile. In contrast, a rival shipper, compelled to use barrels, which were calculated at 400 pounds per loaded barrel, was paying freight at the approximate rate of 12½ cents per mile per 100 barrels, and then had to pay return freightage (a term then much in use) for the empty barrels. Standard, as the only shipper using tank cars in quantity, had a real rate more than one-third lower than that of others. Yet it was now possible for railroad men to assert as literal truth that freight rates were uniform for all shippers.

The High Command Is Pleased

Page's ingenuity was regarded with approval by Tilford and Rockefeller, and he soon extended the new deal to almost all railroads used by Standard. But aside from the obvious benefits to Standard in terms of rail shipping costs the new freight contract had another and indirect value of tremendous importance. It gave strong support to the Trust's pipe line policy. For many years Rockefeller had taken the position that pipe line rates for moving oil should be roughly equivalent to railroad rates and that both should be kept at a high level. Thus, no matter which form of transportation was used for a competitor's crude oil, Standard's advantage was retained. If the competitive oil moved by rail, the advantage lay in Standard's lower net freight charges. If the competitive oil moved through the pipe lines, which Standard owned, the advantage lay in the pipe line's profits. Any significant reduction of railroad rates was always opposed by Rockefeller, for it tended to divert competitive crude-oil shipments away from the pipe lines and to reduce Standard's advantage. Measures which compelled the railroads to keep their rates high were welcome—and this was precisely the effect of Page's negotiation.

O'Day, the head of Standard's pipe line subsidiary, National Transit, was especially enthusiastic about Page's achievement. He recommended to Rockefeller that Page be brought to New York and made coordinator of rail traffic for all the Standard Oil companies; and this was done. Thereafter Standard's pipe-line and rail operations became more and more closely meshed. Whenever one was threatened, the other provided the power needed to maintain Standard's advantage. For example, the Pennsylvania Legislature in 1887 debated a bill which aimed to compel all pipe lines within the state to serve as common carriers. Nearly twenty years would elapse before the enactment of a Federal law to the same effect; the reformers at Harrisburg were hopelessly premature; but not knowing this, they made a very loud noise. The threat was taken seriously by the Trust, which thought it advisable to provide Standard's friends in the legislature with ammunition for countering the attack. At the height of the debate, O'Day signed an agreement with the Independent Producers Association of Pennsylvania, an agreement which seemed to say that National Transit, without coercion, had made itself a common carrier. Under this agreement, the use of its pipe lines was open to any member of the Association who could provide facilities to receive the crude oil as it was pumped and who paid the required fees, which were the same as those paid by Standard's own producing companies.

The new agreement was thought to be a token of a more liberal spirit in the Trust, and it played a part in the defeat of "the common carrier bill." In practice, however, it meant little.

If O'Day could no longer regulate the flow of independents' oil into the pipe lines as closely as before, Page could continue to regulate the rail movement at the far end, which came almost to the same thing. Ownership of most of the storage tanks and tank cars needed to contain the crude oil on its way from the pipe line outlet to the refinery and domination of rail movements of refined products were enough for the needs of the Trust.

A Little Paint Does Wonders

Government, however, continued to poke its nose into Standard's business. The new agreement with the railroads had to be submitted to the newly-formed Interstate Commerce Commission for its approval. The great question was whether railroads would be permitted to charge shippers using barrels for the weight of the barrels—a point hotly contested by independent refiners. To Rockefeller's satisfaction, the ICC's decision favored Standard. Railroads would be permitted to charge freightage for the barrels. Although the Commission added that rates for the oil in barrels were to be identical with rates for comparable weights of oil in tank cars, no question was raised at this time as to the railroads' method of calculating the weights.

The independents, led by the indefatigable Rice, quickly rallied from this blow. Through a friendly railroad employee Rice was able to get hold of several invaluable pieces of evidence against Standard. One was a circular catalogue listing all of the company's tank cars by number and capacity. This he accompanied by records showing that the railroads had accepted these printed capacities as the basis for their freight charges to Standard—"blind billing" was the railroader's term for the practice. And the cars themselves, Rice was prepared to prove by affidavit and physical demonstration, in many instances had capacities more than 25 per cent greater than those listed.

In August, 1887, he brought this factual dynamite before the ICC, which promptly ordered a full investigation. For Rockefeller this was a critical moment. The charge, if substantiated, would be regarded as clear proof of conspiracy between Standard and the railroads. Many of the suspect cars were in the Green Line, which Standard had taken over from Empire, but by no means all. Rice and his friends anticipated a smashing triumph.

The cars could be subpoenaed as evidence by the ICC and would speak for themselves.

It was later said, but never proved, that at this time an order went forth from Rockefeller to bring as many Green Line cars as possible into the shops without delay, paint them red, give them new numbers under the Union Tank stencil, repaint and re-number, too, any UTL cars which might be involved. However that may have been, when a few weeks later the ICC investi-gation began, members of the commission had heard rumors of a great repainting. Startled and shocked, they queried Page: "Has there recently been any general change in the numbering of the cars?"

"Yes, sir," was the reply. "There has been quite a general re-numbering, repainting, and overhauling."

"When did that change take place?"

Page was doubtful. "I think it was commenced some time in July; it may have been later."

If the order had been issued in July it would have anticipated Rice's complaint, and so might have been innocent coincidence; but who was to prove it? Surely Standard had the right to re-paint its cars in the interest of operating efficiency. To merge the old Green Line cars with the Union Tank Line made ex-cellent sense; it was a step which had long been contemplated.

Instructed to deliver some of the cars in question for the in-spection of ICC agents, Standard readily complied. When the agents traveled to the appointed railroad yard, there the cars were, gleaming in fresh red paint, with spotless white new num-bers. Members of the ICC observed that to any railroad man's eye, unaided by instruments, these cars showed capacities greater than the 80 barrels at which they had been billed. But before specific charges could be brought against Standard, the Com-mission had to be able to state definitely which car had been blind billed, on what date, by which railroad, and this was no longer possible.

Their frustration was compounded by the bland candor of Standard's representatives. Had, demanded the ICC, the capac-ities shown in the new listing of cars prepared by Standard been changed from the old? Oliver Payne of Standard willingly acknowledged the fact. The cars had been "changed as to classification, slightly, to get the cars of the same general class as near together as possible ... as to strength, age, and capacity." Everyone knew what had happened; tempers flared and congressional necks burned under their starched collars; but the fact remained that Standard had again turned aside the enemy's ax.

SEVEN

"PERFECTLY TRUTHFUL"

One of the extraordinary political phenomena of the period was the zeal and pertinacity of the enemies of monopoly in the country's legislative halls. The movement against Standard Oil in particular was nourished by a sense of outrage in many hearts. After each defeat the ruined independent refiners and their political friends managed somehow to rise from the ground to challenge Rockefeller anew. In 1888, the Committee on Manufactures of the House of Representatives in Washington began hearings on a bill, later to be known as the Sherman Act, which was designed to rid the country of monopolies by penalizing conspiracy in restraint of trade. A major portion of the committee's attention went to the Standard Oil Trust. It was not easy for its members to get the hard facts they wanted. Their problem was summed up in an article in the *North American Review,* then the nation's leading intellectual periodical: "If there was ever anything in the country that was bolted and barred . . . shielded before and behind . . . with secrecy, that thing is the Standard Oil Company." The committee was especially irked at being unable to renew the attack on blind billing. It was forced to admit that, with the cars repainted, it was "impossible now to identify any of these past shipments . . . to ascertain the exact quantity a tank car contained."

Nevertheless, the congressmen went doggedly about their purpose. Summoning an imposing array of top Standard officials, including John D. Rockefeller himself, it centered its drive on the monopolistic roots of their power, trying to extract from them the admission that they owned virtually all the tank cars of the country. Questioned on the subject, Rockefeller showed himself a master of the policy which one of his associates had written out for the guidance of Standard's officials in their role as witnesses: "Parry every question with answers which while perfectly truthful are evasive of *bottom* facts." He passed to Flagler the question of how many tank cars were owned by other refiners. Flagler was clear. There were, he stated flatly, 6,132 tank cars in the United States. Of these, the Union Tank Line owned 3,833, while "others" owned 2,299. The committee found this hard to believe, and asked how he had arrived at his estimate. He submitted somewhat later a list of companies other than Standard owning tank cars. On this list cars owned by others did indeed total 2,299. But 1,800 of these 2,299 cars, it presently appeared, were owned by companies which, although it was not generally realized, were subsidiaries of Standard. Even the late Green Line was included! Flagler's definition of "others" was obviously not identical with that of the investigators. Yet he had been "perfectly truthful."

The committee made another effort to penetrate the mystery of tank car ownership, this time with Howard Page. He was more cautious than Falgler; the cars owned by others, he thought, might run to 1,000. A careful analysis of his list shows that it, too, described as "others" companies which were actually units of the Standard Trust. The only railroad owning a substantial number of tank cars was the Philadelphia and Reading, with 250; and the only independent refiner with more than a finger-count of cars was Standard's old Cleveland rival, Scofield, Shurmer and Teagle, with 20.

For Every Thrust, a Riposte

Among the questions stirring in the minds of the Congress and the ICC was, could the Standard Trust be compelled to permit the use of its tank cars by the railroads for other refiners? It seemed only right that tank car service should be provided by the roads for independent refiners who could not afford to build and operate their own cars. Transportation of oil was the point at which Standard was most vulnerable, at which there was the best chance of breaking its monopoly. In several important states

—Pennsylvania, Ohio, New York—there was a gathering pressure for legislative action on this issue. If it succeeded and was backed by Federal legislation, the props might yet be pulled out from under Rockefeller's system of rail domination.

The prevailing view among Standard's enemies was that all tank cars should be made common carriers or at least brought under an agreement comparable to that made by National Transit with the independent producers. Let the owner of the cars be compensated for their use by others, the independents urged, but not be allowed to monopolize the cars for his own freight. Their dream was that Standard might thus be compelled to lease or sell a substantial part of its tank car fleet to the railroads, under ICC jurisdiction.

It was another matter, however, to find satisfactory grounds for a direct legislative move against tank car monopoly. The inadequacy of existing laws governing trusts and Standard's legal claim to its right of secrecy made it difficult to draft a law which would separate tank car operation from the refining business. The next attack on Standard when it came was based on an entirely different and shrewdly chosen legal position. In 1890, just as the federal Anti-Trust Act became law, the Attorney General of Ohio raised a new question. Was not any Standard subsidiary, chartered under the laws of a state which forbade monopoly, in violation of that state's laws if it adhered to the monopolistic Trust? If so, it could be compelled to desist from any practices which gave the Trust its power. The Attorney General filed a petition in the state's Supreme Court contending that Standard Oil of Ohio, in transferring its stock to the Trust, had "submitted to dominance by an agency unknown to Ohio law," had become part of a monopoly, and had forfeited its rights to the corporate charter which the state had given it.

This was a suit more difficult to defend and more dangerous in its implications than any in Rockefeller's previous experience. It was especially irritating because he was a heavy contributor to the Republican party in Ohio, and the Attorney General was a Republican. A letter which he wrote at this time to a friend in Cleveland complained that "we have not received fair treatment from the Republican party." He was fully alive to the peril of the situation. If the monopoly charges against Ohio Standard as an element of the trust were proved, the keystone of the entire Standard operation—its domination of oil-transportation facilities—might crumble. Legal title to all of the cars of the Union Tank Line was still vested in Ohio Standard. Unless a change was promptly made, a ruling by the court that the cars were instruments of monopoly might result in denying the use of the Union Tank Line to the rest of the Standard combine. The court might even compel the sale of a large number of Union's cars to railroads and independent refiners.

Out of One Pocket, into Another

The ceaseless struggle to maintain Standard's power in the face of adverse public, governmental, and legal actions was telling on Rockefeller. Underneath his calm, quiet exterior he was full of tensions, which presently expressed themselves in a badly ulcerated digestive tract. He was seriously ill when preliminary court hearings were held in the case against Ohio Standard. Nevertheless, he personally laid down the strategy necessary to save the Trust's tank car operation from legal mayhem.

When the tenor of the preliminary hearings held in Ohio in the early summer of 1891 showed that the situation was grave, he gave orders that ownership of the Union Tank Line be transferred immediately from Ohio Standard to a new and separate corporation. Each Standard refinery would thereafter "rent" from the tank car corporation the cars that it needed. The refinery would itself operate the cars so obtained, to meet its own needs, and, so far as the record went, independently of the other units of the combine. This being done, what legal basis could there be for the allegation that the tank cars used by Ohio Standard or any other Standard refinery were monopolistic in purpose?

Of all the states with which the trust had to deal, New Jersey was the most acquiescent and the least encumbered with anti-monopoly laws. At Rockefeller's instructions, Dodd quietly obtained from the authorities at Trenton a charter for a new corporation, the Union Tank Line Company. The incorporators were James McGee, president of the Standard Oil Company of New Jersey, Wesley H. Tilford, and Howard Page. "The objects for which said company shall be formed," read the charter, "are manufacturing railway cars of all kinds for itself and others, contracting for and buying railway cars and materials therefor, owning railway cars, and letting and hiring the same to railway companies and other corporations and persons for use on railways, and selling railway cars." The capital stock of the new company consisted of 35,000 shares at $100 each; of this stock 5,000 shares were issued to each of seven persons—James McGee, Walter Mc-Gee (a young relative), Tilford, Page, Archbold, Rogers, and Paul Babcock, a director and former president of Standard Oil of New Jersey. On July 16, 1891, a quorum of the stockholders met—Tilford, Archbold, Rogers, and James McGee, and elected three directors—Tilford, Howard Page, and F. Q. Barstow. Tilford, always close to Rockefeller, was then president of Standard of Indiana; Barstow was the right-hand man and intimate associate of John Archbold, who, during Rockefeller's illness, had become tacitly acknowledged as the leader of the Standard Oil hierarchy. Evidently, the new corporation was regarded as having an importance that was not suggested by the amount of its capital.

A week later the directors had their first meeting, with Tilford in the chair. Officers were quickly elected—Tilford as titular president, Howard Page as vice-president and operating head of the company. "On motion of Mr. Barstow," so the minutes of the meeting read, "it was resolved that the officers of the company be authorized to negotiate with the Standard Oil Company of Cleveland, Ohio, for the purchase of the cars, tank cars, and other equipment...." Two weeks later the $3,500,000 capital pledged by the stockholders was recorded as paid in. It was further recorded in the minutes that the price asked by Ohio Standard for its 5,000 cars was exactly $3,500,000. The purchase was formally approved by the directors, and the deal was consummated on August 11, 1891. This left the new company without working capital, but a loan from Standard Oil of New Jersey took care of its modest financial needs.

The seven stockholders in the new company promptly turned over to the Trust all of their shares except for token holdings. The entire financial transaction had, of course, been handled on paper. Money had merely been taken from one pocket to be put into another, but the legal purpose had been served. Ohio Standard no longer owned the cars, since Union Tank, on the record, was the owner and lessor. Although Union was obviously owned by the Trust, it could be legally demonstrated that the cars, once leased to a refiner, were operated by that single lessee, and so could no longer be considered as centrally operated for purposes of monopoly. And there was no reason in law to deny the Ohio company or any other Standard refiner the right to lease cars as needed from the one company which had them to lease.

The California Game

Rockefeller's decision to put Wesley Tilford at the head of UTL, with Page as executive officer, showed that his conception of the role of the tank car in Standard's business was unchanged. Tilford's major assignment as one of Standard's top executive committee was the westward expansion of Standard's domestic business. As each new regional market was opened up—the Mississippi Valley, the Missouri Valley, the Mountain states, the West Coast—Tilford moved into action to assure Standard's predominance. In this task the tank car was an essential instrument of power, as it had been in the days of Rockefeller's beginnings. To put the tank car operation directly under Tilford was to make sure that it would be meshed as closely as possible with Standard's domestic marketing program. New tank cars were ordered by Page almost exactly at the pace at which Standard's sales of refined products in the United States were increasing. In the decade of the 1890s, approximately 900 tank cars were added to UTL's fleet—an increase of 18 per cent. In the same period, Standard's domestic business in kerosene rose 17 per cent.

Under Tilford's policy first priority in the assignment of the cars went to those companies facing competitive situations and problems with railroads in markets still undeveloped. He himself often served as the active head of such companies. In the years in which Standard of Indiana became the great oil marketer of the Midwest he was its president. When he resigned this office to become president of Iowa Standard, it was because the decision had been taken to assign to this company the markets of the West Coast.

During the 1880s Tilford spent much of his time in California, quietly assuring to Standard effective control of the distribution of oil products there. At that time few California oil wells were producing, and the local refineries were small. Most of the West Coast's kerosene and lubricants came from the Midwest and were shipped by rail. At once a major transportation problem arose. How could the operation of tank cars from the Mississippi to the Pacific be made economically sound for Standard? California had no liquid products to send eastward in tanks, so that the cars had to travel empty for 2,000 miles; and the great transcontinental trunk lines, Southern Pacific, Union Pacific, and Great Northern charged $105 per car for the empty back haul. It was an unsatisfactory situation.

Tilford dealt with the problem through the development of a new type of tank car. In 1883, Standard acquired patent rights to a so-called gondola tank car which had been designed some years earlier by a Pennsylvanian named Odell. The purchase of the patent was made through the employee of a small company not then known to be part of the Standard combine, and the price paid was only a few hundred dollars. In Odell's car a section of cylindrical tank was slung below the floor of a box car, the upper part of which "could be loaded with freight at the seaboard for the return trip." Tilford knew that California would in time produce and refine its own oil in quantity for the West Coast market. When that happened, tank cars would no longer be needed in transcontinental freight. In the intervening years, however, cars capable of carrying oil to California and lumber on the return trip would help solve a difficult problem.

Construction of experimental cars of this general type was promptly undertaken, and a few years later 500 of them were in use. Although their relatively small oil tanks made them unsuitable for the short hauls of the eastern trade, they more than justified themselves on the long runs to the West Coast. By allowing the railroad to use the upper part of the car for return loadings Standard escaped the heavy charge for the empty haul, and earned the mileage allowance both ways. But Standard's cash income from the use of these cars was by no means their main value to Tilford. The gondola car, with its two-way freight revenues, meant large profits for the western roads and gave them an excellent incentive for cooperating with Tilford's marketing strategy in California.

He was thus able to prevail on them to reduce or raise their freight rates at times indicated by himself. When he wanted to accumulate stocks of oil in California, the rates went down. In this way he could lower Standard's prices to California dealers and squeeze out local competition. At other times, when it became desirable to raise Standard's California prices, the freight rates also went up, making it uneconomical for West Coast dealers to order barreled oil from other eastern refiners. It was a neat and highly effective system. That the railroads understood it thoroughly is shown by an indiscreet telegram which in time found its way into the hands of federal investigators. It revealed that in 1888 the general traffic manager of the Southern Pacific Railroad, speaking for the association of Pacific railroads, recognized their role in Tilford's scheme.[1]

In addition to the gondola cars Tilford assigned a number of conventional tank cars to the North-South run on the West Coast. By 1888 so much of Standard's rolling stock had been diverted to the California trade that Rockefeller became a little concerned. During the summer, when the Cleveland–Harrison presidential campaign was getting up steam, he wrote a note to Archbold: "I fear we shall be cornered this year for bulk cars, for increase in demand will be more than ordinary owing to torchlight processions." Nevertheless, he did not interfere with Tilford, who was always one of his favorites, and who advanced faster in the company than any other of the younger excutives.

With a Touch of Indignation

California had been made safe for Standard, business was better than ever, but there was no mistaking the peril faced by the Trust. In creating the ICC and adopting the Sherman Act the federal government for the first time had put itself in a genuinely punitive posture; while the suits brought by Ohio and other states were being prosecuted with unprecedented zeal, and the threatening public clamor was at a new peak.

Men less sure of themselves, less aggressive in spirit, and less experienced in the ways of the world than Rockefeller and his associates might have tried to come to terms with their enemies, but it is safe to say that appeasement was not even considered

[1] See Appendix A.

by Standard's high command. These were men accustomed to victory. If they sometimes retreated it was only to prepare for the next advance. They wasted no time in useless anxiety or idle regret over their troubles. The one emotion that comes through their memoranda and statements of the time is a touch of indignation that the government should be so misled as to challenge their purposes. What they had done seemed to them entirely sensible, entirely right. They were quite sure that efficient operation of the oil industry required unified administration, and that the weak had to be dominated by the strong. They were quite sure that in creating and operating their vast industrial structure they had performed an enduring service for the nation, and that the public, if not inflamed by vote-seeking politicians, would not have questioned their policies. The business principles by which they were guided had always been accepted by civilized nations everywhere, and they were not prepared to admit that standards of business morality were changing. Since when was it wrong for men to grow rich in business, if the business labored to provide a wanted commodity at a price that people would pay? This was the essence of the matter, as Standard's leaders saw it. From their standpoint the real menace was not monopoly but the growing radicalism of the country, and they were determined not to be its victim.

PART TWO:

ONE STEP AHEAD OF THE GOVERNMENT

1892-1911

> *"I ascribe the success of the Standard Oil Company to the consistent policy of making its business large through the merit and cheapness of its products."*
>
> JOHN D. ROCKEFELLER

ONE

OLD WINE IN NEW BOTTLES

Rockefeller's corporate legerdemain was never more effective than when he separated the Union Tank Line from his other companies. The common use of tank cars had been the main tangible link connecting Standard's refineries with the Trust. Now this link had vanished, legally, into thin air. UTL, merely owning and renting the cars, could disclaim any responsibility for the use made of them by the refineries which it served, or for their freight contracts. A refinery using the tank cars and routing them to meet its needs could disclaim any responsibility for the arrangements made by UTL to obtain compensation for them from the railroads. The right hand knew not what the left hand did. The Attorney General of Ohio would not now find it easy to justify the barring of Standard's tank cars from the state.

Through the Kindness of New Jersey

Other grave penalties still threatened, however, if the charges of monopoly were proved. Dodd, preparing Standard's answer to Ohio's charges, made it his first objective to save the company's state charter. He felt able to reassure the ailing Rockefeller on this score. The state of Ohio had a five-year statute of limitations. It was possible to claim that, since the trust had been in existence for eight years, the charges against the Ohio company had not been filed in time. Therefore, Dodd contended, whatever the court's finding as to monopolistic practice, the company's charter should not be revoked.

Ohio's Attorney General protested that Standard's use of so narrow a legalism was tantamount to an admission of guilt. The state's Supreme Court agreed. Its decision when handed down was a stinging rebuke to Standard. While the statute of limitations prevented revocation of the charter, the Ohio company, the court said, was wholly a creature of the Trust, the object of which was to establish "a virtual monopoly.... All such associations are contrary to the policy of our state and void." The company was ordered to separate its activities and management from the Trust without delay and to pay all costs of the suit.

The Trust was no longer a safe instrument for ruling Standard's empire. The Ohio decision had breached its legal wall, and other states were moving toward the inviting gap. Dodd learned that a suit similar to that of Ohio was being prepared in Albany against Standard of New York. Forestalling action was urgently needed. He was not, however, caught unprepared. A line of defense had been dug against precisely this contingency. In 1888, even before the Ohio suit, when it became probable that the Sherman Act would be passed by Congress, he and Rockefeller had discussed the possibility that the Trust might have to be dissolved. To replace it they had envisaged a holding company, charatered by a single state but authorized to own companies elsewhere. The question was, in which state could such a charter best be obtained without the payment of high taxes? In none were the laws governing corporate charters quite suitable as they existed. But New Jersey's laws came fairly close to the mark, and the company's relations with the state's political bosses were friendly. Standard's agents had quietly lobbied at Trenton to effect certain technical changes in those laws. New Jersey's legislature obliged. The state Commissioner of Corporations was authorized to issue new charters embodying the features desired by Standard; while state taxes on corporate shares were adjusted downward.

As a result, when in 1892 the Ohio decision forced the issue, the Trust was able to move swiftly to escape further attacks upon it by individual states. At that time, Jersey Standard was one of 92 companies owned and controlled by the Trust and by no means the largest. Now it requested and was granted a revised charter, which in time would enable all of the other Standard units to come under its protective wing.

This great recasting could not, of course, be effected overnight. In its first phase the 92 companies were consolidated into 20. Of these 20 surviving units of the combine 4 were producing companies, 7 were pipe line companies, 8 were refining and marketing companies, and one, Union, a tank car company. Standard Oil Company (New Jersey), as it was now designated, was in the forefront of the new grouping, but technically all of the 20 companies were separate and independent.

High Finance with Mirrors

There followed an elaborate financial operation that set Wall Street buzzing with rumors. A Board of Liquidating Trustees, selected from Standard's major stockholders, was appointed. This group published an announcement, requesting every owner of certificates in the Trust to turn them in and receive in exchange scrip certifying that he owned an equivalent proportion of the shares in the twenty separate Standard companies. Here the gate opened to an accountant's paradise. Rockefeller himself, for example, owned certificates for 256,854 out of 972,500 shares which had been issued by the Trust. In exchange, he received certification that he owned precisely that proportion of the outstanding shares in each component company. In the Union Tank Line, he was assigned $\frac{256,854}{972,500}$ of the 99.17 per cent of the company's shares owned by the Trust—or 9,250 shares plus a complicated fraction of a share.

When all the insiders had exchanged their Trust certificates for the new scrip, about 500,000 Trust shares had been retired. But the shares of the Trust had been traded in publicly, and a large number were owned by people not connected with Standard. Many of these investors resisted the exchange primarily, it would seem, because they did not understand it. Moreover, the dubious stockholders were troubled by the idea of accepting scrip—or in effect receipts for stock—instead of actual stock certificates. A rumor that Rockefeller was preparing to take some mysterious and cunning advantage of them gained currency. Some thought that shares of the twenty companies, which were capitalized in the aggregate at $102,000,000, represented a watering of their stocks, and they hastened to sell their Trust certificates on the open market rather than exchange them. The value of the Trust certificates was known, and they had a ready market. But who could tell the value of shares in, say, Standard Oil of New Jersey, or New York, which had never been traded in?

The new capitalization was, in fact, highly conservative—always the case with Rockefeller's enterprises. Within the decade, the net value of the 20 companies, still figured conservatively, would be shown at nearly $200,000,000. It is worth noting that the Liquidating Trustees made little effort to correct the misapprehensions and overcome the doubts of the outsiders. The falling prices of the remaining Trust certificates on the market created attractive bargains for those who knew their real value. In terms of public policy, also, it suited Rockefeller just then to keep the financial structure of the combine in an amorphous and flexible condition. Another nineteen years would elapse before the Trust's last certificate was retired. Ironically, it turned out to be owned by the estate of Rockefeller's most vociferous enemy, George Rice.

At the end of 1892, while liquidation of the Trust slowly proceeded, a majority of the stock of the twenty Standard companies was held by seventeen individual stockholders, all of whom were top Standard executives or members of their families. This exclusive group had complete managerial control of all of the companies, dominated all of the directorates, and elected from among themselves the Liquidating Trustees for the Trust. Ostensibly each of the companies now managed its own affairs. But in practice the seventeen tycoons worked collectively as in the past. Their headquarters continued to be in the New York skyscraper which had been built by the Trust at 26 Broadway. There they exercised unified control over all Standard companies. But they no longer offered a target for government investigators.

Anyone seeking to demonstrate that the combine was still run as a unit would find the going hard. The essence of the Trust's operation had been its central committees. Where were they now? Testifying under oath, Standard executives denied their existence, and literally they spoke the truth. All intercompany committee appointments had been revoked. When the leaders of the various Standard units met to discuss matters of common interest they did so merely as individuals, as friends. No one in Standard any longer referred, for example, to the old Executive

Committee of the Trust, of which Rockefeller was the chairman. It was now known only as "the gentlemen in Room 1400"—this being the suite of offices which it occupied at 26 Broadway.

Standard showed itself eager to do all that the government desired it to do. A legitimate effort was being made—was it not? —to dissolve the Trust, which had become only a rump of its former self. The 20 component companies had, anyone could see, separate managements, and separate directorates. Was this not proof of their independence of each other? If the officers of these companies chose to make their headquarters in New York, in the same building, and meet frequently, was that illegal? Legal purification had been achieved, but without any significant change in actual operations.

"Small Potatoes"

Of all the companies of the new Standard organization the Union Tank Line was the only one whose activities embraced the entire country, and it was probably the most hated. Moralistic elements of the American public in the 1890s regarded UTL as having been conceived in sin and reared in wickedness. Incorporation had not given it respectability. Together with Standard Oil as a whole, it continued to be the target for congressional and journalistic fulmination. A writer of the period on railroad affairs voiced a popular impression when he spoke of the Union Tank Line's "resistless influence." Yet this company, which stirred up so much righteous wrath, consisted of only 35 people, most of them clerks earning less than twenty dollars weekly. (This was not bad pay; the average weekly wage of American workers in the 1890s was less than ten dollars.) Even the company's treasurer and secretary were not much more than glorified bookkeepers, at salaries of about $3,500 per year. Most of their work was altogether routinized. Such decisions as needed to be made came from the desk of one man, Howard Page. It is noteworthy that UTL's records contain no indication of any salary paid to him. His vice-presidential compensation of $8,000 per year came directly from Standard Oil—a respectable figure for a middle-echelon executive—the equivalent, roughly, of 50,000 depreciated and heavily taxed dollars of 1960.

Although Page never belonged to the golden inner circle,

Tilford did. Always a favorite of Rockefeller's and a strong personality, he not only received $10,000 per year for keeping a shrewd supervisory eye on UTL, but had even larger emolument from Indiana Standard and from his services as a liquidating trustee. Half-a-dozen Standard directorships added further to his earned income, while stock holdings in the 20 Standard companies put his fortune comfortably into the millions. Some clue to the dividends paid by the Standard companies is to be found in an estimate that John D. Rockefeller, owning not much more than a fourth of Standard's shares, had an average annual income in the 1890s of about ten millions, tax free.

Compared to the rest of the Standard group Union was obscure and impoverished. One of Standard's executives, on the witness stand in a subsequent lawsuit, referred to the tank car company as "small potatoes." There was no more glamor in its offices than in a dreary tank car repair shop, or a string of grimy cars rumbling along a railway. The company occupied a few rooms on one of the lower floors at 26 Broadway, where clerks perched on high stools examined reports sent in daily by the railroads and painstakingly recorded the movement of tank cars from point to point. For these tedious and never-ending tabulations the clerks were provided with long roller shades to which were affixed large sheets of paper. There was enough space on a single shade to record the movements of about one hundred cars over five or six years. Each clerk had four or five such rollers, and fifteen clerks could keep track of the entire Union Tank fleet, which in 1895 numbered about 5,500 cars.

These car records were the heart of the operation. Knowing where every tank car was at all times, UTL could make rail transport available with minimum loss of time to Standard's refineries. Standard of Kentucky, for example, might telegraph a request for twenty tank cars to carry kerosene from Louisville to Nashville. In UTL's offices shades would be unrolled, and twenty empty cars moving in the vicinity of Louisville would be quickly identified by number. Telegrams would then go from New York to the roads on which the wanted cars were then traveling, ordering them to be switched to the tracks serving the Louisville refinery. This operation from the beginning was called Car Service. The cars had to be kept in good condition, so a

Mechanical Department maintained repair shops in the larger Standard refineries. Beyond this, all that was needed was to replace old cars as they wore out, or increase the fleet as warranted by business conditions.

Nothing could have been more cut and dried. Page's job was simply to make sure that Standard's refineries could get tank cars promptly and in good condition, while giving the government no basis for legal proceedings. Whether UTL earned money was a secondary consideration. Profits were never the test of its success. From Standard Oil's standpoint, it made no difference how much of its total profit was shown by one subsidiary or by another, for all of its earnings went into consolidated accounts, and finally to the same stockholders. Any losses sustained by UTL would be offset by profits earned by the Standard refiners who benefited by obtaining tank cars at very low rental charges. Those charges, of course, were a company secret. Nor did UTL ever disclose how high a proportion of its revenue came from the mileage allowance paid by the railroads. The fact was that for practical purposes UTL was subsisting on mileage. From data supplied by the railroads UTL's clerks would calculate the total mileage run by the company's cars over each road. The railroads would pay accordingly. The checks would go "upstairs" to the parental offices at 26 Broadway. The books of UTL would be credited with the payments. That was all.

"An Overshadowing Monopoly"

Its inconspicuous outer image, however, did not make people forget the power which UTL's control of the nation's tank cars gave to the rest of the Standard combine. To break that power became more than ever the objective of the independent refiners and the government. A rumor began to circulate that the company was making large profits from the mileage allowance paid it by the railroads. In 1894, independent refiners, led by the single-minded George Rice, filed charges to this effect with the ICC. One railroad specialist published an elaborate calculation designed to show that such payments could not aggregate less than a million dollars a year.

The amount indeed was less important than the principle. The substance of the charges against UTL was that since it was not chartered as a transportation company—since it was wholly owned by the same persons who owned the other Standard companies—since all its cars were in the service of Standard—then any profits which it made were actually illegal rebates paid to Standard by the railroads. There was more. UTL's relations with the railroads, the independents alleged, constituted restraint of trade and so violated the ICC Act. They themselves had to pay high prices for barrels and for the use of such few tank cars as they could get hold of. But Standard refineries got the use of UTL's tank cars free of charge. With the resulting saving in car costs, a Standard refinery went into the market with an unfair advantage. In effect, UTL as a separate company merely served to transmit to the Standard refineries a subsidy paid by the railroads. If it made a cash profit besides, that was insult added to injury, in the view of Standard's enemies.

The press at that time was talking loudly of a great purge of the monopolists. It was a time for reform. Industrial depression once more stalked the land. This was the year 1894, when Coxey's little army of unemployed men marched on Washington and was dispersed on the lawn of the Capitol. It was the year when a strike at the Pullman plant in Illinois and a sympathetic walkout of railroad workers were bloodily broken by the gunfire of federal troops. In Washington, faces were grim. The silver voice of young William Jennings Bryan was loud in the Congress, calling down wrath on the "bloated capitalists" of Wall Street. With public opinion so fixed the law was Standard's only refuge. If the ICC and the courts also took the view that UTL was in violation of federal laws Standard would face a major disaster. Heavy fines and retroactive repayments to railroads might be imposed and, worse, its tank car monopoly might be ended.

The drive against Standard was accelerated by the publication of a book called *Wealth Against Commonwealth,* a sensational indictment of the Trust's operations, with particular stress on its use of the tank car as a competitive weapon. Henry Demarest Lloyd, the author, was a former *Chicago Tribune* reporter turned reformer. He knew how to write for a mass audience. Thousands of readers felt that he had conclusively proved the case against Standard. Public and press enthusiastically followed his lead. In Washington, his book became the bible of the antimonopolists.

Hunters of big economic game seized their guns and closely followed Standard's trail.

The tank car operation provided the easiest target. It was almost a symbol of Standard's alleged iniquity. The new ICC investigation seemed especially timely because of a number of accidents—derailments and explosions—involving tank cars. Some thought that railway workers were taking action against Standard into their own hands. Others contended that tank cars were unsafe and should be ruled off the railroads.

Commissioners of the ICC made no secret of their conviction that UTL was guilty of violation of law. One of them, Judge Schoonmaker, whose term of office was approaching its end, went so far as to declare to a convention of state railroad commissioners that "the gross discriminations that have characterized the transportation of petroleum in barrels and in tanks, and in which payment for the use of tank cars has been a factor, have been developed ... The revenue received for their use is ... a rebate from the rate, which gives the shippers owning the cars a corresponding advantage in the markets.... Tank shippers owning their own cars have enormously prospered and rapidly absorbed the business of their less-favored competitors, until the great combination has become an overshadowing monopoly, representing fabulous wealth with corresponding power and influence ... and accorded on the part of carriers an apparently eager subservience."

The Virtue of Poverty

In the face of this new government line, it became essential to Standard's high command that UTL be shown innocent of profit. The old records of the company show that it had net earnings in 1892 of $209,000, but to eliminate profits from the books was now a matter of high policy. The problem was solved by the directors at a meeting in July, 1893, when they approved the following minute: "Resolved, that the treasurer be instructed to charge Profit and Loss account and credit a Depreciation account on the Company's books with the sum of $500,000 for depreciation of equipment to January 1, 1893."

Here was a beautifully simple device, which Rockefeller must have appreciated, if he did not actually suggest it. Cars depreciated in use, did they not? If cars built in 1869 were still being used in 1892, that did not mean that all cars were so long-lived. If a depreciation of $500,000 in a single year represented 14 per cent on the company's total investment in tank cars, there was none at that period to say that it was unwarranted. In any event, UTL's Profit and Loss statement was not for public consumption; only the top Standard executives saw it. Gone from the books were the profits.[1] Depreciation voted the next year was only $200,000 against earnings of $226,000; but soon afterward, when income stubbornly insisted on rising, depreciation of $800,000 in a single lump took care of the profit. In four years, UTL's depreciation amounted to more than 40 per cent of its capitalization.

It was accordingly possible for Page, when called to testify before the ICC, to declare with a clear conscience that his company operated at a loss. No one was convinced, but who could prove otherwise? The ICC was then a fledgling agency with meager powers; it could not subpoena the books even of a railroad, let alone those of a company which was not under its jurisdiction. For lack of evidence the agency's investigation floundered and finally collapsed.

Revolt in the Midwest

Resistance to UTL, for the moment suppressed in Washington, next bubbled to the surface in Chicago. Aside from Chicago's

[1] UTC NOTE: The motive attributed here for the elimination of the profit is not necessarily correct. Standard's Profit and Loss statement in the period referred to was never published, and was, in fact, restricted to a few top officials. To alter the profit figure would have been meaningless, so far as the government and the public were concerned. It may well have been that, in taking large initial depreciation write-offs, the company was catching up on depreciation which it had neglected to take in the past. If this was the case, the elimination of the profit could have been justified on the ground that, if proper accounting methods had been used from the beginning, no profit would have been shown in the first place.

AUTHOR'S NOTE: The elimination of UTL's profit from Standard's secret accounts, at the very time when the question of that profit was being pressed by the government, was not likely to have been merely coincidental. Even though the Profit and Loss statement was secret, there was still value to the company in wiping out the profit. Now UTL and Standard officials were able to deny the profit without falsifying "the facts." This action removed the onus of bearing false witness from company officials, and it accorded with the scruples of an organization among whose executives the vogue for piety was very strong.

traditional resentment of New York's preeminence, there were powerful economic reasons why it should become a center of independent agitation against Standard. Under Tilford's direction Standard of Indiana was then moving in force to exploit the midwestern and western markets. The largest refinery in the country had been built at Whiting, Indiana. Standard's products, distilled from nearby Ohio oil, were being offered to dealers at lowered prices which brought despair to the hearts of small rival refiners.

Midwestern railroads, too, were becoming hostile to Standard. While their freight revenues were increasing agreeably, their mileage allowance payments to UTL were rising even faster. The reason lay in the comparatively long distances that the cars had to run on empty back hauls. In some instances the roads found that mileage traveled over their tracks by empty cars, and for which they paid, greatly exceeded the loaded mileage and ate up their freight revenues. There was even the suspicion among some railroad men that in the summer season, when the demand for oil as fuel fell off and tank cars were not so urgently needed, UTL had no objection to seeing its empty cars take long and circuitous routes on back hauls in order to roll up the mileage allowance. There was always the possibility, too, that this technique might be used to injure roads which were not sufficiently assiduous in cooperating with Standard.

Many of the railroaders had never forgiven Howard Page for clubbing them into submission in the matter of the empty mileage allowance a few years earlier. Early in 1894 they decided that the time had come to assert themselves. Encouraged by the unofficial blessing of Washington officials, representatives of ninety-five western roads met to consider how they could best force the issue. Some were in favor of declining in the future to pay any mileage allowance for empty cars. The majority, however, felt that it would be unwise to reopen this question and that their interests would be better served simply by a reduction in the allowance paid for all mileage, whether loaded or empty. Among those urging this position was the president of the prominent Chicago and Great Western line, A. B. Stickney. His reputation as a stern fighter for railroad justice had been made when he published a book, *The Railway Question,* in which he inveighed against Standard's power "to play one competing railroad against another" in order to prevent the roads from combining to protect their interests. It surprised no one that Stickney's road had never received any business from Standard. His fellow railroaders listened with respect as he counseled that they refuse to pay UTL a mileage allowance of more than one-half a cent per mile, instead of the three-fourths of a cent which then prevailed. The meeting agreed, and a resolution to that effect was voted, with all the solemnity of a declaration of independence.

The Weak Sister

Part of Rockefeller's financial genius lay in his instinctive comprehension of the importance of fractions of pennies when they were multiplied by millions. To lose even a mill or two in a question of railroad mileage would have been regarded in Standard's inner councils as a serious defeat. Instantly on hearing of the railroads' decision Page went into action.

His first move was a polite request to the officers of the western roads that they reconsider. When they refused, he began to apply pressure. He approached the presidents of the major eastern roads, with whom UTL's relations had long been tranquil. Would they not in the interests of all concerned form a committee to study the question which had been raised, and invite the leaders of the western association to a meeting? The easterners agreed and extended the invitations. A delegation of western railroaders came to New York and listened while their brethren of the East proposed that they compromise with UTL. The terms of the suggested compromise, while they had face-saving elements, turned out under analysis to amount to a surrender. It shook the westerners to realize that such great roads as New York Central and the Pennsylvania were on the side of Standard. Nevertheless, they stuck to their guns and it was in a do-or-die spirit that the next day they met with Page.

In his usual virile style Page went straight to the point. The western roads, he said, could lower the mileage allowance only at cost to themselves. One of the railroad men present later summarized his remarks from memory. "Unless they would restore the mileage of three-fourths of a cent, loaded and empty, on tank

cars, they would get none of the Standard Oil Company's shipments.... The weakest road in moral stamina which could be
found would be selected and all shipments ... concentrated
thereon, whereupon other lines, it was predicted, would soon
cry out for Standard Oil business, which they would not get until
they agreed to restore the concessions heretofore granted." "I
never saw an association," another source reported Page as saying, "but what there was a weak sister among them."

One of the railroad men was ill-advised enough to remark
that railroads were large users of lubricating and illuminating
oil and that, if Union boycotted them, in reprisal they might boycott Standard. Page shrugged. The railroads, he said, were at
liberty to purchase their oil from other sources, if they could find
any. It was perfectly true, and all the railroad men present knew
it, that there were no other heavy lubricating oils on the market
which in quality and uniformity matched those produced by
Galena.

On this ominous note the conference ended. The next development seemed to prove the accuracy of Page's—and Rockefeller's—
estimate of the cohesiveness of voluntary business associations.
The only railroad man to call on Page after the meeting was the
chief of the rebels—A. B. Stickney himself, who now gave point
to the observations in his own book. In return for Page's assurance that large tank car shipments would be made for the first
time over the Chicago and Great Western road, he agreed to
pay the three-fourths of a cent mileage.

When the news became known, the leading railroad publication of the period, *Railway Age*, voiced the despair of the other
roads. "Nothing has occurred in Western railroad affairs for a long
time which has caused so much discouragement.... Once more it
has been found impossible for the railways to stand together.
Once more, after the executive officers of all alike had agreed
upon a certain course of action for the common good, one has
weakened. It is the shattering of confidence that is so bitter...."

Their Word Was Good

During the subsequent month, earnings of the Chicago and
Great Western soared, but not a single Standard tank car ap-

peared on the competing lines of the West. Freight loadings dropped with a leaden thud that was heard on Wall Street. As the prices of the stocks of the Western roads cracked, so did their courage. Another meeting was arranged, this time at St. Louis. Terms of capitulation were agreed on. They were almost precisely those which the eastern railroad men had proposed in the first instance—unconditional surrender, covered by a show of compromise. Page was gracious in his acceptance. Like Grant returning Lee's sword at Appomattox, he restored Standard's tank car business at once to the rebel roads as they came back to Standard's fold.

The railroads did, however, obtain one significant concession from UTL. In return for their agreement on the three-fourths of a cent mileage allowance, Page assured them against having to make excessive payments for empty mileage. UTL undertook to keep records of empty and loaded mileage and to compare them with similar records kept by the individual roads. Any excess of empty mileage accumulated on any road would, the company agreed, be corrected through a periodic audit. When such an excess appeared, UTL would promptly increase the loaded mileage on the road in question until the discrepancy no longer existed, or it would pay the road for the excess miles at going freight rates and would return the allowance collected for such excess empty miles.

In adopting the Mileage Equalization Rule, as it came to be called, Page was not taking much risk. Standard's tank cars then traveled loaded much more than empty, and routings could almost always be arranged to correct any adverse mileage balance which appeared on any road. Cash payments to the roads under the Rule were small and few. Its main purpose was to reassure the roads against the rolling up of unwarranted empty mileage on their tracks by intent or negligence on the part of Standard.

It is a point of some interest that where the keeping of records was concerned there was almost from the beginning an atmosphere of trust and good faith in UTL's relations with the railroads. Scrupulous respect for figures was always a characteristic of Standard's operation. The railroads might and did object to some of Standard's policies and to its remarkable skill in finding

legal escape holes in uncomfortable laws, but they never doubted
that the transportation records kept by UTL and the Standard
marketers were faithful to the facts. At the height of the controversy between Page and the western roads neither side ever
thought of impugning the honesty of the other. Once given, their
word was good.

TWO

PAGE STANDS FAST

The popular agitation against Standard was to some extent offset by respect for its economic advancements. There were many sober men in the nation who recognized that the combine, for all its freebooting style and monopolistic character, was making constructive contributions to American life. It had developed significant new technical processes, built numerous plants, and organized an unprecedented system of distribution. Its hard work and excellent products had made oil a servant in nine households out of ten. If Joseph Pulitzer's *New York World* raged against Standard's disregard for "constitutions, and right and justice," and its "pretense of piety," the *New York Tribune* gave Rockefeller credit for "setting new standards of efficiency for industry." "If you can forgive the magnificence and vanity of a successful politician," wrote E. W. Howe at a later time, "why are you unable to forgive a successful businessman? Every time I strike a match, or turn an electric button, or use the telephone, I am indebted to a businessman, but if in debt to any politician, I do not know it." A similar line of thought was operating in many minds in the 1890s.

In the highest legal circles as well the color of the Trust was seen as something lighter than black. Eminent jurists agreed that Standard, even if a monopoly, did not by that fact necessarily stand in violation of Federal law. Early in 1895, Chief Justice Fuller of the United States Supreme Court handed down a decision that must have uplifted Dodd's heart. Congress, Fuller pointed out, had not, after all, asserted "the power to deal with monopoly as such." The mere fact that a contract, combination

106

of enterprises, or conspiracy resulted in a restraint of trade did not necessarily mean that such restraint was "the object of the contract, combination, or conspiracy." Standard, in theory, might as a monopoly have been conspiring to do something quite legal, and merely stumbled inadvertently into the restraint of trade.

In the Heart of Texas

It is possible that some executives of Standard Oil read more into Fuller's decision than the Chief Justice had intended. Standard's affiliate in Texas, the Waters-Pierce Company, seemed especially to respond with a leap and a bound. At the time, 1895, Standard owned 68 per cent of Waters-Pierce stock, but its management was left largely in the hands of the company's president. This was H. C. Pierce, a flamboyant Texan who believed in the God-given right to do as he pleased with his own business. Legalistic interference with corporate activity was the crime, in his eyes, not restraint of trade. When Texas adopted a stern antitrust law, Pierce was not only outraged but contemptuous. He simply ignored the law. Apparently he knew his Texas courts. On more than one occasion his employees were accused of conspiring to monopolize trade through unfair marketing practices; but no convictions ever resulted. Pierce felt sure of his ground even before Justice Fuller's decision was published. Thereafter he became still more assiduous in thumbing his nose at "pettifogging politicians" in Austin, as he called them in one of his published statements.

Making use of nearly a thousand tank cars obtained from UTL, Pierce in 1895 put unprecedented pressure on Texas railroads to compel them to discriminate against rival refiners and obdurate dealers. Producers of oil also felt his heavy hand. Several firms, finding themselves driven to the wall, appealed to the Attorney General of the state. Court action followed, with Union Tank named as codefendant with Waters–Pierce. The firmness of the state and the skill with which it presented its case evidently took Pierce by surprise. The facts were so damaging that a stellar battery of Standard's lawyers in New York rushed to Austin. But even they could find no valid defense for Pierce. The best that they could do was to arrange postponements and delays in the hope that time would assuage the anger that he had stirred up.

Tornado in Ohio

The early hearings in the Pierce–Waters case, with their gloomy implications, were still being held when Standard was staggered by another shock. In Ohio a new Attorney General, Frank Monnett, had been elected. It had been the general assumption in Standard's offices that Monnett was under the thumb of Mark Hanna, the Ohio political boss, who was a friend of Rockefeller; and that in consequence no further trouble was to be expected from Columbus. Insufficient allowance was made for the fact that Monnett was a natural crusader, with courage and ambition. His move against Standard had its inception when George Rice came to him with facts purporting to show that the old Standard Trust had not been dissolved and that Standard of Ohio was still linked to it. Monnett recognized a chance to achieve fame and serve the people of Ohio at the same time. Ohio Standard manifestly stood in contempt of the court's order of 1892, or so he believed; and he obtained a new order instructing the company to show cause why its charter should not be revoked.

This time no statute of limitations applied. The issue was clearly joined. If Monnett was right, if Standard of Ohio was indeed still tied to the other Standard companies, if the dissolution of the Trust had not been carried out in good faith, then Ohio Standard could be heavily penalized, and every state with an antitrust law, and which had issued a charter to a Standard company, could swing into action.

The subsequent trial evoked tremendous public interest. Testimony by Rice and others and interrogation of Standard Oil magnates brought out the general outlines of Standard's corporate structure. One cartoonist portrayed it as a hydra with twenty heads and a single tail, labeled "The Trust," under the caption, "But Where Is Its Heart?"

Rockefeller and Archbold both took the stand and with the guidance of some of New York's finest lawyers defended Standard with courage and skill. The chief point was that the number of independent refiners and marketers of oil in the country had lately been increasing, not diminishing. One of these, the Pure Oil Company of Pennsylvania, had itself become a combination of substantial size. (At the time, Pure Oil's sales were about 5 per cent of Standard's.) Were these facts compatible with the charge of monopoly? Could anyone deny that the oil industry, under Standard's leadership, was serving the public well with a variety of excellent products, produced in enormous quantities and sold at prices which the people evidently considered fair?

This line of reasoning was brushed aside by Monnett. Other refiners existed only at the sufferance of Standard and could be extinguished at Rockefeller's will. It was only Standard's fear of antitrust actions such as Ohio was then bringing that caused it to tolerate some competitive activity. Was it not true that Standard, through its ownership of pipe lines and the Union Tank Line, continued to control bulk shipments of oil and could and did compel competitors to rely on the uneconomic and disadvantageous barrel?

On this issue both Rockefeller and Archbold were uncommunicative. Each had his own style of evading Monnett's embarrassing questions. Rockefeller appeared calm and indifferent as to whether the court found his answers responsive or not. Archbold found it easier to lose his temper. If they had rehearsed in advance, they could hardly have been more effective in concealing what they wished to conceal.

When Monnett subpoenaed Ohio Standard's books they were not forthcoming. The secretary of the company, cited for contempt, explained that the books and other company records had been lost in an accidental fire. The newspapers left little doubt as to how, in their opinion, the fire had occurred. One of them quoted a line from a popular plantation tale by Joel Chandler Harris: "Youk'n hide de fier, but w'at you gwine do wid de smoke?"

The case abounded with excitements. Some of the Midwestern press had begun to print articles sympathetic to Ohio Standard and extolling Rockefeller. Monnett managed to prove in court that the writer and the pro-Standard newspapers had been handsomely paid by officials of the company. On another occasion Monnett told the court and the country that agents of Standard Oil had tried to bribe him. According to his account he had been offered $400,000 if he would back away from the case and permit hearings to be delayed and postponed until the state's suit could be quietly dropped. Standard's denial was hardly heard in the furore.

The character of Standard as the press was then presenting it to the nation was porous enough to absorb every sin in the calendar. Once the public had read about the harsh tactics used by the monopoly in its efforts to destroy Rice and other independents, the name Standard Oil became a byword. Satirical references to the company on the vaudeville stages of the country of the late 1890s were generally good for hoots of laughter and jeering comments from the audience. The syndicated columnist, Finley Peter Dunne ("Mr. Dooley"), made the country roar with his remark that John D. Rockefeller was "a kind iv society f'r the prevention of croolty to money. If he finds a man misusing his money, he takes it away from him an' adopts it." This was about the time, too, when John D. told his Cleveland Sunday-school class that "it is wrong to assume that men of immense wealth are always happy."

Surrounded

Before the Texas and Ohio cases could be decided, the federal government once more went into action, this time with heavy artillery. Congressmen, especially the representatives and senators from the West, were stirred by the failure of the ICC and the antitrust laws to change the ways of Standard. Seeking a new approach, the House and Senate joined in authorizing President McKinley to create a new temporary agency of the government, to be known as the Industrial Commission, for the purpose of probing the several monopolistic combinations in American economic life, of which Standard was the most notorious.

The President, himself an Ohio man and a stanch conservative, whose political manager was Mark Hanna, and to whose campaign fund Standard officials had contributed handsomely, was not happy over the prospect. In view of the temper of the country, however, he saw no alternative to acceptance of the powers which the Congress was pressing on him. He was especially sensitive to public opinion just then because not long before he had allowed the country to be pushed into war against

Spain and had sent American battleships and troops to Cuba, largely in the interest of the American sugar trust.

Congressional leaders insisted on a considerable voice in the formation of the Industrial Commission. As finally constituted it comprised four senators, five representatives, and ten private citizens of high repute. The nomination of one of these individuals caused tempers to run high at 26 Broadway. He was Thomas W. Phillips, the head of the Pure Oil Company, and an enemy far more potent even than the fanatical George Rice. Phillips could take heart from the certainty that, given the existing state of public opinion, Rockefeller would not try to crush him by economic reprisals. There would never be a better time, he reasoned, to declare open war on Standard. It was largely on the basis of his guidance and information that Congress had renewed its antimonopolistic efforts.

Surrounded by inquisitory probes in Texas, in Ohio, and in the nation's capital, Standard's officials wearily traveled from one battle front to the next. They contended that Phillips's appointment to the Commission showed so obvious a bias as to invalidate its findings even before its work began. This did not prevent the Commission from opening hearings in April, 1899, with Phillips playing a major part in the questioning of witnesses. Those summoned against Standard included not only rival refiners and embittered producers but Attorney General Monnett of Ohio as well. Their testimony lost none of its point by familiarity. The anti-Standard members of the Commission, who represented the majority, were from the beginning determined to bring Standard to task.

To Phillips, knowing as he did the intricacies of the business, there was not much sense in asking questions about Standard's broad policies. It was its detailed practices, especially in oil transportation, that he wanted to expose. When the chairman of the Commission, Senator Kyle, became ill, the Commission appointed Phillips to serve as chairman pro tem. The appearance of John D. Archbold as Standard's chief witness gave him the opportunity he sought. Sparks flew as he hammered his way through Archbold's crust of reserve. In the upshot, making a virtue of necessity, Archbold told more about Standard's operation than had ever before been revealed. Friends of Standard in the press gave him great credit for his frankness, declaring that Standard's managers "now clearly recognized that publicity is the surest safeguard of legitimate manufacturing enterprise."

As the Commission began to piece facts together, it became clear that while its target was Standard's monopoly in general, the bull's-eye was its monopoly of tank cars. Phillips, in particular, was determined to show that Standard's ownership of most of the country's tank cars resulted in the subservience of the railroads. Out of this condition, he asserted, grew the various unfair advantages in transportation by which Standard kept its hold on the market for oil, and which enabled it to make its unparalleled profits. When Archbold reminded him that there was nothing to prevent any refiner from building tank cars, Phillips had a quick counter. Even when the small independent refiners managed to build tank cars they were still at a grave disadvantage, so long as the railroads favored Standard in their rate-fixing and other policies.

With the Commission's questioning centered sharply on tank cars and relations with railroads, Archbold retired from the stand in favor of Standard's specialist in these fields, Howard Page.

"If You Can't Lick 'Em . . . Confuse 'Em!"

The Commission by this time thought it could smell Standard's blood. With the testimony already in hand all that it needed to complete its case was proof that, through the Union Tank Line, Standard dominated bulk rail shipments of oil; and that UTL, by making profits at the expense of the railroads, was not only violating an ICC ruling forbidding the payment of freight rebates, but was conspiring with the railroads in restraint of trade, in defiance of the Sherman Act. The information wanted was essentially simple: what proportion of the nation's oil tank cars did UTL own, and did it make a profit?

Page came before the commission in the spirit of a man with nothing to conceal—bluff, hearty, forthright, positive. When Phillips asked him how many tank cars UTL owned, he unhesitatingly gave the figure—5,900. Then he was asked the crucial question: How many tank cars were owned by others? He replied: "There are in the United States between 170 and 180 individuals and companies, entirely outside of the Standard Oil Company, owning an aggregate of 7,240 tank cars."

The Commission was stunned. Presently one of its members formulated another question:

"Now the testimony is that Standard Oil Company do pretty nearly 90 per cent of the business in the United States. . . . It would look a little curious that they could do that business with 40 per cent of the tank cars in the country, unless they were using the cars of some other company. . . ."

"The explanation of that," Page replied airily, "is that the tank cars used by other individuals are not confined to the use of petroleum. . . ."

Could Page provide a list of owners of these 7,000 "other" tank cars? He thought he could. The list included thirteen tank lines other than UTL, and owning more than 100 cars each. Among them was the Green Line, with 750 cars, which had long since been absorbed by UTL. Nor did Page bother to point out that the Manhattan Oil Company of Lima, Ohio, with 755 cars, was actually a hidden subsidiary of the Anglo-American Oil Company, the address of which was 26 Broadway.

Since the Commission had asked for a list of "tank cars" and not specifically "petroleum tank cars," Page was technically correct in putting on his list a great many cars which carried only vegetable oils and other foodstuffs. There is some reason to think that many "tank cars" on the list were not railroad cars at all, but tank wagons, the tanks of which could, if necessary, be put to use on railroad flatcars. But even after making allowance for such distortions, there had unquestionably been a sharp decline, within ten years, in UTL's percentage of the country's oil tank cars, from 90 per cent to an estimated 70 per cent. Standard no longer had anything to gain and it had something to lose from trying to keep tank cars other than its own off the rails. The rebate system was barred by law. The weight determinations worked out by Page in 1887, to the disadvantage of barreled shipments, had been corrected by the ICC in 1892. It made less difference, thereafter, whether a competitor shipped by tank car or not. Standard, by the volume of its shipments, would still be the beneficiary of the railroads' rate policies. And the fact that more tank cars were available for independent refiners would reduce the pressure on Congress to designate the tank car as a common carrier. Without opposition from Standard, some private car leasing companies and some railroads, as well as a few independents, had ventured into tank car ownership.

A Little Semantics

The Commission sought to show that, while other refiners were forced to use barrels for their refined products, Standard's rail shipments were made primarily in tank cars. Not at all, Page countered. "Standard's shipments in barrels exceed those in tank cars." He then set about to dispel the Commission's astonishment. "The Standard ships its oil in tank cars to a distributing station, it is there barreled to a very large extent, and it goes out in barrels." The phrase "goes out in barrels" was apparently accepted by the Commission as signifying a further movement of the barrels by rail. But Page had said no such thing. Since almost all bulk oil was sooner or later put in barrels or cans, and some oil never was shipped in tank cars at all, it was perfectly true that more gallons "went out" in barrels and cans than in bulk. Whether after being barreled the oil was hauled by wagon, by barge, or by rail for short local deliveries did not enter Page's statement. The fact was, of course, that in terms of actual miles traveled by rail Standard's tonnage of tank car shipments was far in excess of its barreled shipments. But Page, without departing from literal fact, had conveyed an entirely different impression. His statements implied that rival refiners claiming that Standard had forced the railroads to discriminate against barrels did not know what they were talking about—that discriminations against barrels would hurt Standard as much as they would the independents. Ergo, the alleged discriminations did not exist.

The Commission asked Page how it was that, if the tank cars were so unimportant in Standard's scheme, the company had so much influence over railroads. He denied the influence. "The total consumption of oil in tons in the United States is less than one-half of 1 per cent of the total tonnage moved by the railroads of the United States, and it is absurd either to argue or conclude that so small a percentage of the traffic moved . . .

should be of such controlling influence over railroads and their officials." What Page did not say was that the percentage of oil freight to total tonnage carried by some railroads ran 20 per cent and more.

Was it not true, wondered the Commission, that "in certain sections of the country ... local rates are made so that independent refiners cannot enter?" Page was unshaken. "If you mean, sir, because we have refineries ... to supply both the West and New England, I admit we have advantages; but I say we pay the same rate ... from the same shipping point to the same destination as every other shipper." By and large this was true. The Commission, seeking evidence that secret rebates were still being paid, had missed the real point; even Phillips missed it. The railroads no longer needed to make rate discriminations in order to serve Standard's interest. Merely by lowering rates at times when Standard was shipping in large quantities and raising them again thereafter they could put independent refiners at a serious disadvantage. This had long been done by the transcontinental railroads as well as by roads in the East. But it was not for some years after the Commission finished its work that the fact became known.

By stubbornly pursuing the outdated rebate question the commissioners enabled Page to strike telling blows for Standard. At one point they thought they had him. Documents were produced to show that the New Haven Railroad had on one occasion billed a Standard shipment at 48,000 pounds when it should have been 100,000. A matter of $52.98 was involved. Confronted by the apparently damaging facts, Page pointed out quite correctly that the Commission was taking up its time with a clerical error. "Standard Oil Company has shipped thousands of carloads of freight to all points in the United States over nearly every railroad line in the country, and the freight bills for its cars pass through the hands of numberless employees of the railroads and the shippers. ... It would have been impossible to keep such rebates secret had any such been granted. ... The Interstate Commerce Law ... has been in effect for more than twelve years, and at the end of this period the best case that they [the independent refiners] can produce is that involving a clerical error in the billing of three or four cars shipped from Boston to Newport; and I would like to see somebody else equal that record." Standard lost no time in paying the $52.98 in question to the New Haven.

"The Answer Is Simple"

Unable to extract from Page an admission of UTL's monopoly of tank cars, the Commission concentrated on the question of profits. It wished to show, first, that UTL made a profit; second, that its profits went to the Standard Oil ownership. This established, Standard might have been vulnerable to suit under the Sherman Act.

Asked whether his company was profitable, Page said no. Very far from profitable.

With elaborate irony Phillips said, "I should like to ask upon what theory you are able to induce the stockholders to continue their investments and make additional investments from time to time as would seem necessary?"

Page was eager to explain. "The answer is simple. The tank car is a necessary facility in the economical distribution of petroleum and its products. It is one of the means by which we are enabled to ship oil cheaply and supply it cheaply. For that reason the investment, as you see, in the UTL is a proper one, for it is a necessary arm of the petroleum business."

Counsel for the Commission pounced: "Why, then, is the business conducted by an independent company, and not by the Standard Oil Company itself?"

Page's bland answer missed the question by about 90 degrees. "The Union Tank Line Company is simply a corporation that owns tank cars."

His interrogators were not to be put off that way. "What is the purpose or advantage of the separate corporation?"

Said Page, "I am not a lawyer."

"Oh," said the Commission's counsel, "you do not need to be a lawyer to answer a question like that, if you choose to answer it. It is a business question, not a question of law."

"I do not refuse to answer it," Page retorted. "The Union Tank Line Company has been formed to own and run these cars over various railroads of the United States for the transportation of oil."

Doubtless taking a deep breath, Commission counsel began all over again. "You have testified that there is no profit in it at all?"

"I have," said Page. He explained that UTL returned only 4½ per cent on its investment.

"What I am trying to get at is why it is continued as a separate organization instead of by the Standard Oil Company itself directly?"

Page's reply showed his mastery of double talk. "If it is profitable or unprofitable, it would make no difference whether it was conducted in the name of the Union Tank Line Company or in the name of the Standard Oil Company, but it was formed under the name of the Union Tank Line Company and I say it is a necessary adjunct in the distribution of petroleum and therefore continued although it is not profitable."

The Commission evidently felt groggy, for it took a new tack. Who owned the stock of UTL? The stockholders, Page thought. Were the stockholders the owners of Standard Oil? Page did not know.

... "The stock can be bought independently of Standard's stock?" Still Page did not know.

"I mean," patiently asked one of the commissioners, "is it listed for sale?"

"It is a separate company."

"How many stockholders were there?"

"I think," said Page, "there are a great many; I do not know."

The Commission was dissatisfied. It thought that Page was being evasive. He was then asked about the salaries paid to the officers of the corporation. They were modest, said Page. "I should prefer not to say what my salary is, or what the others are ... but I think they are small."

"The point I am getting at," said counsel, "is this. If such an organization ... continues in business when that business is so unprofitable ... there must be some way ... to make it profitable to its officers or stockholders.... Does the UTL do it [remain in business] simply through philanthropic or generous motives toward the Standard Oil Company?"

"I think I have made that clear," Page said "The tank car is a necessary adjunct in the petroleum business."

A New Line of Defense

Here, however, one of Standard Oil's subsidized publicists, Patrick Boyle, who was present at the hearing, whispered to Page, and he amplified his answer. "The present owners of the Union Line and Standard Oil are the same. Now those owners think that the tank car is necessary in the conduct of the general business."

"Do you know of any reasons why Standard should prefer to operate Union as an independent company?"

"I do not."

The questioning took another turn—this time in an effort to determine whether Standard Oil was "technically and legally one company, or . . . 25 different companies."

Page said, "I do not know that I am competent to answer as to that. There has recently been formed, as you know, the Standard Oil Company of New Jersey, which, as I understand—I had rather cancel that answer. I do not know; that is all."

Page had almost given away a plan which Standard was not yet ready to disclose, although it had been widely rumored. Rockefeller, Archbold, and Dodd had come to the conclusion that the separation of the combine into ostensibly independent units was no longer a serviceable device. Not only would a tighter administrative structure be needed to assure firm central control of the operating companies in the future, but it was immediately important to allay criticism of Standard resulting from slowness in liquidating the old Trust. In 1897 the *New York Herald* charged that "under the guise of complying with the law and 'liquidating,' a few men have for more than five years been exercising absolute and arbitrary power over this vast property, and as to what they have done with it, or what it is today, one shareholder's guess is as good as another's." This line of attack was soon followed by Standard's enemies throughout the country. Especially dangerous was the case still threatening to penalize Standard of Ohio on the ground that the Trust had not been dissolved and that, contrary to the court's order, the Ohio company was still a part of it. The time had come for a new corporate structure that would relieve the operating companies from this charge.

While the Industrial Commission's hearings were being held

in Washington, Dodd obtained changes in the charter of Jersey Standard, increasing its capitalization to $110,000,000. Its shares were then exchanged for outstanding stock in the other component companies, and in the summer of 1899 Jersey Standard became the holding company for the entire Standard Oil organization, with the Union Tank Line Company as one of its wholly-owned subsidiaries.

Rockefeller himself assumed the presidency of the Jersey company, with Archbold, William Rockefeller, Flagler, and Rogers as vice-presidents, and Tilford as treasurer. But Rockefeller's stomach ulcer had greatly reduced the energy that he could pour into the business. He was sixty years old, the possessor of the greatest fortune in America, and his mind had begun to turn away from business and toward the tremendous philanthropies which filled the last third of his life. His unpretentious office at 26 Broadway was seldom occupied. Flagler, too, had deserted the oil business; he was busy with the development of the state of Florida, the possibilities of which as a modern resort area he was the first to recognize and exploit on a substantial scale. Archbold had become Standard's chief executive officer; at UTL Tilford and Page continued as president and vice-president, respectively.

"Without Any Manipulation ..."

Page, in his testimony before the Industrial Commission, slowly wore down his inquisitors by his baffling habit of answering questions different from those which had been asked. In an effort to learn what happened to the money paid to UTL by the railroads in the form of a mileage allowance, counsel inquired whether Page's company turned its profits over to Standard in some form. "They do not," he replied. "They get nothing from the Standard Oil Company."

"It has been testified," one of the commissioners put to him, "that in the opinion of several railroad men ... this rate of three-fourths cent a mile ought to be profitable for the owners of the cars." He was referring to calculations which purported to prove that an average UTL tank car earned enough to pay the cost of the car in three years.

Page admitted that if the company's cars were in constant

use throughout the year on long trips, it might make money. But the cars were necessarily idle much of the time. "I tell you honestly that the 4½ per cent, as the average earning on the investment in Union Tank Line, is the exact truth, without any manipulation of the books. . . ."

The Commission was unhappy. "The testimony that you have given here this morning seems . . . remarkable," said its counsel.

Page gave the Commission an explanation of the economic reasons for the existence of private tank lines. "If every railroad were required to have sufficient tank car equipment to do the oil business that at times moved over its rails, it would mean the building of many more tank cars than the business would require. For instance, it would require 200 tank cars . . . to transport oil between Chicago and St. Paul. . . . There are five lines competing for this business, and if each railroad was required to own 200 cars, there would be four times as many cars as the business would require. . . . You might just as well require a railroad to own all the Pullman cars that are necessary to go over its road as to require them to own . . . tank cars." He did not trouble himself over the possibility that the railroads might pool their tank cars—an idea which had not yet been publicly advanced. With considerable virtuosity, he explained how the weight determinations on oil products were arrived at by the railroads, and justified the roads in their acceptance of tank car capacities as published by the private tank car lines. He insisted that the customs of the industry had been evolved to meet the real business situations which existed, and had stood the tests of time because they were effective. If Standard benefited from those customs more than others, it was fundamentally because of the greater efficiencies which its size and imaginative management made possible.

Comparatively seldom did Page depart irrevocably from the truth, but when the questions of net profit and depreciation were raised, facts slipped easily from his memory. At one point the Commission came uncomfortably close to the real reason for UTL's extraordinary unprofitability. Page fended them off. "Since the formation of the UTL," he said, "that company has never paid a dividend, and the . . . average annual return on the capital invested (has been) 4½ per cent per annum. This return has been figured without charging anything off for depreciation." He went on to say that among railroads it was customary to depreciate cars at the rate of 6 per cent per year. It was at that moment highly convenient to forget the depreciation decisions to which Page as a director had been a party, and the fact that UTL's net profit for 1898, as shown by its secret books, had been $330,000, or nearly 10 per cent on its investment. Its net profits from 1891 through 1900, before depreciation, totaled more than $2,000,000. In 1900, the company paid Standard Oil (New Jersey) dividends of $10 per share on its stock—$350,000. The purpose of this payment apparently was to get rid of its cash surplus.

One of the commissioners made a last effort to find out "why a corporation of that sort should be organized and run without a profit. Now it seems to me that for some reason of their own . . . [they] have organized the Union Tank Line for the purpose of running that company in the interest of the Standard Oil Company. . . . They [Standard's stockholders] get their profits [from UTL] by way of dividends on the Standard stock; is that not really the relation?"

Page replied, like a man taking the Fifth Amendment: "The tank car is a necessary adjunct to their general business. . . ."

As sarcastically as possible the Commissioner said, "Of course there is nothing in connection with the Union Tank Line that is worth hedging about?"

"There is not," said Page. "I say to you that for eight years the company has shown an average earning of 4½ per cent. . . ."

A Drop in Temperature

A marked feature of the national scene in 1898–1899 was the sudden subsidence of public interest in Standard Oil. For this the company owed a debt of gratitude to the Hearst newspapers for their part in whipping up the popular excitement that led to the Spanish-American War. Events in Cuba diverted the attention of the country from the problem of monopoly at home to that of tyranny abroad. In the later stages of the Ohio trial the sins of Standard were relegated to the back pages of newspapers filled with reports of victory, with celebration of new heroes— Admiral Dewey, Admiral Sampson, Colonel Theodore Roosevelt's Rough Riders—with the ousting of Spain from Cuba, and with the acquisition of Puerto Rico, the Philippines, and Guam. While the hearings of the Industrial Commission were in progress the country was far more interested in a new wave of sensations—the Boer War, the Filipino insurrection, the Boxer Rebellion in China, and the presidential election of 1900 with McKinley and Roosevelt triumphant. The state courts and the Federal government seemed to feel the lowered pressure of public opinion on Standard. Certainly their findings were far from having the punishing impact that had been indicated.

In 1900, the Supreme Court of Texas did indeed rule that Waters–Pierce had violated state laws, but it contented itself with an order which allowed the company to continue in business after a complicated legalistic juggling of its shares. Ohio's Supreme Court in the same year decided that Standard was not, after all, in contempt of its 1892 ruling. Attorney General Monnett had been defeated for reelection, his successor held other views, Mark Hanna's machine was once more in control of Ohio politics, and Ohio Standard no longer stood in danger of losing its charter. As for the much-vaunted Industrial Commission, it could not prove—did not even try very hard to prove—that Standard was culpable under the Sherman antitrust law. Its report, issued just before the collapse of the Ohio case against Standard, added little to what was already known of Standard's operations, and not the Congress nor the courts nor the ICC saw fit to take any action. By the end of 1900 the agitation of the preceding decade against Standard had fizzled out like a dead firecracker. Its only practical consequence was that instead of the old Trust, Jersey Standard now was the controlling mechanism of the combine. As for the tank car operation, it continued to serve the fundamental purpose for which John D. Rockefeller had conceived it—to assure Standard Oil of favored treatment by the nation's railroads in the transportation of its products. Union Tank Line's capitalization was less than one-thirtieth of that of Standard as a whole, its net worth on the books was trivial as compared with the $200,000,000 net worth of Standard Oil (New Jersey), but its place at the center of the machinery of the vast organization was unchanged.

THREE

"NO TURPITUDE WHATEVER"

As the new century began, interest in protecting the country against monopoly revived. Newspapers once more pointed accusing fingers at Standard Oil. The assassination of President McKinley in 1901 and the coming to the White House of Theodore Roosevelt accentuated the trend. Roosevelt, when Governor of New York, had made trust baiting an essential part of his political program. That he would be an active threat to the Rockefeller interests was taken for granted.

The company continued to deny at every opportunity that it stood in restraint of trade. Such accusations one of its spokesmen, C. M. Pratt, described as "a palpable absurdity." How could it be a monopoly when it controlled only a "very moderate percentage of the crude-oil production of the United States?" When there were more than 125 competing refiners in existence? When it owned, or so it said, only 40 per cent of the tank cars of the country? Whatever measure of prosperity Standard enjoyed was, Pratt insisted, "not traceable to illegal or reprehensible methods, but to its economic and elaborate industrial organization, covering, as it does, every detail of transportation, manufacture, and administration." All this in the early 1900s was literally true. Reformist legislators and journalists were convinced that Standard was violating federal laws, books were written to prove the company's moral guilt, but the fact remained that no business was more careful to examine the letter of the law and search for legal ways of circumventing it.

Of the actual rebates there was little evidence, except in California, where they were paid by the roads under a plan established by Tilford. In time this arrangement came to light, but Standard Oil's attorneys were able to point out to the ICC that these rebates were paid entirely within a single state, were not involved in interstate commerce, and were outside federal jurisdiction under the existing law. In the words of Archbold, the California rebates "involved no turpitude whatever."

Increasingly critics of Standard had come to suspect that its power over the markets derived largely from its control of pipe lines and tank cars. But it was one thing to suspect and another to prove. By some sorcery, it appeared, Standard was able to transmute an iron tank car into a pistol pointed at the heads of its competitors or suppliers. To fathom the secret of this magic required an intimate knowledge of railroad practice which few among Standard's enemies possessed. Even refiners like George Rice and T. W. Phillips, or ICC agents who knew more or less what was going on, were unable to get hold of telling facts until long after the deed which they described had been done and its benefits absorbed by Standard.

"Now You See 'Em, Now You Don't"

Perhaps Standard's most subtle device for slaying competition through manipulation of tank cars was worked out by Tilford in California during 1901. The facts of this operation, when they finally emerged into the light of publicity five years later, were taken by the country as conclusive proof of Standard's diabolical cunning in ruining competitors, yet in reality the company had done nothing which deviated in any way from permissible business practice, as then regarded.

In 1898, Tilford found that in order to counter independent competition in the fast-growing California market, Standard of Indiana, of which he was president, needed the cooperation of the powerful Southern Pacific Railroad. A contract was worked out which, while it did not give Standard preferential treatment, assured Tilford that UTL's expanding fleet of tank cars in California would be hauled and serviced by the road as required for Standard's business. He was compelled, however, to make important concessions. The mileage allowance paid by Southern

Pacific would be less than that paid by other roads and would be paid only on loaded cars, when used to haul Standard's oil. UTL agreed to let Southern Pacific lease 325 of its cars for the service of oil shippers in general, for a three-year period. No UTL cars could be reserved exclusively for Standard's use on Southern Pacific tracks.

During those years the situation changed to Standard's advantage. A large California refinery, Pacific Coast Oil, was acquired, greatly increasing the supply of refined-oil products available to Standard and enhancing Tilford's power as a shipper. What followed was reminiscent of Rockefeller's early days in Cleveland. Playing competitive railroads against Southern Pacific, Tilford put himself in a greatly improved bargaining position. He was further aided by the fact that the California oil industry as a whole had expanded so rapidly as to create an incessant clamor for tank cars. When in January, 1901, as the expiration date of the leasing agreement approached, he gave notice that he expected the return of the 325 cars on schedule, he was well aware that he was dealing the Southern Pacific a body blow.

The railroad's California managers seemed to have nourished the delusion that UTL would agree to renew the leasing agreement and had made little effort to build up a tank-car fleet of their own. Now they found themselves in sudden danger of losing, for lack of tank cars, a great deal of highly profitable business. After an appeal to Tilford the San Francisco manager of the Southern Pacific telegraphed Charles Hays, the road's president, who was in New York. "There is urgent demand for oil cars. . . . Standard offers cars but wishes to keep control and use them wholly in their business. . . . If we could temporarily lease 300 tank cars we . . . would save a good deal of embarrassment."

Hays evidently did not at first sense the gravity of the situation, for his reply said, "Want to keep private cars off our line except we lease and control them." Subsequent telegrams from San Francisco, however, altered his thinking by their evident desperation.

"SO Co. demand we let them run cars local subject to their orders and control, and pay 7½ mills mileage loaded or empty . . . on 300 cars now under lease. . . . They threaten that Atchison [the Atchison, Topeka and Santa Fe Railroad] will concede their terms." "Standard Oil now demands immediate return of . . . tank cars we have leased from them."

Thus prodded, Hays consulted lawyers, got in touch with Tilford, and sought a compromise. Graciously, on February 28, 1901, Tilford outlined in a letter to Hays the terms of a new agreement which would be acceptable to Standard. The essence of the deal was that for six months more the Southern Pacific would be allowed to retain 325 UTL cars in its service for all customers. Over and above these 325 cars, Standard would provide an unspecified number of cars for its exclusive use. A mileage allowance of three-fourths cent per mile was to be paid to UTL on loaded and empty cars alike, and whether they served Standard or its competitors.

In terms which radiated cooperation Tilford advised the Southern Pacific "to build for service in California such tank cars as you deem proper. . . ." But the Southern Pacific executives were well aware that there was no hope of solving their tank-car problem within six months. The breathing spell was well enough, but it was evident that the independent refineries along the road's tracks would shortly be deprived of tank car service. Apparently, however, the road gave little or no warning of the impending doom to the oil shippers. Instead, it took the opportunity to acquire a refinery of its own, the output of which could be handled by its own small fleet of tank cars after all UTL cars had returned to Standard's exclusive service.

Meanwhile production and refining of oil throughout California were soaring. Refineries had no trouble in getting crude oil by pipe line and tank car; and rail transportation of refined oil was adequate, if barely so. Then on September 1, 1901, the boom was lowered. Southern Pacific was compelled to tell its customers that they could no longer supply tank cars, certainly not in the former quantities. Independent refiners with orders in hand, plants in operation, and storage tanks full, were aghast and helpless.

Standard, merely by exercising its legal rights, now dominated the West Coast market. Tilford's agents promptly offered to relieve competitors of their surplus oil and oil products—paying from 25 per cent to 50 per cent of the going market price. Bitterly the independents recognized the nature of the trap into which they had fallen. To add to their anguish, even as they sold and took their loss they were able to see surplus UTL tank cars, exclusively employed in Standard's service, standing for days at a time at sidings. Protests to the Southern Pacific brought only polite regrets—there was nothing, they were told, that could be done.

Genius to the Rescue

While Tilford was making California secure for Standard, Howard Page was running UTL single-handed at 26 Broadway. The results were not altogether satisfactory to the masters of the combine. Page's error was one of fundamental outlook. Like everyone else, he knew Rockefeller's love of frugality, and sought to prove himself a worthy disciple. He was managing UTL like a conventional business, keeping outgo to a minimum and expanding income. His trouble was that he lacked the feeling of men like Rockefeller and Archbold for the times of expansion when money had to be spent freely and even hugely. To them UTL's financial position, in the final test, was unimportant. What counted was its service to Standard. While they were disposed not to interfere with Page, they kept an eye on his operation.

The specific mistake that Page made was in over-restricting expenditures for new tank cars. He was adding cars to the fleet at the rate of only a few hundred a year, and those built to ordinary specifications, and at the lowest possible cost. In his effort to avoid an oversupply of cars he was creating a shortage. Even more serious, UTL tank cars, in a technical sense, were no longer abreast of the requirements of oil transportation. Advances in locomotive design had resulted in marked increases in the speed at which freight trains were moving, and tank cars were being subjected to unprecedented vibration and strain in transit. In consequence, the iron tanks with their riveted sections were leaking more than in the past. The leakage became more serious as the cars grew older, and as they began to carry increasing quantities of volatile substances, especially gasoline. But perhaps the worst of the technological problems grew out of the fact that the heavily-loaded tanks, traveling at high speeds, would often shift their position longitudinally on the wooden underframes of the cars, in spite of iron tank bands and bolsters. When this happened, riveted sections of the tanks sprang leaks which were responsible for serious losses, fires, and explosions. Railroads, especially the Pennsylvania, strongly urged that safer tank cars be built; and there was even an implied threat that the issue might become public if the problem was not solved.

The infant automobile industry, feeding on gasoline, was already revealing its Herculean future to the farsighted Standard chieftains. It could be taken for granted that, American inventive talent being what it was, if UTL did not produce a better tank car one of the other private car lines would eventually do so, to Standard's detriment.

UTL could no longer delay an effort to bring the design and structure of the tank car into closer harmony with advances in railroading and refining. The urgency of the need made Archbold and Tilford turn for assistance to one of Standard's most remarkable personalities, John W. Van Dyke. He was the Trust's greatest technician and trouble shooter in the field of mechanical design, a man of extraordinary inventive genius. His creative contributions to the development of oil refineries had made possible significant progress in the elimination of impurities from crude oil and in the production of paraffin and gasoline. It is said that when confronted with a technical difficulty of the oil business he had never failed to find an original solution.

From the beginning it was evident to Van Dyke that the iron tank which had prevailed in the industry since 1869 would have to go. Only steel had the required strength and resistance to corrosion. New processes of fabrication made it possible to fit steel tank sections more closely than iron sections; leakage could be greatly reduced. This was not a new idea. As early as 1893 an independent car builder had exhibited a tank car in which a steel tank was fastened to a steel-and-cast-iron underframe. In actual test, however, the mountings of the tank in this model had been found dangerously insecure, and no one had been willing to risk capital on steel cars until the related technical problems were solved.

Van Dyke went to work, and the result was the construction to his design, in 1900, of an all-steel car which represented the first fundamental and successful structural change in tank car design since the days of Densmore. Since then vertical wooden tubs had given way to horizontal iron tanks; the flatcar had been replaced by a massive wooden-and-iron underframe; but the principle had remained unchanged; the tank continued to be fastened to a flat surface.

Van Dyke broke with this tradition. His car dispensed with the underframe. Instead, the double-riveted steel tank was riveted to strong iron saddles. These, in turn, were directly connected to the center plate of the truck. Since the tank saddles had the approximate shape of a V, the new car was promptly nicknamed the V-car.

Progress—But Not Enough

Tested in 1901, the new design was found well able to withstand the shocks of service. Old-time railroad and tank car men, however, were highly skeptical of any car that did not have an underframe. Because Van Dyke's model looked at first glance less sturdy than the conventional car, its reception was on the whole unfavorable. Among the skeptics was UTL's chief operating technician, C. M. Bloxham, a veteran who had the title of Master Car Builder. He was himself a pioneer of tank car construction, with a number of technical innovations to his credit; and his word carried great weight with Page.

The latter was in a quandary. Urged to push ahead with a new car-building program, he hesitated to back the V-car unreservedly in the face of opposition from within and outside the company. Orders for its construction were placed, but on a scale too small to satisfy the need. Then, in the spring of 1902, came crisis. A train of UTL tank cars exploded at Sheridan, Pennsylvania, with loss of life and heavy property damage. An outcry in the press against the use of obsolete equipment on the railroads followed; and angry fingers were pointed at Standard.

That more new cars had to be built was clear enough to Page. But to what design? The old-type cars would no longer do. The V-car was regarded as a dangerous gamble. Once again Van Dyke came to the rescue. Early in 1903 he revealed a model of a conventional underframe car in which all hazards were greatly reduced. The tank and underframe were both of steel. But instead of relying on the old type of tank fastenings, Van Dyke had connected the tank to the underframe by a patented device, an anchor which firmly gripped the tank at its center and prevented it from shifting its position. Known from the design of the underframe as the X-car, Van Dyke's model offered Page his first real hope of extricating UTL from its embarrassing shortage of new equipment.

Although orders were placed for construction of the X-car with the Van Dyke anchor, the company's progress in this area was slow.[1] The first tank car line to offer all-steel cars to its customers was not UTL, but an independent rival, the German–American Transportation Company, whose cars bore the stenciled initials GATX. No one in Standard then dreamed that this comparatively small concern would grow into the huge General American Transportation Corporation, but it was already displaying, in 1903, a vitality and aggressiveness which would soon challenge UTL in tank car transportation, while developing the country's largest fleet of refrigerator cars, and reaching out into many other fields.

The Midgley Affair

Technical questions aside, Archbold and his intimates had reason to feel that Page was no longer the man to run UTL. For one thing, it was doubtful that he could in future properly represent the company in its conflicts with government. The testimony he had given in past hearings was too vulnerable to let him take the witness stand again as a spokesman for the combine. His offhand style might have met the needs of the 1890s, but it would not do in the changed political climate of the 1900s. If there had been no other reason for retiring him, his persistent public denial of UTL's ability to earn a profit would have been enough. For in 1900 and 1901 under his regime the company had paid substantial dividends to SONJ; and although this was was considered a secret, it was known to enough people so that further refusal to admit the fact of UTL's earnings would be highly inadvisable.

---

[1] Despite the lag in car production, UTL was at this time taking some forward technological steps which were to have profound effects on the tank car industry—notably in developing the heater-piped tank car and in calibrating tanks. See Appendix B.

Concern over Page became acute when, late in 1902, the magazine *Railway Age* published a series of extraordinary articles by an experienced former railroad executive, J. W. Midgley, in which the past sins of the private tank car lines, and especially of UTL, were exposed for all to read. Although factually inaccurate at many points, Midgley's articles went further than any previous public statements in revealing the specific ways in which Standard had made use of its tank cars to dominate the rail transportation of oil and to maintain its monopoly. Two of his points were particularly effective. He purported to prove by citing figures that Page's claim of UTL's unprofitability could not possibly be true. And without mentioning names he told the story of A. B. Stickney and the "weak sister," in which Page was recognizable as the man who had single-handed dictated to the railroads.

Page reacted like a wounded bull. Feeling that he and the company had been outrageously misrepresented, he urged Tilford to authorize a published reply to Midgley. The question was referred to the sagacious Samuel Dodd, and the result was a flat negative. Dodd was well aware that in business affairs the effect of most published denials is to enlarge the number of people who are aware of the original accusation. "In my opinion," he wrote, "it is not now worth while to publish a refutation of his [Midgley's] statements. The matter is ancient history, and rehashing it will serve no good purpose."

Midgley's articles were, however, making a large stir in the world of railroading. Soon he was asked to appear before a session of the Interstate Commerce Commission and give his views as to ways of correcting the abuses of the public interest which he had described. His recommendation was so radical for its time that it took away the breath of even the boldest of the commissioners: let the government outlaw private ownership of tank cars, all of which would then be purchased by a new corporation owned and controlled by the railroads and regulated by the ICC. The roads would "thus resume functions which have been usurped by shippers and other private car owners." A fair purchase price would be determined by the government. That this procedure might be inconsistent with the theory of the private enterprise system did not appear to trouble Midgley. He knew parties in New York, he said, who were ready to put up $50,-000,000 to launch the undertaking.

And there was more. Regardless of the question of ownership, he had strong convictions about the need for new methods of operating the tank cars. Specifically he believed that the mileage allowance ought to be eliminated. Midgley had already been given credit for persuading railroads to abolish troublesome mileage payments for freight cars which they themselves owned. As a result, when a freight car owned by Railroad X traveled over the tracks of Railroads Y and Z (to the increase of their freight revenues), Y and Z paid for its use simply on a straight per-diem basis, at that time 20 cents per day. Thus the costly accounting required by interrailroad mileage calculations was eliminated. Now he proposed that tank and refrigerator cars also be paid for by the day—at the rate of 30 cents per day, he suggested—since their cost was somewhat higher than that of ordinary freight cars. The railroads had provided him with statistical evidence which indicated that they, and presumably the public, would save $6,500,000 a year by this change. "Excessive earnings" of the private tank car lines—UTL especially—would thus be curtailed, he contended.

Throughout 1904 Midgley led a crusade to form the new corporation that he had proposed, only to find himself without a following. The railroads whose support he had been counting on let him down with a thud. Collectively and privately they had been willing to urge him on; but individually they would have nothing to do with him. All at once he, who had been a major personality in railroading, found himself an outcast. Not only was he forbidden to use the names of railroads in his articles, he was virtually ostracized. His office in Chicago, once a gathering place for railroad executives, was now avoided like a plague spot. Bitterly he complained that the word had gone out from Standard—no railroad friendly to Midgley could expect UTL tank cars to run on its tracks—but this he could not prove. After a year of struggle he gave up, abandoning the project. The private tank car lines continued in existence, mileage allowances continued to be paid, and all went as before. As Dodd had told Tilford, "it was not worthwhile" to publish a refutation of Midgley's statements.

Muckraked

The services which Page had rendered Standard in the past by his stanch defense before investigating bodies could not offset the plain fact that he was becoming an embarrassment. The issue was further crystallized by the appearance in 1902 and 1903 of installments of Ida M. Tarbell's famous *History of the Standard Oil Company,* published first in *McClure's* magazine, and subsequently in book form. Cogent passages of the Tarbell study analyzed the past statements of Page and other Standard officials, with devastating effect.

Unlike Henry Demarest Lloyd's *Wealth Against Commonwealth,* and another best-selling book which had attacked Standard, Thomas Lawson's *Frenzied Finance,* Miss Tarbell's work was written with calm confidence and from an apparently objective viewpoint. She was, in fact, hardly an unprejudiced critic. Her brother, Franklin Tarbell, was a leading executive of the Pure Oil Company, and she was writing for S. S. McClure, whose magazine depended for circulation on the violence of its muckraking articles. For all that, she succeeded in avoiding the shrill denunciatory style of Lloyd and Lawson. Heavily documented and cogently organized, her book penetrated deep into the mystery of Standard's phenomenal success of the three preceding decades. Although she lacked detailed knowledge of the peculiar and crucial role of the tank car in Rockefeller's operations, she correctly pointed to his control of oil transportation as being the key to the Standard story.

A number of contradictions, errors of omission, and evidences of bias in her work were instantly perceived at 26 Broadway, but it was not possible to contest the main line of her argument. Recognizing that in the 1870s the law had not forbidden most of the practices by which Rockefeller had driven his company ahead of competition, giving him credit for great abilities and useful accomplishment, she nevertheless drove home the point that he and his associates had used their power to bully and persuade the nation's railroads to serve their private interest and annihilate competitors.

The replies made to the Tarbell history by journalists who served Standard's interests were ineffectual. Her book was a

country-wide sensation, and it was known that President Roosevelt himself had been deeply impressed by it. When the elections of 1904 returned him to the White House, Standard's high
command had few illusions about what was in store for them.
In the first years following McKinley's assassination Roosevelt
had been somewhat cautious in his attitude toward big business,
and his 1904 candidacy had even been supported by powerful
financiers. Once elected, however, he promptly showed that he
did not intend to let their campaign contributions shape his
policies, leading one of them, Henry C. Frick, to remark in disgust, "We bought the son of a bitch, but he wouldn't stay bought."
It was unmistakable that all of Standard's defensive strength
would have to be mustered to face imminent attack from the
government.

Wanted—A New Witness

Roosevelt moved promptly. In a tart message to Congress he
criticized past negligence in extending the powers of the ICC.
At his urging a bill authorizing the ICC to determine reasonable
rates for common carriers engaged in interstate commerce was
introduced into the House. Its passage by the House of Representatives put Standard in extreme danger. If as it stood the
Hepburn bill (it had been drafted by the former New York State
legislator) were now to pass the Senate, obliging railroads would
in future be unable to raise and lower rates at Standard's behest,
and the combine might even be deprived of its tank cars, its last
instrument of power over the roads.

Rallying their political influence, Standard's officials counted
conservative heads in the Senate. At first they felt some hope
that the Hepburn bill might be defeated there but they were
quickly disillusioned. A new senator from Wisconsin, Robert M.
La Follette, a nominal Republican, had come to the Senate fresh
from victories over the railroads in his own state, and he was
primed for battle. His oratorical assaults on the evils of monopoly and plutocracy startled his party and the country. When indignant right-wing senators tried to stop him by walking out of
the Chamber during his speeches, he shrugged them aside. Their
"temporarily empty seats," he prophesied, "would soon become
permanently vacant."

The conservatives fought him tooth and nail, deriding anything he favored, regardless of its merits. On one occasion, when he proposed a simple amendment to the Hepburn bill forbidding judges to sit in cases involving railroads in which they owned securities, only three Republicans voted with him. In the nation as a whole, however, his efforts bore fruit, and under pressure from the press and constituents a number of previously uncommitted senators began to turn against Standard.

President Roosevelt personally intervened to aid the attack by bringing out new evidence of wrongdoing by the great trusts. Operating through the newly created Department of Commerce and Labor, he instructed Commissioner of Corporations J. R. Garfield to study and report to him on monopolistic controls in American transportation. It was well understood that special emphasis would be given to relations between Standard Oil and the railroads.

To Rockefeller, Archbold, and Tilford it was evident that the Hepburn bill in some form would probably become law eventually. If so, if pipe lines fell under ICC authority, if freight rates ceased to be readily susceptible to Standard's pressure, then it was all the more important that Standard's tank car fleet be kept free of Federal regulation. UTL had to be saved. Regardless of what happened to sleeping cars and express cars, Congress had to be convinced that privately owned tank car lines ought not to be classed as common carriers.

Standard's need was to assure a defense of its tank car operations so tight and consistent in its legality as to stand against all the old accusations and any new ones that might be forthcoming. It was easy to predict what these new accusations would be. In the past it had been possible for UTL to contend that its cars were exclusively in the service of Standard Oil. But this position was no longer secure since Tilford's now notorious tank car operation in California. That Garfield would fasten on this episode was a foregone conclusion. A way would have to be found to justify Tilford's action. On the whole, the high command considered that it might be better if, when the time came for testimony, he himself were busy with other matters and no longer connected with UTL.

The times called for new leadership in UTL—a man who had

no earlier testimony to live down, who would not merely thwart inquisitive legislators by evasion and shrugs, but would defeat them with carefully selected facts.

The Careful Man

In 1904, Tilford announced that UTL would have a new vice-president for Car Service, in charge of relations with refineries and railroads. The man selected was Henry Felton, who as traffic manager of Standard Oil of New Jersey was already one of the overlords of transportation. Standard had given him large discretion over the shipment of both its crude and refined output, and it was his responsibility to coordinate the use of pipe lines, water carriers, and railroads. By playing one mode of transportation against the other he was able to keep the costs of all to a minimum. One of his techniques was to warn recalcitrant railroads which ran through regions where shipment by water was feasible that, unless their rates were reduced to a level competitive with barge transportation, he would thereafter ship by water to the cities which they served; and the phrase "water-compelled rates" had become a bitter byword in railroad offices. By this and similar means Felton was in a position to influence railroad freight rates without recourse to illegal rebates and secret agreements. Commanding as he did a vast tonnage of freight, he had become a feared and respected figure in the railroad world.

Without giving up his post in SONJ Felton, as vice-president of UTL, relieved Page of his responsibilities. The latter retired, to become one of the first beneficiaries of a pension plan which the Standard Oil companies had adopted and which entitled him to "an annuity equal to 50 per cent of his average pay for the ten years preceding retirement." As in the instance of his salary, his pension was paid by SONJ, not by UTL.

It would have been hard to find a sharper contrast between two executives. Page, who had recently turned sixty, was ebullient, aggressive, bluntly outspoken; while Felton, in his middle forties, was restrained in manner, careful in his choice of words, uniformly courteous, and a teetotaller of fastidious habits and decorous life. Seeking an executive who would "play it safe,"

Archbold and Tilford could not have made a better choice. If it can be said that a man was passionately cautious, that man was Felton. The recollections of one of his early associates afford a significant glimpse of his psychology. "Mr. Felton had a phobia about germs. He was reluctant to shake hands with anyone. He would avoid it if he could possibly do so without appearing discourteous. At the very first opportunity after having engaged in a handclasp he would rush back to the washroom and thoroughly scrub his hands. If anyone but himself used the telephone on his desk, after that person had left the room he would ring for the office boy and order him to swab out the mouthpiece and the receiver as well, using a disinfectant, which was light blue in color. When he went to a restaurant, he would always take his napkin and wipe the rim of his water glass before drinking."

With this quirk of personality went very considerable administrative abilities and an exceptionally strong will. An autocrat by nature, Felton could be relied on to shape UTL in his own careful image and to assure the company's correct demeanor in the troubles that loomed ahead.

Simultaneously with the decision to bring in Felton, a new financial policy was adopted by UTL's directors. Beginning in 1903, the annual profits which had been consistently shown in UTL's secret financial reports since 1894, averaging about $250,000 after depreciation, gave way to a series of heavy losses, averaging about $300,000 per year. No public explanation of these sudden losses was ever made. It is true that UTL at this time reduced its rental charges for tank cars almost to zero, but this could not have much affected revenues, for rentals had previously been very low. A not unreasonable surmise, but one which cannot be proved, is that the rate of depreciation was arbitrarily raised. Since construction orders for hundreds of new steel tank cars were then being placed, the resulting write-offs could have accounted for the losses. Whatever the reason, the losses appeared on the books, and it became possible for Felton, in giving later testimony before investigating committees, to swear to the unprofitability of UTL's operations without having to forget, as Page had conveniently forgotten, the company's private accounts. For Felton, a deeply religious man, this was a point of importance. He prided himself on telling the truth, even though it was only the literal truth.

Late in 1905 Tilford resigned the presidency of UTL, to devote himself wholly to Standard's marketing problems until his untimely death a few years later; and Felton formally assumed command of the tank car operation.

FOUR

DEEP WATER

A few weeks after becoming president of UTL, Felton appeared
before Commissioner Garfield in Washington. In contrast to
Page, his manner in the witness chair was a marvel of correct-
ness. There were no questions that he would not answer, and
every answer was responsive to the question. More, his statements were factual, precise, complete; he was positively eager
to acquaint Commissioner Garfield and his associates with the
realities of the tank car business. Unruffled by pressure, respect-
ful in tone, serene in the assurance of his personal and corporate
virtue, he made the investigation seem like the unjustified intrusion of bureaucrats into the time of a busy but polite gentleman.

Felton's testimony came late in Garfield's investigation. Most
of the government's effort to this point had consisted of interrogation of competitive refiners, producers, and railroad men, in
an effort to prove that Standard "has habitually received from
the railroads, and is now receiving, secret rates and other unjust
and illegal discriminations." With his facts assembled, Garfield
invited Archbold to testify for Standard, or to send someone in
his place. Archbold, knowing only too well how much depended
on the nature of the replies made to Garfield, selected Felton for
the task. He could not have done better. When the commissioner's attack on Standard's practices grew warm, when a Page
or an Archbold would have shown resentment and lost ground,
Felton parried Garfield's thrusts without emotion or perceptible
anxiety.

The questions aimed at him on the matter of freight rates were specific and factual. Why had the rate between such-and-such points on this or that railroad been established at an abnormally low level benefiting Standard? In some instances, Felton had no personal knowledge or recollection of the matter, but when he had he gave it unhesitatingly, and always Standard emerged from the testimony wiped clean, or fairly clean, of the charge. Yes, Felton said, it was true that an exceptionally low rate for petroleum was in force between Rochester and Olean, New York. The reason, he believed, was that nearly twenty years earlier Standard had threatened to build a pipe line between these two points, and the railroad had kept its rate low ever since. In contemplating the pipe line Standard had certainly violated no law; and the concession made by the railroad was voluntary; no doubt it found that a lower rate with a higher volume of freight was more profitable than a higher rate with lower volume.

"The Evidence Was Wrong"

Allowing his incredulity to show, Garfield cited another example—rates on railroads running westward and southward out of Chicago—as proof that Standard was dictating "the policy of the railroads, both East and West." His evidence showed that Standard had ruthlessly compelled the lowering of these rates.

If that was the evidence, Felton replied, then the evidence was wrong. The matter of railroad rates was at bottom one of simple economics. The railways had to decide whether their total revenues would be increased or diminished by lower rates, and they had made their own decision. To be sure, midwestern roads had to recognize that if their rates were excessive, refiners might turn to Mississippi barges for deliveries. But these "water-compelled rates" were no more remarkable than any other aspect of pricing to meet competitive situations. Certainly Standard could not be held responsible for the existence of America's waterways. The uneven railroad rates for oil freight, as between one railroad and another, could not well be understood unless each individual rate was considered on its own merits, in relation to the location of refineries, plants, and pipe lines, and the size of the market served by the road. If on some roads on which they shipped heavily Standard enjoyed advantages in low freight rates, independent refiners had similar benefits from other roads. In the heavy oil traffic running westward out of Pittsburgh, for example, the independents shipped at precisely the same rates as Standard. Was not this evidence that railroad rates, like prices in business generally, were merely being adjusted in each instance to the railroad's best interests, irrespective of pressure from Standard?

Unable to shake Felton on the subject of rates, Garfield narrowed his attack from Standard as a whole to the tank car operation in particular. From the first one of his main purposes had been to prove that UTL enjoyed the privileges of a common carrier, and ought to be made subject to ICC authority. To this end he had chosen Tilford's "now-you-see-'em, now-you-don't" trick with tank cars as a prime example of the danger of permitting unregulated operation.

Felton found himself confronted with full documentary evidence of the California story—the files of the Southern Pacific Railroad and woeful letters from independent refiners and producers who felt that they had been reduced by Tilford's manipulations to mere pawns in Standard's game. "We had contracts for about 35,000 barrels of oil a month," wrote a refiner. . . . "Just about the time we were trying to get cars to fill the contracts, Standard called all their cars in, and kept some of them lying idle . . . for months. The Southern Pacific claimed they were very short of equipment because of this withdrawal. . . . The Standard came to us and offered to take our oil at 20 cents a barrel. We were forced to accept. . . . The Standard then took over all our contracts."

Another refiner wrung his typewriter to this effect: "Before the Standard Oil entered the field we had no trouble getting tank cars . . . and we got a good price for the oil, namely, 62 cents. . . . Today we are obliged to sell . . . at their price, namely, 15 cents a barrel." Producers were similarly indignant. "In the summer of 1909, I saw a hundred empty cars in the Kern yard, when neither I nor any other shipper could secure a car." And yet another: "At a time when we were short of cars, I counted 87 empty cars in the Southern Pacific yards. . . . My partner . . . asked the Southern Pacific why they didn't send those empties. They couldn't answer. . . ."

With a large stockpile of such ammunition to support him, Garfield established the essential and, to his mind, conclusive facts. "Prior to about the middle of 1901, the Union Tank Line's cars were available for the use of shippers generally in California. About that time they were suddenly withdrawn from general use and reserved for the exclusive use of the various Standard Oil companies."

"They Were Very Generous"

Felton allowed himself to look surprised—not at Tilford's action, but at Garfield's naïveté. "The wonder to my mind," he replied briskly, "is that the Union Tank Line's cars ... were ever put into general use ... Union Tank Line is a subsidiary of Standard Oil of New Jersey.... If they ever allowed their competitors to use those cars in California they were very generous."

This, then, was his case: that Standard had no legal or moral obligation to let others use UTL's tank cars, and that when any such use was permitted it demonstrated only Standard's high-minded regard for the customer's welfare. He did not deny that the tank car withdrawal had occurred at a time very convenient for Standard. But, he reasonably pointed out, Standard did not, after all, control all the tank cars of the country. Had it not been testified a few years earlier that UTL owned only about 40 per cent of the nation's tank car equipment? It was up to the other California refiners and to the Southern Pacific to find their own tank cars.

The Commissioner stuck to his guns. For him the essential fact was that after the sudden withdrawal of the tank cars "the independent producers had to sell their oil to Standard at reduced prices or else close their wells."

Felton, however, did not believe that Tilford had necessarily anticipated any such result of his action. He had merely done what the requirements of his company demanded that he do. "I suppose," UTL's president said quietly, "the Standard Oil Company, with the increase of production, needed all of that equipment for its own business. There is no reason why it should furnish equipment to a competitor."

The charge was made that the Southern Pacific had favored UTL and Standard above all independent owners of tank cars in California. "This is news to me," said Felton, "... we know absolutely nothing about it...." And then, reprovingly, "We ought to hesitate before accepting the complaint of producers on that subject." Garfield, he said, had let himself be misled by prejudiced testimony. "When a great production of oil comes along in any territory, and a man is not equipped to handle it with his storage tanks or his tank cars ... he is very prone to accuse the railroad and the people who have facilities.... In every case that comes to my attention these charges have proven to be absolutely without foundation."

Unable to demonstrate that there had been any violation of law in the handling of tank cars, Garfield shifted his attack, reviving the charge that UTL was profitable; and that its profits, passed on to Standard, could be regarded as an illegal rebate paid by the railroads and a violation of federal law. The completeness and earnestness of Felton's denial made it difficult to pursue this question. "It has been alleged that the Standard gets great benefit through that service [tank cars].... In answer to the wild and reckless charges ... I would say that the Union Tank Car Line today is bankrupt as an individual corporation."

Precisely how this state of bankruptcy had been produced Felton did not feel called upon to explain. Never deviating from the literal fact, he went on to assure Garfield that his company "had not paid a dividend since 1901. It is very heavily in debt." If Garfield had probed into the nature of the debt, he would have learned that it consisted of funds advanced by SONJ for the purchase of new tank cars; but he did not, and Felton raced ahead. It would be outrageously unfair on the part of the government, he conveyed, to make UTL a common carrier. How could the ICC insist that UTL carry the oil of competitors, when it could not even make money as a member of the Standard family? In fact, Felton made it clear, no one could earn a profit out of so difficult a business. "There is not a railroad in the United States that can afford to acquire tank-line equipment." It was far cheaper for the roads to pay the mileage allowance. "The hauls are short ... the cars do not ... pile up heavy mileage.... The expense of keeping up a steel car to handle ... oil over the railroads in an absolutely safe manner is something enormous. The tank car must be perfect, and if it meets with any slight accident

... the car must go into the shop, and all the expense is very, very heavy."

To put tank car lines on a par with other private car lines, such as Pullman cars, would be an atrocious error of judgment —this was the sense of Felton's testimony. The complexities of the tank car business were such that any departure from the established and familiar system of operation would mean chaos on the railroads. Garfield had to understand the methods by which UTL operated; so Felton described in detail how reports of every tank car were kept and transmitted by the railroads; he explained the function of every piece of paper, every clerical form; he elaborated on the company's methods of accounting. It is doubtful that the Commissioner was able to follow him through the maze of minutiae; but one unmistakable point, the point that Felton was intent to prove, emerged from the welter of explanation: it would be an extremely ticklish matter for the government to meddle with so complicated a mechanism.

Saved

In May, 1906, Commissioner Garfield presented the report of his investigation of Standard Oil to President Roosevelt. Its most damaging sections consisted of data gathered by ICC agents and showing in detail that certain subsidiaries of Standard had made secret freight-rate agreements with various railroads in violation of Federal law. But when it came to the operations of UTL itself the results of Felton's precise testimony were plainly to be seen. Although the report rehashed many old allegations and brought out the whole story of Tilford's relations with California railroads, it contained no evidence that the practices which it criticized were still employed. Its text was replete with such terms as "formerly," "in previous years," "at that time." Garfield felt obliged to point out that although "at the present time ... the tank car shipper in many cases enjoys a considerable advantage over the barrel shipper," the Trust no longer had a monopoly of tank cars. If "Standard and its affiliated concerns in 1904 had a little over 10,000 tank cars," competing refiners had 3,000 cars of their own, and were further serviced by private tank car lines. "Many competitors," the report stated, "seem to be fairly well supplied with tank cars." Such statements tended to reduce congressional interest in protective legislation for the users of barrels. Garfield, it was evident, had uncovered nothing in UTL's current activity to justify denunciation.

As for Garfield's findings on Standard as a whole, they were presented in a high-pitched tone which made it easy to question his fairness. Charges by Standard's friends that Garfield and Roosevelt were guilty of bias and politicking gained a large audience. Some writers portrayed the struggle not as that of government against a violator of law but as a personal duel between Roosevelt and Rockefeller, or between "the two great houses," the White House and 26 Broadway. Garfield, wrote one economist, had been unable to "resist the temptation to tell the people what the popular prejudice demands." Many journalists who had previously joined in the outcry against Standard began to retreat to a more objective position.

Not altogether satisfied, Roosevelt nevertheless rewarded Garfield by making him Secretary of the Interior. Then he appointed a new Commissioner of Corporations, Henry Knox Smith. The first assignment given Smith was to carry on the study of the Standard combine in its relation to the American economy.

In spite of its insistence on Standard's misdeeds, the first effect of the Garfield report was to aid the friends of big business in the Senate. A compromise was then in the wind. Pro-Standard senators had expressed themselves as willing to agree to ICC's power to regulate pipe lines, as long as tank cars were exempted from regulation. Their position was supported by senators close to the great meat packers or owners of refrigerator cars, whose position was somewhat similar to that of Standard. If Garfield's report had been able to point an accusing finger at UTL, it is doubtful that this compromise would have been accepted by the bill's proponents. But having been given no new ammunition to use against the tank car business, and being eager to push the bill through after so long and wearisome a struggle, they reluctantly made the deal. A few weeks later, when the regulatory bill was passed, sleeping cars and express cars were included in it, but tank cars and refrigerator cars were not.

Bloody but Unbowed

Standard's sudden decision to drop its fight to keep the pipe lines out of the Hepburn bill had surprised many. The surrender was undoubtedly dictated in part by belief that the bill would finally pass, regardless of protests, and that it was better to save tank cars in a compromise than to risk total defeat. But another element also entered strongly into the combine's calculations. Before the Hepburn bill was signed by the President, Standard had quietly replaced its interstate pipe line subsidiaries by new companies whose physical properties were entirely contained within the borders of individual states. A pipe line running from Pennsylvania to New York no longer was operated by one company, but by two. At the state line ownership of the pipe changed hands, even though the oil continued to flow continuously as before. By this device Standard challenged the ingenuity of the government's lawyers. Could the power given to the ICC by the Hepburn bill to regulate pipe line charges be exercised over companies which were technically not engaged in interstate commerce? It was a nice legal point; and eight more years would go by before the Supreme Court upheld the constitutionality of the regulation of pipe lines in intrastate as well as in interstate commerce. Meanwhile, the separate state pipe line companies set their rates as before.

Standard came out of the bruising fight over the Hepburn Act bloody but still unbowed. The high command, however, Archbold, Rogers, Pratt, Tilford, knew that the worst of their troubles lay ahead. Roosevelt was an unrelenting enemy, and the nation's press, on the whole, was with him. An effort to turn the publicistic tide was made when a number of journalists were put on Standard's payroll with instructions to offset the incessant attacks from the antitrust forces, but theirs could be no more than a rear-guard action. The heat was on. The Federal administration was now backed by the governments of a dozen individual states in the drive to break Standard's power.

Largely on the basis of information contained in the Garfield report no fewer than twelve separate suits against Standard companies for violation of state antitrust laws were brought in the six months that followed passage of the Hepburn bill. Nine others had been launched shortly before. From Texas to Connecticut, from Kansas to West Virginia, from Chicago to Jackson, Tennessee, the federal and state courts kept the top echelon of Standard executives continually on the move, and under great strain. Never before in the history of the United States had there been so far-reaching a struggle between industry and government.

FIVE

"WELL, GENTLEMEN, SHALL WE PROCEED?"

There is some evidence that the central strategy of the government's campaign to dismember the Standard combine was laid out in the White House. That federal and state actions were closely coordinated is certain. The President himself played an important part in shaping public opinion in the matter through his vigorous speeches and statements. Many newspapers and magazines, having found that their readers would accept with enthusiasm almost anything derogatory to Standard, whipped up public opinion to such an extent that in the popular oratory of the day the corporation was bracketed with Benedict Arnold, Aaron Burr, and John Wilkes Booth.

Early in 1907, Roosevelt infused new energy into the anti-Standard forces by releasing in close succession two damaging reports. The first of these, prepared by the ICC, extended the findings of the Garfield report in the matter of secret railroad rates. It claimed that Standard's offenses lay not only in the past but in the present; that the corporation was currently violating the Hepburn Act and many state laws as well. While the congressional fight flared again, the second report, prepared by the new Commissioner of Corporations at Roosevelt's behest, was published. For all the rise of competition in the oil industry, Commissioner Smith contended, Standard still controlled 85 per cent to 90 per cent of the production, refining, and marketing of petroleum products, as well as almost all pipe lines and a large preponderance of tank cars. Its monopoly was for practical pur-

148

poses as formidable as it ever had been. The public, said the Commissioner, was being gouged by the Trust's prices, "averaging much above the competitive level." And he made it plain that he still had not exhausted the charges against Standard. His main conclusions were reserved for another section of the report, to be published a few months later.

The Big Barrage

The press hardly had time to digest and summarize Smith's material when it was given even juicier meat for its columns. The Supreme Court of the state of Missouri accepted the findings of a special investigator to the effect that certain Standard subsidiaries had entered into a conspiracy to defy the state's anti-trust laws. The expected penalty, which soon materialized, was an order from the court requiring Standard to cease all operations in the state.

A week after this adverse news from Missouri, on June 1, 1907, Standard's Texas affiliate, the Waters–Pierce Oil Company, was convicted on a similar charge, ordered to pay a fine of over $1,600,000, and to place its affairs in the hands of a receiver appointed by the state. Another Texas antitrust suit was decided shortly thereafter and led to an injunction which came as a shock to Felton. UTL was forbidden to remove any of its tank cars which were then in the service of Waters–Pierce and other Texas units of Standard Oil. These cars, numbering nearly 1,000, with a depreciated value of $350,000, were ordered sold by the state; in addition, UTL was fined $75,000, and barred from doing business in Texas. To replace the lost equipment, Felton was forced to borrow $500,000 from the SONJ and commission 500 new steel cars.

But these blows, heavy as they were, were mere love taps compared to the haymaker which was in preparation. On August 3, 1917, Federal Judge Kenesaw Mountain Landis found Standard of Indiana guilty of numerous violations of the Elkins Act forbidding secret railroad rates. His decision stated that on 1,462 separate occasions, cited in detail, loaded UTL tank cars had passed between Whiting, Indiana, and East St. Louis, Illinois, at rates lower than those published by the railroads. For each such violation Standard was to pay a fine of $20,000. The staggering fine, assessed at $29,240,000, delighted the American press, with its passion for broken records, and made headlines all over the country. As the *Chicago Tribune* pointed out, the fine was equivalent to a payment of 35 cents for every man, woman, and child in the United States.

News of the fine came to John D. Rockefeller as he was playing golf in a foursome at a Cleveland country club, and about to tee off for a drive. When a messenger hurried up to him and put a yellow envelope into his hand, everyone in the group knew what it contained. Rockefeller, according to the legend, gave the boy a dime, tore the envelope open, read the message without a change of expression, put it into his pocket, and said to the silent men around him, "Well, gentlemen, shall we proceed?" One of his fellow golfers, a Standard executive, blurted out the question in all their minds: "How much was the fine?" About to concentrate on his shot, Rockefeller murmured, "Twenty-nine million dollars," hit a fine, long drive down the center of the fairway, and finished nine holes in 53, the lowest score he had ever made.

"Absolute Innocence"

Following time-honored laws of military strategy, never giving Standard a chance to catch its breath, the governmental forces struck again. Only two days after the Landis decision Commissioner of Corporations Smith released the final section of his report to the President. In a volume of nearly 1,000 pages Smith analyzed a great body of statistics and came to some familiar conclusions. Standard's policy, he averred, had been "to sacrifice the interests of the American consumer" to its own purposes. It had done this in part by charging higher prices in the United States than it dared charge in foreign markets. It had connived with railroads to strangle its competition. It had practiced price discrimination to the detriment of the rest of the petroleum industry. Above all, it had made outrageous profits—alleged to be $700,000,000 on a capital of less than $70,000,000, over the twenty-four years from 1882 to 1906—or an average of over 40 per cent per year.

A sharp drop in the prices of Standard securities attested the effect of all this on the public and goaded top management into a reply. A special report to stockholders from the directors protested their "absolute innocence of wrongdoing in any of the prosecutions lately instigated against it [Standard] in the Federal courts." Keep calm, was the implied message of the pamphlet. Landis' decision had been appealed. The company was confident that fair judgment would rescue it "from the domain of vindictive politics." "Socialistic outcry from below and political pressure from above" were blamed for Standard's bad press. Commissioner Smith was "illogical and partisan."

The *New York World,* one of Standard's foremost enemies, had a field day with this attempt at rebuttal. "STANDARD OIL WHIMPERS, *Says It's a Victim,*" the story was headlined. Although the *New York Times* gave credit to the corporation for its large achievements by "some of the best business brains in the world," and agreed that Smith's conclusions were "in many substantial respects unreasonable, unfair, and not sustained by the evidence," the press as a whole had no doubt that the days of the Rockefeller combination were numbered. Many of the metropolitan reporters, recognizing the peculiar importance of the part played by UTL in Standard's situation, tried to interview Felton but were firmly turned away. Every Standard employee had long since learned to keep his mouth closed about company business in the presence of outsiders, but at this period, so wary was Felton of the lurking danger of unfriendly ears, it became customary for UTL's personnel in the ordinary course of their daily business to speak in hushed tones, even in whispers.

Yet for all the weight of aggressive prosecution, legal decision, and public opinion, Standard did not yield an inch without a hard contest. The Rockefeller spirit was still alive, with its will to fight and its sharp perception of legal loopholes. Every charge against Standard was argued with all the fervor of conviction. Unreasonable prices? How dared the government say so? People were urged to consider a statement by Joseph French Johnson, professor of political economy and dean of the School of Commerce of New York University. Upon careful study, Professor Johnson had concluded that Standard's price for kerosene to dealers had risen less than the average price of 258 other leading commodities.

Unfair profits? Why, pointed out Standard, the net assets of

SONJ in 1907, as shown by its books, were only $360,000,000—representing about 500 per cent on the 1882 capital of $70,000,000. And this sum was only what $70,000,000 would have earned if invested at compound interest of 7 per cent. Therefore, said Standard, it had been earning only a paltry 7 per cent on its investment—far from the 40 per cent figure then being bandied about. Skeptics observed that no reference was made in this statement to dividends paid out, and which had enabled Standard's owners to acquire immense wealth.

The Public Is Disappointed

Considering that the average pay load of a tank car was worth about $450, a fine of $20,000 per violation was emphatic enough. To many it suggested that Landis was seeking to make a Rooseveltian reputation for himself at Standard's expense. In fact, however, the immensity of the fine, while elating enemies of the Trust, was actually a legal protection for it—a point which Rockefeller almost certainly recognized from the first. For the fine, if sustained in the courts, would not be merely punitive; it would be confiscatory. Although few newspapers reported the fact, there were then standing against Standard Oil companies in Missouri, Louisiana, California, and New York indictments which brought the total number of separate violations of the Elkins Act charged against UTL cars to over 8,000 for the nation as a whole. If Landis' fine were allowed to set a precedent, the final assessment against Standard might reach the total of over $160,-000,000. Even Roosevelt, with all his determination to dissolve the trusts, was unwilling to advocate the bankrupting of the nation's greatest corporate enterprise. Although Secretary of the Interior Garfield publicly praised Landis' decision, the President himself refrained from comment. At that time, late in 1907, he had to be especially cautious, for a financial panic had gripped the financial markets and New York banks and threatened to swamp even some large corporations. In fact, to help prevent a business crisis Roosevelt sanctioned the United States Steel Company, then dominated by J. P. Morgan, in making new acquisitions which brought its power dangerously near monopoly. Under the circumstances he was hardly in a position to maintain an uncompromising stand against Rockefeller, especially since it was known that the latter had cooperated with Morgan in stemming the tide of panic, putting up $10,000,000 for the purpose.

The change in the attitude of the press toward Rockefeller was sufficiently marked so that even some senators and representatives opposed to Standard urged Rooosevelt to use his influence to have Landis' fine reduced, on the ground that it was weakening the government's position and playing into the combine's hands. For a time he was inclined to follow their advice, but political expediency intervened. William Howard Taft was then running for the Presidency with Roosevelt's progressive mantle draped around his portly conservatism. Republican political leaders felt that Taft's chances of beating William Jennings Bryan would be lessened if the President were suddenly to relent toward Standard—that no St. George ought to show softness toward the Dragon. In the upshot, Roosevelt decided to leave the matter to the courts, and Taft went on to victory at the polls.

The courts were besieged by Standard lawyers. The Landis decision was appealed not only on the merits of the case but also on the size of the fine. The penalty, contended the Standard lawyers, had been imposed under a misapprehension on the part of the judge. If there had been an offense against federal law by Standard of Indiana—and this was not admitted—it had been an offense in principle, and should have been so considered; each separate tank car shipped did not constitute a separate offense. The judgment rendered by Landis was therefore invalid.

A higher court agreed and went even further, reversing Landis' decision, on the ground that some of his technical rulings at the trial had been prejudicial to Standard's case. A series of appeals culminated in the Supreme Court, where the reversal was sustained and a retrial ordered. Thereafter Landis, stung by judicial criticism, declined to preside at the new trial and another judge, A. B. Anderson, took his place. In February, 1909, one week before Taft's inauguration, Anderson ruled that on the evidence submitted by the government Standard of Indiana was not guilty of violating the Elkins Act.

Most of the American public were grievously disappointed; there were loud protests; but the case was closed. Soon afterward, by one legally permissible device or another, companies affiliated with Standard worked their way back into Missouri and eventually into Texas.

Painless Finance

While the fortunes of Standard were being entrusted to its formidable battery of legal counsel, UTL was quietly proceeding to expand its car fleet. Regardless of courts and politicians, the American people wanted their kerosene stoves, their gasoline motors, their asphalt roads, their well-lubricated machinery. Standard refineries were clamoring for tank cars. In the five years following 1906 Felton asked his board of directors for, and was granted, authority to buy an average of nearly 1,000 new steel cars per year, many of them to replace old cars built in the 1870s and 1880s.

Since the company had no capital of its own and was losing money, Standard of New Jersey had to provide funds for the new equipment. Each year saw UTL borrowing large sums from the parent company. To cover the obligation Felton in 1908 was authorized to recapitalize UTL. Instead of the 35,000 shares of $100 stock outstanding, 120,000 shares, representing a $12,000,000 capitalization, were deposited in Jersey Standard's treasury. This was a formidable jump. The $8,500,000 worth of additional shares was evidently considered to represent equity for and repayment of money borrowed from SONJ since the original capitalization.

Once the recapitalization was completed, Standard did not stint Felton in the further amounts that he could borrow. Rather, he was encouraged to bring the tank car fleet to a high peak of size and efficiency. In this, "Room 702," as the policy-making office at 26 Broadway was then known, was undoubtedly anticipating a possible fragmentation of the combine. Combined or separated, a first-rate tank car operation was essential to the prosperity of all the Standard companies. Properly managed and with an adequate fleet, UTL could be expected to continue to serve the separate Standard refining companies much as it was serving the combine. The chief difference would be a raising of car rental charges sufficiently to permit UTL to earn a reasonable profit and to finance its future expansion.

In deciding on the new types of equipment to be added to the fleet, Felton found himself facing a difficult choice between

V-cars and the somewhat more costly X-cars. He himself believed in the sturdiness of the V-car. He could not, however, ignore the feelings of railroad men and refinery tank car handlers who refused to trust a car without an underframe. On one occasion the directors of UTL—Felton included—approved an appropriation for 500 V-cars. Immediately thereafter Felton went to Chicago to attend a meeting of railroad executives and upon hearing what they had to say telegraphed his office to countermand the order; X-cars were to be built instead. One reason for this choice was that running boards, which ICC regulations required on all tank cars, could be provided in X-cars without having to rivet them to the sides of the tank, as in the V-car; the more rivets in a tank, it was considered, the greater the chance of leakage.

Van Dyke apparently regarded Felton's change of mind with disfavor. In his judgment the V-car was the better and the cheaper of the two, especially since its construction, like that of the X-car, had been strengthened by his patented anchor. There is no evidence of heat in their disagreement; but his resignation as a director followed soon thereafter. The contributions he had made, however, proved to be of major importance to UTL's future.

The Final Battle

On September 17, 1907, soon after the Landis decision against Standard of Indiana, the Federal government struck its hardest and most direct blow against the Trust. Bringing suit against Standard of New Jersey itself, it charged violation of the Sherman Anti-Trust Act and of the related acts designed to protect the American people against monopoly. The grand hierarchy of the corporation was summoned to testify, among them John D. Rockefeller, H. M. Flagler, and John D. Archbold.

Testimony was taken in Washington, New York, Cleveland, Chicago, and St. Louis, for the government's case was based on evidence from many different parts of the country. Four hundred individual witnesses were called by prosecution and defense, and Henry Felton was prominent among them, testifying, in his precise, assured fashion, to the strict legality of Standard's use of tank cars.

In spite of his efforts, however, the chief government prosecutor, Frank B. Kellogg, clearly established that pressure exerted on railroads through manipulation of tank cars had contributed fundamentally to Standard's monopolistic power; and that, taken in conjunction with control of pipe lines, the tank car had been a formidable instrument for the restriction of competitors. And it was the ability of Standard to keep competition to a bare 10 per cent of the total petroleum industry that was the main target of the prosecution. Kellogg, who, largely on the strength of his victory in this case, was to rise to eminence as U.S. senator and Secretary of State, was highly effective in making this point. He claimed that with its transportation advantage and ability to squeeze competitors by price cuts in any local contest Standard had gained an ascendancy that could be shaken only by government action. It had used that ascendancy to keep its prevailing prices at a level so high as to assure enormous profits. The resulting power of the combine was an unwholesome factor in—even a threat to—the life of the free American society. Since Standard stood in violation of various Federal acts, as many witnesses had testified, and also had often transgressed state laws, it was the duty of the court, Kellogg averred, to rescue the nation by inflicting penalties so far-reaching as to assure an end to the danger.

The distinguished New York lawyer, John C. Milburn, who led counsel for the defense, made a valiant effort to stall the attack by a variety of legalistic maneuvers and logical arguments. He cited the statute of limitations. He objected to the introduction of hearsay evidence. He denied the responsibility of Standard for the actions of its affiliate, the Waters–Pierce Company, whose management was not under Standard's control. Through examination of ranking Standard officials he brought out the tremendous scope of the organization, its remarkable constructive achievements, its extraordinary efficiency, and the essential part it had played in putting the American oil industry in a position of unrivaled world leadership. It was strange, he said, that a company which had spread an American industry not only throughout the nation but all over the world should be considered in restraint of trade. For almost every charge of illegality made against Standard he contended that there was a reasonable explanation, and he drew these explanations from his witnesses. Those cases of unfair practice that could not be explained away he dismissed as mere "incidents in the conduct of a great business," evidence perhaps of the overzealousness of some employees but not of monopolistic intent.

The crucial decision rested in the Federal Circuit Court in St. Louis, and in November, 1909, the presiding justice handed down the court's opinion. It represented a complete defeat for Standard. The combine was held to be exercising power to prevent competition in its field. It was in effect a conspiracy to maintain an unlawful monopoly. Therefore it must be dissolved. The directors and officers of Jersey Standard were told that they could no longer "exercise any control, direction, supervision, or influence over the acts" of subsidiary companies. Subsidiaries, in turn, were warned not to pay, in future, any dividends to Jersey Standard and not to permit their stock to be voted by Jersey's directors.

Not too Many Tears

By this time the Rockefeller forces were prepared for whatever might happen. Initial gloom at anticipation of the breakup had given way to mere regret that so beautifully efficient an economic organism as the Standard Trust should be slain by radical demagogues, who had never met a payroll or struggled for a market. Come what might, the plans of the Standard hierarchy were laid. Even if they could never again formally control the constituent companies, their tacit influence would be felt in all of them for a long while to come; and they could count on great rewards for past enterprise. Yet although philosophically ready for the worst, they did not cease to fight until the end. Their last stand was an appeal to the Supreme Court. There the justices reviewed the thick volumes of evidence given in past cases and listened to the solemn pleadings of counsel for both sides, while months went by. One justice died; delay followed delay, until President Taft publicly expressed his concern over the slowness of the judicial process. Then at last the court acted. On May 15, 1911, the last hope for the Standard combine vanished, as Chief Justice White pronounced it guilty as charged and allowed six months for its dissolution.

By autumn the formal separation of the constituent companies was under way. The method employed was to give each stockholder in Jersey Standard his *pro rata* proportion of stock in each company. For Felton's company the proportion was $\frac{119993}{983383}$: that is to say, each holder of one share of stock in Jersey Standard received that fraction of a share of stock in UTL.

As to the real value of a share of UTL stock at that time, it is suggested by a note in *Moody's Industrials* to the effect that the price of the $100 par stock on the date of quotation "nearest to March 1, 1913," was $67 bid, $69 asked.

Morale of the forty employees of the company was at a low ebb. Except for Felton, the little office force was as frightened and uncertain and as homesick for the maternal womb as any unloved babe. Years of unprofitable operation, of psychological battering by an unfriendly press and stern judges, had left their mark. Without the power of the combine behind UTL, what was it? The company had been cast off owing Standard of New Jersey $1,500,000. There was hardly any office equipment aside from desks and chairs. It had only been within the past few years that UTL had been allowed to have a telephone, and it still lacked an adding machine of its own, although there were many in the Standard offices. Clerks asked, in whispers, whether they ought to start looking for other jobs. Young men who went to work for UTL soon after the dissolution were warned by their fathers against joining a company reported to be on the verge of bankruptcy. This was the darkest hour in UTL's history. Felton, however, maintained his customary aplomb. He alone in the company knew that there was nothing to worry about. The essential fact was that the Standard refiners had no recourse but to deal with him, no other quarter to which they could turn for tank cars in the required quantities. They needed UTL as much as UTL needed them. As a result, it was comparatively easy to make practical arrangements for the future. All of the separate Standard refiners stood ready to do business with UTL as in the past, and to pay reasonable car rentals calculated to put the company on a sound economic footing.

Standard stocks that were being traded in on the exchange proceeded to surprise the general public, which had expected them to slump. Instead, they rose to unprecedented heights. Few outside of the organization realized how conservative Rocke-feller's financial statements had been for fifty years past, and how huge were Standard's hidden assets. The stock of Standard of Indiana, capitalized at a mere $1,000,000, provided some of the most dazzling fireworks in Wall Street's explosive history as its actual worth came into view. On the eve of the dissolution speculators became frenzied. Up and up went the price, jumping as much as $100 from sale to sale, until the old $100 par shares were selling for $700 each. And even after the company was recapitalized at thirty times its former figure the price of the new stock continued to soar. It was a happy time for the in-siders. Wall Street estimated that three months after the dis-solution, the market value of the publicly-traded stocks of the Standard companies had risen by $200,000,000. John T. Mc-Cutcheon, the famous cartoonist of the *Chicago Tribune*, ex-pressed the country's feeling. Now that other trusts could see from Standard's experience what dissolution really meant, he said, they were all eager to be dissolved.

PART THREE:

HANDLED WITH CARE

1912-1929

"Commerce is a game of skill, which every man cannot play, which few men can play well."

RALPH WALDO EMERSON

ONE

ORPHAN—WITH BIG BROTHERS

Dissolution or no dissolution, the belief was widespread that UTL was still linked to the Standard Oil group, not legally, perhaps, but by strong ties of common interest. And it was a belief with a reasonable foundation. If UTL no longer had a parent company, if it was financially puny and undernourished, unprepared for the struggles of the competitive world, it was at least surrounded by any number of corporate big brothers, all of them attentive to its needs and willing to smooth its way.

The company was soon to detach itself physically from 26 Broadway, moving into a separate office miles uptown; but the plain fact was that Felton and the Standard Oil refineries conceived UTL's function to be unchanged. That function was to serve Standard as in the past. No "outside" business was solicited or wanted. Some of the newer oil companies which were then springing up made inquiries: would UTL lease tank cars to them? The stock reply which all UTL personnel were instructed to make on such occasions was, "Sorry, but all of our cars are assigned and actively employed. We are not in a position to help you."

This was true enough. UTL's refusal was not merely a matter of policy. Despite its large construction program in the years preceding 1912, it found itself woefully short of cars. Other private car lines were growing faster than UTL. Eight years earlier UTL had 10,000 cars to 3,000 for all other private car lines combined. By 1912 its advantage had sharply diminished, with 13,000 UTL cars against 10,000 for the other lines. Railroads over the past decades had built their fleets to a total of 8,000 cars. In part UTL's comparatively retarded growth was due to financial caution, in part to a desire to avoid charges of monopoly; but it was also due to the simple fact that the company had no facilities for building its own cars. Having come as a matter of business economy to rely on independent car builders, it was forced to compete for new tank cars with the other private lines.

The great rush of industry to oil was then getting under way, car builders were working overtime, and UTL had to stand in line. To make matters more difficult, by far the largest tank car building facilities in the country were owned by GAT, Union's most formidable competitor. To have to order new cars from a competitor was humiliating, but Felton had no choice; no choice, that is, unless he chose to establish his own car-building shops, and this would have required a financial outlay for which his already indebted company was unready. Under the circumstances he could not obtain cars from GAT until after it had provided for its own needs, and the rate of its expansion continued to exceed that of UTL.

A Single Sheet of Paper

Yet Felton was far from unhappy. A new schedule of car-leasing rates had been issued to the various Standard companies. In the days when it had been essential to show a loss UTL's cars had been rented out within the family at 11 cents per diem and less. Now the typical charge was $3 as an initial fee for furnishing the car and 75 cents per loaded day. The resulting revenue from lessors assured UTL of a profit that would quickly enable it to repay its $1,500,000 debt to Jersey Standard while showing a net profit of over $1,000,000 in 1912.

Moreover, unlike other car lines, which had to solicit business on a competitive basis, UTL had no sales problem. Where there was a Standard company there was a customer; and although some Standard refineries were occasionally dissatisfied by UTL's inability to let them have all the tank cars that they needed at peak seasons they did not dream of utilizing the services of UTL's competitors. For one thing, no competitor, not even GAT, then had enough cars to improve on UTL's service. For another, large stockholders in the various Standard companies were also large stockholders in UTL and naturally preferred to see the old tie sustained. For yet another, traffic managers of many of the Standard companies had been Felton's assistants in the days when he headed the traffic department of the old combine. Gratitude for the training and positions he had given them, the habit of deference, reliance on his judgment and personal esteem were enough to keep them loyal to UTL.[1]

As to the formal, contractual relationship between UTL and the refining companies, it was of the lightest and most tenuous nature. The contracts which Felton had negotiated with each of the now-separated Standard Companies consisted of a single page with a minimum of legalisms. It was actually nothing more than the statement of a few general principles. The customer agreed to look to UTL for his tank car requirements; UTL bound itself to deliver tank cars in the quantities needed by the customer, at the times and places specified by the customer, and at a given per diem rental;[2] and either party could cancel the arrangement at any time on six months' notice.

This simple document was, in fact, an inspired legal conception. Initiated by Felton, it was worked out by Douglas Campbell, an attorney who had done excellent work for Standard in the Missouri antitrust case, and who had caught John D. Rockefeller's practiced eye. Before the dissolution Campbell had established his own law firm in New York, with UTL among his clients. It was clear to him that in the uncertainties that would

---

[1] UTC NOTE: It should be recognized that these men had been raised by Felton to their positions as traffic managers in the various Standard companies because they were experts on regional freight rates. While well disposed toward Felton, they had neither obligation nor inclination to favor his company as against their own. They were all ambitious executives, eager to make good records, and they insisted on competent service at fair prices from UTL. Friendship or no friendship, disagreements between them and UTL were resolved on their merits, by arm's length negotiation. After the dissolution, UTL stood on its own feet in customer relationships. It was a firm policy of the company never to bring its problems to the attention of "26 Broadway."

AUTHOR'S NOTE: It is true that the company abided by the dissolution order of 1911, and that legally its customers were not captive. But the old tradition was unmistakably a force in the relationship—and the fact is that UTL never lost a customer.

[2] The per diem rental charge permitted the company to maintain the operating system which had been in force from the beginning. See Appendix C.

follow the dissolution the Standard companies would want to keep as free as possible from binding obligations, while they established themselves on their new footing. The contract was essentially a device to keep customers tied to UTL without exposing either Standard refiners or UTL to charges of antitrust violation.

All or Nothing

Felton recognized that as new executives came up in the Standard companies, men who had no personal feeling for the old combine, they might try to put pressure on UTL by threatening to give their tank car business to its competitors. UTL needed protection against a possible weakening of the old ties of friendship. And this the contract provided by assuring that customers would lease their per diem tank cars from UTL only. At a later period, when one or two oil companies proposed that they be allowed to divide their tank car requirements between UTL and other lessors, they found the company adamant. It was impractical, Felton pointed out, to try to split responsibility for a single refiner's daily service between two tank car companies. With demands for tank cars constantly shifting to correspond with shifts in seasons, weather, refinery competition and expansion, new products and new pipe lines, UTL's responsibility to maintain an adequate supply of tank cars at all times for all customers was no light matter. The task could not be efficiently performed, advance calculations would not be dependable, unless the company were responsible for all of its customers' tank car needs.[3]

The contract form in effect bound UTL to provide enough cars to meet each customer's "peak requirements." If some other tank car lessor's cars had been hired by a customer for ordinary requirements, UTL might have been left "holding the bag," with a costly surplus of cars. "Keep us in entirety or give us up in entirety" was thus the essence of the company's contractual policy for its per diem fleet, as put into effect by Felton. The argument was recognized as valid by almost all oil men. The

---

[3] UTC NOTE: In dealing with oil companies which owned some tank cars of their own, UTL had a gentleman's agreement that, as such shipper-owned cars wore out, they would not be replaced.

company made it clear that it would not stand in the way of any refiner who wished to give up its service; that, on the contrary, it would cooperate in making the period of transition as painless as possible; but the offer was never taken up by any customer.

The essential fact in the eyes of the great refiners was that UTL's charges were reasonable, its cars good, and its service competent. There was little cause for any customer to wish to cancel; and if sometimes they felt themselves to be captive customers, the captivity at least was not rigid. On more than one occasion ambitious new executives in the oil companies, eager to make reputations as shrewd traders, criticized UTL's service and threatened to give it up unless more cars were put at their disposal at lowered rates. But since the inconveniences of a changeover to another lessor were formidable and since Felton's desire to serve them well could not be mistaken, the critics invariably ended by accepting his assurances and easing their pressure.

The New Look

It was imperative, in Felton's opinion, to dissociate the new UTL as much as possible from the old in the eyes of the world. No informed person could see the company's familiar red tank cars without recalling the Standard Trust—a memory that neither UTL nor its customers cared to perpetuate. In the autumn of 1912 an order went out: every UTL tank car, as it came into a shop for repair or cleaning, was to be repainted, this time in black. An official explanation was given for this decision: the cars needed to be repainted in any event, and black graphite was a low-cost, long-wearing paint; but there can be little doubt that the change was mainly motivated by a desire to shed a symbol of the past. The repainting, carried out over a period of years, caused a wit within the company to remark that it had "lost on the red, so it shifted its bet to black."

The change was not entirely on the surface. Felton realized that UTL's relations with all the Standard companies would need to be scrupulously correct. It had always been a part of company policy in the old days to pass along to interested Standard executives any information that UTL gained about the activities of competitors. Now, however, some of the Standard companies themselves were coming into competition, which was bound to increase as time went on. It would be only natural for the executive of one customer-company to play on the old family feeling and try to extract from UTL news of activities of other customers. Once begun such a practice could lead only to confusion and distrust. Felton accordingly established a firm rule: all customer relationships were confidential; no customer—no matter who—would be given information about UTL's dealings with another. Few grumbled. The men who ran the Standard companies were quick to recognize that their own future security was enhanced by Felton's position. Rates, charges, conditions of service, and confidentiality were identical for all. No one could accuse any Standard company of obtaining secret benefits from UTL.

The point was especially important because the nature of the business made it desirable, essential, in fact, for UTL's customers to confide to Felton their plans for expansion or for changes in their marketing patterns, so that additional tank cars would be ready for them as needed. Given Felton's recognized integrity, no executive of a refining company had to worry about premature disclosure of his intentions. Felton took the position with each customer that UTL was in effect his tank car department, with loyalty as a primary ingredient of its service. Every one of the company's employees—numbering, in 1912, nearly 100—was trained in this tradition.

The Government Strikes Again

The need to demonstrate the company's legal purity was acute in the years immediately following 1912, for the country's economic situation was then giving great encouragement to advocates of government regulation of the private car lines. Railroads in particular, suffering from watered stocks and inefficient management, were in distress. In 1913 and 1914 more than 15 per cent of the entire railroad trackage in the United States, measured in miles, went into the hands of receivers. As bankruptcy followed bankruptcy among the roads, public attention focused once more on the mileage payments which they were making to the private car lines. The reformist administration of President Woodrow Wilson was then generating great zeal and expectation among government regulatory agencies. It was confidently expected by those close to the President that the anti-trust activities of the Theodore Roosevelt era would be extended.

Closer public regulation and even government ownership of railroads and utilities was freely discussed, and the tank car lines were an attractive target. The undercover stratagems by which they had kept clear of the Hepburn Act and ICC regulation in the preceding decade had not been forgotten. And the public was interested in anything connected with oil. "Black gold" was again the topic of the day, as in the 1870s. The great Texas and Oklahoma fields had begun to produce at the very time when the mass-produced automobile was coming into its own. Oil stocks, like automobile stocks, were the pets of Wall Street.

To make sure that transportation of oil products in all its aspects were regulated in the public interest seemed a manifest duty of the government. There was evidence that small shippers of oil products were still unable, as in the past, to obtain cars for bulk transportation, and in the spring of 1914 the ICC opened an investigation into the practices of the private car lines. Simultaneously court actions were begun by independent shippers of oil products against certain railroads, to require them to provide tank cars as needed. Their attempts to obtain such cars from the private lines, the plaintiffs alleged, had been rebuffed. If the courts should decide against the railroads, it seemed likely that either the tank and refrigerator fleets would be legislated out of private hands and turned over to the roads, or the private car lines would be made subject to close ICC regulation.

The burden of testimony for UTL fell on Felton. Appearing in Washington in May, 1914, he came supported by a brief which Douglas Campbell had written for use in the pending court cases involving UTL. It was in its way a masterpiece of concise logic. Would the public be better served if the requirement to provide tank cars was placed on the railroad, instead of on the shipper? Not at all, said Campbell, speaking to the ICC through Felton. Tank cars, to be of value, needed to be available at the exact places and at the times and in the quantities required by the shipper. They were used for many different commodities and had to be designed specifically to carry those commodities safely, efficiently, and without contamination. Hence there was "a value to the shipper in owning or otherwise controlling by rental his supply of cars over and above what he would receive if the carrier supplied the cars. This value consists in an assured and regulated supply of cars and freedom from the danger of contamination to his commodity, both of which . . . are essential to his business."

The railroads had never wished to assume the heavy burden of running their own tank car fleets. The private lines as they stood had a deserved reputation for efficiency. Would the fleets be as efficient, would they serve the shippers as well, under the reluctant management of the roads? This was the question implied in Campbell's brief—a question calculated to make any judge think twice.

As to the mileage allowance, Campbell was equally cogent. Far from costing the railroads money, he conveyed, it represented an actual saving to them. If they were compelled to own and maintain their own tank cars their costs would be higher than their mileage payments to the car companies. In view of the advantage to the carriers of having tank cars provided without capital outlay by themselves, "something less than the total saving to the carrier . . . should be the measure of the compensation to be paid by the carrier for the use of the car."

Said Campbell, "It is conceded by car owners that they are not properly entitled to make a profit on their cars used by carriers." Profits, if any, would come from rentals paid by shippers. All that the car lines wanted in the way of payment by the railroads was "a return sufficient to pay all costs of the cars including interest on the investment." The mileage allowance at that time, he made clear, was not large enough to meet this reasonable demand.

A Time of Harvest

After an initial hearing, the ICC investigation was deferred to await the outcome of the pending shippers' suits against the railroads. But long before the court's decisions could be handed down the attention of the country and the administration was diverted to larger and graver issues than the legality of the private car lines. World War I began in Europe, and the newspapers were filled with sensational accounts of invasions, great battles, U-boat raids, the sinking of the *Lusitania,* and high diplomacy. The excited climate of opinion was not favorable to radical social and economic legislation. After August, 1914, it became plain that the private car lines were unlikely to be tampered with while the war lasted. Oil was urgently needed in Western Europe, and the American oil companies put every available tank car into service to carry their products to the Eastern port cities. There they filled the holds of waiting tankers which, U-boats or no U-boats, carried their high-priced loads to the desperate Allied nations.

Every tank car builder in the country was working overtime to fill the insatiable demands of the car lines, which, in turn were harassed by their eager customers. From the standpoint of profits it was a time of harvest. Car rental rates rose by 75 per cent, and the number of tank cars on the tracks increased at the average rate of nearly 20 per cent a year. Although UTL's costs also rose, with the total employee force expanding to 500, they were far outstripped by revenue, and between 1914 and 1916, a time of low taxes, the company's annual net profit increased from $1,000,000 to nearly $4,000,000.

UTL was cheerful but the railroads were not. Unprepared for the sudden onrush of freight and poorly coordinated, they soon found themselves facing chaotic conditions in the marshaling yards and terminals. Traffic tangles on the Eastern seaboard delayed so-called fast freights for days at a time. Entire freight trains were "lost" as the recording systems of the roads broke down. Complaints poured in to the government from all sides, until in August, 1916, when America's entry into the war was becoming increasingly probable, Congress authorized the President to take over the railway system of the nation and use it, if necessary, exclusively for war needs. This development Felton and Campbell regarded with foreboding. It seemed only too probable that if the government assumed control of the railroads the private car lines would quickly be brought under ICC's power.

"You Cannot Compete with Standard"

Their fears were deepened by a new attack specifically against UTL from its ancient enemies, the small refiners of petroleum.

No sooner had Congress made the railroads liable to governmental seizure than the independents raised loud voices demanding that the President's power be extended to include the private tank car lines. The animosity of the independents, it soon became clear, had not been lessened by the dissolution of the Standard Trust. On the contrary, they were enraged by the conviction that the separation of the Standard companies was deceptive and illusory. As proof they cited a single fact: no one except a Standard Oil company could lease a Union Tank Line car.

The issue boiled over into the public press in September, 1916, at a convention of the National Petroleum Association, which had been organized largely in the interests of Standard's rivals. Among the speakers was an independent refiner named John Ames, known for his sensational platform style. Ames had taken to himself the sling formerly swung by the late George Rice, and he sought to play David even after Goliath had been dismembered. Before his talk it was widely rumored that he would "take off on Standard," and a large crowd, including reporters, filled the auditorium. He did not disappoint them. His speech was a long, withering blast against the Union Tank Line. Its essence was that the private car lines would not, and the railroads could not, serve the independents adequately. Out of more than 50,000 tank cars in the country, he said, the railroads owned only about 9,400—"only one tank car to every 29½ miles of road," or "one for every 320 square miles." The rest of the cars were in the service of the big refiners, the Standard companies mainly. "No wonder," Ames roared, "you cannot compete with the Standard Oil group. You are unable to deliver your goods, even if you have them to sell." He pointed out that the motor manufacturers did not provide their own automobile freight cars. These were supplied by the railroads. Why should the principle be different when it came to tank cars? "We are forced to the conclusion," he said, "that the neglect of our industry is due to the existence of some subtle influence which prevents any expenditure by the railroad managements ... for equipment that would enable competitors of the Standard Oil group to enter their vested territories."

One might think, said Ames, that since the railroads would not build tank cars themselves they would provide every inducement for the small private owner to obtain his own cars, "but such is not the case." The railroads, he implied, were in conspiracy with the big private tank car lines to push the cost of tank cars to prohibitive levels. "The Master Car Builders' Association, composed of the mechanical representatives of the railroads, is now voting . . . on specifications . . . which will increase the present cost from $150 to $200 per car. . . . On the Tank Car Committee of the MCBA you will find no independent marketer or refiner represented, but the Union Tank Line is there." And it was not only that the small refiners could not afford to build expensive cars in the quantities required. New tank car specifications were being imposed which would condemn the few old but perfectly usable tank cars which they already had. "Sitting in the committee and directing the trend of affairs, they [UTL] have undoubtedly already so constructed their cars that these tests can be met without additional expense to them."

The remedy? Simple, said Ames. Bring private tank car lines, like pipe lines, under governmental control, if not actually under government ownership. Let the government provide or compel the private car lines to provide enough cars to meet the requirements of the entire petroleum industry.

Although the press picked up Ames' diatribe, Felton made no public reply. Privately, however, in the inner circles of the oil industry, he and others spoke up in UTL's behalf. The Standard Trust had been dissolved. UTL was now a separate, privately-owned corporation. As such, so long as it complied with the law it was entitled to lease its cars in the way which would best protect its long-range interests. In a period of national emergency, especially, the assignment of UTL's cars to the largest refiners was necessary to assure the movement by rail of the greatest possible amount of oil. Even under government ownership, even under socialism, the tank car could not do more to serve the petroleum industry and the public than it was doing under the existing scheme. As for Ames' charges about the rising cost of tank cars, was it not obvious that such costs were bound to go up with all other costs in basic industry? It was entirely in the interest of safety, efficiency, and the public interest that the new specifications had been adopted by the railroads on the recommendation of the MCBA. If unsafe and inefficient cars had to be condemned, could the owners of efficient and safe cars be blamed? Surely Ames' motive in his attack was obvious. As the owner of a few old and condemned tank cars he was in a vulnerable position. He was venting a private grudge, not defending a public cause.

Opinion in the petroleum industry and railroading strongly supported UTL, and little more was heard from Ames. Nevertheless, it was clear that a strong undercurrent of feeling against the private car lines was again running in the country and would almost certainly reappear at the surface of politics before long.

The Daring Young Man

The prevailing spirit in UTL's small executive group was optimistic; problems there were, but business had never been better, nor profits higher. Misgivings about the future were seldom expressed, for Felton shared his own intimate thinking on the problem of the company's status in the courts only with Campbell. He was accordingly the more surprised when, early in 1917, one of the junior members of his staff asked to see him privately and disclosed his concern over UTL's legal purity.

The young man's name was B. C. Graves. Felton paternally called him "Clifford." Since he was not yet thirty years old, in a company where a well-established rule of seniority gave every advantage to age, he was considered something of a phenomenon. In only fourteen years he had climbed from office boy at three dollars a week to assistant to the vice-president at fifty dollars. Felton regarded him with approval, for there was unmistakable vitality and intelligence in Graves. But Felton recognized, too, the marks of driving ambition and an urge to power, which he thought it best to restrain.

Already there had been signs that Graves did not trot easily under the weight of his immediate superior. This was E. C. Sicardi, who had come to UTL in the early 1890s as a stenographer, and who was one of the few employees of the company who did not have an English, Scotch, or Irish name. Shrewd, hard working, and with a good eye for detail, Sicardi had made himself acquainted with every aspect of UTL's all-important

car-record system, and in 1913 had been put in charge of this
function. He went on from there. A barrel-shaped man who loved
good food, good wine, and good cigars, he had proved especially
effective in dealing with railroad officials, known for their hearty,
robust style at table and bar. Soon he became a specialist in relations with railroads, an authority on such matters as switching,
demurrage, and mileage payments. Executives of the oil companies served by UTL increasingly deferred to his knowledge.
Seeking to relieve himself of some of his responsibilities, Felton
had decided at the beginning of 1917 to make Sicardi vice-
president in charge of Car Service, with Car Records also under
his command. As reinforcement, he had given him Graves.

The ambitious young Graves respected Sicardi for his knowledge of the business, but their relationship had never been easy.
Felton, therefore, was not entirely surprised at finding the
young man in a state of rebellion. It was no light matter that
Graves presented to him. Sicardi, it appeared, had found an
ambiguous phrase in a railroad tariff under which UTL shipped
considerable quantities of steel car parts for its own use; and he
had interpreted this phrase to the company's advantage. It was
Graves' view that Sicardi's interpretation was "too clever," and
if it became known could result in serious criticism. When he had
tried to remonstrate with Sicardi, he was waved aside. From
Sicardi's standpoint the company was technically within the
law. In any event, only a few thousand dollars were involved.
But Graves demurred. It was the principle that was important,
not the money, he said. So far as the letter of the law went perhaps Sicardi would be supported in the courts, but the company
was nonetheless in jeopardy if the suspicion grew that it was the
beneficiary of rates not available to others. This argument appeared to have no effect on Sicardi.

Graves was not a man to drop under duress an issue on which
he felt strongly, especially when the duress was applied by a
man whom he did not much like. At the time there was no legal
officer whom he might have consulted with UTL's own organization. He had therefore gone straight to Felton for a review of
the problem.

The Flying Trapeze

When Felton heard the facts, he showed irritation, but less against Sicardi than against Graves, for putting him in a delicate position. "You may have a point," he said. "I'll take it under advisement. But that doesn't excuse your insubordination." In breaking the company's line of authority, he said, Graves had violated a fundamental principle of business. There were, he hinted, other ways by which the matter could have been brought to his attention without forcing him to choose between a vice-president and an underling.

On this note, Felton sent Graves away and conferred with Sicardi. A little later Graves was called back into the president's office. Felton's manner now was friendly but his decision was stern. "I think," he said, "you had better find other employment. I want you to understand that this is no criticism of your work. It's entirely a disciplinary action." Graves was taken aback; the last thing he wanted or had expected was to leave UTL; but he saw no point in protesting. He thought he detected Sicardi's pressure behind Felton's decision.

But Felton, it appeared, was not inclined to throw the young man into the economic jungle without guidance. He turned to the telephone, asked to be connected with one of the officers of the Standard Oil Company of New York, and explained the situation. If any executive opportunities suitable for Graves should come to light, Felton said, he would be glad to hear of them. He had not long to wait for a reply. Some years before the United States Industrial Alcohol Company had been formed, largely with capital provided by sources friendly to Standard Oil, and it was expanding rapidly. The president of USIA, F. M. Harrison, had asked acquaintances in Standard to recommend a bright young man for his staff; and with Felton's recommendation there was every reason to think that Graves could qualify.

It was perfectly clear to all concerned except Graves that Felton would retain an interest to his future. A talented short-stop sent to the minors for additional training could not have felt worse than the young exile. He was especially incensed when he heard that Sicardi had rescinded, as if on his own initiative, the dubious agreement that had caused the trouble.

There was no way for him to foresee the future linking of his life story to that of UTL.

From Felton's standpoint the loss of Graves came at a bad time. The country's shortage of trained manpower was being especially felt in the executive areas of business. Here and there an able young man could be found, largely by accident, but it took years to train new executive personnel in a business so complicated and so full of pitfalls as UTL. Beset on all sides by clamor from customers for more tank cars and faster service, every man in the company had to work at a feverish pace. And this in the face of a railroad crisis of frightening proportions.

TWO

THE GREAT DECISION

In April, 1917, when America entered the war, the railroads made an effort to clear up the worsening traffic jam on their tracks. Under government auspices the presidents of leading roads came together to form the Railroads' War Board, which sought to coordinate freight movements on all the tracks of the country. For a brief time it appeared as if the Board was making headway, but this was an illusion. Its initial gains were swamped in another immense surge of wartime traffic, as troops and munitions trains joined the flow of commodities to the ports. To make matters worse, underpaid railroad workers were leaving their jobs by the thousands for the glittering pay of war plants. Confronted by demands for higher wages, the railroads contended that they could not meet them without raising freight rates in a similar ratio—and this the ICC would not permit.

By autumn the roads were in despair. Their financial plight made it impossible for them to provide the enormous amounts of new equipment and to offer the higher wages required to improve their situation. In the East, 158,000 freight and tank cars were standing loaded on the tracks for want of locomotives to move them. On the Pennsylvania and the Baltimore and Ohio, freight traffic was almost completely at a standstill. The marshaling yards were in a state of chaos. Frenzied employees volunteered for the Army, saying that they preferred to dodge bullets at the front rather than maverick freight cars in the yards. New England was on the brink of a coal famine. British and French diplomats wrung their hands over the very real possibility that

178

the American railroad crisis, by depriving the countries of essential supplies, would force their surrender.

December, 1917, saw the crisis at its peak. The railroads no longer wanted to delay government operation; on the contrary, they were eager to be rescued. The more farsighted executives recognized that, if the government would provide the necessary funds to restore the roads to efficiency and if they were able to recapture ownership after the war, they stood to gain much and lose little. Felton and his associates in UTL were of similar mind. Whatever future dangers they faced from the ICC, their first need was to satisfy the aggravated Standard refining companies. Oil shipments were being especially hard hit by railroad congestion. Exports of fuel oil in 1917 were up 20 per cent over 1916, of motor gasoline up 80 per cent; and domestic consumption was increasing at comparable rates. The country's supply of cracked gasoline rose from 2 million barrels in 1914 to nearly 12 million in 1918. A large part of this immense output came from the refineries of a single UTL customer, Standard of Indiana, which held the patent on the only commercial cracking process then known.

It was clear to Felton that UTL could no longer afford, any more than the railroads, to tolerate existing conditions on the tracks. The problem was not so much a shortage of tank cars as it was the slowness of the hauls. Government intervention in the railroad crisis had become a necessity so obvious that even so stanch a protagonist of free enterprise as Felton could no longer oppose it.

The Biggest Job

The man appointed by President Wilson as director-general of the American railroad network, William McAdoo, Secretary of the Treasury, was confronted by what has been described as "the most prodigious job in industrial management ever undertaken, before or since, by an American citizen." Under the Congressional act of authorization the railroads retained their corporate structure, but had nothing to say in the management of their properties. Temporarily the ICC also yielded up its power to McAdoo. He acted with extraordinary speed and on every sector of his problem.

Congressional sanction for a loan of $500,000,000 from the Treasury to his office, to be used in rehabilitating and adding to needed equipment and facilities, solved the basic financial problem. Seven transportation areas were established in the nation, with a regional director for each and with all services consolidated. Wages were raised sharply and a promotional campaign was launched to recruit railroad workers, with gratifying success. McAdoo pacified business opinion by making it clear that he regarded the "leasing" of the railroads to the government as an emergency measure, not as an experiment in socialism.

A freight-rate increase of 25 per cent was accepted by industry without a murmur. With everyone cooperating he was able to show phenomenal results within a few months. Immobile loaded cars disappeared from the tracks. Freight and passenger trains resumed scheduled operation. The locomotive and freight-car shortage was met by more efficient distribution of cars and huge production of new equipment.

Within a year McAdoo's methods of consolidation had saved the railroads about $110,000,000 in operating costs. Freight revenues were large enough not only to meet the interest on the carriers' funded debt, but to pay 8½ per cent on their capital stock. Hosannas were heard on all sides. The only question remaining in the minds of the railroad men was: how soon would their convalescent properties be restored to them?

The Attack Renewed

As the war entered its last year proponents of government regulation recognized that there would never be a more favorable time to extend the powers of the ICC to include the private car lines. To be sure, the courts had shown themselves inclined to agree with the railroads that as the law stood it was the shipper's responsibility, and not theirs, to furnish tank cars. But under sufficient pressure the law might well be modified by Congress through a simple amendment to the Hepburn Act. And to make Congress move there could be no better prod than a recommendation from the ICC.

Some officials of the Wilson administration let it be known that they favored an early resumption of the 1914 ICC investigation into the tank car business. It was their hope that the probe would result in a scorching indictment of the private lines and pave the way for governmental action against them. The question was raised: why should there not be a single company, owned by the railroads, and which would acquire all privately-owned tank cars and provide them for the use of shippers? This was a revival of the Midgley plan of 1902. Theoretically, at least, it seemed feasible and in keeping with the spirit of the times. It was linked in the minds of many to the expectation that the railroads, instead of being returned to their former owners, would remain permanently in possession of the government.

Early in 1918, the ICC announced that it would again look into "the rules, regulations, and practices governing the operations of private cars on the railroads of the country." Articles in the press suggested that new interpretations of the existing law would enable the ICC, even without further legislation by Congress, to extend its authority over the private car lines.

Felton immediately turned to Campbell, who took on the task of restating UTL's legal position to meet the new threat. The result was another brief of extraordinary vigor and penetration. It pointed out that the legally-established authority of the ICC to regulate the mileage allowances for shipper-owned or leased cars was a limited power. "The commission has jurisdiction over the relation between the carrier and the shipper in regard to the private car, but that jurisdiction does not extend to the relation between shipper and car company. All of the dealings of the carrier . . . the shipper or car owner in respect to the car are a matter of public interest, but how or where the shipper acquires the car . . . is of interest to no one but himself. . . . No one would contend that the commission has or should have the power to say what the shipper should pay for cars which he buys. It is only as to what he pays for cars acquired by lease that there seems to be any doubt. Yet one is as closely associated with transportation as the other, and affects the cost of transportation in the same way." If the ICC proposed to regulate the charges and practices of the private car lines to oil refiners, they would in logic be obliged to regulate the charges made by railroad-car manufacturers to shippers, and no one would suggest that this was a legitimate function of the government, under the Constitution.

Ordeal of a Young Attorney

Campbell's argument struck Felton as fundamental and unassailable, but sensing the mood of the country and the administration in all matters connected with railroads in that year of war, he was far from optimistic. Adding to his worry was the fact that Campbell, who was supposed to go to Washington with him for the hearing, suddenly fell ill. His place was taken by a young associate of his firm, Edward N. Goodwin. Although Goodwin was regarded as a lawyer of great promise and he was thoroughly familiar with UTL's affairs, his experience in trials and hearings was limited. Felton, always courteous, gave no outward sign of worry, but Goodwin himself was disturbed by the enormous responsibility that he felt to be resting on his untried shoulders. The thought was in his mind that, if he failed, government seizure of the private tank car lines might well follow.

The atmosphere of the committee room in the offices of the ICC on the first day of the hearings was tense. Present also were representatives of UTL's chief competitor, General American Transportation, with its attorney, a middle-aged man named Mayer, from Chicago. Felton and the GAT executives greeted each other formally; there was at that time some strain between them arising out of arguments over technical details of an order which UTL had placed with GAT for the construction of a large number of tank cars.

After the chairman of the ICC had made an opening statement outlining the formal purpose of the investigation, he called on Mayer, as the senior of the attorneys present, to present the views of General American. Mayer made a deliberate, thoughtful, and reasoned statement which, it was evident, profoundly impressed the commissioners. Hearing him, Goodwin more than ever felt his own limitations and was certain that Felton shared his misgivings.

When the chairman addressed him and invited an opening presentation for UTL, Goodwin began with a rush to amplify the thoughts in Campbell's brief, citing precedents, urging analogies. To his alarm he saw nothing but stony faces among the commissioners, while others in the hearing room were openly inat-

tentive. He felt compelled to go on, but long before he concluded
he was in a mood of deep depression, and his statement trailed
off into insignificance. He sat down heavily, stabbed by a sense
of failure; he had, he felt, gravely damaged UTL's case and his
own law firm. At the thought of what lay ahead for the next day,
when the hearing would get down to serious business, he found
himself breathing hard.

Felton, with whom he dined that night, was, as always, courteous and friendly, but Goodwin was not deceived; he knew what
the UTL president was thinking. Tired and depressed, he went
to his hotel room. It came to him that he needed advice, profes-
sional advice, such as Felton could not give him. To whom could
he turn? Pacing the floor, he had an idea—Mayer, the experienced GAT attorney, had a wise and amiable face—they were
on the same side—perhaps he would listen and respond if properly approached.

A few minutes later Goodwin knocked at the door of Mayer's
hotel room, was told to enter, and found the older man preparing
for bed. He swallowed his embarrassment and blurted out his
anxiety. "Sit down," said Mayer; "sit down, Mr. Goodwin," and
he offered a cigar. "You want to know what is wrong? I can
speak only for myself, but I'll be glad to tell you what I think."

Gently but frankly Mayer went on to say that Goodwin had
prepared a good statement from a legal standpoint, but that
he had not sufficiently considered the viewpoint of the commissioners. The subject was complicated. It was important to realize
that they were not familiar with all the intricacies and fine legal
issues of the case. Goodwin had spoken rapidly and he had tried
to cram a great deal of information into two hours. His auditors
were not antagonistic—merely uncomprehending and thus bored.
What he had said was perfectly sensible but he had left them
confused as he raced from point to point.

Advice? Mayer's was very simple—to slow down. Emphasize
the important points, he recommended, by deliberate statement,
and if need be by restatement. Make sure that every commissioner knew what he meant. Then go on to the next point.

It seemed to Goodwin that he had never heard any counsel
that made more sense. With a feeling of permanent gratitude
he went back to his bed and a good night's rest. The next day,

when he rose to speak, it was with a new confidence. After his first few measured, simple, slow-spoken remarks he could see that the commissioners were responding, and that Felton was pleased. When he finished his statement it was obvious from the appreciative acknowledgment of the chairman that he had won the respect and approval of everyone present. UTL's case was, as Mayer subsequently put it, "back on the track."

At the end of the session, the impressed Felton whispered, "What happened to you overnight?" Goodwin told him. Felton, recalling recent sharp correspondence with GAT on production of tank cars ordered by UTC, smiled grimly. "That's the only good thing they ever did for us," he said.

Reward of Virtue

The commissioners then turned to Felton. In a long, searching interrogation he gave testimony so clear, concise, and candid on every aspect of UTL's business that no one could any longer accuse the company of concealing facts. Thanks in part to Graves' insubordination the year before, Felton was able to tell the ICC, without fear of dispute, that since the dissolution UTL had not been the recipient of any rebates or other favors from the railroads. Its profits came entirely from shippers. As for the rest, it was an essential business. It was efficiently run. It served the interests of its clients and of the nation without excessive payment. It performed functions which no one could realistically expect the railroads to perform for themselves.

The hearings concluded, Felton waited anxiously for the ICC's report. When it came, at the end of July, 1918, he felt that virtue, even if recent, was not without reward. The ICC findings incorporated every major point that Goodwin and Felton had made. "No class of cars in railroad service," the report averred, "is used more effectively than the cars owned by large railroad shippers. They have organizations of men to see to it that their cars move as promptly as possible, both loaded and empty. The carriers of the country could not as effectively handle the entire . . . tank car equipment as is now done by the intervention of private owners. . . . The oil refiner produces certain kinds of oil and desires to reach certain customers. No carrier could inform himself as to his needs and insure that he would have the kind and number of cars to enable him to conduct his business economically and efficiently. If private ownership or control of cars of particular types results in greater economy and more efficient use, the whole public is to that extent benefited....

"Some years ago carriers paid excessive allowances for use of cars to certain shippers.... There does not [now] appear to be any unlawful practice, so far as payments by carriers to shippers are concerned."

The ICC then went on to reduce to ashes the hopes of independent refiners of the Ames persuasion. "There is a demand upon the part of certain shippers of petroleum oil that the commission require carriers to furnish tank cars on request.... The contention is that if the commission has not the power, it should be given it by the proper legislation.

"The system of the use and supply of private cars that now exists cannot be at once and radically changed, without serious consequences to shippers, carriers, and the public...."

The private car lines, the report implied, were essential to the national economy. "In practice, the shipper either buys the cars used by him, or rents them.... If a request were referred to a carrier for a kind of car it did not own, considerable delay might occur...." It was incumbent on shippers "to expedite the movements [of the cars] to enable them to meet their contract obligations out of the total number of cars they own.... Shippers realize that through the efforts [of private car lines] ... they secure a larger use of the cars they lease, and for that reason find it more satisfactory to lease than to own them....

"There seems to be no sound reason why shippers should not continue to secure cars through independent car companies ...

"Under the law as construed by the courts, car lines and others engaged in leasing cars to shippers are not common carriers and thus do not come under direct control by the commission."

Emphatic and Complete

The ICC did, indeed, leave itself a loophole for a possible future change of mind. "As a means of removing ... unjust discrimination we have the right to require the carrier to provide specifically in its tariffs the terms under which all ... shippers may demand ... even terms for the use of cars employed upon the carrier's line. We do not feel that...under present conditions the requirement should be ordered." The charges made for leased cars were not considered unreasonable. "To change the basis of compensation for use of private cars would create great uncertainty...whereas, with the experience of years under the present system, the result from operation may be measured with substantial accuracy...."

There was more. In the course of the hearings, questions had been raised about theory and practice in the payment of mileage allowances by railroads. The relevant section of the ICC Act permitted railroads to pay a reasonable allowance to a shipper for a facility which he provided for the transportation of his freight. This principle had never been questioned, since the railroad's revenue from the freight could not be earned without the use of the shipper's facility. But the ICC commissioners pondered the propriety of the custom under which the mileage allowance might be paid not to the shipper but to a private car line which leased the facility.

The position taken by Felton and Goodwin was that UTL acted merely as a collection agency for the shippers, who benefited from the mileage allowances paid by the railroads through lowered net charges for tank cars. If the mileage allowance were paid directly to the shipper, UTL would of course cease to credit its customers for mileage run by cars in their service. Customers would then have to remit the full rental charge to UTL. Neither shippers nor carriers would save money, while both would have to assume the burden of elaborate accounting which only the tank car companies then bore in connection with the mileage allowance. A change in the existing system would therefore require costly clerical duplications which all of the parties concerned wished to avoid.

The ICC saw no reason to overthrow this theory of the mileage allowance. The only question that remained was the rate on which the allowance was based. Felton had supplied figures demonstrating that, in view of the increased cost of tank cars, the long-existing rate of three-fourths of a cent per mile on loaded and empty mileage was no longer adequate to defray amortization and interest charges for the cars. The commissioners agreed and forthwith increased the allowance to one cent per mile, loaded or empty.

The victory was emphatic and complete. With publication of the ICC report, a move then afoot in Congress to amend the Hepburn Act at the expense of the private car lines came to an abrupt halt. Some members of the House had been urging that the railroads be compelled to provide tank cars for shippers within a period of five years. Under such a law the private car lines would be forced to sell their cars to the roads on whatever terms they could make. The ICC report knocked the wind out of this plan.

The Ground Stops Shaking

There remained some doubt as to the position of the railroads themselves. If they remained much longer under government control, further attacks on the private car lines were to be expected. Felton followed developments in this area with close attention. The crisis came during 1918, when William McAdoo proposed that a peacetime test of government operation be made and that to this end Congress extend federal control for five years. In this way he hoped that the government might be reimbursed for its financial outlay for the railroads, wartime operation of which had cost the Treasury nearly a billion dollars.

Opinion in the country was sharply divided. Liberals and radicals hailed McAdoo's plan on theoretical grounds. Some railroad executives and shareholders were quoted as favoring it because they believed that dividends paid by the roads under the government's policy would be greater in the long run than if the roads were privately managed. In the opposite camp were defenders of the free-enterprise principle together with strong financial interests, which wanted a prompt end of wartime controls —especially since the railroads had been substantially reequipped at a low net cost to the owners.

Political commentators in Washington asserted that Congress in the end would follow the wishes of President Wilson, then at the zenith of his popularity. Many of his supporters waited for him to speak out for McAdoo's proposal. They were soon disillusioned. The President's economic convictions were at root conservative. Governmental operation of the roads in his mind had never been more than an unfortunate necessity. It has been suggested, too, that he felt some personal irritation with his son-in-law McAdoo, whose growing popularity in many quarters was encouraging him to reach out for power without waiting for the Presidential blessing. In the upshot he firmly declined to back McAdoo in the matter, and congressional advocates of government ownership were compelled to yield.

There remained some congressmen, however, who thought that before 1920, when the wartime Transportation Act would expire, another and more successful attempt might be made to extend it. This hope too was dashed. The congressional elections in November, 1918, showed a strong conservative wave rising in the country. Even more decisive was the deflation which immediately followed the end of the war and which caused railroad traffic and revenues to melt like last winter's snow. McAdoo, recognizing that a drastic rise in freight rates was required—he thought by 76 per cent—feared a dislocation of industry if he took such a step and compromised at 28 per cent. As a result, the government's operating losses soon ran into hundreds of millions. His opponents were full of glee: it was obvious, they contended, that Uncle Sam "had neither the experience nor the ability to bring order out of chaos."

With the ICC report published and the defeat of the McAdoo plan assured, Felton could breathe easy. For the first time UTL and the other private car lines felt that the legal ground on which they stood had stopped shaking. And the economic ground as well. All the auguries were now favorable. The company while no longer monopolistic was the largest owner of tank cars in the country, with more than 18,000. Its rental rates and loading charges, which had put the company on a profitable basis in 1912, were increased again, and substantially, in 1917. Typical charges for an 8,000-gallon tank car in 1918 were $4.20 for each time the car was loaded and $1.40 per day of use. Rates for special types of pressure cars carrying volatile substances such as casinghead gas and naphtha were double those for ordinary cars.

A Change of Name

The ICC decision was all that was needed to transform UTL's financial situation. As long as the company's life was endangered by mooted legislation, even its excellent wartime earnings could not offset doubt in the minds of investors. But after the ICC decision those familiar with UTL's position recognized that the speculative element in the company's securities had been almost eliminated, and the full importance of UTL's wartime earnings could be recognized. Those earnings exceeded every prewar expectation. In 1914, the company had a net income of $687,000. Two years later its net had tripled. Its 1917 profit was $3,700,000, representing more than 30 per cent on its common stock. In 1918, profits would have been still higher but for payment to the Federal government of an income and excess profits tax of approximately $1,000,000, and a drastic change in methods of calculating depreciation, which permitted the company to write off more than $3,000,000 in 1918 as against $700,000 in 1917. Through the war years the company had paid a steady $5 per share on its common stock, but when 1919 showed a net profit of $3,600,000, it increased the common dividend to $7.

Felton sensed that the time was ripe for a series of moves that had long been in his mind. One was the listing of the company's shares on the New York Stock Exchange. With earnings high and tending higher, and with the public in a speculative mood, an active market for the stock was very much in the interest of the owners. The comparatively small amount of stock outstanding was a disadvantage, but one which could be corrected by splitting the stock as soon as its price was stablized at a sufficiently high level.

Shortly before the stock was listed, Felton ordered a change in the name of the corporation. The word "line," he felt, was unfortunate, connoting as it did a railroad or transportation company. It was natural for the the public to assume that any "line" was a common carrier and ought accordingly to be under ICC regulation. To continue with the old name would be to invite future misunderstanding. In June, 1919, the corporate name was officially changed to Union Tank Car Company.

Ready Money

These steps, however, were of secondary importance. The big fact of the time was the rapid postwar growth of the American economy, and especially of the oil business. The resulting demand for tank cars took the company by surprise. No fewer than 11,000 new cars were needed, representing a numerical increase of more than 50 per cent in the size of the company's fleet. Many of these cars were ordered in 1917–1918 for delivery in the years immediately ahead. To pay for them Felton estimated that the company would have to borrow $24,000,000. Fortunately, the company's credit had greatly improved in the years just past. In 1919 Felton raised half the needed amount by a plan reminiscent in some respects of Rockefeller's Tank Car Trust of the 1870s. So-called Equipment Trust Gold Notes were issued to the amount of $12,000,000. Paying 7 per cent and due serially over the succeeding ten years, they were secured by the value of the cars to be built; and they were quickly snapped up by investors close to the company.[1] The rest of the needed money was obtained in 1920 by issuing 120,000 shares of preferred stock at $100 per share—an amount and par value identical with those of the outstanding common stock. The preferred shares were offered only to holders of the common, on a share-for-share basis. Yielding 7 per cent cumulative, with preference over the common in important respects and with a call value of $115 per share, the new offering was attractive, and almost all of it was sold within a few weeks.

Every cent of the money thus raised was needed, for rising costs in industry and advances in tank design to meet the changing needs of shippers had rapidly increased the price paid by UTC for new tank cars. In 1912, the average new car cost less than $800. By 1920 the price was almost $3,000. Most of the increase reflected rising labor and material costs, but in addition the cars themselves had been upgraded. New and improved safety valves; forge-welded tanks to carry gases under pressure; insulation to minimize temperature changes in the contents of the tanks; improved coil piping for rapid heating of tanks; safer construction of the camel-hump domes of the cars; double riveting—improvement followed improvement in swift succession. Among other qualities which the new UTC was discovering within itself was that of pride in its technical performance. UTC engineers, spurred by aggressive competition in improved car design from other tank car companies, strove to match or outstrip them at every point.

However, except in the case of a few patented items such as

---

[1] Five years later these notes had been completely retired ahead of schedule.

the Van Dyke anchor, the advances made by any one company soon became standard among all, for in the final test the detailed specifications of cars were laid down by the Association of American Railroads under the authority of the ICC. It was especially difficult for UTC to produce an improvement much ahead of other companies since, lacking its own construction facilities, it was compelled to rely largely on its competitors for production of new cars. The notable technological progress in tank cars during the years just before and just after World War I represented a more or less involuntary pooling of engineering talents in the industry. But no one at UTC was greatly concerned over the situation. With business good, profits high, and the price of the stock rising, what was there to worry about?

THREE

EXECUTIVE SUITE

One of Felton's chief problems at the end of the war was the finding of qualified executives. Especially he needed someone who could relieve him of some of the burden of top management and eventually succeed him. None of the men close to him measured up to the job. Sicardi, the senior vice-president and a personality of considerable force, was the ablest. The question remained—what would the powers in the petroleum industry, where prejudice was known to flourish, say to a UTC president of Italian origin? A man of "five-by-five" physique with an abnormal interest (from Felton's point of view) in food, especially Italian food, of which he consumed tremendous quantities? More than once Sicardi had come back from lunch with stains showing on his vest, which no napkin was large enough to protect. It was all too plain that his personal style did not conform to the manners and attitudes of the clubs, city and country, where the personal foundations of UTC's business relationships were generally established.

If Sicardi was a dubious choice, the caliber of other UTC executives was even less presidential. Not that they were incompetent. They ran their departments well enough. Nevertheless, it was far from being a satisfactory roster, in Felton's view. One man was narrow-minded and could not see beyond his own job. Another was creating an office problem because of his practicing opposition to the Volstead Act, which had just been passed by Congress. Hypocrisy was the fault of a third; knowing Felton to be strongly religious, the man sought to ingratiate him-

192

self by pretending to a piety which, it was easy to perceive, he did not feel. And so down the list. Sicardi perhaps excepted, there was not one among the company's ranking executives whom Felton was ready to trust with presidential responsibilities.

A Touch of Nepotism

Serious as was the need for new blood, Felton was not altogether pleased when a solution of the problem was imposed on him. That it was imposed there can be little doubt. Late in 1918 he brought into the company with the rank of vice-president a comparatively young man named William A. Barstow, who had no experience of tank car operation or railroading. He was, however, a son of the F. Q. Barstow who had been a director of UTL from its incorporation in 1891 to 1908. By inheritance young Barstow belonged to the golden circle of the old Standard Oil hierarchy, which had a reputation for looking after its own. Moreover, he had served with distinction in the American Navy overseas; and he was personable and reasonably intelligent. If the appointment smacked of nepotism, who could say that a good bloodline was not a sensible test for executive quality?

Most of Felton's staff accepted Barstow's coming if not with pleasure at least with philosophy. Fifteen months later he was president of the newly-named Union Tank Car Company. Felton took to himself the title of chairman of the board and continued to serve as chief executive officer.

In all of this Felton was free to act without worrying about the views of his board of directors. For practical purposes, in matters of policy he was the board. The dissolution of 1912 had compelled representatives of Standard Oil to resign their directorates in UTL. Soon afterward most of the UTL shares belonging to the Rockefeller family and constituting about 20 per cent of the company's stock had been turned over to the Rockefeller Foundation as a small part of its enormous endowment, which consisted largely of stock in oil companies served by UTL. With Felton in the presidency there was no need for the Foundation to worry about UTL's policies. Conditioned as he was to think in terms of Standard as a combine, it was safe to say that he would do nothing that was not consistent with the long-range interests of the great Standard refiners who were then UTL's only customers. And he could be counted on, if he were ever in doubt, to follow the established practice of corporation presidents and consult informally with his largest stockholder before committing himself. The Foundation consequently adopted a hands-off policy from the first, and UTL's board of directors was shaped to a pattern which guaranteed Felton a virtually free hand. There was no director from outside the company. Proxies provided by the majority stockholders enabled Felton to select the men of his choice for the board, and these were all his subordinates.

Too Many Cars

Barstow's presidency, as it turned out, commenced at a difficult time. No one in the company foresaw that the postwar deflation would come as suddenly and as violently as it did. Not that UTC's earnings were much damaged. On the contrary, net income for 1920 reached $3,400,000, or $28 per share—and this after depreciation of $2,500,000 had been taken and federal taxes paid in the amount of $1,300,000. Even the 1921 drop, while acute, could be shrugged off, for it was followed by rapid recovery. UTC's real problem came from another source.

Felton's great new car-building program had been launched during the hectic war years. Orders for thousands of new cars had been placed with three suppliers—American Car and Foundry, General American, and Standard Steel Car. The largest of these companies, General American, was also building tank cars for its own use; and this fact, combined with wartime steel shortages, slowed delivery.

Late in 1920 the new cars began to appear in quantity. By that time business was slumping badly. The velocity of the drop caught Felton, like many another executive, by surprise. The consequence was that in 1921–1922 UTC had to accept delivery of thousands of cars, while lacking any way of using them. Immediately a pressing problem arose: where could they be stored?

The company quickly filled its own storage yards dotted throughout the country, and then had to look elsewhere. At Felton's instructions Barstow arranged to lease the U.S. government's railroad trackage at Hog Island, site of a wartime merchant shipbuilding program near Philadelphia. More than 1,000 of the new tank cars went there, but immediately thereafter the storage crisis again became acute. Desperately Barstow made deals to rent whatever trackage was to be found. A little railroad in New Jersey took care of 150 cars, a steel company in Buffalo 100 more. A feeling of panic gripped many in UTC's ranks. When would these cars ever be used, even if stored? There they were, beautiful 10,000-gallon cars of the latest design, many of them with heating coils—costing millions to build, and expensively gathering rust on scores of rented tracks scattered all over the country. Was it for this that the $12,000,000 worth of 7 per cent Equipment Trust Notes had been issued?

At this period Barstow took up an idea then held by several of UTC's executives—that for the company's future protection it needed to have its own car-building and storage facilities. Felton agreed, and a move was set afoot to acquire facilities for this purpose. Inquiries revealed that Standard of Ohio still owned a tract of land at Lima, where, in the 1880s, John D. Rockefeller had constructed a shop for building and repairing tank cars. After a short negotiation the property was bought and plans drawn for the construction of the necessary buildings. Barstow was enthusiastic; this was to be his first significant contribution to UTC's progress.

"Mamie? You Are Now Talking to the President"

Here, however, Fate intervened. For a gallant sailor and young corporation executive to succumb to chicken pox was perhaps ironic; at any rate, never having contracted the disease as a child, he was vulnerable; pneumonia set in, and the tale was told. His death came so soon after his appointment as president that hardly a trace of his activities was left in the company's files. The only important forward administrative step made in Barstow's regime was a change in UTC's method of recording the movements of tank cars.[1] As for the Lima project, no one else was

[1] Ten years earlier the old roller-shade tabulations, which dated back to the 1880s, had been replaced by large ledgers. These gave an effect of neatness, but the laborious system of entries still required awkward and time-consuming searches down long lists of figures whenever data were wanted. "Efficiency" in the 1920s was becoming a watchword of office management, and one member of Felton's Car Record Department took it seriously—John Harley, then in a subordinate capacity, later a vice-president and director. Harley devised a card system which proved a notable cost saver, and which remained in use thereafter, with few changes.

sufficiently interested to fight for it, and within a few years the land acquired there was put on the market and sold.

With Barstow's abrupt passing the executive personnel problem loomed up once again as Felton's major concern. This time no pressure was put on him by any of the Standard Oil or Rockefeller interests; he was given a free hand. Temporarily resuming the presidency himself, he considered his problem. He was in his sixties. The time for his retirement was near. The only man in the organization even remotely competent to succeed him was Sicardi. As far as the railroad end of the business was concerned, Sicardi was fully qualified. The need was to offset his lack of social polish in relations with the petroleum company executives. Felton conceived a solution—to recall Clifford Graves from his exile, make peace between him and Sicardi, and let them function together, the older man as president, the younger as the head of Car Service.

He spoke with Sicardi, who said he held no hard feelings toward Graves, and would be glad to have him back. Forthwith a meeting of the board of directors was called and Felton proposed Sicardi as his successor. Assent, of course, was unanimous, and the meeting ended with congratulations for the smiling Sicardi. Then with an air of great purpose he went to the telephone which stood in a corner of the directors' room and with several of his associates within earshot asked the operator to call his home. When his wife answered he said, "Mamie? You are now talking to the president of the company."

Felton then sent for Graves.

Prodigal's Return

To Graves the reason for the summons was plain enough. When he sat down with Felton and Sicardi he sensed his advantage and was prepared to use it. In the five years since his departure he had gained knowledge and experience as well as maturity. Harrison, the president of U.S. Industrial Alcohol, had made him his personal assistant, paying him $5,000 a year. Other men had also sensed his ability. A leading executive of Standard Oil of New York had at one point "borrowed" Graves to carry out certain secret stock-buying operations running into millions. The shrewd broker with whom Graves had dealt on that occasion

offered the young man a partnership with large and immediate
cash rewards, but he had withstood the temptation.

Facing his former bosses at UTC, he knew what he wanted. To
the salary that was offered him, $7,500 a year, he made no demur,
but he stated his other demands boldly: a seat on the board of
directors, a vice-presidency. To the directorship they agreed, but
thereafter he ran into resistance from Sicardi. "Superintendent
of Car Service" was as far as Sicardi would go on official titles
for Graves. When Graves argued the point, Sicardi showed himself adamant. "It doesn't make any difference how much ability
you have," he said, "you've got to have seniority. You'll have to
wait."

Graves hesitated, but Felton's warm paternal attitude strongly
suggested to him that he would be foolish not to accept the
offer. "I have always kept a string on you," said Felton confi-
dentially. "I wanted to give you time to mature. Now you are
ready." After a day for consideration Graves made up his mind.
He would serve as contact man for customer relationships in
Sicardi's administration. Privately, however, he was resolved to
continue striving for an early vice-presidency—and for the presidency, when the time came.

Clouds on the Horizon

As Graves caught up with events since his departure five years
earlier, he began to wonder whether UTC's prosperity was quite
as secure as Sicardi and even Felton portrayed it. The competitive
situation was changing rapidly. In 1911, there had been about
22,000 privately-owned tank cars in the country, of which nearly
half belonged to UTC. By 1923 the UTC fleet was close to 30,000,
but now this figure represented only 35 per cent of the privately-
owned tank cars in use. The rate of growth of General American
Transportation was much higher than that of UTC. GAT, which
had been launched in 1898 with a net capital of $1,000, had built
more than 15,000 new tank cars for its own use since 1910, and
in 1923 was said to own more than 25,000. Another rival, Shippers'
Car Line Company, had come up fast since its formation in
1917. These aggressive competitors and others of lesser size drew
most of their business from oil-refining companies which had
come to prominence since the dissolution of the Standard Trust.

UTC, bound as it was to the Standard companies, had never even seriously considered soliciting business outside of the family.

Business was good, yes, but Graves could see clouds on the far horizon. The fact that UTC did not propose to try to take major customers away from other tank car companies by no means signified that competitors would be similarly restrained. Already there had been reports from Standard companies of tempting offers made to them. While Standard executives were strong in their assurances that they had no intention of breaking the old tie with Union, yet they were not above dropping hints that, all things considered, UTC might be wise to cut its car rental prices.

Even more worrisome to Graves at this juncture than competition within the tank car industry were developments in other modes of petroleum transportation. Crude-oil pipe lines no longer threatened UTC's interests, since tank cars had long since ceased to haul crude oil in any considerable quantity. The breaking up of Standard's oil pipe line network, under ICC control, had not seriously disturbed Felton and his associates. In fact, the rapid expansion of pipe lines then taking place under separate corporate ownership had been regarded as a good omen by the tank car companies. New pipe lines for crude oil meant the construction of new refineries, and more refineries meant, by and large, a greater demand for tank cars to carry their output. But now there were rumors of pipe lines to be built for the transportation of refined oils, gasoline, and the like. The technology for such lines was reported to have been successfully worked out. This, for UTC, was another and depressing story. Products pipe lines, as they were called, would be directly competitive to tank cars.

At bottom the problem was one of cost. As rail tariffs had risen, a gap of more than 25 per cent had opened up between the cost of shipping crude oil by rail and of pumping it through a pipe line over the same distance. If products pipe lines were to have a similar cost advantage, they would drive tank cars off the tracks on any rail route they paralleled.

The danger was compounded by the likelihood that products pipe lines would be linked to waterway transport. By 1924 refined oil could be shipped by water at rates nearly one-third below those charged by railroads. In areas where water carriers could penetrate oil markets, as along the Mississippi, the demand for tank cars was falling sharply. If a product pipe line were to carry the output of a refinery to a waterway, and barges then transported the cargo to the marketing area, what would be left for the tank car? Merely short hauls from the waterway terminal to regional distributing points.

Glimpses of the Future

And even in regional distribution, where there were no pipe lines or waterways to worry about, the tank car was about to be challenged. The adversary in this instance was the specialized motor tank truck. Until then, like the tank wagon of former days, the tank truck had been used only in local distribution, carrying oil from storage terminals to retailers. Now automobile manufacturers in Detroit were manufacturing larger and more powerful trucks than had ever been seen before, and in quantity.

A few venturesome men were experimenting with huge tanks fastened to truck chassis, and were using them to carry waterborne oil products from dockside to regional distributing points in the Midwest for distances up to 30 miles, in direct competition with tank cars. Why should a refiner go to the trouble of loading a tank car with gasoline and then transferring the cargo into small tank trucks at a storage terminal, when large trucks could pick up the cargo at the original handling point and bring the contents directly to the doors of the service station? Especially when by so doing he could save time and part of his loading charges?

Although the obvious hazards of heavy trucking in those days of poor roads and inadequate tires might serve for a while to deter the oil companies, such problems were bound to be overcome. It disturbed Graves to observe that most railroad men, and Sicardi, for that matter, did not take the threat of the truck with sufficient seriousness. Most of them accepted the reassurances of the U.S. Secretary of Agriculture, who administered the Federal Highway Act and was supposed to be an authority on motor traffic. This gentleman, W. M. Jardine, told railroad executives not to worry. He could see no likelihood of serious competition for them from motor carriers, he said, except for distances under

30 miles—and then mainly for comparatively light-weight and fragile items not suited to rail handling—household goods, for example.

It seemed probable to Graves that, as time went on, the tank car would be increasingly confined to hauls of intermediate length, with products pipe lines and waterways taking the long hauls and trucks gaining ascendancy in shorter hauls. Could the company, squeezed by competition on both sides, hope for much growth? Only, Graves believed, if it faced reality. As early as 1924 he began to dream of an expansion of UTC into the water-borne freight business, with barges and terminals on the Mississippi River, and into the trucking business, with a fleet of trucks to supplement tank car service.

Business Was Good

This vision found little encouragement in UTC's offices. Felton was not far from retirement, and Sicardi had no intention of experimenting with new ideas. The old ways were good enough for him. UTC would remain a tank car company pure and simple. It would grow with the growth of the oil business. Why worry about tank car competitors and outside oil companies? The Standard companies were expanding; they were loyal to UTC; let UTC be loyal to them, and confine its service solely to their interests. It would be absurd to rock the boat. Business was good. Annual net income was running nicely around three millions. In December, 1922, shareholders were made happy by a stock dividend of 50 per cent and issuance of an additional 10,000 shares rounded off the total outstanding at 250,000. The new shares, with par value still at $100, paid $5 annually—equivalent to more than a 10 per cent yield on the $12,000,000 capitalization of ten years earlier. Selling on the New York exchange at the beginning of 1923 for $90, the stock slowly but steadily moved upward.

One or two officers of the company, it was later discovered, had in the period 1918 to 1922 enriched themselves via UTC stock without much effort. The stock-purchase plan established by Felton in 1918 allowed executives to apply 20 per cent of their salaries toward the purchase of stock, with the company putting up 50 per cent of the cost of the stock. In this way an official earning $10,000 a year could in a single year accumulate $4,000 worth of stock, toward which he himself paid only $2,000. This was legitimate, if generous; but it shocked Felton to realize that the plan was so loosely administered as to invite abuses. In 1922, word came to him that a bank with which UTC had long done business was making large loans for which employees' stock, not yet fully paid for, and supposed to be held in the company's treasury, served as collateral. Even worse, the proceeds of these loans were used by men who knew the size of the company's earnings to acquire still more shares in the certain knowledge that they would advance in price. While their action was perhaps not illegal, it seemed to Felton highly improper. The stock split of 1922 enriched these ingenious men, but only at the cost of their jobs; their early resignation from the company followed. The stock-purchase plan was thereafter modified and tightened. But by the time the stable was locked the unbroken horses were feeding nicely in other pastures.

Such annoying incidents aside, the company ship was on an even keel and Sicardi's hand on the helm seemed reasonably steady. Improving business was rapidly bringing the company's idle cars back into profitable use. UTC's credit was superbly sound. The times were again full of easy money and easy optimism. Against this background Graves' tendency to anticipate future problems seemed to Sicardi overimaginative.

FOUR

"A HELL OF A LOT OF NERVE"

The years 1924–1925 brought with them the first major crisis that UTC had to face since the ICC hearings of 1918. This time, however, it was not the government that applied the pressure. It came from the most unexpected of sources—the Standard Oil family itself. Colonel Robert Stewart, the forceful and ambitious chairman of Standard Oil of Indiana, let it be known that he was prepared to jettison his contract with UTC.

The shock could hardly have been greater if John D. Rockefeller himself had withdrawn his paternal blessing. Among UTC's siblings Standard of Indiana had always been the stanchest of supports, providing an enormous volume of business. Felton and Sicardi could recall the time when both companies had shared the same president, Wesley Tilford. The defection of Stewart threatened to wipe out a large fraction of UTC's revenue. Even worse, by breaking the solid phalanx which the Standard companies still presented to the world it set a terrifying precedent.

"When I Look Out of My Window..."

The first question in the minds of the top UTC executives as they contemplated this disaster was: had Stewart acted entirely on his own responsibility? Or had he obtained the concurrence of the Rockefeller interests for his unprecedented action? Felton's personal inquiries quickly revealed that key men in other Standard Oil companies knew nothing of the matter. To this extent UTC could breathe easier.

202

Protesting letters, telegrams, and telephone calls made no impression on Stewart. His explanation was blunt and succinct. He was dissatisfied with UTC's service. Specifically, he had been plagued by tank car shortages. While UTC's fleet had grown, it had not kept pace with the growth of the Standard refineries. He accused the company of failing to acquire enough cars, and of "dividing the shortage" of cars among its customers. He could get better service, he said, with cars that he could control. "When I look out of my window," he told Felton, "I want to see a thousand cars available for service whether they are being used or not."

Accordingly, he had placed an order with General American Transportation Company for the construction of 1,000 tank cars of the most modern types. He believed that his tank car needs above this figure could be met by cars purchased or leased from one source or another. The fact that such action would be in violation of the exclusive-service clause of his contract with UTC bothered him not at all. "I'll be God-damned," he roared, "if I'll put all my eggs in one basket. If you won't build the cars I want, I'll have them built by somebody else."

The top men at UTC realized that Stewart's action had implications that went far beyond the tank car business. A temporary tank car shortage in itself would never have prompted so shrewd a man to so drastic a move. A hint of challenge to the Rockefellers, of an assertion of his individual power, was discernible in his rejection of UTC.

The Road to Popularity

There were strong reasons why Stewart might feel warranted in proving his independence of the Rockefeller influence. The direct holdings of the Rockefeller family in Standard Oil of Indiana amounted to only 4½ per cent of the outstanding stock. Through shares held by others, including the Rockefeller Foundation, the University of Chicago, and a trust company, control of an additional 11½ per cent was in the hands of John D. Rockefeller, Jr., who was a director of Indiana Standard. It was not by any means certain that even 16 per cent of the stock and the Rockefeller name could in a crisis outweigh Stewart's personal hold on the company. The man had made money for his stockholders beyond any expectation. In 1920, outstanding shares of the $100 par Indiana stock issued in 1912 were multiplied by a stock dividend of 150 per cent. Thereafter the stock was split again, four for one. The newest stock, representing a par value of $25, soon sold for $74. Investors found that for each $1,000 they had put into Indiana Standard stock in 1912, eight years later they owned stock worth $7,400, exclusive of the dividends they had received. It was a situation calculated to make stockholders think highly of a company head.

Beyond this, Stewart had acquired a popularity within the company that gave him extraordinary power. A profit-sharing plan which he had established for Indiana Standard's employees surpassed in its generosity all comparable plans of the time in American industry. It enabled the employee to acquire company stock to the amount of 20 per cent of his annual compensation, with half of the cost of the stock paid by the company. Moreover, the stock was bought by the employees at prices well below the going market price. In the early 1920s more than 15,000 Indiana Standard employees owned shares worth nearly $35,000,000 for which they had paid less than $12,000,000—and their enthusiasm for Stewart was proportionate to this profit.

Stewart himself was exalted by his achievements. Addressing a meeting of employees, he spoke of Indiana Standard as "the world's greatest democracy." And he went further: "Someday," he said to them, "and it is my wish that it be so, the chairman . . . and all of the directors of Standard Oil of Indiana may be elected by a vote of the employees." Asked whom they would elect as chairman if they could, the men at the meeting unanimously roared, "Stewart!"

Behind the Scenes

It is doubtful, however, that success and popularity alone would have driven Stewart to so dangerous a position as he took when he began to separate himself from the rest of the Standard family. A deeper reason for his action was sensed by those following the news from Washington. Information had leaked out tying Stewart, no one could tell how closely, to other oil magnates deeply involved in the so-called Teapot Dome Scandal. Ugly rumors were rife. In 1924, President Calvin Coolidge had been prodded by angry senators into launching a prosecution of certain oil companies which had obtained the rights to Teapot Dome by bribing Secretary of Interior Albert Fall. Liberty Bonds used in the undercover transaction had been traced to a shadowy and mysterious Canadian concern known as the Continental Trading Company, which was established to supply low-cost Teapot Dome crude oil to chosen refiners, and in which, it was presently revealed, Stewart was a stockholder. Two of his associates in this ill-omened venture fled to Europe to avoid testifying.

Stewart, however, appeared in 1924 before a grand jury and vigorously denied knowledge of any wrongdoing. To the Rockefellers as well he stoutly protested his innocence. Accordingly, it came as a surprise to many when the next year he, too, joined the ranks of missing witnesses. Government investigators were informed that he was in Mexico on important business, so secret that no one could be told his whereabouts.

John D. Rockefeller, Sr., had retired, and his son, John D. Rockefeller, Jr., had become the acting head of the family. His concepts of business morality were perhaps the higher because of the harsh criticism to which his father had been subjected for so long. He was not so much concerned with Stewart's ambition for power as with his use of power. The spectacle of the president of a great Standard company seeking to make a secret killing by acting as a middleman in selling oil to his own company outraged Rockefeller and many another in whom the sense of business decency was strong. It was a foregone conclusion that if Stewart could not exonerate himself and scotch the rumors circulating around his name he would find himself sternly opposed by all the power of the dynasty.

Peace Treaty

It was against this background that Felton had to consider Stewart's violation of the UTC contract—the first overt signal that he was preparing to break with the Standard tradition and defy the Rockefellers. One thing was sure—whatever Stewart's future, UTC could not afford to lose Indiana Standard's business. What could be done? And by whom? Felton was not inclined, at his age and in his state of impaired health, to cross swords with Stewart. The limitations of Sicardi for the purpose were all too evident. Accordingly, the weight of the burden had to fall largely on the shoulders of young Graves.

Consulting with Felton, Graves developed a straightforward line of argument. UTC had to deal with Stewart in purely economic terms. Stewart claimed that he could get more cars and better service with his own fleet. He had ordered 1,000 new cars from GAT. What deal could UTC offer him sufficiently tempting in business terms to make him reconsider? Graves' proposal was simple and direct. Let UTC buy and pay for the new cars. Every criticism made by Stewart would be met by a demonstration of willingness to meet his demands, while saving his company money. His final costs would be substantially less than those which he would incur if he broke with UTC. If, rejecting these obvious benefits for his company, he still resisted UTC's proposal, it would be apparent that his motive was not, after all, economic, but rather political—proof that he had thrown down the gauge to Rockefeller.

It was in a mood of grim determination that Graves drafted UTC's formal offer to Stewart and informally communicated its contents to friendly officials within Indiana Standard. He was fortunate in that during the period in which the matter was considered the tension between Stewart and John D. Rockefeller, Jr., diminished, if only temporarily. The two men met in New York and Stewart again averred his absolute innocence of wrongdoing. His participation in the Continental Trading Company, he said, had been solely in the interest of Standard. The possibility that he had his tongue in his cheek and his fingers crossed was all too evident, but Rockefeller could hardly refuse to accept his word. A few weeks later the cloud over Stewart seemed to be thinning away when a federal district court pronounced the Teapot Dome leases valid and found no fraud in connection with them.

In the changed atmosphere there was no reason for Stewart to reject Graves' proposals. The word went forth: let UTC draw a new contract on the terms outlined, and Stewart would sign it. Thereafter he went to considerable lengths to prove his personal friendship for UTC. After the tank car negotiation had been amicably completed, he invited Graves to a reception for some of the nation's leading industrialists at a Chicago hotel. In that atmosphere of plutocratic celebrity the young man was understandably shy; and observing this, Stewart went up to him, put a protective arm across his shoulders, and led him around the room, introducing him as "Mr. Tank Car."

The crisis had passed, but it was some time before the waves of emotion stirred up by Stewart subsided. UTC now had to buy the 1,000 cars which the Standard president had ordered from GAT. Specifications for these cars did not in all instances conform to UTC's preferences, and heated exchanges of the past between engineers of the two companies were still fresh in memory. A. E. Smith, the head of UTC's Mechanical Department, insisted on putting squads of inspectors in the GAT car shops—a demand which resulted in a certain crossing of slide rules by irritated technicians of both companies. On the whole, however, the car-building program progressed smoothly. With UTC's cash surplus fat and growing fatter, the outlay of a few unexpected millions was not excessively painful.

From Graves' standpoint, the essential thing was that the ranks of his customers remained unbreached. Even in the subsequent headline-making struggle between Stewart and Rockefeller for control of Indiana Standard, culminating in Stewart's resignation in 1929, there was no revival of the threat against UTC.

Sales Resistance

But although the struggle with Stewart had ended favorably, Graves was still uneasy. The affair had sharpened his conviction that UTC was unwise to limit its service entirely to old customers. Who could tell how far astray from the fold some of the Standard companies might wander in the future? Surely it was advisable to begin to build up business in the rest of the oil industry and to try to grow at a faster rate.

Graves believed that it was feasible to increase UTC's list of customers substantially. There was, of course, a question of the company's position under the antitrust laws. Since it was the largest unit in a business with very few competitors, an attempt on its part to increase its dominance at the expense of other tank car lines might well cause them to ask the Department of Justice to intervene. Under the Harding and Coolidge administrations antitrust activity had been insignificant, but their indifference to monopolistic trends offered no guarantee for the future. With a reputation still tarnished by the bad publicity of the generation past, UTC might be vulnerable if it grew too large too soon.

Caution would be necessary in seeking new business. Certainly, it would be inadvisable to reach out for the larger of the new oil companies, such as Texas, Gulf, Sinclair, or Shell. Since the nature of the business made it almost essential for a tank car company to handle all of a refiner's per diem rail freight if he handled any of it, the capture of a major customer from a competitor, even if it were possible, would be taken as a declaration of war within the industry and would be bound to bring reprisals.

There were, however, numerous smaller oil refiners and distributors whose individual business was not large enough to cause anyone much concern, but which, in the aggregate, might represent substantial revenue. It was these companies that Graves proposed to approach.

When he presented this idea to Felton and Sicardi he was disappointed by their lack of interest. They had no objection to his soliciting "outside business" if he wanted to try. But as to results they were skeptical, Sicardi especially. "The independents still hate our guts," he said. This was undeniable. Nevertheless, Graves went ahead, selecting as his first point of call a comparatively small Philadelphia concern, the Schock Oil Company.

Received by Mr. Schock himself, Graves proceeded to state his case. Union Tank, he said, was now no longer part of the Standard combine. It was prepared to serve independent refiners exactly as it served its older customers—thoroughly, carefully, and in a spirit of mutual confidence. At this point he was interrupted by an explosion. Schock, an elderly gentleman, rose from his chair as if with the intention of flinging the younger man bodily out of his office. "You've got a hell of a lot of nerve," he roared, "coming in here with the Standard Oil collar around your neck and looking for my business! Get out!"

Graves had not expected an easy time. Still, the violence of the outburst took him aback and roused his own combativeness, a quality with which he was well supplied. "Do you think," he retorted, "that I would come in here asking for your business only in order to lose it again?"

"Give Us a Chance..."

The question momentarily halted Schock, and Graves seized the moment. "I want to get you as a customer and retain you as a customer," Graves went on. "Stop and think. We can't afford to violate the confidence of any customer, big or little. If you'll give us your business, you'll find out that is so."

He explained why, in terms of economy and quality of tank car service, Schock would benefit from an arrangement with UTC. Schock sat down again. "You say you've changed. I don't believe it," he said.

"Give us a chance to prove it," Graves persisted.

"That's asking a lot. But I'll think it over and let you know."

With this Graves had to be content. On balance, he considered the outcome of the talk encouraging, and he had no hesitation in approaching other refiners up and down the East Coast. In time several of them, Schock included, agreed to sign contracts with UTC.

Graves soon found, however, that he was stirring up a tornado of antagonism. Hatred of Standard Oil was still intense among most independents. There existed at that time a trade association of independent oil companies, formed many years before, and which served the interests of companies outside of the Standard family. Its existence was predicated on the assumption that leopards did not change their spots—that the old Standard companies, including UTC, were still secretly combined and had not really given up their monopolistic intentions. Graves' progress in soliciting independent business became a major issue in this quarter. Whenever an independent refiner transferred his tank car business to UTC, the association received word of the move so promptly that Graves suspected the source of the information to be the losing tank car company. However that may have been, the association's trade journal launched a violent campaign against UTC. The line taken was that no customer of UTC could be truly independent of Standard. Photographers made trips to railroad sidings where UTC tank cars serving independent refineries might be found. The resulting pictures were spread across the front page of the journal under funereal headlines. These cars proved, the editors asserted, that such-and-such companies, formerly independent, were now part of the Standard Oil group.

Graves, who shared Felton's religious belief in the eventual triumph of truth, refused to be daunted. The attacks on UTC and its new customers were false; therefore they would break down. He did not intend, however, to sit back and wait for truth to emerge from its well. Instead, he addressed himself to the central problem—how to overcome the fears of independents, who, however they might have welcomed UTC's service, feared to use cars which still bore the controversial letters UTLX. The solution was not long in suggesting itself. A new tank car company came into existence—Products Tank Line, incorporated in New Jersey in 1926—and soon a score of small independents were cheerfully using PTL cars. The fact that PTL was a wholly-owned subsidiary of UTC could not be concealed—the anti-Standard forces hastened to expose the connection—but they found that the public was not very interested. Most of the steam had gone out of their campaign.

To all appearances, UTC had settled down to a serene life.

FIVE

THE OLD SCHOOL TIE

As chairman of UTC's board, Henry Felton viewed some aspects of Sicardi's handling of the presidency with misgivings. These grew as the government reopened its attack on the Teapot Dome contracts, and the trouble between Rockefeller and Colonel Stewart once more flared in the early months of 1926. If, as was rumored, a contest for power was taking shape in Indiana Standard, the personal influence of officials and leading shareholders in the other old Standard companies might need to be invoked on Rockefeller's side. There was no doubt of Sicardi's loyalty— but what kind of impression would he make on his peers? His grasp of the business and his intelligence were not in question, only his manner. Sicardi's eccentricities of style startled his associates, and, it might be presumed, would startle the great men of the oil industry still more.

The Sicardi Legend

In the idiom of a later day, Sicardi was offbeat. His ways were the talk of UTC's employees. A great part of the time he seemed so beset by his problems of office that he was hardly aware of the presence of others. A reminiscence of one of the company's secretaries of the period (in the old Standard Oil tradition, all of UTC's secretaries were then male) catches this characteristic. "Sicardi would walk by you, and you could look him squarely in the eye and say 'Good morning' and he would not see you. It wasn't rudeness. He was just thoroughly preoccupied."

It was gossiped that at a board meeting, when a vice-president's

211

212 HANDLED WITH CARE

secretary was brought in to take notes, Sicardi, ignoring him, sent for his own secretary. After the meeting the vice-president said, "Why did you have to call Jim? Here my boy was right alongside of you." Sicardi turned, startled, and looked at the concerned young secretary. "Why," he said to him, "you sat there so dignified, I thought you were one of the board."

The essential trouble with Sicardi, from Felton's point of view, was no fault of his. The fact was that he broke with the tradition of the old school tie—the Standard tie. But although his social limitations may have created a problem the man had an engaging simplicity and honesty. There were some aspects of company life which repelled him, and to which he simply refused to conform. While no one ever accused him of neglecting an important duty, he was impatient of the duller rituals of business—the ceremonial luncheons, for example, where a man had to gulp a tasteless meal in order to hear a twaddling speech.

Once, just before such an occasion, he suddenly remembered an urgent previous engagement with a railroad official and rushed off, sending an associate in his place. That day one of UTC's young clerks decided to take his lunch at a new Italian counter restaurant, a considerable distance from the office, but where he had heard that the food was good and also cheap. During his meal he looked along the counter and there, at the end, saw the president of the company sitting on a stool perilously small for his wide bottom, and concentrating on an enormous plate of spaghetti, which he wound around his fork with expert ease. It was too good a secret to keep, and soon everyone in UTC heard whispers that Sicardi's important luncheon engagements were not with customers but with *pasta*.

He took to the presidency of UTC with the same single-minded gusto that he brought to one of the fine Italian dinners that he was accustomed to give for his friends among the railroad officials, savoring his privileges with the smacking satisfaction of a gourmand cutting into an aromatic *scaloppini*. Coming back to the office after a mammoth lunch, with perhaps a fresh spot or two on his bulging vest, he would often lie down on a leather sofa in his private office, and puff at a fat cigar with the unalloyed pleasure of an Oriental potentate at rest in his domain. Not that he neglected his work. The business filled his mind at such moments as it did always. But he saw no reason why a man could not be as good an executive supine as vertical—better, if by rest he aided digestion.

Lying on the sofa, he would often send for a secretary to take shorthand dictation. This was something of an ordeal for the young man who got the assignment, for Sicardi would generally keep his cigar in his mouth while dictating, and it was necessary to translate the resulting sounds much as a dentist has to guess at the words of an open-mouthed patient. Fortunately for the stenographer, Sicardi seldom was satisfied with his first attempt at a letter or document and there was plenty of opportunity to correct mistakes. It was so habitual for Sicardi after dictating his first sentence to say, "Strike that out," that UTC's more experienced secretaries seldom bothered to write the sentence in the first place.

"It's No Use Talking..."

There was another chink in Sicardi's executive armor. He had not been trained young in the subtle techniques of power, and when authority was his at last he tended to strut a little more than was wise. There was a moment early in 1926 when this weakness impressed itself unpleasantly on Felton. The Internal Revenue Bureau had questioned some technicalities in the method which UTC was then using in depreciating its tank cars. The rate of depreciation, which since 1918 had stood at 5 per cent, was not itself in question, but the issue was touchy. Sicardi, somewhat out of his depth, consulted with Felton and with Goodwin, of Campbell's law firm. It was decided that all three should be present at a meeting which had been arranged at the New York office of the Internal Revenue Bureau.

Possibly Sicardi felt that Felton doubted his ability to deal with the situation. From the beginning of the meeting he took the lead. The IRB agent was given almost no opportunity to state his views. Citing facts and figures, of which he showed a good grasp, Sicardi overbore all interruptions. The company was absolutely in the right, he said, and could prove it.

The agent demurred; he had examined the evidence, and was

not altogether convinced. At this point Sicardi rose abruptly from his chair and said, "It's no use talking any more. Let Goodwin take it from here. Let's go." And he walked out.

It was a florid gesture such as he loved to make. In those days of rugged individualism many business executives disdained the low-paid clerks of government. Sicardi had never been one to conceal his feelings of superiority. The government man, from his viewpoint, could safely be squashed—so he squashed him. As his dubious associates followed him out of the IRB offices he said loudly, "I know just what has to be done to win this case."

In the upshot the depreciation question went into a labyrinthine process of review by the government, and Sicardi felt that he had been justified. But the effect of the incident on Felton was unfortunate. It revealed Sicardi once more as deficient in the area of human relations, where many a corporation president is made or broken.

The Razor's Edge

At this point in the little drama that was unfolding in UTC a potent offstage voice was heard. Early in 1926 Bertram Cutler, a representative of the Rockefeller interests, invited Felton and Sicardi to visit him at his prim, old-fashioned office. There, as was his custom, he served them coffee and settled down for an amiable chat. Its ostensible purpose was to discuss a question then to the fore and on which Felton and Sicardi disagreed—the advisability of transferring UTC's headquarters to Chicago, where the company would be closer to the center of oil transportation and its customer network.

Cutler was meticulous in pointing out that he was in no sense intervening in the company's decision. His status was unofficial. It could not be said that he spoke either for the Rockefeller Foundation or for the Rockefeller family. But personally, and as a friend of the company, he was naturally interested in their thinking on the subject.

Felton was inclined to favor the move. In the years since the dissolution a considerable feeling of competitive jealousy had begun to show itself among the various Standard Oil companies. Executives of customer companies west of the Alleghenies had been asking Felton, "Why the hell don't you fellows move out to the Midwest where you belong?" Behind the remark he sensed a suspicion that UTC was too much under the influence of eastern shippers; and although he could truthfully deny the charge, he felt that the company might be weakening its position by remaining in New York.

It was unprecedented for Cutler to concern himself in such a matter, which normally would have been settled by Felton's decision. Sicardi, however, was not inhibited on that account. Asked for his opinion, he rose instantly to the bait. In later weeks the UTC grapevine reported that in his earnestness he got to his feet and paced Cutler's office, gesticulating as he spoke. He thought the move to Chicago was unnecessary and would be costly and injurious. Many in UTC believed that his strong feelings on the subject grew in part out of the fact that his family life, on which he set great store, was strongly rooted in New York.

Subsequently, conflicting rumors circulated as to Cutler's real reason for the meeting. Some said that he had heard derogatory remarks about Sicardi's "lack of polish" from influential stockholders in UTC and from top-flight executives of customer companies. There were others who thought that Felton had asked for the appointment in order to expose Sicardi to Cutler's view. Yet another school of gossip held that Cutler wanted to make sure that the executive leadership in all companies in which the Rockefellers had an interest was competent to play a constructive part in resisting the imminent rebellion by Colonel Stewart. This last motive may well have been the more important. Cutler's meeting with Sicardi and Felton took place—it could hardly have been coincidence—just at the time when the Stardard hierarchy had another scion of the old guard for whom it wanted to find an appropriate place. This was Lauren J. Drake, whose father had been one of the great chieftains of the days of the Trust, a former president of Standard Oil of Indiana, and a good friend of John D. Rockefeller, Sr. The younger Drake himself had been president for seven years of the Galena Signal Oil Company, which was just then being liquidated under his direction.

By tradition, experience, and acquaintance with leading stockholders and officials in the Indiana and other Standard companies, Drake was suitable for the UTC assignment. Under the

circumstances Cutler's mind was likely to have been closed
against Sicardi before they talked. But Sicardi, after all, had
been Felton's choice, and policy required that Cutler at least
go through the motions of judging the man for himself at firsthand.

Sicardi, flattered by the invitation, his first, to meet with
Cutler, evidently sensed nothing of the undertow running against
him. Although he argued for his stand, when he found that
Cutler agreed with Felton on the move to Chicago he yielded
with good grace and without misgivings.

There was at the time a popular World War I story about a
German soldier and an American Negro who were fighting, the
former armed with a rifle and bayonet, the latter only with a
straight-edge razor. The doughboy swings the razor, and the
German says, gleefully, "Ach! You missed me!" The Negro grins
and replies, "Just wait till yo' wiggles yo' head." After the meeting with Cutler, Sicardi's head had been severed, but he did not
yet know it. He went back to his office with no suspicion that
Cutler was even then telephoning Felton, expressing the emphatic opinion that Sicardi was not the kind of man to be president of UTC, that it was essential to replace him with someone
who had tradition behind him—who would be acceptable to the
Standard company executives, bankers, and other persons of influence with whom UTC's president had to deal. Lauren Drake,
for example.

Felton had no disposition to argue. There are indications that
he was not happy over the advent of another president without
firsthand experience in the tank car business. His own plan
seems to have been to let Sicardi serve a few years more and be
succeeded by Graves. Now matters were out of his control. All
that remained was to make the transition as painless as possible
for all concerned.

The board of directors agreed with Felton that the Chicago
move should be made as quickly as possible, and Sicardi was
delegated to go there at once and look for office space. While
he was away Felton met with Drake and reached a prompt
understanding. A telegram went to Sicardi, instructing him to
return to New York at once. Even now he had no inkling of the
truth. When he entered the chairman's office Felton went straight

to the point with surgical directness. "Ed," he is reported to have said, "I would like you to write your resignation."

There was, of course, some discussion, but Sicardi knew better than to try to fight against the forces that he suddenly realized were arrayed against him. Arrangements were made for his honorable retirement to his Long Island home. The reason given out for his resignation was that for family reasons he did not wish to leave New York—a true statement, so far as it went.

Ready For The Worst

To the surprise of many, Felton, too, resigned, leaving the chairmanship vacant. There were those in UTC who thought he had been forced out—that Drake had made the resignation a condition of his acceptance of the presidency. Whatever the truth, with the retirement of Felton an era ended. His had been the father image for all of the company's executives except the new president. Eleven years later, when he died, there were still many to mourn in UTC's offices.[1]

Graves was hit harder by Felton's resignation than was anyone else in UTC. His state of mind was somewhat turbulent. On the one hand, he had benefited by the new deal—the long-coveted vice-presidency was at last his, conferred by Drake. But this was minimal consolation for withdrawal of the greater prize to which he had aspired. Drake was a younger and more vital man than Sicardi—the kind of man who lasts long—and he quickly showed an aggressiveness which suggested that he would not be easy to get on with. It was clear to Graves that if the presidency of UTC were ever to be his it would come only after many painful years in which he would have to play second fiddle to a tune that he could not call. At one point he even considered resigning, especially since his family did not relish the idea of leaving their comfortable New York home; but the company had become the center of his life and he quickly put down the rebellion within himself.

Drake was then in his late forties—a man with an average

---

[1] His will contained a provision which was entirely in character: a bequest to St. Thomas's Episcopal Church, on New York's Fifth Avenue, for a set of huge and handsome stained-glass windows, which thereafter were a feature of the edifice.

figure and average features but with a disarming smile, which he knew how to use to good effect. Sometimes when he chose to "turn on the charm" it seemed to his associates that a valve had suddenly been opened. His inner drive, however, was not to please but to command. It was he who selected the new Chicago offices in a Loop building and who personally allocated the choice executive rooms among his subordinates. After the move Graves found that he had been put on an equal footing with A. E. Smith, the grizzled vice-president in charge of the Mechanical Department. However close his relation to Felton had been he was to have no special claim to authority. The business would be as nearly a one-man show as Drake could make it.

The dictatorial spirit in Drake in itself did not unduly disturb Graves. Felton had also been an autocrat, and the feeling for power was strong in Graves himself. He respected men who could bend others to their will. The difficulty, which he perceived early, was that Drake's need to command was stronger than his grasp of the complex tank car business. The problem would be to get him to accept the lessons of experience without making him antagonistic. When in March, 1927, Graves settled down to his job in Chicago, it was in a mood resembling that of General Grant as he led the Union Army southward, inwardly determined and hoping for the best, but ready for the worst.

The New President

Drake's presidency began with a colorful display of financial fireworks. Almost his first move was to arrange with bankers for a $13,000,000 issue of Equipment Trust Gold Notes at 5 per cent. The proceeds were used to redeem the outstanding preferred stock, saving the company a substantial sum annually in interest. In December, 1926, taking advantage of the company's excellent financial condition, he ordered a stock dividend, this time of 33⅓ per cent. Stockholders were delighted; for while the outstanding number of $100 par shares rose to about 330,000, the annual dividend remained at $5.

From the beginning Drake showed considerable native shrewdness in the financial side of the business, and also toughness. These qualities proved especially useful just then, for a major problem centering on the company's financial policies was coming to a head. In 1927, the Federal government revived its inquiry into the question of depreciation practice which Sicardi had believed settled. This time the rate of depreciation was involved, and the case became much more serious than before. Since the imposition of substantial Federal income taxes in 1918, the company had been writing off between two and three millions a year for depreciation. Its calculations from 1918 to 1924 had been based on an average life expectancy of nineteen years for its cars, a figure then generally in use in the industry. The resulting 5 per cent rate of annual depreciation (which took into consideration the salvage value of scrapped cars) struck most of UTC's officers as satisfactory. It was well known that many tank cars of the time had been in use for more than two decades, but the average life expectancy was to some extent conjectural.

It came as a shock to the company when the responsible field agent of the Internal Revenue Bureau claimed that the tank car industry had understated the life of its cars, and urged that in future they be depreciated at 3 per cent a year, the rate used for other types of freight cars. It was a proposal that threatened to raise the company's current Federal income tax, even at the comparatively low tax rates then prevailing, by hundreds of thousands of dollars.

The question at issue was not the amount of the tax that the government would collect over the full life of a tank car at going tax rates. Regardless of whether the average car remained in service twenty years or thirty years or even more—and its life span to some extent would always be a matter of conjecture—it would presumably earn money, and the government would tax that money. The real point was that the government preferred to collect as much of the tax as possible, as quickly as possible; and a low rate of depreciation meant a higher current net income for the company and thus higher current taxes. Conversely, the tank car company was inclined to defer as much as possible of the tax payments on the earnings of its cars to later years. A higher rate of depreciation meant, for practical purposes, lower current taxes and more cash in hand.

This was a matter on which Drake felt strongly. Like Napoleon, he believed that the best defense was an attack. Did the government claim that a 5 per cent rate of depreciation was too high? Nonsense, said Drake, it was not high enough. Forthwith the company's statisticians sat down to "prove" that tank cars had on the average a life expectancy of only about sixteen years, justifying a 6 per cent annual depreciation; and Campbell's firm took the resulting analysis as a basis for a powerful brief, presented to the government on behalf of UTC.

A legalistic running fight ensued, with Drake leading UTC's strategy in a strong rear-guard action. He was aided by the fact that, however dubious his new 6 per cent figure might be, the government was on difficult ground in holding that tank cars could be equated with ordinary freight cars in calculating their working lives. The result, reached in 1929, was a compromise on a rate of 4½ per cent, based on an annual tank car longevity of twenty-two years.

In time to come, the average life of a tank car would be established at twenty-five years, later at twenty-nine, and still later at thirty-five, with Drake fighting all the way. But the 1929 decision left him far from dissatisfied. The result might have been worse.

While he did not confine himself to the financial side of administration, it was his chief area of action. He drove UTC's treasurer of the period into a state of near panic by demanding monthly financial statements. Until then such statements had been given to UTC's president only at comfortable six months' intervals. But with a large effort the financial department speeded up its sedate pace and met Drake's requirements.

When it came to the mundane problems of getting business, servicing customers, and dealing with railroads he had to force himself to show interest. Corporate life appealed to him most in its grander financial aspects. Where Graves would have liked to see more money spent on new tank cars, Drake took pride in the fact that UTC was redeeming its Equipment Trust notes at the rate of well over $1,000,000 annually, while paying good dividends and building its surplus.

Proxies and Rubber Stamps

It gave Drake especial pleasure that he was able to play a role in the sensational struggle between Rockefeller and Stewart, whose name had been sadly tarnished by the later Teapot Dome investigations. Early in 1929, the crisis at Standard of Indiana

came to a head. Although the doughty Colonel knew that the
odds were heavily against him, he had decided to battle for
control of the company, and all of Rockefeller's cohorts were
mustered for the great proxy fight that followed. Drake proved
effective in soliciting proxies for Rockefeller from Indiana Standard stockholders, many of whom had known his father. The result
was a further strengthening of his prestige and power. Following Rockefeller's victory and Stewart's resignation everyone in
UTC felt that only a very bold man would seriously challenge
Drake's authority.

The fact that he had access as a friend of the family to the
Rockefellers themselves deeply impressed all of his associates.
The "yesism" of his board meetings surpassed anything that had
been seen even in Felton's day. There had been some changes
made among the directors, but they were all still drawn from the
executive personnel of the company. Drake hardly bothered to
conceal his feeling that the board, as a whole, was his rubber
stamp. Among the directors it was only to Graves and Smith that
he turned for counsel, and then always in private session. All
of UTC knew that most of the company's important policy decisions were shaped by Graves; but to the assembled board Drake
turned the face of a man who knew his mind and intended to have
his way. The meetings were conducted with clocklike formality;
minutes and statements were read, motions made, votes taken,
but the results were always predetermined. Although each officer
would be given a chance to report on his problems, the opportunity was rarely used. Anything of importance had already
been communicated to Drake, Graves, or Smith, and settled.
The big moments came when dividends were voted, and this
procedure, too, was entirely perfunctory.

The year 1929 offered Drake another chance to startle his associates by a display of financial sagacity. In the soaring market of
the late twenties UTC's stock, which generally sold above $100
per share, had been little noticed by the public. Sales were few
and far between. The stock lived up to the description of it in
Moody's Industrials as a "businessman's investment ... entirely
sound," with a "good or improving" record—a "regular dividend
payer" which showed "consistent progress toward true investment standards."

"A Very Temporary Setback"

While Drake was intent on maintaining the investment quality of the stock, at the same time he was aware of the practical disadvantages for UTC's shareholders in having comparatively few shares outstanding. As in the boom years of 1928 to 1929 the price per share gradually rose, carried along in Wall Street's tide of enthusiasm, the market for the stock thinned until a single buyer or seller could by a transaction of a few hundred shares cause a rise or drop of several points. A move to give the stock more ready marketability was clearly indicated.

The unexpected and violent crash of stock prices in the autumn of 1929 made action imperative. In a few transactions the price of UTC stock tumbled from a high of 163 to 121. Moving fast, Drake decided on another stock split, which would give stockholders four new no-par shares for every old $100 share. The split was carried out in December, 1929, and with 1,250,000 shares outstanding Drake established a quarterly dividend rate of 40 cents, or $1.60 annually. The new shares, in a period of slumping values, came on the market at about $25. Demand was small, but the stock was still held in so few hands, comparatively, and these for the most part the hands of people of such large means, that it remained remarkably steady. In the brief recovery of 1930 it rose to $38 per share. This was equivalent to a price of $360 for the $100 par shares which had sold for $67 seventeen years earlier. The new stock would not again reach the $38 figure for another seventeen years, and in the interim it would sell below $10 per share.

Drake did not sense the imminence of bad times. As the new decade began, he was optimistic. He had proved himself to the company's stockholders. UTC was making more money than ever before. Its fleet stood at 34,000 cars. The oil business was still booming. The stock market crash was regarded in UTC as a very temporary setback to the economy. No one there had been badly hurt. It was felt that after the overextended speculators had stopped jumping out of windows and the bootblacks and ribbon clerks had got out of the market, things would soon settle down again and well-grounded businesses such as UTC would move steadily forward. UTC's thinking on the subject of economic crisis had not advanced much, if at all, beyond Calvin Coolidge's classic line: "When more and more people are thrown out of work, unemployment results."

But the heyday of crusty conservatism was coming to an end. The great social forces unleashed by depression were not to be denied. Neither the United States nor UTC would ever be the same again.

PART FOUR:

THE TWISTING LINE
OF FATE

1930-1952

"Believing that fundamental condi-
tions of the country are sound ...
my son and I have for some days
been purchasing sound common
stocks." JOHN D. ROCKEFELLER
(*October 30, 1929*)

ONE

THE ART OF CASHMANSHIP

Drake's close attention to the company's finances meant inevitably that his treasurer had to be highly responsive to his requirements. In 1929, the post was assigned to a man whom Drake considered sufficiently dependable to work with him. Russell Eustice, the new treasurer, had been assistant to the previous incumbent. Short and stocky, he had a terrier's alertness and shrewd insight into his master's ways of mind. It was his view that to deal successfully with Drake "you had to have the hide of an elephant." Their first exchange after Eustice's promotion was highly educational. Drake demanded certain figures, and Eustice hastened to assemble them. Taking the paper from the treasurer's hand, Drake glanced at it, flushed, and pounded his desk. "God damn it!" he roared, "why the hell can't I get what I want around here?"

It turned out then that he had asked for one set of figures, while actually wanting another. Thereafter Eustice devised a technique for self-protection. Whenever Drake demanded a report from him, he would make notes on the spot. Frequently Drake, on seeing the data brought to him by Eustice, would repeat his temperamental performance of their first meeting. Eustice learned to wait until the storm had passed and then bring out his careful notes of the original request and read them back. "This is what you asked for—and that's exactly what I gave you." On such occasions Drake would subside, growling, "Well, you ought to know what I want."

As the depression gained ground during 1931 to 1932 the excel-

lent financial position of UTC looked even better, relative to the
declining fortunes of other companies. Drake had by then learned
an important secret of UTC's strength—the extraordinary ability
of the company to generate considerable amounts of cash even
in times of slack business. In periods of expansion the heavy cost
of new cars might tax UTC's resources and compel the borrowing of capital; but when construction of new cars was no longer
necessary the company was able rapidly to accumulate substantial
surpluses. And it had no credit problems with its customers. Depression or no depression, the Standard Oil companies paid their
bills. As a result the company's financial health was excellent at
a time of endemic bankruptcy. Even at the worst of the depression, when the movement of oil products by the railroads fell
by more than 50 per cent, UTC was able to continue in the black
and to pay a regular return to stockholders—becoming a member of a comparatively small corporate group with an unbroken
record of dividends. At the bottom of the depression Drake
retired well ahead of maturity all of the outstanding 4½ per
cent Equipment Trust notes issued in 1926. By 1934 the company was entirely free of debt.

"We Made too Good a Deal"

For Clifford Graves UTC's surplus had a significance that
went far beyond the merely financial. His biggest problem lay in
the area of new business. One large fact never ceased to nag at
him. UTC was being outpaced by its chief competitor. In 1919,
at the end of World War I, General American had owned fewer
than 6,000 tank cars, compared with UTC's 20,000-car fleet. But
a decade later, when UTC's fleet stood at 35,000, GAT's numbered 24,000. That a competitor should be growing faster than
UTC not only in percentage terms but in actual tank cars put
into service struck Graves as a serious blow to the company's
prestige and pride. By comparison with GAT's notable additions to its list of customers Graves' success in adding a few
dozen small independents to UTC's portfolio seemed unim-
pressive.

Once more UTC's cash surplus provided the basis for a major
new development. The first years of the great depression had
struck hard at many of the independent oil refiners. Banks on

which they relied for credit were unable or unwilling to lend
them funds for their operations and for the acquisition of wanted
properties. Graves knew that a number of the independents who
owned their own tank car fleets had begun to find them a costly
burden in a time when large numbers of tank cars were idle and
when corporate ledgers were being written almost entirely in red
ink. In such a situation UTC was uniquely qualified to help. It
had the cash that the refiners wanted; it could relieve them of
their troublesome tank car fleets; it could assure them of competent tank car service at fair rates. The satisfactory experience
of the small independents who now for some years had been
customers of the company showed that all customers, large and
small, Standard or independent, were treated alike, their con-
fidences respected, their needs fully met. Those refiners who still
thought that the Union Tank name signified Standard Oil to the
public could be supplied with cars bearing the Products Tank
Line stencil.

With this formula Graves made an approach to the Barnsdall
Oil Company, which owned a small tank car fleet. Barnsdall's
president, Edwin B. Reeser, was a key figure in Graves' strategy,
for he was also president of the American Petroleum Institute
and one of the best-known figures in the oil industry. If he
accepted Graves' offer, the doubts of other oil companies would
be allayed. And he could be readily approached, for he was a
friend of Drake.

Graves' talk with Reeser gave him the satisfying conviction
that a door had opened for UTC. Beyond he could see a new
pattern of future growth through the purchase of large refiner-
owned fleets. His work in the 1920s to prove UTC's integrity to
smaller refiners would now begin to yield significant results. The
oil business would learn from practical experience that UTC no
longer wore Standard's collar around its neck. What remained
was only to shape the right kind of detailed proposals for independent refiners who were in positions similar to Barnsdall's.

Some problems inevitably would arise, but they could be
solved. It was not easy to work out a fair price for a tank car fleet
or to set prices for tank car service in a period of acute economic
instability. In the case of Barnsdall, Reeser and Graves disposed
of the price issue by a simple agreement: if either company

found that it had unintentionally taken advantage of the other it would make a voluntary adjustment. A short time later Reeser had a pleasant surprise when UTC turned over $250,000 to Barnsdall. "We made too good a deal," Graves told him.

The fact was that Barnsdall had given UTC more business than Graves had expected when he established the rates for their contract. Drake winced to see his beloved surplus reduced by the refund but gave way. The resulting demonstration of UTC's integrity turned out, not surprisingly, to have substantial values for the company. Reeser, profoundly impressed, radiated good will, and became an important reference point for other independents who were considering UTC's services.

The Uses of Cash

Other independent refiners owning their own tank car fleets soon followed Barnsdall's lead—first Skelly Oil Company and then the ancient enemy of the old Standard combine, the Pure Oil Company. By 1935 UTC had regained something of its former lead over GAT's fleet, 39,000 to 25,000. Graves saw no reason to stop there. At one point he thought that he had worked out an agreement to purchase the large fleet of the Sinclair Oil Company. With high hopes he rushed back to Chicago to lay the proposition before Drake. Here, however, he ran into unexpected opposition.

Asked for a decision on the Sinclair matter, Drake summoned A. E. Smith, who shook his head. It was not a good deal, he thought. The Sinclair tank cars were old—the purchase price was too high. He insisted on computing the average life of the Sinclair cars from first to last at twenty years. This, Graves felt, was a serious underestimate. But Drake sided with Smith, and all Graves' arguments demonstrating that the price was actually fair flattened against their opposition. Not without irritation, Graves had to give up the project. More than twenty years later the episode afforded him some ironic amusement when UTC finally bought the Sinclair fleet for a price far higher than that for which it had been offered to him and in the same general condition—and regarded the price and the deal as sound.

The extent to which Graves had assumed leadership in the company was all too evident to Drake, and he may well have felt some desire to curb the younger man; but he had deeper reasons for resisting the Sinclair ideal. For some time he had been employing UTC's accumulated cash in an unusual way, which sharply reduced the amounts available for Graves' expansion program. In 1930, when the price of UTC's stock, as of all stocks, plummeted in the deepening depression, Drake took an unprecedented step, purchasing for UTC's treasury 45,000 shares of the company's own capital stock at more than $25 per share— the first of many such purchases. He justified this move on the ground that, since the company would not have to pay dividends on the purchased stock, enough money would be saved to make the investment a sound one. It was not necessary for him to add that the support which this policy gave to the price of the stock in the 1930s and early 1940s was helpful to stockholders who wished to use their stock as collateral for bank loans or to sell it.

For the next twelve years, with the approval of the board of directors, Drake continued to follow this course, until more than 250,000 shares had been bought in, at prices between $15 and $28 per share, the average price paid being about $25.[1] The saving to the company in dividends represented an approximate average of about 5 per cent per year on capital thus invested. Some additional faint color was given to Drake's reasoning when, in 1955, twenty-five years after his first purchase of company stock, UTC sold to certain institutional investors stock equivalent to about 100,000 shares as bought in by Drake, at a price nearly twice what he had paid for it. But later studies of Drake's operation by financial specialists suggest that it may not have been so beneficial to the company as he seemed to think. The elimination of more than 6 millions of capital in a period when many companies were willing to sell assets cheaply was undoubtedly a factor, not only in UTC's failure to acquire the Sinclair fleet in the 1930s, but in its more general reluctance to adopt a policy of broad expansion. Many enterprising companies, including UTC's strongest competitors, were then seizing opportunities to grow and diversify, but for UTC such possibilities were inevitably foreclosed by Drake's insistence on using much of the company's available cash for the purchase of its own stock.

[1] This $25 figure is equivalent to $12.50 per share for UTC stock as it has stood since 1954, owing to a 2-for-1 stock split in that year.

Graves' disappointment over the Sinclair deal was intensified when it was announced that GAT in 1936 had acquired more than 12,000 additional tank cars from various sources, and that its fleet was larger than UTC's. This was a mortifying blow. During the later years of the decade UTC was able to reestablish a slight lead, but it was clear that the two companies now stood neck and neck in the rail transportation of liquids.[2] It was hard to escape the conclusion that the days of UTC's ascendancy were over, even if one did not admit that the days of its decline had begun.

[2] In one respect only could UTC feel that it was maintaining its position as the leader of the industry. At the bottom of the depression, it successfully pioneered in improving tank car construction by the use of fusion welding. See Appendix D.

TWO

"WE DID NOT CUT BACK"

The National Industrial Recovery Act adopted by Congress in 1933 at the urging of President Franklin D. Roosevelt for a while gave modest encouragement to the petroleum industry and the tank car business. Under this act marketers of petroleum products established a code to stabilize the industry, largely through the purchase of surplus stocks of oil products. With the approval of the government, the larger refiners began a systematic buying and storage program which called into play many hundreds of idle tank cars. A committee of the petroleum industry known as the Tank Car Stabilization Committee played a leading role in this effort, and succeeded for a time in firming up prices of petroleum products.

In 1935, when the Supreme Court rejected NIRA on constitutional grounds, the rug was pulled out from under the industry's plan of action. About the same time the Department of Justice began a long-drawn-out prosecution of several leading oil companies which had been represented on the Tank Car Stabilization Committee. They had, it was claimed, violated the Sherman Anti-trust Act. Thereafter, most oil shippers found themselves returned to the chaos in which they had been three years earlier, and the tank car business suffered with them. From 1932 through 1935 UTC's annual average net income was only $1,300,000—less than half of net income for the preceding four years. Thousands of the company's older tank cars were dismantled or remained immobilized for months, even years, at a time. Despite the acquisition by purchase of many thousands of

233

shipper-owned cars, the over-all size of the UTC fleet increased little during this period, largely because of dismantlings.

As Graves viewed the company's position in the middle 1930s, the continuing low level of business was less ominous as a long-range threat to the tank car companies than was the force of competition from other forms of oil transport. Fears which he had felt in the 1920s were now rapidly being justified by events. The 1930s saw new pipe lines built in many parts of the country to carry gasoline and other oil products, while the motor truck was beginning to capture a significant share of the nation's oil traffic. These developments accelerated the decline in railroad revenue and gouged into the business, both long haul and short haul, of the tank car lessors.

What could be done? It seemed clear to Graves that the hope of the railroads and of UTC lay partly in a revision of the rail freight-rate structure, a revision that would make the roads more strongly competitive with products pipe lines, water transport, and trucks.

The ICC Says "No"

Some of the larger oil companies were then advancing the argument that existing ICC regulations were hamstringing the railroads and unfair to themselves. Specifically, they considered it wrong that railroads were not allowed to give freight discounts for large oil shipments—wrong that a refiner shipping 100 tank cars at the same time had to pay as much freight per tank car as a refiner shipping one tank car. Was this not prejudicial to the competitve position of the railroads? Was it not contrary to general business practice? Was it not inconsistent with other rail tariffs? The ICC authorized railroads to charge slightly less for each 100 gallons in a full tank car than for each 100 gallons in a partly full tank car. Why should not this principle be extended to permit trainloads of a single commodity in tank cars to be shipped at lower rates than were fixed for single tank cars?

By no means all of the oil companies agreed in the matter. A few flatly opposed the change. One of UTC's major customers, a Standard company, considered it "a very dangerous proposition," sure to stir up much bitterness, and far from beneficial to big refiners who were in a position to make extensive use of water and pipe line transportation.

In 1935, a group of railroads favoring trainload discounts asked the ICC for a ruling on the question. The Commission replied promptly and emphatically. The proposed new rate was forbidden on the ground that it tended to injure the competitive position of the small shipper. Tank car freight rates would continue to be based on single tank cars, regardless of the number of cars in a shipment.

A few years later the ICC made certain exceptions from this rule, notably with respect to shipments of molasses in freight cars. But where oil was concerned the railroads, whatever their own need, were forbidden to modify rates if by so doing they might strengthen the hand of big shippers. The old days of the Standard monopoly had still not been forgotten, regardless of the amount of oil that had flowed out of the wells since then.

Rough Going

The large worries of the time were made especially acute for Graves by UTC's leading competitors. Like everyone else they were desperately convassing the field for business. Reports came to Graves that first one customer company, then another, and yet another, had been approached by other tank car lessors with extremely tempting propositions—and what did he intend to do about it? The fact that the competition was offering tank car service at prices below cost—a condition with which no company could long survive—strongly suggested to Graves that the purpose of the price war was to destroy UTC. The danger called out all his combativeness. Hopping one train after another, he rushed across the country and back again to put out the competitive sparks before they could ignite.

The strength of his relationship with UTC's customers was tested as never before. In a carefully prepared and rehearsed talk, he told the traffic managers of the oil companies: "We have long served you, under many difficulties and through thick and thin. When the demand for our cars was high and we could have raised our prices, we did not. The law of supply and demand is a two-edged instrument. We never permitted it to dictate our prices. You have been served economically over the years. Now, as a result of hard times, you are in a position to exert pressure on us. But the depression will not last forever. You will not serve your own interests if you exercise your advantage at our expense. There is always danger that the same person who uses price competition in a destructive way may later seek to profiteer at your expense. You are not safe under those conditions. In the long run it will not improve your position to leave us. We served you well in the 1920s when the demand for cars was at its highest. We managed to provide the cars you needed, and we did not increase our charges. Now, when the shoe is on the other foot, is the time for both of us to prove the benefits of loyalty. Don't make the mistake of transferring your business for a very temporary advantage."

It was an effective argument. Once his customers had grasped the principle involved they dropped any notion they might have had of turning elsewhere for tank car service. It was unmistakable that if tank car rental charges were reduced below a safe level, in the long run an injury would be worked on the efficiency of tank car service as a whole. Not one customer served by UTC in this period of stress took its business elsewhere.

In the fury of the competitive battle, Graves conceived the idea of fighting fire with fire. Approaching some of the companies served by UTC's competitors, but which also owned tank cars of their own, he offered to buy their fleets, on the assumption that the purchase would bring UTC their leasing business. He had a strong argument. He was not, he said, looking for a horse trade. He was prepared to pay a fair price for the fleets. Experience showed that companies which had sold their tank cars made more money with the capital payment received than they could have made by keeping the fleets. And UTC, through the increase in its leasing business, also profited. What could be better for both parties?

For a time he thought that he was close to success, but he soon learned that he was wading in dangerous waters. The encouragement that he was receiving, it dawned on him, was mainly for the purpose of extracting low prices for tank car service from UTC's competitors. He had a similar experience when he made advances to certain chemical companies which were customers of other tank car lessors—a field in which UTC had not previously tried to compete. The companies which appeared to be beckoning him had little real interest in transferring their business. His bids for their business were being held as a club over the heads of other tank car companies to which they were committed.

UTC was now in a position to take the offensive, but Graves saw that there could be no benefit for anyone in a price war. The future of the private tank car lines would be imperiled if, under the stress of depression psychology, they allowed themselves to engage in throat-cutting competition. UTC, he decided, had to resist temptation and oppose any such trend. Once this perception had come to him he swiftly withdrew from all negotiations with the customers of competitors; and he firmly adhered to this policy throughout the remainder of the depression.

Comparatively Happy

Among the beneficiaries of Graves' energetic measures during the depression were UTC's rank-and-file employees. The car fleets purchased and the revival of crude-oil movements in tank cars kept many men busy in the company's shops and offices— men for whom it might otherwise have been difficult to find work. Twenty years later one of the company's executives recalled that "we did not cut back personnel to any great extent. After the depression had become really bad, our salaries were cut 10 per cent. At the time, as well as now, I felt that UTC people got better treatment than employees in most other American industries. Many of my friends in other companies were fired. Others had their salaries reduced more than once and by large amounts—25 per cent on the first round, and then another 25 per cent, and they were happy to hang on at half pay. But, as I recall, we didn't lay anyone off. There were certainly no mass terminations." For this comparatively happy condition the company's cash surplus and Graves' creative effort shared the credit.[1]

The middle 1930s were years in which Graves had to make closer calculations of rates and charges than ever before. Although he kept the general structure of UTC's rental charges

[1] Drake kept his office staff nearly intact, but he could not avoid reacting to the economic pressure of the time. Seeking to reduce costs, he focused on the Employee's Retirement Plan, which was then taking an increasing bite out of the company's income. See Appendix E.

intact, he made one important exception. Crude-oil shipments were put in a special category. The greatly reduced production and movement of oil during the depression had sharply impaired the efficiency of pipe line operations; and railroads had dropped their freight rates for crude oil so far that the tank car was once more becoming competitive in moving petroleum from the wells, as it had not been for a generation. Graves, believing that it was the company's obligation to encourage this tendency, for a time even eliminated the rental charge for crude-oil cars entirely and accepted in its place the mileage allowance paid by the railroads to the shippers. His broad pricing philosophy held that UTC's rental charges must never be permitted to deter shippers from using the railroads. As he repeatedly told his associates, he preferred to "take it in mileage," if by so doing he could reduce competitive pressure from trucks, waterways, or pipe lines.

A Defeat or Two

In his determination to tap every source of available business Graves planted one or two seedlings of enterprise which for a time showed promise, but which never flowered into substantial revenue. One of these was the purchase in 1931 of two aluminum tank cars, for use in carrying chemical products for which steel cars were unsuitable. It was a step full of potential significance. At the time the young American chemical industry was already giving hints of its later phenomenal growth, and Graves hoped that from this small beginning would come an important future enlargement of the company's scope. Unfortunately, the experience of the men designing UTC's cars at the time had been wholly limited to steel cars for the oil trade. They knew little of other metals; and from among the few aluminum alloys then developed for industrial use they accepted one not ideally suited to the purpose. The tanks, moreover, were riveted, for the aluminum welding process was then at a primitive stage. The result was that the new cars produced more headaches than income. Used mainly to carry hydrogen peroxide and acetic acid, they leaked at the rivets to a troublesome degree and required frequent repair. Two years later, in 1933, Graves tried again, ordering two aluminum cars made of stronger metal. From a technical standpoint these were more successful, but by that time the depression had reached so deep a point that in Graves' opinion there was no incentive to expand chemical car construction.

The modest cost of the early experiments with aluminum was not important, but its psychological effects were. For years thereafter a cloud of misgiving surrounded the subject of tank cars for chemicals in UTC. Graves' recurrent thoughts of entry into this field were stifled by the prejudices of others. Drake, in particular, wanted nothing to do with chemical cars, and reports that rival tank car companies were making progress in the chemical field did not cause him to change his mind. Let others, he said, handle such business; UTC did not need it; and it required technical skills, he thought, that the Mechanical Department lacked. Nearly twenty years would go by before the company finally shook off its feelings of inferiority with respect to this area of its business and began to produce in quantity tank cars designed specifically for the transport of chemicals.

Another of Graves' experiments, also in 1933, was the first attempt in the company's history to make cars for the purpose of hauling other than liquid products. On his instructions, 26 petroleum tank cars were rebuilt with hoppers to carry powdered cement and lime for leading producers of building materials and were rented on a monthly basis. In later years, as better hopper cars were designed and built by other companies, these 26 cars became obsolete, and UTC retired from the field.

There were few signs, during the dreary depression years, that UTC was still capable of effort on the grand scale. But at least it had not lost its fighting spirit. It fought hard times, it fought competition, it even fought a foreign government, and won.[2] No one within the company had any doubt as to who was providing its combative energy. Drake might be president, but Graves was the active force.

[2] See Appendix F—"Controversy with Mexico."

THREE

THE BIG TEST

Before the European war was formally declared in the summer of 1939, rail transportation of oil products to the East Coast had been steadily dwindling. Product pipe lines and ocean-going tankers were providing the coastal cities not only with crude oil but with gasoline and other refined products, which a few years earlier had been carried in tank cars. According to a report issued by the AAR, on an average day in 1938 no more than 5,000 barrels, or 200,000 gallons, were carried in tank cars on the Atlantic seaboard—an insignificant fraction of the 1,500,000 barrels consumed daily in the area by industrial, institutional, and residential users, and an amount which could be handled by fewer than 1,000 tank cars in short-haul service.

The tank car lines had adjusted to this situation. In 1939, there were 15,000 fewer tank cars in the United States than in 1930. The privately-owned tank car fleets, totalling only 140,000 cars, were used primarily in the Middle West and on the West Coast. The average age of all tank cars had risen to eighteen years, and their maintenance and repair demanded increasing vigilance and expense.

In the light of the experience of World War I it was easy to foresee the probable effects of the new European crisis on tank car requirements; but the war in its first months was widely dismissed as "phony" by an optimistic press; and the tank car companies had not yet shaken off the depression psychology of the mid-thirties. With many of their cars still idle, a highly cautious attitude prevailed. Profits were improving, and stockholders were eager for dividends; surely it was advisable to keep investment in new cars as low as possible until the situation had been further clarified.

Not until the war suddenly roared into full blast in 1940 did UTC's executives become aware of the full weight of their responsibility. It was with profound concern that Graves, among others, observed the worsening conditions of American freight transportation. Costly delays and confusion on railroads were slowing deliveries of oil to tankers desperately needed by the Allied nations. Was the United States to experience a repetition of the disastrous railroad crisis of 1916? If so, there would be little hope for England or for the future of democratic government anywhere.

The railroads, fearful that the government might seek once again to assume management of their business, made vigorous efforts to coordinate and improve their operations. The movement of oil, however, continued to present jagged-edged problems. When in May, 1941, President Roosevelt appointed Secretary of the Interior Harold Ickes Petroleum Coordinator for National Defense, one of the main tasks with which Ickes was charged was "the elimination or reduction of cross-hauling of petroleum and its products and the development of transportation facilities and of methods by which more efficient use can be made of existing transportation and storage facilities...."

From this moment the tank car companies were engaged in a ceaseless effort to provide more and ever more cars. The difficulties were formidable. In the summer of 1941, America's loan to oil-starved Great Britain of 50 huge ocean-going tankers provided by major oil companies posed a critical problem for the tank car industry. To load the tankers and create a storage surplus for their later reloading required that about 850 tank cars carrying approximately 185,000 barrels of crude oil and oil products move daily on long hauls, as much as 2,000 miles, from the Gulf and Midwest refineries to the East Coast. An estimated 20,000 tank cars were required for this emergency operation.

The Government Is Surprised

Secretary Ickes promptly asked the American Petroleum Institute to organize a fact-finding committee of major figures in the petroleum industry to advise him in the matter. The petroleum industry's statistics of available tank cars gave little hope. When the API asked the nation's oil companies how many cars they might be able to release for emergency service without disrupting the domestic economy, the replies totaled only a small fraction of the quantity needed. As for the tank car lines, most of the people working on the problem felt that little help would be forthcoming from them, that privately-owned tank car fleets had deteriorated and diminished to a point where they could not rise to an emergency.

Nevertheless, the effort had to be made. It was in a grim mood that the API committee invited each of the large tank car companies to send a representative to Washington. UTC's choice for the assignment, inevitably, was Graves.

When he came into the committee room for his first meeting he had an instant sense that it was charged with tension. He had hardly sat down at the table when members of the committee began to ask questions which, while outwardly courteous, were plainly intended to put him on the defensive. Was it true that his company's tank car fleet was smaller than it had been ten years earlier? Graves admitted the fact. It was then explained that the country needed to move about 200,000 gallons of petroleum daily on emergency long-haul service, over and above the regular requirements of oil transportation. What could the tank car industry contribute to the solution of the problem?

Graves looked around the table with the bland gaze of the ace-holding poker player. "We can supply enough cars," he said, "to move 200,000 gallons daily. If necessary, we could move 500,000."

The committee was stunned, but as Graves went on incredulity gave way to enthusiasm. What the government and the API had not realized was that thousands of old tank cars retired from active use in the 1930s were still standing on unused railway tracks all over the country. Destined for the scrap heap, they had not yet been dismantled. It was those forgotten cars that Graves, with the backing of his colleagues in the industry, now proposed to recall to service.

"What are we waiting for?" a relieved member of the committee asked. Orders were given, and all over the country rusty tank cars were hauled to the nearest car-repair shops, where crews went frantically to work, sealing tank leaks, lubricating axle journals, getting sticky valves to operate. At first, even with the utmost effort, the work went too slowly for comfort. It seemed for a time as if Graves might have to eat his words, for by the early days of September, 1941, only 50 tank cars per day were being provided for the emergency assignment. At this rate it would take more than a year to get 20,000 more tank cars into service—and England could not afford to wait even a month. The British Ambassador was alarmed, and Secretary Ickes, in no mood to accept explanations, heated the telephone wires. But more was being done than they could know, and another two weeks brought reassurance. From 50 cars per day the figure shot up to 400 cars, 600, 800, until the requirement was fully met. Soon 20,000 tank cars were in continuous movement between the Midwest and the East Coast ports, filling the great tankers, many of which were doomed to be sunk by submarines. Later observers expressed the belief that had it not been for the desperately needed American oil carried by tank car in the autumn of 1941 England could not have been saved; and the United States might have had to fight alone the combined might of Germany and Japan.

Hard-pressed executives of the tank car industry had a sense of triumph. They thought they had done everything that could be expected of them. They were wrong. A few weeks later came the Japanese raid on Pearl Harbor, and the real pressure began.

The Key

In December, 1941, President Roosevelt used the emergency powers granted him by Congress to establish the Office of Defense Transportation (ODT) with Joseph B. Eastman as its director. Without delay Eastman plunged into the search for ways to meet the vastly increased transportation requirements of the country. The tank car especially was a focus of his attention. Once the United States was in the war, German U-boats began to raise havoc with coastal as well as with ocean-going tankers. During the winter of 1941 to 1942 an oil famine threatened the Eastern seaboard. Pipe lines alone were unable to meet the need. For every tanker sunk or transferred to an Allied nation, it was estimated, 210 tank cars had to be found and corresponding railroad movement had to be provided. In all, it was estimated that 1,000,000 barrels a day would have to be moved overland by rail in the United States to keep the economy and war production at the required level of performance.

The success of the tank car industry in finding 20,000 tank cars for the earlier British emergency had not completely dispelled the government's skepticism about the willingness and ability of the private car lines to cooperate fully in the war effort. Secretary Ickes, in particular, believed that the tank car companies would resist any measure that interfered with their ordinary operation or that appeared to threaten their competitive position. It was one thing, he thought, for the companies to bring 20,000 old cars into service; no great credit could be claimed for that; the cars were there, after all. But now the government needed a great many more tank cars, which could be obtained only if oil companies and tank car companies joined in removing these cars from the regular service on which their profits were based. What did the industry plan to do about that?

Even before Pearl Harbor a committee of the American Petroleum Institute was created to deal with the problem, and Graves, as one of its members, had been asked to present his ideas. Working under great pressure, he submitted to the API a memorandum designed to serve as a proposal to the government from the oil industry. It was a far-reaching document. The oil-trucking industry, he pointed out, had made great recent advances in the quantity and quality of its equipment. Let movements of oil under 200 miles,[1] in which thousands of tank cars were engaged, be handled by trucks wherever possible, displacing tank cars. The latter could then be promptly diverted to long-haul emergency use. If, as seemed probable, this action would result in the capture by the trucking industry of an additional large share

[1] UTC NOTE: The original figure in Mr. Graves' memorandum was 100 miles. After consultation with government officials, it was revised to 200 miles.

of the petroleum transportation business, that could not be helped. The tank car industry would have to deal with its competitive problems as best it could when the emergency was over. Meanwhile, it recognized its obligations to the country. The plan was capable, Graves asserted, of making 50,000 more tank cars available for government service.

Not every oil company represented in the API committee was favorable to Graves' proposal. Some did not relish the problems which it threatened to create for them. No one had a better plan, however, and the memorandum went to the offices of the Petroleum Administration and Office of Defense Transportation for review.

Intrigue in High Places

At a later time the fact came to light that UTC in 1941 had begun to negotiate for the acquisition of substantial interests in the oil-trucking industry. Some observers drew the not-unnatural inference that the company's wartime policy was self-serving, that it sought to throw business to the trucking industry because it intended to profit thereby. The company, however, took the position that the move was calculated in the national not in the company's interest—that even with a trucking subsidiary UTC in the long run stood to lose far more than it stood to gain if short-haul transportation of oil left the rails and took to the roads. As matters turned out, the volume of business done over the years by the trucking subsidiary acquired at this time was minor as compared with the tank car operation, while profits from trucking were even less impressive. But in the atmosphere of the early 1940s any expansionist move made by UTC was bound to be suspect.

A further suspicion of an ulterior motive arose in the mind of Secretary Ickes and certain industrial groups interested in rushing to completion the great oil pipe line known as the Big Inch, then under construction. Since the Big Inch was bound to take away from the railroads a heavy tonnage of crude oil moving by rail from Texas to the Atlantic seaboard, some of its proponents assumed that the tank car companies would attempt to block the pipe line or slow its progress.

The rumor began to spread that Graves' proposal to the ODT

was an indirect attack on the Big Inch—that in proposing to find 50,000 more tank cars for crude-oil traffic he was trying to demonstrate that the pipe line was not urgently needed. Backers of the pipe line promptly rallied to what they believed to be its defense. Whether or not they actually attempted to undermine the ODT tank car program will always be a matter of surmise; but certain events made Graves incline to this view. At the height of the crisis he was disturbed to receive from some of UTC's customer companies a number of telegrams worded much alike and all requesting more tank cars for immediate use. It seemed to him that this unexpected wave of demand had been deliberately stimulated by the pipe line's advocates in order to prove that there was so great a shortage of tank cars in the domestic economy as to rule out any huge shift of cars, such as Graves had proposed, to the emergency crude-oil traffic.

To these suspect telegrams he replied with care, explaining that UTC could not comply with the new demands lest they interfere with the orderly procedure then being established by the government to meet the crude-oil emergency. Summoned to Washington to meet at dinner with officials of ODT concerned in the matter, he presented the essential facts. He did not oppose the pipe line but felt that emergency action could not be postponed until its completion; that the need was immediate, the tank cars were available, and that his program represented the shortest route to victory. When the men who had the power of decision supported him, the issue was closed. The tank car plan, much as Graves had outlined it, was announced by the ODT in May, 1942. Movements of petroleum tank cars were rigorously limited. No tank car could be used for a haul shorter than 200 miles without special permission.

For the Country—More or Less

The official tank car order as promulgated by the ODT required the cooperation of railroads, tank car companies, and oil companies. A huge equipment pool was to be established, into which every available tank car would be put regardless of ownership or contracts with shippers. Tank car trains would be assigned to runs as dictated by the nation's need and would be given priority by the railroads. All tank car routes would be determined by the railroads in cooperation with ODT, utilizing the most rapid and efficient movements. In view of the huge freight revenues involved the railroads agreed to cut their rates drastically. Similarly, recognizing the enormous mileages which their cars would run, the tank car companies consented to certain reductions in the mileage allowance for the duration of the emergency.

A new difficulty promptly arose over ODT's assumption of the right to dictate routes for all tank cars. This right had always been vested in the shipper, a point specified in UTC's contracts with customers. A voluntary concession by oil companies was thus essential in order to modify their tank car contracts and give support to the ODT emergency program. No oil company traffic manager contested the necessity of shifting from railroads to trucks for short hauls. But to give up the prerogative of routing was another matter. Their established custom was to assign their freight wherever possible to railroads which bought their company's products, or which provided some other direct benefit. This profitable practice was now suddenly threatened. Under the emergency system, with ODT and the railroads in charge of all tank car movements, reciprocity would have to go out of the window. Confronted with this threat to their sovereignty, the traffic managers of several oil companies resisted strongly. The government, they felt, was going too far; and a good deal of time and energy had to be spent in reminding them of their patriotic duty.

In one large company, which had been served by UTC for many years, a crisis arose. The traffic manager flatly refused to yield up his contractual right to dictate routes, and no argument budged him. Graves realized that he would have to appeal over the traffic manager's head to higher authority—a painful situation, since by so doing he might incur costly enmity for UTC. Pointing out that a matter of high policy was at stake, he suggested that the traffic manager accompany him and that together they put the problem before the company's president. This the official flatly refused to do; he preferred to stand on the contract.

Seeing no alternative, Graves went alone to the office of the oil company's president, who was a figure of consequence in American industry. It was a tense moment; if the president chose to support his traffic manager, or even hesitated to make a decision, his example, as interpreted by other oil companies, might gravely embarrass the ODT program and UTC's legal position, not to mention the Allied cause. As soon as he had grasped the facts, however, the president dispelled Graves' anxiety with a word. The oil company would, of course, cooperate fully with the government. From this moment there was no doubt in Graves' mind as to the success of the ODT program. Over the next few weeks the same response was forthcoming from every other UTC customer. A steady flow of tank cars, released from the service of the oil companies, passed under ODT control, until 50,000 more cars were available for the emergency.

Antiques and Makeshifts

Executives of other tank car companies had comparable experiences as they rallied to the support of the ODT program. All for a time were concerned over the possibility that the car-pooling arrangement might injure their regular business. Many customers were agitated at being told that none would be allowed to have a surplus of cars. A tank car company which firmly refused to yield to threats or blandishments from its lessees could not help wondering if perhaps one of its competitors might not secretly promise the extra cars that it had refused. The fear was the greater because it was not possible to keep the cars of any one tank car company exclusively in the service of its own customers. Under the accepted arrangement each company could bill any user of its cars, even though there was no contract between them. For practical purposes not only the cars but all tank car customers had been pooled for the duration of the emergency.

Long accustomed to think in the hard and often cynical terms of commercial advantage, it was natural for tank car men to expect that their rivals would plunge a knife into every chink in their armor. Each was prepared to see the others seduce his disgruntled customers away. It was not so. No instance was reported of a customer lost by any tank car lessor as a result of the pooling arrangement. Gradually the realization came home to the industry's executives that their competitors, like themselves, were able to resist temptation in time of national need.

Eighty-hour weeks of unremitting strain were for a time the norm among officials in the industry, as every tank car that could be repaired, no matter how rusty and dilapidated, was restored to service. Cars nearly fifty years old, long scheduled for the scrap heap, rumbled back onto the tracks. Others were hastily reassembled from dismembered parts. The industry even reverted to practices of the distant past in order to find cars. Kerosene was shipped in metal drums loaded into boxcars. The shades of the Densmore brothers were invoked when the Missouri Pacific Railroad fitted up flatcars with huge metal water tanks, in order to release 13 tank cars which had been in water-transport service. Even the compartmented boxcar reappeared. The antiques and the makeshifts, together with the working tank cars extracted from shippers, gradually brought the government's pool to 70,000 tank cars, for the hauling of which the railroads provided 1,500 locomotives, steam, diesel, and electric.

Zealous as they were to serve in the war effort, the tank car companies were also businesslike. They continued to require every shipper to pay a rental charge for each individual car in his service; for it would have been totally impractical in the middle of the war emergency to try to develop an efficient substitute system. For the same reason, the mileage allowance also was paid by the railroads as before, on a per car basis. In certain respects, however, UTC altered its practice. Wherever the length of haul was sufficient to provide a mileage allowance adequate to compensate the company, it waived charges for the use of its per diem cars. Established accounting procedure was also modified. The Mileage Equalization Rule, requiring that loaded and empty mileage be periodically balanced on individual railroads, could not apply under the pooling arrangement; so it was suspended, as it had been in World War I.

The All-out Effort

Once the tank cars had been found, the need was to hurry them to loading points, organize them into trains, speed them to their destinations, rush them empty back to loading points, and repeat the process day after day. By August 11, 1942, the railroads had worked out a plan of action which startled even themselves by its efficiency. It called for the bulk movement of oil in solid blocks of tank cars, each train traveling from a given loading point to a given destination. These were known as "symbol trains" from the fact that they were designated by code letters—"G" for loaded "going" trains, "R" for empty "returns"— and by numbers standing for the order of travel on a given route on a given day. Thus, the second loaded train traveling on October 9 over the route designated as 45 would become for all railroad men Train "2nd-45-G-9," and would be so reported from all points on the route.

More than 60 of these symbol trains were scheduled per day from the oil-producing regions to various ports on the Atlantic seaboard, each train comprising on the average about 60 tank cars. For example, a typical symbol train—101-G—running from Pine Bluffs, Arkansas (a concentration point), to Buffalo, New York, had to cover a distance of 1,133 track miles over three different railroad systems. Often traveling in two sections, it would make the run in sixty-seven hours, the movement being carried out as if only one road were involved. Previously such a run for a typical oil train would have taken more than twice as long. All switching en route was eliminated except when a tank car had to be cut out because of disability.

Making up the symbol trains was in itself a complicated problem. They originated at any one of eight concentration points in Texas, Oklahoma, Louisiana, Arkansas, and Missouri; but in order to assemble at the concentration points the tank cars had to carry their loads from any of 40 major loading stations in the oil fields or at the terminals of midwestern pipe lines. In addition, many tank cars were constantly coming in from more than 100 lesser loading points. Each day's inflow of tank cars to the concentration points had to be organized into the all-tank-car trains for the long haul east.

When a symbol oil train was on the tracks, movements of other trains on all of the railroads involved were regulated to avoid delay of the oil. Even passenger trains would be shunted aside for the oil express. The exact time required to move each train over the tracks of each railroad from point to point was calculated to a fine point, and schedules were set up accordingly. Troop trains were not supervised more closely. At every junction point where one railroad received a symbol train from another, it would arrange beforehand for such locomotives, inspectors, and crews as were needed, so that the train would not be held up.

The AAR's Tank Car Section established a record system enabling it to trace the movement of every symbol train almost minute by minute, by telegraphed or telephoned reports from points along the road. Any delay, due to whatever cause, instantly called corrective measures into play. If bad weather, power shortage, congestion at unloading points, or some other emergency threatened to hold up the train, it could be diverted while in transit to another destination where the oil was needed.

Thirty Drops a Minute

Given the dubious equipment which had been put into service, tank car disabilities were inevitably frequent. To save time the tank car companies agreed to forego their right to have the defective cars brought back to their own shops for repairs of consequence. It was arranged, instead, that such cars go into the nearest railroad shop and that the tank car companies would accept repair bills not exceeding $250 per car. This proved to be no small item. One railroad had to put more than 4,000 tank cars into its shops for overhaul in a single month.

It was essential to keep to a minimum time losses due to the cutting out of loaded tank cars, the transfer of their cargoes, and their repair. Yet everyone agreed that no tank car should be kept in a train if its troubles threatened to disrupt schedules or imperil safety. The latter point was especially troublesome, for there were countless instances of seepage from some of the old tanks that had been put into service. Old-timers could remember more than one tragic explosion that had been caused in past decades when gasoline dripping from defective tank cars had trickled into city streets, or caught fire in a train yard. Some railroad men felt that even slight seepage justified the "shopping" of a car. Others insisted that wartime needs justified keeping a car in service unless its troubles were manifestly dangerous. The question soon arose: at what point did a leak from a tank warrant a train crew in cutting out the car? It fell to the AAR's Mechanical Division, in cooperation with the tank car companies, to work out a rule-of-thumb answer. On the basis of evidence at hand they determined a critical point for a gasoline leak. Cars with small leaks yielding less than 30 drops per minute could be allowed to proceed to their destination without attention and would be repaired after unloading. If a car leaked more than 30 drops per minute, the leak should, if possible, be temporarily sealed while the car was in transit, possibly by rubbing yellow laundry soap into it or driving a chip of wood into the hole. If such homely measures did not suffice and the leak persisted at a rate of more than 30 drops per minute, then there was no help for it—the train had to be stopped, the car cut out, and its cargo transferred.

"A Revolution in Transportation"

Oil, in railroad parlance, had become "hot cargo." Fifty railroads had joined to provide 66 express routes for oil—which, as one traffic expert said, were "handling oil across the continent faster than they used to move perishable California grapefruit." One railroad, the Boston and Albany, reported that its freight of crude oil, which in 1939 had been 527 tons, was more than 1,500,000 tons in 1942. In all, 154,000 tank cars were on the rails. Shipments of oil from midwest to east rose at their peak to nearly 1,000,000 barrels per day. UTC's tank cars alone, in the first six months of 1943, moved 56,000,000 barrels of oil to the eastern seaboard from distant points. The tank car had always been the dirty drudge of transportation; now it was hailed as "the stopgap between the dark threat of disaster and ultimate victory." The railroads enlarged their yards, put on extra crews to help move "oil for the democratic way of life." Petroleum companies increased their facilities, provided round-the-clock service at loading and unloading points, sent out expediters to check cars in transit and supervise rapid repairs.

The result pleased even the curmudgeon Secretary Ickes. The extraordinary cooperation of the railroads, the tank car companies, and the petroleum companies with the responsible government agencies had resulted, he said, in a "revolution in transportation." A Senate committee investigating gasoline and fuel-oil shortages was similarly impressed; "a magnificent job," it termed the oil-transport performance. One fact had been made plain: the tank car had proved itself a pillar of national defense, and would be counted on in any forseeable national transportation emergency of the future.

Big Inch

Early in 1943, oil, railroad, and tank car men fixed their eyes on southern Illinois, where the world's largest and longest crude-oil pipe line, two feet in diameter, and known as the "Big Inch," was crawling steadily northward toward a town called Norris City, where rail terminal facilities awaited it. Eventually it would be extended to serve the New York and Philadelphia refineries, but the war effort could not wait for its completion. As the pipe line began to pump its Texas oil to Norris City, more than 10,000 tank cars were rushed into the region. At the peak of the movement, 39 symbol trains carried 300,000 barrels of oil every twenty-four hours from Norris City to the North Atlantic seaboard.

Now another problem was created for the tank car companies. The powerful locomotives provided by the railroads to haul oil from the Big Inch were designed for high-speed travel and could pull a long string of loaded tank cars at passenger express speeds. It was found by test that at speeds of more than 40 miles per hour a tank car's oil cargo, instead of sloshing horizontally, began to "dance" vertically up and down. Newer cars had been provided with snubbers to absorb the stresses resulting from the dancing of their oil, but a number of the antiques could not survive the unaccustomed strain and broke in two. The first few accidents of this kind startled the industry. Tank car shops set to work at an unprecedented pace to install snubbers in thousands of old cars which had been brought in for other repairs. Meanwhile, for safety's sake, an order was issued forbidding oil trains to travel at more than 40 miles per hour. Soon the difficulty was overcome, but it left a lasting impression, for it brought home to tank car executives that after nearly a century of experience there was still much that they had to learn about the technical side of their business.

With the completion of the Big Inch the need for tank cars for the run from Midwest to East fell sharply. By September, 1944, the hauls could be managed by a mere 43,000 of the 70,000 tank cars which had been provided for the purpose. Average daily oil-car loadings dropped from 4,400 to 2,400 in a few months. The remainder of the cars were diverted to use in other sections of the country or sent back to idleness or the scrap heap.

It had been a great achievement, in which the railroads and tank car companies could take legitimate pride; but they were not blind to its implications. Ruefully wrote the *Railroad Magazine* in July, 1943, "Besides the Big Inch, more than 1,500 miles of additional pipe lines are under construction or planned. All of this new development is helping to win the war. What it will do to tank car traffic afterward is something that no railroad men like to think about."

FOUR

A REMINDER FROM THE GOVERNMENT

A clear sign that the postwar position of the tank car in petroleum transportation would be increasingly threatened by the truck was the wartime order of the Office of Defense Transportation giving trucks an uncontested hold on oil hauls of under 200 miles. Entry into the trucking business, Graves was convinced, would strengthen UTC's defensive position, as a hedge against any future decline in the demand for tank cars. In addition there would be a gain in finding out at firsthand the inner problems and real potentialities of oil trucking, as a guide to possible improvements in UTC's customer service policies.

Drake agreed that it might be sound strategy to acquire one or more trucking firms. His motivation, however, differed somewhat from Graves'. Expansion through the acquisition of other companies did not in itself greatly interest Drake. Growth potential was not then so highly valued a factor in corporate thought as it was later to become; and Drake's almost Victorian abhorrence of debt made him uneasy about borrowing from banks even to assure future earnings. But at the time there was no need to borrow. UTC was continuing to generate sizable amounts of cash which, owing to wartime shortages of materials, could not be invested in tank cars. To put surplus funds into a going concern in a field close to the company's existing business made excellent sense to him, and he authorized Graves to proceed.

Late in 1940, an oportunity arose to buy stock in a moderately successful Detroit oil-trucking firm, Refiners' Transport and Terminal Corporation (RT&T). Over a period of thirty months UTC was able to accumulate a substantial majority of RT&T stock, 83 per cent, through private negotiation with former owners, at an average price slightly less than the book value of the shares. Drake and Graves recognized that RT&T's past average earnings represented only a modest return on the $1,300,000 paid for the stock. But it seemed reasonable to expect that UTC's resources, connections, and managerial experience would improve RT&T's prospects and make the investment a sound one.

The situation seemed especially hopeful since E. S. Turner, the president of RT&T, had a clearly defined plan for the expansion of the company. It was thought that capital made available by UTC would enable him to unite a substantial group of oil-trucking firms under the RT&T banner, and greatly multiply the scope and potential earnings of the company. This possibility had, in fact, been a major factor in arousing Graves' initial interest in RT&T. As he took the dominant place on the RT&T board of directors, he felt satisfaction in knowing that he had helped to bring UTC the first non-tank-car subsidiary in its history. His hope was that by keeping a fatherly eye on RT&T's management he could help assure the company's progress without disproportionate inroads on his time.

"We Would Like to Know..."

Although in 1942 the oil-trucking business, with its government-conferred monopoly of short-haul transportation, was doing well, RT&T's somewhat antiquated internal organization, service policies, and accounting practice were handicapping its progress; and rising costs of operation and keen competition from other truckers were cutting into earnings. It struck Graves that no time should be lost in putting Turner's plan of expansion into effect. Gains in efficiency could be made much more profitable if the scope of RT&T's operation was enlarged under strong unified management.

Graves discussed the problem with Drake. The response was instant and affirmative. Drake, his mind always on the constructive use of surplus cash, agreed that RT&T should act at once to acquire new trucking firms and combine them into a single large operating unit. With this encouragement, Graves authorized Turner to take action. Within a few weeks good progress had been made, as Turner opened negotiations to buy trucking firms in Massachusetts, Vermont, New York, Pennsylvania, West Virginia, and Florida, the subsequent contracts being subject to approval by the Interstate Commerce Commission. From the trucker's standpoint the eastern states then appeared to be a more promising field for expansion than the midwest.

Turner foresaw that this move would generate a certain amount of worry among competitors of the proposed new trucking combine. But their objections, he felt, could be fairly met. A letter written in November, 1942, gave his view of the matter: "It is not our policy to try in any way to eliminate competition.... There are not any overlapping interstate rights.... [We] feel that we should be considered as welcoming competition by competitors who operate efficiently...." But Turner recognized that protests by competitive truckers might cause the ICC to take a long look at the RT&T application to buy additional trucking properties. He wrote: "If this can be made a reality through controlling governmental agencies' approval, we would like to know as quickly as possible so that we may proceed...."

Campbell Is Cautious

UTC believed that it was entirely justified under the law in seeking through RT&T to protect itself against a possible decline in future tank car revenues resulting from strengthened trucking competition. Since it was only one of several private tank car lines and not even the largest, and since its proposed acquisitions in the trucking field represented only a small percentage of that industry, UTC's management had no reason to feel that it was in any way transgressing the antimonopoly laws. However, the question was put to Douglas Campbell in New York. Promptly a letter came back: in terms of legality the move might prove sound enough, but Campbell felt that its timing was inadvisable. Expansion into the trucking field, he thought, ought to take place only gradually and with due regard for the surrounding political and economic atmosphere. That atmosphere in 1942 was hardly favorable for such a venture. The national mood of antagonism toward bigness in business which had become prevalent in the early 1930s had not ended with the depression. Although UTC was comparatively a minor corporation, its customers included the mammoths of the petroleum industry. Ancient suspicions of its purposes could easily be revived.

A survey conducted by the public opinion expert, Elmo Roper, showed that in 1943 most Americans believed that Standard Oil was still a single company. Even otherwise well-informed businessmen, some in the oil industry, clung to the view that the policies of the separate Standard companies, UTC among them, were somehow dictated by a common authority. It was not surprising to find in government circles a residual feeling that wherever a unit of the old Trust was involved, the guard against monopolistic intent had to be doubled. A number of the ICC commissioners of the time, with their watchdog responsibilities, had a natural tendency to growl whenever UTC crossed their path. In a period of wartime excitement, when the public was being asked to remember national rather than private interests, a proposal by UTC to move strongly into the trucking field could easily be misunderstood.

After years of exemplary behavior and patriotic effort the company was perhaps more aware of its virtue than anyone else. Certainly it was less conscious of its vulnerability than was Douglas Campbell. Graves was somewhat taken aback by Campbell's negative counsel. It was a delicate moment for him. Although he had been the original proponent of the move, his respect for Campbell's judgment was unbounded, and he was inclined to abide by it. When he said as much to Drake, however, he encountered unexpected resistance. Lose a golden opportunity, after so much good spade work? In Drake's view, Campbell's caution was excessive.

RT&T thereafter made application to the ICC for the right to acquire ownership of selected trucking companies, which simultaneously sought permission to sell. The first hearing in Washington appeared to justify Drake's optimism. The responsible ICC examiner filed a report recommending that the requested permission be granted. By this time, however, several trucking firms competitive to those which RT&T proposed to buy had filed protests with the ICC. Their very existence, they alleged, would be threatened if UTC became the overlord of a large trucking combine operating in their territories.

As a result the ICC deemed it necessary to submit the matter for an opinion to the Department of Justice, where it had the personal attention of the assistant Attorney General, Thurman Arnold. Known for his strong defense of the competitive rights of small business, Arnold was unsympathetic to UTC's position. In a memorandum dated January 18, 1943, he expressed the view that UTC through its relations with railroads might so manipulate its trucking interests as to prevent true competition between "the two modes of transportation," and he advised the ICC to reject the RT&T application.

"The Real Party in Interest"

To Drake, Arnold's finding came as a shock. As he saw it the protesting truckers had set up a straw bogeyman. Did they really believe that UTC would be so reckless as to permit their trucking subsidiaries to try to drive competitors out of business and so give ground for new governmental attacks upon the parent company? To invite trouble of this kind would be total folly. Why, then, should the Attorney General attribute to the company a purpose which it did not have? How could he ignore the competitive realities of the oil-transportation industry? It was inconceivable to Drake that the government would base its decision on so biased a statement as he believed Arnold's to be. When Campbell again counseled that the issue be dropped, Drake persisted in rejecting the advice. "Full steam ahead and damn the torpedoes" was the essence of his response. He felt that to withdraw the RT&T application at this stage might lend credence to Arnold's opinion. Campbell's firm accordingly arranged a hearing on the application before the full commission of the ICC.

It fell to Edward Goodwin to appear for UTC before the commission, as he had done in the private car case fifteen years earlier. This time, although his style left nothing to be desired, he found most of the commissioners firmly against the company. Their report, issued in August, 1943, rejected the application. The decision was not, however, grounded in Arnold's memorandum. Although one of the ICC commissioners thought Arnold right, and expressed the fear that "the proposed transaction is

the beginning of an effort to obtain monopolistic control...
contrary to public interest," the others did not subscribe to this
view. Instead, they emphasized a technical point. RT&T, said
the commission, could not properly act alone in applying for
the right to purchase additional trucking companies. The application would have to be signed also by "the real party in interest,
the controlling corporation, Union." UTC, if it chose, would be
provided with an opportunity "to file an appropriate application."

The implications of this offer were clear for all concerned, and
the company and its counsel united in rejecting the invitation.
Why, merely in order to enlarge an interest which was after all
secondary, should they imperil the company's prized freedom
from government regulation—freedom which the ICC itself had
conferred in 1918, when it ruled that private tank car companies
were not common carriers? If the ICC should obtain jurisdiction
over one aspect of UTC's business, might it not seek to extend
that jurisdiction to other aspects, especially to tank cars?

The Government's Watchful Eye

Even after the adverse ICC ruling Drake continued to insist
that UTC's position was legally right, that the government was
out of bounds in turning down the RT&T application. No one,
he felt, could properly ignore the real intent of the application,
which was not to seek monopoly but to strengthen UTC's future
defensive position against a worsening competitive situation. For
the government to use the RT&T application as a lever for imposing government regulation on UTC struck him as unreasonable. Let the matter be pressed in the courts, Drake told Goodwin;
and in September, 1943, suit was filed in the U.S. District Court
at Baltimore, contesting the legality of the ICC decision.

A month later Drake thought that his judgment had been vindicated. After hearing arguments on both sides the District Court
had filed an opinion reinstating the RT&T application before the
ICC. But the sense of triumph was premature. It was still the
ICC's conviction that whether or not the charge of monopolistic
intent could be sustained UTC was obliged, in the public interest,
to come forward as the prime mover behind the application and
to sign it. Holding to this point, the government's lawyers appealed the case to the U.S. Supreme Court.

Time passed, a hearing was held, the Court deliberated. Finally in April, 1944, Chief Justice Harlan Stone announced the decision. With a single justice, Owen Roberts, dissenting, the Court upheld the ICC decision. If UTC wanted RT&T to acquire the proposed properties, it would have to join in the application to the ICC.

There was nothing more to be done, and Drake in disgust turned his back on the matter. It fell to Graves to tell RT&T to drop negotiations for the purchase of other trucking companies. Even though he had not been wholly at one with Drake's strategy, it was a mortifying moment for him. The company had suffered a defeat, and he was not a man to take defeat lightly.

The war had hardly ended when Graves was reminded once again of UTC's need to tread carefully where public opinion and politics were concerned. Congressional committees were then hunting on all sides for evidence of malfeasance or turpitude in industry's relations with the wartime administration. Some congressmen, recalling the great trust-baiting days gone by, were inclined to revive the popular sport, if they could find a living example of the species. Inevitably the Standard companies and UTC came in for a share of attention. Late in 1945 Graves was summoned to testify before a congressional committee seeking ways to assist small business. At the Washington hearing he found himself subjected to questioning reminiscent in some ways of the days of Howard Page and Henry Felton. Counsel for the committee appeared to believe that UTC still operated only for the benefit of the Standard companies and would not permit others to use its cars. The charge was an interesting illustration of the persistence of a widely publicized belief long after the grounds for it had been removed. Quietly Graves pointed out that over the previous twenty years many refiners, large and small, who were in open competition with one or another Standard company, had become and remained UTC customers, satisfied that they were being conscientiously served and their confidence fully respected. Small customers and large alike received equal treatment.

Although some of the committee's members may have been chagrined at losing the chance of a headline-making probe, the committee as a whole rose to the occasion and expressed itself satisfied, its doubt allayed. Counsel had no further questions, and Graves departed with the chairman's thanks. His mood as he left the hearing was compounded in equal proportions of grimness and satisfaction.[1]

Faced with an obscure outlook for the postwar period, UTC's executives were not disposed to worry. UTC's financial position was excellent. The dividend was well protected. To be sure, in terms of growth potential the company had little attraction for new investors. But then it did not particularly want new investors. Why not admit that the days of big achievement were past? Considering the competitive difficulties ahead, if the company merely succeeded in holding its own, that would be a kind of triumph. Such was the general attitude in UTC's office at the war's end.

---

[1] Another indication that the government's watchful eye was still on the tank car came a few months later, when the ICC raised the knotty problem of "switching." See Appendix G.

FIVE

WITH A LITTLE BIT OF LUCK

Graves would not have been human if he had not been troubled by the knowledge that at the beginning of 1947 he was over sixty—and not yet president of UTC. It was perhaps some consolation that since 1944 he had held the rank of executive vice-president; that for more than a decade his authority as the active center of the company had been tacitly acknowledged by everyone around him; and that his salary was not much below the presidential level. But Drake had passed the age of sixty-five without giving any hint of retirement. There was no reason to think that he would choose to retire in the near future. So far as Graves could tell, he might be compelled to remain in a subordinate relationship to Drake until he himself was near retirement. In the past Drake had tried to offset Graves' growing power by encouraging the presidential ambitions of A. E. Smith, of the Mechanical Department. Smith had now retired, but there was always danger that Drake would seek to bring some new henchman into the company and put him in line for the presidential succession.

How Many Cars?

Much more than personal ambition was involved. Without the powers of the presidency Graves could not be free to establish new policies as his own judgment and intuition dictated. For example, he differed with Drake on the question of an economically sound size for UTC's tank car fleet. The time-honored policy of the company was to maintain the fleet at a level which would permit the company to meet the peak demand of its customers. In the 1920s the popularity of the oil burner for heating had definitely established the peak in winter. The crucial decisions—how many old cars to retire and new cars to build?— rested largely on estimates made by the oil companies as to their peak requirements for the coming winter.

In 1946, many economists of the petroleum industry were unenthusiastic in their business forecasts and estimates of next year's demand for tank cars. Drake, whose natural tendency was always to preserve a maximum cash surplus while keeping new capital investment and outlay for maintenance at a minimum, was glad to accept these estimates at their face value. The time had come, he held, to remove UTC's older cars from service. Depreciation and tax calculations led to the same conclusion. Ready for dismantling were many so-called Z-cars, acquired through purchase of shipper-owned fleets in the 1930s, and which had proved considerably less sturdy and more costly to maintain than cars built to UTC's specifications; and also a number of Van Dyke's old V-cars, which had been resurrected for wartime service.

Although Graves had always urged replacement of old cars whenever possible, he had been consistently cautious about dismantling without replacement. Even at the worst of the depression, when thousands of old cars had been earmarked for the scrap heap, he had insisted on holding some of them intact in "dismantling suspense"—a policy which had proved its value when the war came. In his view some surplus of cars, even if kept at the expense of increased maintenance costs, was good insurance. Demand could change at any time, and it would be difficult to obtain new cars in quantity during the postwar reconversion period, with its shortages of materials and manpower. Graves was also concerned over the psychological effect of excessive dismantlings on UTC's customers. Sophisticated oil men, regarding UTC's aging and diminishing fleet, might read into it a sign of an aging and diminishing company. These were some of the considerations which made him nervous about the scope of Drake's dismantling program in 1946–1947.

In view of the oil industry's forecasts, however, Graves had insufficient ammunition to oppose Drake vigorously on the issue.

Misgivings or no misgivings, he instructed the Mechanical Department to scrap thousands of Z- and V-cars. By the end of 1946, the fleet had been reduced to 34,000 cars from the wartime peak of 39,000.

The Moment Comes

It was in situations of this kind that Graves most keenly felt the limitations of his position. He had learned to value his intuition as a factor in policy making and was uneasy when he had to suppress it. Conservative himself in financial policy, he was yet alarmed by what he considered Drake's cash-mindedness, which he thought tended to sacrifice UTC's future competitive position to immediate financial considerations.

This was by no means the only issue on which they stood opposed. Another was introduced by the Internal Revenue Bureau. From the moment of his advent in the company a major factor in Drake's handling of UTC's earnings statements had been a high rate of depreciation on its tank cars. Large amounts of depreciation deducted from gross earnings resulted in lower net income as shown on the annual earnings statements, but this did not bother Drake, for it meant that the government's take was also lower. He was perfectly willing to defer present earnings to the future if by so doing he could keep present taxes to a minimum— the policy of many American corporations. It was therefore his constant effort to keep the depreciation rate as high as possible. In 1927, he had begun by asserting that the average tank car lasted only sixteen years, and over the years only grudgingly had compromised with the Internal Revenue Bureau at progressively higher figures.

The year 1947 found the government pressing for yet another revision of the life-expectancy figure, this time to thirty-five years, indicating a drop in the depreciation rate to below 3 per cent. Drake's first reaction was that he would go to court and fight to the last ditch rather than accept such a ruling. Here, however, he ran into opposition from Graves, who held that the thirty-five years' figure was realistic and ought to be accepted. The depreciation rate, Graves maintained, should be determined strictly in terms of the facts of experience. There were statistics to show that thirty-five years was a fair approximation of the average tank car's life; and it would be unwise for the company to contest the issue.

Both men had strong wills, and their disagreement over the size of the fleet, depreciation, and other matters soon began to brew a crisis. Drake would have liked to see Graves resign; Graves had no doubt that the time had come for Drake to step down from the presidency, or at least allow himself to be kicked upstairs to a position where he could enjoy prestige without exercising power.

In the upshot Drake decided to avoid an open test of strength. How he arrived at this decision he confided to no one, but in the summer of 1947 he unexpectedly cleared the air. The subsequent transfer of authority was carried out with due regard for his dignity. That autumn he was elected chairman of the board of directors, a post unfilled since Felton's day. Graves became president and chief executive officer. The moment toward which he had been working for forty years had come at last.

The change in authority ended the internal argument over the depreciation rate. The government's position was no longer contested, and the lowered rate, based on a thirty-five-year life expectancy, went into effect. Thereafter a higher proportion of the company's annual gross revenue became immediate net income on its earnings statements. At the same time the immediate "tax bite" became larger than ever before in the company's peace-time history.

Too Much Business

Graves liked action, and he was to get it. Within a few months after he became president, his earlier doubts about reducing the size of the tank car fleet turned into certainty. The winter of 1947–1948 arrived early and with a frigid insistence that startled the oil industry. By December, 1947, a critical fuel shortage was at hand. Several states, in an effort to prevent panic, appointed conservators, whose task it was to prevent the waste or hoarding of fuel stocks. Conditions in the northern states, especially in the Midwest, soon became so alarming that the Federal government had to intervene, reviving the wartime mechanism for the emergency routing of oil trains to the stricken regions.

Once again the tank car was in the forefront of the national consciousness. Heating oil and liquid petroleum gas were in such demand that shipments had to be made from many producing areas to far-distant markets which they could not ordinarily serve. At the peak of the demand small refineries close to the Mexican border found themselves routing tank cars to frozen towns on the Canadian border, regardless of the cost of transportation.

The demand caught UTC and, it would appear, competitive companies unprepared.[1] Oil companies cooperated by releasing for emergency use thousands of tank cars employed in their normal business, but it was physically impossible to provide the number of cars wanted. Refineries which had never before used UTC's services and which now offered to sign contracts had to be regretfully refused, lest the diversion of even a few tank cars from scheduled hauls impair service to established customers.

The FBI Investigates

The problem was complicated by the increasing demand for special-purpose cars, notably pressure cars used for the transportation of liquid petroleum gas. The search for more LPG cars, as they were known in the trade, led Graves to Washington. He knew from his wartime experience that the government had underwritten the construction of hundreds of such cars for the use of the new synthetic-rubber industry.[2] It occurred to Graves that if the government's LPG cars had become surplus property after the war they might be purchasable in far less time and for far less money than it would take to build them.

[1] UTC NOTE: It would be more correct to say that the demand caught the petroleum industry unprepared. The tank car problem in the winter of 1947–1948 was due to miscalculation on the part of the refiners, who had failed to forecast their tank car requirements accurately. The severity of the winter, taking them by surprise, resulted in a shortage of fuel oil at the regular points of shipment. Rail movements had to be greatly lengthened in order to bring oil to the distressed areas. The tank car industry responded promptly to the need and met its responsibility to the full, cooperating with the oil companies to alter established distribution patterns, diverting cars from the usual sources of supply to any point where oil stocks were to be found.

[2] These were domeless cars of 11,000-gallon capacity, built to sustain bursting pressures of 750 pounds per square inch, more than three times that of the general-service cars. With fusion-welded tanks made of exceptionally thick steel plate and specially designed safety valves they were costly to produce.

Inquiry revealed that he was on the right track. A hurried trip to the responsible government agency in Washington resulted in agreement on price, and the purchase was effected. Graves was especially pleased because he had reason to believe that some of UTC's competitors were hot on the same trail. Possibly it was their disappointment that led to the sequel. The former government cars had not long been in UTC's service when an agent of the Federal Bureau of Investigation called on Graves in Chicago to inquire into the details of the transaction. The Surplus Property Administration, it appeared, had become the target of a sweeping congressional investigation.

Since Graves had kept a careful record of the negotiation, the facts were easily ascertained. Letters, memoranda, and financial records told the story. The subsequent FBI report was a source of satisfaction. UTC had at every point of its dealings in the matter abided by the law and the principles of ethical business. But if Graves had ever been inclined to forget the complexity of the company's relations with government and its competition, this episode would have served to remind him. There would always be some to view with suspicion any move made by UTC. The sins of the fathers were being remembered unto the third generation.

The government's surplus cars eased the strain on UTC slightly, but only slightly. The need was for more cars and more, and pressure from customers kept the company in a state of continuous agitation.

Snares and Wily Birds

Perhaps the most awkward fact in the company's situation was that it had to order its new cars from competitors who were enlarging their own fleets. Under the circumstances UTC could hardly expect to be given priority for its orders, or low prices for such cars as were produced for its account. The problem was brought to a head when an urgent request came from a high executive of one of the country's large oil companies for scores of additional LPG cars. These became part of an order for 1,000 LPG cars which UTC placed with one of its competitors, the cars to be distributed among its customers as delivered. The supplying company, however, was somewhat vague about the date of delivery. It would do the best it could, it told Graves, but he had to remember that the shortage of steel still set the pace of production.

It was an excuse difficult to contest. Graves, in turn, asked his customer for patience, but patience is not a quality for which oil men, faced with the need to move their products, have ever been noted. The oil company executive refused to accept the steel shortage as a valid reason for delay.

No customer in UTC's long history had ever been lost to a competitor, but the possibility that this comfortable tradition was about to be broken could not be shrugged off. The strain had become acute when Graves awoke one morning with a fresh thought, which he promptly put into action. Telephoning the customer, he suggested that the oil company order its tank cars directly from the same builder who held UTC's order.

The customer was startled; was he being invited to take his business elsewhere? Graves, however, had no such intention. It was simply his hope, he said, that the customer in this way would get his LPG cars more quickly. This assurance was accepted, and the oil company placed its separate order forthwith with UTC's car builder, and added an urgent request for speed in production.

The oil executive may not have grasped the subtlety of Graves' maneuver, but the car builder did. It was clear to him that if he took the bait being dangled before him—the hope of getting the oil company's tank car leasing business away from UTC—and if he thereupon completed the oil company's order before that of UTC, he would be open to a serious claim for damages by UTC. The bird in this instance was too wise to enter the snare. Instead, the builder informed the oil company that it could not expect to get its cars until prior orders placed by UTC had been completed; and that the steel shortage was delaying completion of all orders. Since this was precisely what Graves had been telling his customer, UTC stood vindicated. The oil company then canceled its own order for the cars and resignedly waited to be supplied by UTC as the new cars were delivered.

In the course of the prolonged exchange Graves had caught an implication on the part of the oil company that he did not like: that UTC, by remaining at the mercy of competitors in respect of new car production, was failing in its responsibilities to its customers. It was a charge not easy to evade and which, if it were to gain circulation in the industry, might be highly injurious. Graves was led to the conviction that with another surge of car building ahead UTC could no longer afford to depend on its former suppliers for new equipment.

The Spirit of Independence

His feelings about the need for independence were intensified by the fact that the American Car and Foundry Company, UTC's chief supplier of new tank cars, had many years earlier purchased a fast-growing tank car subsidiary of its own, Shippers' Car Line Corporation. This development further complicated UTC's problem of car supply. GAT and ACF then had the only facilities in the country capable of producing tank cars in large quantity, and now both were lessors as well as builders. Thus the company was in a position where it could not place a substantial order for new cars without contributing to the coffers of one or the other of its chief competitors—and also to their engineering know-how, since UTC's innovations in car design automatically became available in all their detail to the car builder.

Even this was not the full extent of the difficulty. If competitors could determine the period required for construction on UTC's new cars and their cost, they could also materially affect UTC's sales. Graves in 1947 was taken aback by the prices he was compelled to pay and even more by the time required for delivery of car orders placed. One or two curious incidents caused a suspicion—perhaps unfair—to grow in his mind that when it became known that UTC was about to place an order a similar order was hurriedly placed by the builder's car-leasing subsidiary, and predated to give it the appearance of priority. In this way—so it seemed to Graves—the competitor was providing himself with a legal excuse for deferring production of UTC's cars and hampering the company in its customer relations. He made this blunt accusation in a face-to-face interview with an executive of the car-building company, and an earnest denial did not content him.

A Matter of 1 Per Cent

The unpleasant thought was inescapable that UTC had become a captive of the car builders. Its chances of future expansion would be materially narrowed if its ability to supply customers with tank cars at acceptable prices was to be governed by its rivals. Early in 1948 he discussed the matter with Charles Hardy, the president of ACF, with whom most of UTC's new car orders had then been placed. Hardy tried to be reassuring. ACF, he told Graves, wanted UTC's new car orders, which were much larger than those placed by its own subsidiary, Shippers', and would stand by its contracts at every point. But Graves was troubled by the fact that Hardy, a lawyer by profession, seemed to view the problem in a legalistic light. (Nor did it soften him when Hardy, making a display of friendship, persisted in calling him "Clint" instead of Cliff.)

The time had come, Graves was convinced, to free UTC from its dependence on competitors, regardless of their fairness. Could he gain a voice in determining the delivery dates and prices set by ACF? A promising idea occurred to him. Why should not UTC and ACF unite in joint ownership of a separate corporation, which would buy ACF's tank car-building facilities and thereafter provide cars for both UTC and Shippers' Car Line, without discrimination of favor?

The more he thought about it, the sounder this conception seemed to him; and on the day when he first presented his idea to Charles Hardy he came back to his office with, he thought, reason for encouragement. The next step was to make a study of the car-building operations of the two companies, evaluate and appraise the tank car shops to be acquired, and outline the structure of the new corporation. Graves prepared a plan that satisfied him and submitted it to Hardy.

His proposal was calculated to win agreement on every point except perhaps one, but that one was crucial. As he saw the matter UTC was entitled to own 51 per cent of the stock, for it would certainly provide the new company with much more car-building business than would be available from the smaller Shippers'. To this end UTC stood ready to put up 51 per cent of the new corporation's capital, in cash at 100 cents on the dollar. The argument did not, however, overcome Hardy's dislike for being a minority stockholder even by 1 per cent in a business venture dominated by a competitor. He asked for time to think about the matter. Although neither he nor Graves was willing to yield

on the point of control of the new company, they kept the ball
of negotiation in the air, while weeks stretched into months.

Stalling for Time

Hardy, it occurred to Graves, might be sitting tight because
he believed that UTC was bluffing and had nowhere else to go.
It was true that at the outset Graves' hand in the poker game
had been poor, but he had been studying to improve it. The
question was: in the event that the deal with ACF fell through,
could UTC obtain cars from sources other than its competitors?
For the company to set up its own tank-fabricating facilities was
out of the question. Demand for tank cars was not continuous; it
was cyclical. From time to time, as the oil economy entered a
new period of expansion, customers would ask for more cars
by the thousands, but in the interval UTC might go for three
or four years without needing to expand its fleet. Tank manufacture could be profitable only if it were part of a more general
plate-fabricating business with a dependable market for other
products.

Was it not possible, however, that the company could purchase tanks and structural parts for underframes and assemble
them itself? He discussed the matter with Ray Smith,[3] who had
replaced A. E. Smith [3] as head of the Mechanical Department,
and found encouragement. Smith had no doubt that UTC's shops
at Philadelphia and Whiting, Indiana, could be enlarged to permit
assembly of cars. Parts for underframes could be obtained from
steel companies. The big uncertainty was the tank. If tanks could
be obtained promptly and at fair prices from steel-plate fabricators not connected with UTC's competitors, there was every
reason to believe that UTC could put its cars together at substantial savings.

This was hopeful, but Graves was too cautious to force a
showdown with Hardy on the basis of hope alone. He asked
Ray Smith to pretest the operation, especially the procurement
of tanks. A trial run made at Whiting with tanks obtained from
an independent fabricator proved discouraging. Tank deliveries
were so slow and tank prices so high that by comparison the old
relationship with ACF looked attractive.

[3] They were not related.

UTC Draws a Full House

For a time it seemed that Graves would have to accept ACF's terms if UTC expected to get tank cars. But Graves had one more card to draw before he could gauge the power of his hand. From time to time he had dealt with a firm the name of which was not much different from his own—The Graver Tank & Manufacturing Company, one of the country's old and important plate fabricators. Among Graver's more important activities was the construction of petroleum storage tanks and pressure vessels for refineries; but it had never been a large producer of tanks for tank cars. It seemed to Graves that with intelligent planning UTC's interests and Graver's might be made to coincide.

Early in 1949 he sought out Graver's president, E. N. Gosselin, and put a proposition to him. Given reasonable guarantees, would Graver agree to produce tanks for UTC? Gosselin saw no reason to hesitate. Assured of an amount of business that would justify the necessary investment in additional facilities, he said Graver could organize to produce any welded tank that UTC wanted, including the all-important pressure tank for LPG cars.

The remaining problem was that of cost. When Gosselin found it difficult to estimate accurately the cost of producing the large quantity and variety of tanks wanted by UTC, it occurred to Graves to tell him of his gentleman's agreement with Reeser of the Barnsdall company fifteen years before. If their negotiation should result in a contract, let the same principle apply. "Quote me fairly from your knowledge," said Graves. "If you have quoted too low, I shall make you whole. If you quote me too high, I shall expect a refund from you." Gosselin agreed.

When Graver's initial quotation proved to be less per tank than UTC had been paying, Graves felt reassured.

With a Flourish

Now, for the first time, he was able to present an ultimatum to Hardy, setting a deadline beyond which there would be no further negotiation between UTC and ACF for the proposed jointly-owned corporation. Hardy apparently had no inkling that Graves was prepared to go ahead without ACF. When he continued to stand pat the project was dropped, and UTC made its commitment to Graver.

The operation proceeded more smoothly than Graves had dared hope. Tank deliveries by Graver were on schedule; so were deliveries of underframe parts by steel companies; the Whiting assembly plant was operating with reasonable efficiency; and final costs per tank car represented a distinct saving as compared with the past. His pleasure increased when some months later Gosselin came into his office and with a flourish dropped a check for $50,000 on his desk. It was precisely the kind of gesture that appealed to Graves. Gosselin explained: the initial billing by Graver had been on the basis of rough figures, before cost estimates had been completed; the check represented a subsequent readjustment after actual cost figures were in. In effect the contract had been put on a cost-plus basis, with any unforeseen excess in Graver's profit voluntarily returned to UTC.

Subsequent payments of this nature brought the total of Graver's refunds to nearly $500,000. In the years following 1949 the tie between the two companies became very strong. UTC's savings in tank car costs ran into millions of dollars, while Graver profited handsomely. It occurred to Graves more than once that Graver seemed to have become increasingly dependent on UTC's orders, to the weakening of its enterprise in other areas of plate fabrication; but this, after all, was to UTC's advantage, and he saw no reason to meddle with someone else's business.

As the decade approached its end, UTC's earnings were good, its dividend was steady; and yet Graves was fully aware that the company had made comparatively little real progress since its great period of growth between 1915 and 1925. The peak earnings of the 1940s were no greater than those of the 1920s if one considered the intervening depreciation of the dollar. Graves himself had become philosophical about the company's future, had begun to accommodate himself to life on a business plateau. If he occasionally glanced longingly at the distant hills and wished that the company had dared a little more in the years past, he did not dwell on such useless regrets. As the decade of the 1950s began, the words of Lewis Carroll's Red Queen—"It takes all the running you can do to keep in the same place"—summed up UTC's prospects so far as the rational eye could see.

SIX

CHEMICAL REACTION

With the outbreak of the Korean War in June, 1950, the company found itself confronted by a new problem. Cross-country tank car traffic rose sharply in order to fill West Coast oil stocks depleted by trans-Pacific shipments for the armed services. Alarmed by the threat of a bottleneck, the government urged railroads and tank car companies to increase the size of their car fleets. As far as petroleum cars and LPG cars were concerned, UTC was ready to cooperate to the full; its fleet had, in fact, been steadily expanding since the 1949 arrangement with Graver for tanks.

There was one area of expansion, however, in which UTC hesitated to commit itself. In 1951, with the Korean War at its height, the government's Defense Transport Administration was deeply concerned about the need for tank cars for the rail transportation of chemicals. A DTA report, published in April of that year, "The Tank Car Story," stressed the serious shortage of cars for "special chemicals whose production has been increased faster than cars for their transportation can be built." The chemical industry was praised for its cooperation and efficiency in the use of its tank cars; but, said DTA, "if a critical shortage ... is to be averted, it is imperative that the tank car manufacturers produce the maximum number of cars.... Reporting companies indicate a need for 4,461 additional tank cars [over and above several thousand already under construction] ... and it is possible that the number ... may be increased."

In these factual statements DTA put the tank car industry on notice that it was expected to invest without delay scores of additional millions in modern tank cars especially designed to carry a wide variety of chemicals. At stake was the efficiency of the chemical industry, with its crucial role in the nation's military program.

With a Shaking of Heads

In UTC the government's prodding created a certain amount of discomfort. The company was reluctant to build chemical cars. In a sense, it was already in the chemical field, since it owned many cars which if need be could be adapted for the transportation of chemicals, including thousands of costly pressure cars, which carried liquid petroleum gas for oil companies served by UTC. Special linings and coatings permitted tank cars to carry substances other than oil products without corrosion of the tank or contamination of its contents. To this extent, the company could properly say that it had met and would continue to meet requests from customers for chemical cars. But in fact, where the chemical industry was concerned, UTC had never offered much of a challenge to its larger competitors. It felt that the time had passed to become a major contender for chemical business, that the large financial outlay required could not be economically justified.

The question had to be considered, too, whether the government's impressive forecast of future tank car requirements was dependable. Suppose the apparent need for thousands of additional chemical tank cars were to disappear before UTC could produce them? And even if the demand persisted for a time, was that enough to warrant UTC in going ahead? In the last board meetings that Drake attended in 1951, prior to his retirement, he pursed his lips over the financial data presented to him on the subject and counseled against any important construction program for chemical cars.

As a former consultant to the ODT, Graves was sensitive to the government's concern; and he believed that the company's earnings might be improved by getting some additional chemical tank car business. But he, too, was inclined to make caution his watchword. His chief fear was that by building chemical cars in quantity the company might create a surplus of such cars in the industry, leading to a competitive price war. It was, he felt, important to make sure that the new cars would not displace cars already built, that the demand would be sustained, and that their construction could be financed at low cost.

Painless Compromise

A gradual entry into chemical transportation was the right solution, in Graves' opinion. This was also the view of executives of the Car Service Department, especially since the chemical business differed greatly in its service requirements from the familiar patterns of the oil industry. Ranking executives of the Mechanical Department were concerned over the ability of their staff to cope with the new problems which would be involved. Their experience had been almost entirely confined to the production of more or less traditional cars for the petroleum industry. These were produced in quantity to familiar specifications. Once the prototype had been built and approved, once the Graver plant was producing tanks at the requisite speed, it was a comparatively simple matter to push a few hundred petroleum cars through the assembly procedure at the Whiting and Philadelphia shops.

The chemical cars posed a very different problem. Tank cars for specific chemical products and for individual shippers varied widely in specifications. The range of interior linings, claddings, and coatings—rubber, plastics, nickel, and other metals—went far beyond UTC's previous experience; and the company employed no chemical engineers. The use of new materials, such as aluminum and stainless steel, was a complicating factor. Other variations occurred in tank capacities, in types of valves, in color of paint, and in the insignia of customer companies. What would be the result if the Whiting shop, for example, were confronted with the need to produce not one type of car at a time, but perhaps 25 or 30 types, differing in design, capacity, linings, valves, construction details, and paint jobs? The thought daunted the stoutest hearts among UTC's engineering heads.

No one flatly said that the job could not be done. It was simply that in the view of the responsible executives the company's relative inexperience in construction and repair of chemical cars threatened to put manufacturing and maintenance costs at a prohibitive figure. Engineering manpower and production facilities would have to be sharply expanded.

The first result of UTC's internal debate on the subject was a painless compromise. The Mechanical Department was instructed to emphasize production of new cars, and in order to stimulate progress in this direction Graves in 1951 brought into the company one of the industry's most experienced designers of special-purpose cars, Clyde Folmsbee. Beyond these moves, however, he did not think it necessary or expedient to go. No effort was made to solicit chemical business. In 1951–1952 ownership of a major fleet of tank cars for the chemical industry appeared to most men in UTC as not much more than a pleasant dream. Between the dream and its fulfillment stood the habit patterns of two generations.

Squeeze from Three Sides

Chemical cars or no chemical cars, the fact remained that something had to be done to increase revenue. UTC was caught in a triple squeeze: competition, taxes, costs. Truck transportation in all fields was experiencing a sensational boom. Ever since the end of the war the inroads of truckers into short-haul oil transportation had realized Graves' worst fears. Water-borne transport of oil was similarly undergoing an unprecedented rise. At the same time taxes—federal, state, local—were steadily climbing. Even more serious, the cost of equipment and its maintenance had soared. By the early 1950s 1,000 new cars of the kinds most in demand required the investment of at least $10,000,000.

Not that the demand for UTC's tank cars had declined. The difficulty arose not so much in keeping the cars busy as in earning a satisfactory profit on them. Other businesses, similarly faced with high costs and high taxes, had raised their own prices. Graves, however, was inhibited in this respect. While recognizing that tank car rentals were only a small fraction of the cost of the rail movement of oil as compared with freight rates, nevertheless it was his contention that any substantial rise in rental charges would open the door to sharper competition from other modes of transportation, and especially from trucks. His experience as a director of Refiners' Transport had convinced him that representatives of trucking companies made a practice of emphasizing the cost of tank car rentals when soliciting business from shippers, and that for UTC to raise prices would be to lose business. "Keep rental rates down, build up the use of cars" was his reiterated theme in UTC's policy meetings. No one opposed him.[1]

The company's financial position was aided, if only temporarily, by an Act of Congress relating to depreciation of certain kinds of new equipment. To encourage new capital investment related to the Korean emergency the Department of Defense joined with other interested government agencies in working out a plan to permit selected industries to write off such investment rapidly for tax purposes, as had been done during World War II. The heart of this plan was the issuance of so-called Necessity Certificates, authorizing companies that were putting out capital for new equipment serving the national interest to apply a higher rate of depreciation to such equipment for tax purposes. The certificates granted to UTC made it possible to write off in five years 70 per cent to 85 per cent of the value of the new cars built under the government's program. Since higher depreciation meant lower immediate taxes, it made more cash available for current use. In this way the Necessity Certificates, together with bank loans, permitted new additions to the tank car fleet.

With oil refiners able to use all the equipment they could get, the enlarged number of cars soon had a favorable effect on earnings. Net income in 1952 stood close to that of 1947, a peak year. If the company's future seemed limited, at least it was holding its own.

Everything Was Satisfactory

The atmosphere of UTC's executive offices in 1952 was that of a sailing ship which has had a long and difficult crossing, weathered many a storm, and anchored at last in a snug harbor. UTC's officers and crew felt that they had earned the right to bask, together with many another serene American corporation,

[1] See Appendix H.

in the rising sun of national prosperity. The company saw no need to assume more responsibility than it already had. After all, President-elect Eisenhower had promised an early end to the Korean War. Pressure from the government for more tank cars could be expected to lessen. Given time, other tank car companies already serving the chemical industry on a large scale would be able to meet its full requirements.

Why venture back into choppy waters and the cold winds of competition? The company was doing well, still growing, even if not spectacularly. Between 1950 and 1952 it had acquired 3,000 more tank cars. Many of these were pressure cars, which had come to constitute almost 16 per cent of UTC's rolling stock. At a total of 45,000 cars, in 1952 the fleet was numerically not much smaller than that of GAT. The company's 300 corporate customers were satisfied with the service that they were getting, as were its stockholders with their dividends. Income was good. In 1950, total revenue had been $18,600,000; two years later it stood at $25,300,000. Annual net income, more than $4,300,000 in 1952, meant that more than $1,500,000 could be retained in the business after the regular dividend had been paid. Under these agreeable conditions, the company felt no urge to explore new worlds.

Graves at this period believed that UTC's best hope of expansion lay in additional purchases of shipper-owned fleets. There was nothing to deter him from an effort in this direction. No responsible person in the oil industry worried any longer about UTC's ancient tie to Standard. Perhaps now and then an oil man playing a game of golf with a UTC executive might revive the old canard, "You Standard fellows," but only as a friendly gibe.

The traditional lines of expansion which Graves had laid down in the depressed 1930's still seemed sound in the prosperous 1950s. True, the remaining oil companies owning their own tank car fleets no longer needed UTC's cash. But they were responsive to facts and figures which showed that they could save money and release capital for more profitable investment by divesting themselves of their tank car operations and entrusting them to UTC. When in 1953 the company acquired one of the larger shipper-owned fleets, that of the Imperial Oil

Company of Canada, numbering more than 2,200 cars, the transaction was taken as additional evidence that UTC was on the right track. In spite of the problems created by the Korean War, nothing had really changed. The established ways and habits of life in the company remained comfortably the same. No one had the slightest inkling of the revolutionary changes that lay immediately ahead.

PART FIVE:

YEARS OF ASTONISHMENT[1]

1953-1961

> *"Our chief want in life is someone who shall make us do whatever we can."* RALPH WALDO EMERSON

[1] AUTHOR'S NOTE: The rushing events described in this part of the book are for the most part too recent to permit valid judgments as to their relative importance, let alone their final effect on UTC's position in industry. They do, however, reveal the extent to which a company's history reflects the personality of its leaders, the surprising impact that can be produced by a change of leadership, and the problems, economic and psychological, that are created when businesses are abruptly forced out of their established habit patterns and compelled to adopt new ways.

ONE

"THE OLD ORDER CHANGETH . . ."

In 1949, UTC was being compelled by customer demand to embark on a large program of fleet expansion, including hundreds of pressure cars costing on the average $10,000 each. Even when tank cars had cost only two or three thousand dollars each it had not been possible to meet the costs of expansion out of earnings. Now borrowed money running into the tens of millions was needed to pay for the new equipment.

Graves had no doubt that the vast sums called for would be well spent. The company's customers wanted the cars, and for him this was the decisive fact. Customer need and not the size of the company's cash surplus had to be allowed to shape its building program. Even Drake, as chairman, with his aversion to debt, gave way.

A prominent insurance company, invited to discuss the problem, proposed an immediate loan of $20,000,000. But a point of disagreement arose. UTC wanted the right to draw on the money as and if needed. The insurance company insisted that the money be taken all at once. Although Graves could not know it, this was a turning point. If the insurance company had been content to meet his views, UTC might well have followed another fork in the path of destiny. As it was, he broke off the negotiation.

A Man Named Locke

A few days later, when Graves was out of town, Drake received an unexpected visit from a vice-president of the Chase

285

National Bank of New York, which had long been the company's principal bank. This man, Edwin A. Locke, Jr., surprised Drake partly by his youthful appearance and partly by what he said. Chase had learned—how, Locke did not explain—that UTC was interested in a loan, and would be glad to be helpful in the matter.

It pleased Drake to find that Locke seemed to understand UTC's problems and to appreciate the company's financial soundness. The loan structure that he proposed was realistic and convenient. Drake raised some perfunctory objections to the interest rate, but he was inwardly satisfied that the company was on the right track. As soon as Graves returned to the office, they boarded a train for New York, to complete the deal in a meeting at the bank.

Graves also was pleasantly impressed by Locke's approach to what he had anticipated would be an irksome chore of negotiation on petty points. He and Drake asked Locke for a letter of commitment. When Locke dictated it then and there, in the simplest possible form, leaving the details to be worked out subsequently, Graves nodded approvingly. This was a way of doing business that appealed to his instinct. A banker who understood the needs of business and who thought in broader terms than those of conventional banking was, he felt, a happy discovery.

The thought crossed his mind that Locke was the kind of person whom he would like to groom for future leadership in UTC, and although he regarded the possibility as remote he was curious enough to make some inquiries. The resulting information surprised him. Locke, as a New Englander fresh out of Harvard, had begun his business career with Chase in the 1930s, but in 1941 had been called to Washington. There he had become executive assistant to the chairman of the War Production Board, Donald Nelson. In this capacity he had accompanied Nelson on war missions to Russia and China which had received considerable attention in the press.

All this was creditable, Graves considered, but he was less certain about what followed. Locke had subsequently been invited to join the staff of the White House under President Roosevelt, and after the war had served as a special assistant to President Truman for two years before returning to Chase. Graves found it hard to reconcile Locke's personal style and business position with what he considered the radicalism of the Truman administration, but he recognized that his White House service did not necessarily reflect on his soundness and conservatism. After all, respectable Democrats were not unknown!

From time to time, after their initial conference, Graves met with Locke to work out a program of credits, and UTC was enabled to borrow without difficulty as payments for new equipment had to be met. By 1952, the company's obligation had climbed to $40,000,000. Rates of interest and the requirements of amortization were moderate, however, and UTC's treasury felt no strain.

The Choice

Finance was becoming increasingly important to UTC, and Graves was hopeful that in Locke he had found a valuable ally. Their frequent talks in New York and Chicago produced a rare sense of intimacy and mutual confidence. He was accordingly disappointed when he heard early in 1951 that Locke had been tempted back into government service and had resigned from the bank. It was, from Graves' standpoint, an unsound move. The assignment which Locke had accepted was unenviable. As special representative of the Secretary of State, in charge of United States economic and technical aid to the Middle East, he was to coordinate, and make effective, programs intended to aid both the Arab states and Israel. It seemed to Graves that Locke was unwise in reassociating himself with an administration that most bankers and industrialists regarded with critical eyes. In his view a good man had been lost to business.

And more particularly lost to UTC. As Graves came closer to the age of retirement the question of finding the right successor was more and more in his mind. There were experienced men in the company, but he was looking for something more than experience. Granted, his own vigor and health were such that he could reasonably anticipate years of unimpaired activity, yet the fact had to be faced—sixty-five was sixty-five.

It was with keen interest that late in 1952 he came across Locke's name in a newspaper, and learned that he had resigned his Middle Eastern post and was returning to the United States. Even better, to Graves' mind, Locke had differed with the Department of State on a point of policy and had made a speech strongly critical of the government's Middle Eastern program. To Graves this suggested that Locke had got back on the right track, that his penchant for government did not represent an actual aberration, that he was, in fact, a sound man, after all. The result was that shortly after Locke returned to the United States he received an invitation from Graves to come to Chicago for a talk.

The meeting that followed was altogether satisfactory. Locke's personality and mind made the same favorable impression on Graves as before. Would he be willing to come in, Graves asked, as executive assistant to the president? Locke raised only one question. Was this to be a limited assignment or would he have a "full opportunity," based on results attained? Graves assured him that the full opportunity was there, implying that Locke was in line for succession to the presidency, if his performance lived up to expectations.

Locke was satisfied. As to salary, he would leave that to Graves. There was nothing more to be said. Graves perceived, not for the first time, that underneath Locke's frank and engaging style there was a formidable will and a strong inner drive to achievement. But Graves had no way of foretelling how drastically that will and that drive were to alter the structure and scope of the company that he led.

The Opening of Minds

For Locke, as in the first months of 1953 he involved himself in the company's affairs, one of the striking facts about UTC's management was its obvious preference for not rocking the boat. He himself was convinced that it is only the becalmed boat that does not rock, at least a little. In particular it seemed to him extraordinary that UTC had not moved actively and extensively into the transportation of chemicals, an industry which for years past had been undergoing a vast expansion.

The company's reluctance to break out of its accustomed pattern was reminiscent of events in his own experience. In 1942, after Pearl Harbor, many a patriotic American industry had found it extremely difficult to give up the ways of peacetime commerce and reorganize for war production. One of the chief tasks of the War Production Board, in which Locke had served, had been to fill industrial leaders with a will to do what was necessary and with confidence in their ability to do it. Once they made the effort they were often startled by their own ability to achieve "the impossible."

Locke did not permit himself to form a definite opinion in the matter of the chemical cars until he had become familiar with the intricacies of the company's business and had established working relationships with its personalities. Much of his time initially went into arrangements for UTC's registration with the Securities and Exchange Commission and first public offering of securities—a $20,000,000 debenture issue quickly bought up by investors, and a milestone in UTC's financial history. Thereafter, during most of 1953 and 1954, while working on a variety of projects, he ranged through UTC's departments, looking for buried talent among the more than 300 office employees. It seemed to him that the company was underestimating its own potential. He believed that it could, if it tried, put not a few scores or hundreds but thousands of tank cars into profitable service for chemical manufacturers—and that by so doing it would enter a new and sustained period of growth.

Except for Graves, who agreed in principle but thought the time was not yet ripe for action, the response of UTC's executives to Locke's ideas on chemical cars was on the whole tepid. Locke did not press at once for a decision, but he kept the issue alive. Little by little, the realization sank in that an extraordinary opportunity was beckoning to UTC, and that it would not beckon much longer. The gist of Locke's argument was that

> "There is a tide in the affairs of men
> Which, taken at the flood, leads on to fortune,"

and he urged his associates to follow Shakespeare's counsel and "take the current when it serves."

Some of his associates were startled by his tendency to use classical quotation to back up business judgment, but if teeth were gritted, minds were opened. First one UTC executive, then another, found himself drawn to support Locke on the issue against the uninterested majority. The change in attitude was undoubtedly accelerated by the appearance of new faces in managerial meetings. At the time of Drake's retirement in 1952, three of the company's departmental heads, all respected and influential figures, were approaching the age of sixty-five. They were men who had been with the company since youth, who had matured under Drake's administration, and for whom he, even more than Graves, represented the image of authority. It was natural that they should continue to reflect Drake's views after he had gone.

The retirements of these older officers, coming close together, altered the atmosphere of the executive offices. Although their successors also had been in the company's service for decades, the change of personalities made it possible to consider familiar questions afresh, with fewer preconceived ideas, and with greater responsiveness to facts and opportunities. Since Graves encouraged more freedom of expression than had been customary under Drake, there was an increasing interchange of views on the subject of the chemical business.

Well-guarded Secret

Another, more subtle psychological influence bearing on the company's attitude in the matter of the chemical cars during 1954 came from Wall Street. The company's stock, even though it was listed on the New York Stock Exchange, had little appeal for investors interested in capital gains. Selling typically around $45 per share, and paying in the years 1951–1954 an average annual dividend of $2.70,[1] it yielded a pleasant 6 per cent, but it behaved more like a bond than a common stock. While the shares of many other less stable companies were rising fast, UTX, as it was coded in market transactions, stayed in a very narrow range. Purchases of the stock by the company itself with surplus funds under Drake's administration had left little more than a million shares outstanding. Of these, the Rockefeller Foundation now owned 22 per cent; the rest was owned, mostly in small lots,

---

[1] For comparison with subsequent dividends and stock prices, the dividend and price-per-share figures shown here should be halved, to give effect to the two-for-one stock distribution of 1954.

by only 7,000 stockholders, who included many of the company's employees. There was little trading in the stock. Any stockholder who wished to sell a few hundred shares might have to wait days for a buyer at a fair price, or take a lower price.

To increase the number of outstanding shares and their marketability was obviously desirable. UTC's management made its decision in the spring of 1954—a highly secret decision. Everyone knew that in the vast majority of the stock splits of the period Wall Street rumors of the impending actions had played into the hands of canny speculators, who, at the first hint of a split, moved swiftly into the market.

The directors of Union Tank were determined to avoid this gratuity to speculators with no real interest in the company. Any financial benefits resulting from the stock split, they felt, should accrue to the advantage of the stockholders who for the most part held their shares as long-term investments, rather than to the pocketbooks of the in-and-out traders with inside information.

Rarely, if ever, has a publicly-owned corporation so successfully guarded against a leak of its plans for a stock split. In the period preceding the split there were no substantial purchases of UTC stock to arouse the curiosity of sharp-eyed brokers. Through the early months of 1954 the price of the shares on the New York Exchange was firm in the middle forties. Then on April 29 it was announced that the stock would be split, two for one, bringing the number of outstanding shares to 2,153,000; and that the dividend on the new shares would be at the annual rate of $1.45, representing an increase of 20 cents per old share.

Another Corner Turned

It had been a long time since traders had seen an almost forgotten stock come to life so spectacularly. The news of the split caught the investment community by surprise. More than 3,000 UTC shares were traded that day—about 15 times more than in a typical day of its previous record. In a few hours the price of the as yet unsplit stock rose by more than $14 to a high of $63 per share, and it closed at $57. The new stock came on the market in June, 1954, at a price of more than $28 per share. From that time on the interest of investors produced sustained daily transactions in the stock—a pattern very different from the past, when sometimes days had gone by without a single trade.

Wall Street's reaction to the stock split struck the imagination of the company's executives perhaps more sharply than they themselves realized. UTC had at last been discovered by the investment public. A feeling that more was possible than had been thought possible seeped without being articulated into management's discussions of policy. Even those who had been most negative with respect to the proposed entry into the chemical-car field now found it less difficult to accept. That summer of 1954 there ceased to be any difference of opinion as to the desirability of initiating without delay a program of chemical car construction. The only question remaining was the size of the program. On this point Graves and most of the department heads continued to regard as unrealistic Locke's view that the market would absorb thousands of additional chemical cars if UTC would build them.

A few months later the company received another sign that "the old order changeth, yielding place to new." From New York, in October, came word that the Rockefeller Foundation had decided to sell part of its stockholding in the company. It had long been public knowledge that the Foundation had been reducing its corporate investments where they exceeded 10 per cent of any one company's outstanding stock; for under the law a holding of stock above 10 per cent exposed the owner to certain special regulations of the Securities and Exchange Commission. UTC had for some time understood and taken pride in the fact that it was the last company represented in the Foundation's portfolio by a stockholding of more than 10 per cent. There was, consequently, no surprise for the directors in the Foundation's decision to dispose of 380,000 UTC shares out of its total holding of 480,000. The company joined in the preliminary legal formalities and on November 8, 1954, the sale was quickly carried out through a public offering underwritten by leading investment bankers.

The Foundation had been remote from company affairs and, seeking income rather than power from securities, had not even wished to be represented on the board; so that the reduction of its holding from 22 per cent to about 5 per cent had no direct significance for UTC's management and policy. Nevertheless, expected though it was, the development made a strong impression on UTC's directors. There was a feeling that another corner had been turned. Thousands of new names were appearing on the company's list of stockholders. Investment analysts had begun to scrutinize UTC's annual reports on behalf of their clients. From this point on the company's management might feel greater need than ever before to justify publicly its actions or omissions to act.

The Company Surprises Itself

By the end of November, Graves, reviewing the facts, came to the conclusion that the time had come for an all-out plunge into the chemical tank car business. He was influenced in part by the development of new petro-chemical products requiring tank cars for shipment and manufactured by companies which were already using UTC cars for oil. Another major consideration was the feeling that, if the company delayed, potential customers would become fewer and fewer. Chemical business still available in 1955 might well be in the hands of competitors by 1957. Even more dangerous, oil companies served by UTC, and which had now entered the chemical business, might be forced to turn to other tank car companies for chemical cars if UTC proved unable to satisfy their needs.

UTC's shops were not yet fully prepared for the task ahead of them, but Locke was convinced that once the die was cast everyone would do what was required of him for success. The decision was taken on this premise. As one executive put it in the words of the old children's game, "Ready or not, here we come."

Events moved as if predestined. Many chemical concerns, when informed that UTC was preparing for large-scale production of chemical cars, quickly placed orders for delivery in 1955 and 1956. A new debenture issue at a modest rate of interest took care of financial requirements. Although the new cars demanded an outlay of many millions, it was calculated that the monthly rentals would yield enough revenue per car to justify the investment.

As demand for the chemical cars ran into the thousands and

continued to mount, everyone in the company realized that the company had entered its greatest year of expansion since the 1920s. The company's executives threw themselves into the task of getting the chemical cars produced, and obstacles went down before them.

By the end of 1955, the venture had all the earmarks of success. The men responsible had something of the feeling of mountain climbers who had reached the top. But they soon found that they stood, not on Everest, but only on a foothill of the future. Ahead of them was a formidable range of higher peaks, and they were expected to keep moving.

TWO

NOTHING SACRED

Late in 1955, Graves felt that the time had come to lighten the load of his administrative work. The chairmanship of the board had been vacant since Drake's retirement, and as soon as Graves indicated his intention to resign the presidency, the directors elected him chairman and Locke president. By and large, Locke's promotion was expected and accepted without murmur. If there was some disappointment among men who had been with the company longer and who may have aspired to the presidential succession, it did not show on the surface. The older executives felt especially secure since, while turning most of his responsibilities over to Locke, Graves had retained authority as chief executive of the company. The power of decision in departures from established practice was still his.

Locke's challenge to UTC's conservative tradition had startled but not disconcerted Graves. The evident surge of new life within the company was what he had hoped for. He saw grounds for optimism. Gross revenue in 1955 had reached a new peak at more than $30,000,000. So, too, with net income, at more than $6,000,000. Once Graves had satisfied himself as to the merits of the new ideas generated by Locke, he was willing to let the new president run with them, and enjoy the ensuing excitement. He could not help sympathizing, however, with some of the older employees, whose minds turned back nostalgically to the peaceful years when the ability to keep quiet, obey orders, and avoid conflict had been fully appreciated. Theirs had been a comfortable world. What was happening to it? UTC's long-term indebtedness, which in 1955 stood at $55,000,000, horrified financial officers for whom Drake's no-debt policy had represented the acme of financial acumen. Even more alarming to some was the crumbling of the mossy walls of the ancient seniority system. Departmental reorganizations and realignments were bringing young men into key positions which in other times they might have had to wait a dozen years to obtain. An intensive recruiting program was under way. Strangers from outside the company, without previous experience of the tank car business, appeared in key offices. Clerks who had grown gray in the recording of data shook their heads as batteries of sorting and data-processing machines were installed to take care of work previously done by hand.

The sense of upheaval spread even to the company's far-flung repair shops, as old-line superintendents and foremen found themselves called upon to introduce improved procedures and reach higher standards of efficiency. Although the output of cars at the Whiting assembly plant achieved unprecedented levels, it did not satisfy the demands of the home office. Labor relations came under review, job specifications were rewritten, training programs were instituted for shop supervisors. To add to the sense of pressure, the spring of 1956 brought the first strike in the company's history to the Whiting shop.[1]

Although costly both to the company and the Whiting employees, the strike had some constructive results, notably in pointing up the need to strengthen the managements of all the shops. To aid in establishing a firm basis for action, the company undertook a survey of employee morale. The findings were emphatic. The company, said the survey report, ought to lose no time in promoting better mutual understanding between supervisors and employees, providing stronger incentives, minimizing feelings of insecurity, and improving shop conditions, among other objectives. Before the end of the year UTC had initiated several programs designed to raise the level of relations between management and employees.

"In All Candor..."

At about this time, in 1956, Locke became chief executive officer of the company. His personality was a source of be-

[1] See Appendix I.

wilderment to some of UTC's executives. In ordinary con-
versation he was casual, gracious, soft-spoken, with an easy
laugh and a twinkling eye. As soon as an example of ineffi-
ciency came into view, however, the twinkle could become
a steely glint and the voice take on a cutting edge. Most of
UTC's older men had been conditioned to think of "the office" as a kind of club, where it was bad form for one executive to critize another's work openly, or to expose his
areas of weakness. Locke's impersonal, objective, detached approach to business situations troubled those who in their business
lives had never known any but breezy paternal authority. Especially irksome was his insistence on getting fast, direct answers
to questions of fact. He would ask a question, listen silently to a
reply which circled the issue, and then quietly ask the question
again, until the essential information was forthcoming or, as was
not unusual, a red-faced executive rushed out to get it. And
many a man who thought that, in obtaining information, he was
fulfilling an assignment was startled to find that he had been
expected to take action. "I'm afraid I haven't gotten across my
point. This isn't at all a question of 'asking' a third party. It is
something that must be done. The problem is 'how,' not 'if' or
'what.' ... It will be futile to tell me it can't be done." Memos
of this type were calculated to stir the adrenal glands of the
recipients.

In private conversations, old-time departmental heads admitted
that they hated to hear Locke's voice on the telephone or go into
his office because they "never knew what was coming next." It
might be praise: "This report is full of meat...." "You are making good progress...." But it was not easy to earn such presidential approbation. Locke was criticized as trying to get too
much done, as expecting too much, as not making sufficient allowance for human fallibility, as a perfectionist, as being too
concerned with detail, as thinking in too large terms. Never in
all its previous history, except perhaps briefly in wartime, had
UTC's staff been compelled to work so many extra hours, even
nights and weekends. The Purchasing Department, in the midst
of its struggle to meet demands for materials for chemical cars,
suddenly found its traditional inventory controls subjected to
damning criticism, and radically revised.

Veteran statistical officers were appalled not only by the number, variety, and depth of the reports demanded on every phase of the company's operation, but by the unprecedented urgency attached to them. "Why was not the July report completed until September 11?" "Why has not the August report been distributed?" To answer such blunt questions meant more self-revelation than one or two executives could bear, and they sought refuge in early retirement.

Technical specialists especially were under pressure. "I must say to you in all candor," wrote Locke to one official, "that I hear nothing about new developments in the railroad equipment field ... except when I read about them in the public prints." It was essential, he insisted, to improve the technological position of the business. "I do not propose to preside over the slow obsolescence of the Union Tank Car Company." Whether or not the Churchillian humor was appreciated, the implication was unmistakable. Something had to give.

"Where Does He Think He Is?"

Particularly baffling to most of Locke's staff was his emphasis on the use of language. Men who had been dictating letters most of their lives were taken aback by suggestions that brevity in phrasing would be a relief, or that the company's reputation deserved better grammar. Since when had grammar been a presidential responsibility? Said one resentful employee, as he left the president's office with a letter that had been blue-penciled to death, "Where does he think he is—at Harvard?" This was shortly after Locke had been elected to the Board of Overseers of Harvard University.

Locke's insistence on accuracy, especially in the written word, went down hard in a company where, as in most businesses, loose and approximate usage had always been taken for granted. Not all of his associates grasped his point that carelessness in language could conceal serious defects in attitude or understanding. When an official reported, not without satisfaction, that "production schedules are filled beyond capacity," and hence that "we will be unable to accept any additional business," he was shocked by the intensity of Locke's reply. What was meant by the "capacity" of a production schedule? "That is the language, apart from its inaccuracy, of defeatism. . . . Our production...is basically limited by the *productivity*...and not by the *capacity* of our shops...." Accurately defined, the situation called for improvement in productivity as the road to increased business. There was no justification, said Locke, for "passiveness and complacency," and he would appreciate it if the memo in question were withdrawn by its author. "I cannot accept some of the statements made and I do not want them to have the chance of creating the wrong impression among our staff."

On another occasion department heads who had recommended increases in the salaries of certain subordinates in recognition of their "aggressiveness" were amazed to have the word challenged. Locke suggested that the qualities to be rewarded were rather "initiative, drive, energy, follow-through, or the habit of working hard." "Aggressiveness," he commented, "is more for the bill collector, the warrior, or the wolf." To some who read his memo this seemed almost like heresy.

Gradually, a noticeable change took place in the prevailing UTC attitude toward the written word. At a later period, it was not uncommon, when Locke sent draft copies of his own reports to his associates for their suggestions, to have them come back from men whose use of language he had formerly criticized, with stylistic notes penciled in the margins—"redundant"—"euphemistic"—"needs cutting"—a repayment in kind that gave him considerable pleasure.

"Hot Dog"

The agitations of the time were augmented by major technical innovations profoundly affecting the company's operation. The most important of these was a new and radically different tank car evolved by a small task force of UTC engineers between 1954 and 1956. Aided by some fortuitous circumstances,[2] they built the model of an all-welded, general-purpose tank car with revolutionary features—a car without a dome and without an underframe, and with a long, perfectly cylindrical, sausage-like tank that impelled Locke to give it the nickname of "Hot Dog," by which it eventually became known to the trade.

Inevitably, the Hot Dog provoked a great deal of technical controversy among UTC's engineers. Was it strong enough?

[2] For the step-by-step story of this development, see Appendix J.

Would it meet the tank car specifications established by the government? Ought UTC to experiment with new models at a time when the chemical car program was in full swing and taxing the company's productive resources, as some felt, to the full?

Some of the points raised were creative and constructive, others merely captious. Underlying Locke's and Graves' enthusiasm for the new design was a conviction that it would lend itself to efficient production, especially of very large tank cars. If so, this could be an economic factor of considerable significance for railroads and shippers, and hence for UTC.

Since World War II, competition from trucks, barges, and pipe lines had seriously weakened the position of the railroads in the haulage of liquid freight. The pressure was bound to continue until the roads found ways to serve the American oil and chemical industries more economically, while maintaining a realistic level of earnings.

The size of tank cars directly affected the costs of the railroads and their freight rates. Although freight rates were charged only against the contents of the tank, the railroad also had to haul the dead weight of the entire car—a source of considerable expense. Since a single 20,000-gallon tank car weighed much less than two 10,000-gallon tank cars, the big car meant a less expensive haul—that is, a larger percentage of the total load hauled was payload than if it had been carried in two cars. Thus the railroads were enabled to earn their freight charges per gallon of liquid moved while spending less in the haulage of the non-paying weight represented by the cars themselves. In addition, by handling only one car instead of two, the railroads effected economies in switching, in repairs, and in the assembly and break-up of trains.

With the Hot Dog a 30,000-gallon tank was technically practicable, so the railroad's savings would be even greater. Such a mammoth tank would be a partial offset to the inflationary trend of the economy, with its rising costs of materials and labor. If the saving for the railroads should prove large enough to justify the lowering of freight rates for large cargoes carried in single cars, it could go far to strengthen their competitive position in liquid freight, as against barges, pipe lines, and trucks. It was also predictable that the big streamlined Hot Dog cars would make possible significant savings of time and money for shippers in loading, gauging, and unloading. Tests showed that they were exceptionally strong and safe, and their streamlined appearance was strongly in their favor. Carrying the insignia of the company to which they were leased, they could serve as impressive traveling advertisements.

These considerations eventually led UTC to standardize production on the Hot Dog design in three diameter sizes, attaining a record capacity of 30,000 gallons. The response was a prompt surge of demand from customers. By 1960, a number of shippers using the huge new cars were able to obtain significant reductions in freight costs.

Big Dome

Technical arguments over the Hot Dog had not yet quieted down when UTC's executives were asked to follow Locke to another break with the past. This time the issue was a new type of tank car repair shop, unprecedented in size, shape, appearance, and technical features. The first of these new shops, built at Baton Rouge in 1957–1958, attracted national attention. Circular in shape, uniquely modern and efficient, it was covered by a vast golden "geodesic" dome, made of steel and in a hexagonal pattern, without internal supports—described as the largest circular free-span structure in the world, and a breakthrough in industrial architecture.[3]

In one respect, however—cost—the new shop was open to criticism within the company. The expected cost for the dome of $5 per square foot of enclosed area had been 100 per cent short of the mark. The actual figure was $10. UTC's experience had been not unlike that of the bold householder who experiments in housing, and who finds that the architect's original estimate is one thing and the contractor's final bill another. No tank car repair shop in the past had cost anything like the Baton Rouge shop. To be sure, times had changed, and what was wrong for the UTC of the previous generation might be right for the

---

[3] For the sequence of events leading to the new type of shop, and a description of its dome, see Appendix J.

UTC of the future. Still, figures were figures; and although the dome in a sense was only incidental to the shop as a whole, its dramatic character caused attention to center on it.

Seen by hindsight, the reason for the high cost was obvious enough. In constructing the dome there had been no previous experience to fall back on. No builder in the history of the world had had to face the particular problems involved in lifting the huge steel panels into place and securing them, and at the same time assuring the stability of the enormous structure. It had been necessary for the dome's engineers to experiment with methods never tried before. Only in the latter stages of construction, after many unexpected obstacles had been overcome, could the work go rapidly and costs be held somewhere near reasonable levels.

Pain over the cost of the new shop was only partially eased by the undoubted success of the venture in other respects. The dome was being hailed by newspapers and magazines. The soundness of the design, if not its economy, had been proved, and techniques for producing, transporting, and erecting the individual panels had been developed. Most important, the round shop covered by the dome showed considerable promise of efficiency, notably in the speed with which tank cars could be repaired, and the greatly increased number of cars which could be handled at a given time. Personnel of the former Baton Rouge shop had been carefully trained in new operating procedures which were expected to cut costs and improve technical performance.

Locke considered the venture sufficiently promising for UTC to begin work promptly on a second round and dome-covered shop of the same size to replace an old shop at Wood River, Illinois. The Wood River dome, it was hoped, would be built more rapidly and would cost less than the one at Baton Rouge. There a recently developed principle of construction was to be used. If all went well, the dome would literally be built from the top down, with the aid of a balloon.

At Baton Rouge, the individual steel panels which, when welded together, formed the dome, had been hoisted into place by tall cranes, and the welders worked far above ground level. At Wood River, the welding would be done at ground level, on the surface of an enormous, partially inflated nylon bag; and as more and more panels were joined, more and more air would be pumped into the bag, until finally a great part of the steel dome would be carried aloft to the desired height.

But at Wood River, too, as construction progressed, costs substantially exceeded estimates. Torrential rains and jurisdictional labor disputes, delaying work for months, made this dome as expensive as that at Baton Rouge. Here, at last, was a dollar-and-cents issue on which, some thought, the Locke administration might be vulnerable. For a time a warm argument on the subject was pursued in UTC's executive offices. Protagonists of the domes pointed to intangible values. The money that had gone into them was a nonrecurrent expense, while their publicity value was large and continuous. No one could look at the great shining hemispheres without respect. They were in a sense symbolic of the transformation taking place within the company. The gauntlet had been thrown down to the past. The domes bespoke the company's new vision, new spirit, and new energy. Even on the financial side, it was necessary to suspend judgment. Henceforth the company's experience with the dome represented potential earning power. UTC could now build domes for others far more economically than it had built them for itself. To what extent other industries would turn to the dome could not be predicted, but there were continuous stirrings of interest.

Not everyone in the company, however, was convinced by this line of reasoning. As late as 1960 there were those who said that the domes had cost too much, and who did not tire of saying it. Beginning in that year, however, a few prominent corporate customers contracted with UTC for construction of domes made of steel or anodized aluminum; and as time went on, and new and more important events dominated the interests of the company, the issue gradually evaporated.

THREE

POINT OF NO RETURN

As the year 1957 unfolded, the general expectation in UTC was that the tempo of events would gradually return to normal. Everything, after all, was going pretty well. The company was firmly in the chemical car business. In the Hot Dog it had the most advanced tank car in the business. The shops were improving in efficiency. Labor relations had been strengthened. Some good new executive personnel had been recruited, while many of the veterans had revealed abilities and inner resources of great value to the company in its development.

Tank car business in the United States was holding fairly well, in spite of some signs of recession in the economy as a whole. The Canadian division, Products Tank Line of Canada, Inc., called Procan in company slang, was expanding its repair-shop facilities. The tank truck subsidiary, Refiners Transport and Terminal, seemed to be on an even keel. Taken as a whole, the company was doing business at the rate of $35,000,000 a year—a new peak. Although no one doubted that further improvements in efficiency could be made, there was a widespread opinion that Locke had gone about as far as he could in the way of major innovation. It was an erroneous opinion. Within four years, UTC would embrace 10 divisions covering a broad range of industries, and with annual sales of over $100,000,000—a growth which would be accompanied by a new crop of misgivings, uncertainties, and travail within the organization.

Marriage of Necessity

That the stable earning power of the tank car business provided an extraordinarily strong base for the acquisition of additional enterprises was a familiar thought to Graves and Locke. But the new enterprises, they felt, should be related to the present activities of the company so far as possible. UTC did not need diversification so much as integration and a faster rate of growth.

To pay out large sums of cash for the assets of other companies was unnecessary. Owners of such companies, it could safely be taken for granted, would prefer to exchange their stock for UTC's. Both parties stood to gain by this form of transaction. The seller would benefit from a tax advantage which he could not have had if he received cash, while in UTC stock he acquired a security of proved dependability. UTC, by using stock for such purposes and so making it unnecessary to borrow cash, would minimize the increase of its long-term debt and its interest payments on the debt. If properties purchased in this way produced an adequate return on the investment, UTC's stockholders would gain more from rising earnings per share than they would lose per share by increase in the number of outstanding shares.

As early as 1955, Graves and Locke prepared to give substance to this conception of the company's growth. In that year UTC's stockholders authorized the issuance, at times to be determined by the board of directors, of additional shares of UTC common stock to make a total authorized stock issue of 6,000,000 shares, as compared with 2,350,000 shares then outstanding. This increase would be ample, it was felt, to take care of any realistic growth program over a period of years.

Despite these financial preparations, the first major acquisition by the company was made largely because of circumstances beyond its control. The roots of the extraordinary transformation which UTC was about to undergo reached back to 1949, when Graves worked out his first agreement with the Graver Tank & Manufacturing Company. Since then, Graver had been producing virtually all of UTC's tanks. The extent to which the two companies had become important to each other revealed itself in 1957. In that year E. N. Gosselin, the president of Graver, raised

the question of the possibility of a merger—a subject which had
been hinted at more than once in the past, but which was now
put forward for serious consideration.

Graver was a wholly owned subsidiary and the larger part
of the Phoenix Manufacturing Company, which made a variety
of steel products.[1] A large Chicago bank which held half of
Phoenix's stock in trust was understood to be concerned over
so heavy a concentration of the trust's investment in a single company. Rumors were heard that other stockholders also were restless and uneasy over what seemed to be signs of serious ineffi-
ciency and the slowness of Graver's older leaders in developing
qualified younger men for important posts. There was a feeling
that only a formidable effort could correct the situation—and all
the evidence pointed to a strong probability that Graver's owners
would seek to avoid the looming problem simply by selling the
company.

From the first UTC's management regarded the purchase as
a marriage of necessity. If UTC did not buy Graver, some other
company almost certainly would. This was a danger that had to
be avoided. Studies showed that it would not be sound economically for UTC to build its own tank shop, since tank production for tank cars alone would not provide a sufficient return on the investment. With its large tank requirements, UTC
was vulnerable. Already its two principal competitors, owning
their own tank building facilities, had a cost advantage in tank
car manufacture. That advantage would be increased if Graver
fell into the wrong hands. An unfriendly owner would not hesitate to hold UTC up, in both senses of the phrase—by raising
tank prices and by limiting production of tanks urgently needed
by UTC.

Graves and Locke did not propose to see the clock of progress
turned back ten years, and the company again become dependent
on competitors for its tank production. To have Graver as a
source of tank supply was of the utmost importance, especially
with the Hot Dog looming on the horizon as the industry's most
advanced car. The Hot Dog's success as a competitive instrument would depend in large measure on the company's ability
to keep its tank cost uninflated, for the tank represented about

[1] For the story of the Graver Company, see Appendix L.

60 per cent of this car's total cost as contrasted with only 40 per cent of the cost of the pre-Hot Dog model.

A Tail That Could Wag the Dog

"We have no choice. Buy and make the best of a difficult situation," Locke recommended to UTC's board of directors, and there was no dissent. But a great deal of cautious preliminary exploration was necessary. Graver, although smaller than UTC in terms of investment was, with Phoenix, by far the larger in terms of dollar sales and employees. In buying it, if it could be bought, UTC would be crossing a point of no return, a corporate Rubicon. Owning Graver, the entire nature of UTC would be importantly changed.

Could a formula of purchase be found which would not impose too great a financial burden on UTC and which would be fair to Graver? The long friendship of the two companies and their intimate knowledge of each other's business put UTC in a preferred position to carry on a negotiation in a frank and pleasant atmosphere. But the first talks with Gosselin gave rise to an obstacle. Not that he was unwilling to sell for an adequate price; but he was determined that he would not sell Graver without its parent company, Phoenix Manufacturing.

For UTC this was a proposal requiring reflection. The idea of owning Phoenix did not appeal. True, the company had a merchant bar mill in a good location at Joliet, Illinois, where it produced hot rolled carbon steel shapes—flats, angles, channels, reinforcing bars, and the like; and also a forging plant in Pennsylvania, where steel pipe, tank flanges, and other products were made. But Phoenix was a small company; it lacked facilities for producing its own raw steel supply; and the fact was that UTC did not need it or want it. Neither Graves nor Locke was at first certain that the purchase should be considered, even to make possible the Graver acquisition. Eventually, however, they decided to yield the point, rather than risk acquisition of Graver by another company.

Early in September, 1957, UTC stock worth about $12,600,000 was exchanged for all of Phoenix–Graver's assets.[2] The acquisition produced a remarkable change in UTC's balance sheet and

[2] How this price was arrived at is described in Appendix M.

earnings statement for 1957 as compared with the preceding year. Although only the final three and one-half months of Phoenix-Graver's income for 1957 was included with UTC's, it brought the gross income figure to $63,000,000, from the $35,000,000 of 1956. Net income before taxes was up more than $4,000,000. After taxes, and after dividing profits by the full number of shares outstanding at the end of the year, net earnings per share for 1957 were $2.64 as compared with $2.40 in 1956.

No One Predicted It

Locke took a highly conservative position in reporting the 1957 figures to stockholders and public. It was important to prevent any inclination in Wall Street to use the year's increased earnings to promote an unwarranted rise in the price of the company's stock. In answering inquiries from the financial community, he made it plain that although long-range benefits to UTC from Phoenix–Graver were certainly hoped for, so far as the immediate future was concerned management saw no reason for marked enthusiasm. This insistence on discouraging rumors of increased earnings and dividends acted to dampen speculative interest in the stock, and its price remained almost unaffected by the radical changes in the company's financial statement.

It was, in fact, no time for self-congratulation. A sharp recession in business had begun in mid-1957. However, in the last quarter of the year and the first quarter of 1958 Graver's situation seemed by no means dark, for it was then completing a number of contracts, with good profit margins, resulting in the sudden rise of UTC's profits for that period. To be sure, there were those in UTC who were acutely aware of weaknesses in the Graver situation. But it is hard to take a gloomy view of an enterprise that is reporting large profits. When Graver executives spoke of good sales prospects, UTC was encouraged. For those months, not Graver, but Phoenix, appeared to be the trouble spot, and there was a heavy concentration of UTC's executive attention on the Joliet mill.

Then, as the second quarter of 1958 showed an accelerating slump in the nation's business, and industry sharply reduced its capital expenditures, Graver's sales and income fell away. It became unmistakable that management there greatly needed strengthening, and that many changes in policy and practice had to be made. By late 1958, UTC's concern over Graver was serious and persistent.

Meanwhile, however, in another sharp turn of fortune, Phoenix, regarded as a sore spot in 1957, had become a strong point. Within a year, strenuous executive effort to improve efficiency began to produce profits, and these were soon augmented by a nationwide steel strike in which Phoenix was one of the few mills left operating. As a result, while Graver was dropping into the red, Phoenix was moving steadily ahead, well in the black—a development which no one in UTC had foreseen.

To the West—To the North

It now appeared that the company, having begun to expand, was being carried along almost by momentum. Locke felt that one of the weaknesses of the Graver operation was its failure to cover two geographic areas of increasing importance—the western part of the United States and Canada. Partly as a result of these gaps in its marketing structure, he believed, Graver's volume of business was not large enough to support an adequate program of research and development. Consequently, when early in 1958 he learned that a well-known plate-fabrication concern in the West might be purchasable—the Lang Company, of Salt Lake City, Utah—he was strongly attracted. The company was small as compared with Graver, but it served the area in which Graver was least effective—an area which appeared to be in the early stages of a long-range industrial development—the 11 states of the West and Northwest. It seemed probable that unified management of Graver and Lang would effect economies while strengthening sales and production in both companies.

Lang's owner-president was interested. A man well into his sixties, he recognized that his small firm, standing alone, would find the going increasingly arduous in a field of growing complexity and evolving skills. Negotiations began early in 1958. A rapid study convinced UTC that the business was soundly based and that at a reasonable price it would be a useful acquisition.

An offer of 80,000 shares of UTC stock—then selling at $30 per share—was approved by UTC's board as a fair price for Lang's assets. When it was finally accepted, UTC found itself owning and operating in Graver–Lang an established nation-wide plate-fabrication business of unusual scope. For 521,000 shares of stock—about one-fourth of the previously outstanding shares—UTC had acquired a business that in good years was expected to earn much larger returns for the shares paid out than the tank car business had been earning. It was recognized, however, that in bad years the story might be very different—unless the new divisions were sharply reoriented, reorganized, and re-staffed on a broad scale.

Reasons similar to those that had made the company decide to buy Lang next directed attention to a Toronto plate fabricator, the Sparling Tank Manufacturing Company, Ltd. Locke believed that Sparling would provide UTC's Canadian tank-car operation with needed manufacturing resources. Canada was then in the first year of an economic slump, but the country's prospects were good. Population was growing steadily. Oil consumption was on the rise. For years previous there had been a steady rise in Procan's tank car fleet, and in the number of its shops. With Sparling, as Locke saw it, Procan would be able to develop its opportunities more fully, and in 1958 he pressed the deal through to a conclusion.

No Call for Cheers

How sound were the expansionist moves of 1957–1958? Behind closed doors men debated the question without reaching a firm answer. Locke himself felt that the chief problem was to find the right men to head some of the more troublesome operations of the expanded company. But by the end of 1958, only the tank car division seemed to be responding as hoped to the changes made. There the average executive age level had been brought sharply down from the sixties to the forties. Men of capacity had been lifted out of the company's ranks to key positions. An in-fusion of strength had come through the hiring of executives who had proved themselves in other industries, and who brought a new professionalism into crucial aspects of the company's opera-tions. Behind them stood a new crop of younger men of talent who were being trained for later major responsibilities. There was an unmistakable drive and zeal in the organization. At the same time the company had not lost the benefit of its voices of experience. Although the frozen hand of the old seniority system had been lifted, every major department still had at its head, or close to its head, an executive of many years' service in UTC. Clifford Graves himself, who in 1958 resigned from the chairmanship of the board, was elected honorary chairman, and continued to give counsel on vital issues.

It was Locke's conviction that UTC's managerial group was competent to deal with the problems that lay ahead for the tank car operation. But he could not say as much for the Graver, Lang, and Sparling acquisitions. The company might have to wait until the early 1960s before the new properties would begin to produce significant earnings—and even then the financial showing would necessarily be linked to prevailing economic conditions.

The unpleasant fact had to be faced: it was still anybody's guess whether UTC had added to its future earnings per share through its new acquisitions. And if not, it was easy to surmise at whom the finger would point.

FOUR

NO LETUP

When confronted by a specific business problem for which there was no apparent solution, Locke believed that the best course was to surround the problem with good men. His search for men capable of providing strong leadership for UTC's ailing divisions was continuous for several years after 1957. It took time to find such men, and even more time before they could begin to prove themselves. But once he was satisfied that the right man was in the right spot, he felt secure. "You are tackling this new job of yours in just the right way," he wrote to a recently appointed divisional head. "The results will show up in the profit-and-loss statement in God's good time; meanwhile, I am the opposite of worried or impatient."

The process of change continued with no letup. Between 1957 and 1959 the policy of secrecy and silence inherited from the old Trust broke down. Newspapers had not been much concerned with UTC for forty years, and such few inquiries as reporters made in that period were generally met with laconic caution reminiscent of the attitude of Felton or Tilford in the old days. The concept of "public relations" as a corporate activity had been ignored. Now an interested press discovered that, far from being rebuffed, it could get responsive replies to its questions, and hardly a month passed without news accounts of UTC's bustling affairs. It was at this period, too, that the company ceased to be aloof from community activities, setting up a program of aid to education and social welfare, both nationally and in localities where UTC had shops. A decision to advertise was

312

even more of a break with the past. In the years since its separation from Standard Oil in 1912, UTC's total effort in this area
had consisted of occasional technical announcements in railroad
and engineering magazines, and of metal-backed calendars and
specially-designed decks of playing cards sent out at appropriate
times to executives of customer companies. As long as UTC's
executives had to think only of about 300 customers with whose
key executives they generally had close personal relationships,
there had been little need for anything more. But the acquisition
of new companies with a specific need to advertise demanded a
radical change in the company's approach to the business community and the public as a whole. In 1959, a campaign of color
advertisements in national magazines began to tell the American
business community about the functions of the various UTC
divisions.

Dark Question

The launching of research programs in the various divisions at
a cost of hundreds of thousands a year was a further sign of the
ferment in the company. A hunger for achievement was revealing
itself in many of the executive offices. "Men are conservatives
after dinner," in Emerson's phrase, and the new UTC had not yet
dined. The mood of the younger men especially was futuristic;
for them "will be" had replaced "used to be." In 1959, when a
sweeping reorganization of the new companies was carried out,
the pace of action steadily increased to the point where the wife
of more than one executive made her voice heard on the sub-
jects of long hours and short weekends. At the end of the reorganization, UTC stood as parent to six major corporate divisions
with distinct operations: Tank Cars-U.S.; Refiners Transport &
Terminal (tank trucks); Graver Tank, which now included Lang
(plate fabrication); Phoenix (steel products); Graver Water
Conditioning (water treatment); and Products Tank Line, which
included Sparling (Canadian tank cars and plate fabrication).
A central executive staff provided all the divisions with specialized services.

The ride was exciting but the road was rough, and some felt
the bumps. Deep-cutting personnel changes in several of the
new divisions, and a closer control of costs in all, created tensions.

And the feeling of discomfort in many quarters grew as 1959 showed itself a difficult year. Several of the plate-fabrication operations were still in retreat against heavy competitive pressure in a slow market, and were losing money. Only the old stand-bys, UTC, Procan, and RT&T, plus the newcomer Phoenix, were turning in satisfactory performances. How serious was the problem?

The gloomy answer came in the earnings statement for the first quarter of 1959. The company had netted only 41 cents per share —barely enough to meet current dividend requirements. True, the number of shares had tripled since then to 3,200,000; true again, the expansion of the past few years made comparisons with the past unreliable, and Locke had warned against premature optimism. Nevertheless, disappointment was inevitable. Although no one in UTC admitted openly to pessimism, in the background was a dark question: was this to be the result of all the effort of the past two years—a lowering of net income per share? The question became even more aggravating when earnings for the second quarter of 1959 were announced at a bleak and paltry 40 cents per share. More than one person close to UTC privately expressed the opinion that "Locke had overreached himself," that he had gone "too far, too fast."

In that summer of 1959 some members of UTC's board of directors gave Locke a rougher time than any previous president of the company had ever experienced in a board meeting. Criticism focused on the failure of recent acquisitions to show much progress, but the cost of the geodesic domes was not forgotten. Locke's reply was that the company was becoming stronger in fundamental ways which were bound to show presently in its earnings. In this belief, and in spite of voices urging him to retrench, he carried his associates with him, both the willing and the unwilling, into yet more unprecedented ventures. As one executive put it, "Tomorrow was here before we had a chance to get used to today."

To Faraway Places

One of the new enterprises in particular caused eyebrows to rise—UTC's expansion into foreign markets. The embryo of the overseas operation was an order obtained by the Graver Tank division to erect the storage tanks for a large new refinery to be constructed near Oslo, Norway—a project financed jointly by American and Norwegian capital. Running into millions, this order had tested the ability of Graver's new management to compete successfully abroad against low-cost bids from European plate fabricators, and earn a profit. It was no light challenge. Graver's success was not achieved without much ingenuity and hard work, but it was achieved. Utilizing Norwegian welders, Japanese steel delivered in a Japanese freighter, and American technical supervision, and fabricating the plate in a Norwegian shipyard, the work was driven through to successful completion.

If an overseas assignment could be brought off once, why not again, and many times? To be sure, other companies already were in this field on a large scale, and competition was sure to be severe. As Locke saw the picture, however, the foreign market was growing, and there was room for an energetic newcomer. From another standpoint, in terms of America's strategic and economic interests, there was every reason to promote American investment abroad, the use of American techniques in foreign construction projects and the establishment of foreign licensees for American products and patents. A brief announcement heralded the establishment of what was to become Graver's far-flung international department. Recruitment of a headquarters staff went forward rapidly, and by autumn of 1959 a group of men thoroughly experienced in foreign industrial methods and international trade were organizing a strong drive for business all over the world.[1]

An Interest In Water

Development of the international operation was still in progress when the company reached out for still larger responsibilities. It was Locke's intention to associate UTC with fundamental trends within the country, as well as in the free world as a whole, so far as the company's capabilities and resources permitted. One such trend that particularly caught his interest was the growing shortage of water in many parts of the United States and other nations, where population, industry, and agriculture were pressing hard on available supplies. For many industries it was

[1] For UTC's foreign affiliations, see Appendix N.

becoming increasingly important to use purer and purer water—
a need requiring highly specialized skills. The obvious possibilities in this field had impelled Locke to devote a good deal of
effort to the Graver Water Conditioning division, which, under
new leadership, had begun to respond efficiently to its opportunities. In 1960, investigation brought word of two other young
companies concerned with water, and which might be purchasable. One was the nation's leading manufacturer of home-owned
water-softening appliances—the Lindsay Company of St. Paul,
Minnesota. The second company, Smith & Loveless, Inc., of
Lenexa, Kansas, had successfully pioneered the manufacture of
factory-built equipment for sewage systems used by municipali-
ties, in industry and in residential construction. Both companies
had achieved remarkable sales and profit records within a comparatively brief period, operated efficient factories, and showed
every likelihood of continued growth.

UTC did not hesitate long. Comparatively brief negotiations
in 1959 resulted in the absorption of Lindsay at a cost of 225,000
shares of UTC stock, issued for the purpose, and of Smith and
Loveless for 100,000 shares.

For the first time, through the Lindsay Company, UTC had
entered the consumer market—and a substantial segment of it.
With the majority of American homes facing a hard-water problem, the water softener showed signs of becoming an essential
of modern high-standard residential life. Smith & Loveless also
touched the consumer market through the manufacture of equipment for use in residential sewage lines, but by far the larger
part of its fast-growing business was in the production of sewage
lift stations, ejectors, and sewage-treatment plants designed for
communities and real estate developments.

"When Will the Upturn Come?"

When, for the year 1959, UTC's income from sales and services
soared to $115,500,000, as compared with a gross income of only
$18,600,000 in 1950—an increase of 600 per cent in ten years—
everyone was stimulated. But the comparison for net income was
another matter. In 1950, on its puny $18,600,000 gross, the com-
pany had netted $4,200,000. The $115,500,000 income of 1959

had yielded only a $6,500,000 net—representing an increase of less than 50 per cent. Dollar earnings per share stood at $1.86; and only special circumstances had made possible the attainment of even this modest figure.[2]

The fact had to be faced: the year had been worse than anyone expected. Viewing the total situation, some of UTC's executives felt a good deal less than optimistic. To be sure, it was comforting that in the face of the adverse-earnings statements the price of the company's stock remained steady, suggesting that the stockholders were not seriously disturbed by the 1959 report. But the big question within the company was: "When will the upturn come—if at all?"

In executive meetings during late 1959 and early 1960, Locke took the position that, without being unduly optimistic, there was reason to believe that a corner had been turned, that the trend had become favorable. The intensive restaffing of a number of the newer divisions in the higher echelons was showing results. Careful analysis of sales and production costs was pointing the way to important savings and more realistic policies. Earnings in the second half of 1959 had been distinctly better than in the first half, and in the first quarter of 1960 better still. The long-term debt had been reduced. Capital expenditures, declining sharply, were at the lowest point since 1952. The order backlog of the non-tank-car divisions was substantially better than the year before.

Those who were ready to take a long view were struck by a remarkable increase, certainly not in earnings, but in earnings potential. In 1957, 64 per cent of the company's total net revenues had come from the tank car divisions. In 1959, these divisions had done more business than ever, yet they represented only 37 per cent of UTC's gross income from sales and services. Nearly two-thirds of the company's business now came from the non-tank-car divisions. Locke in the 1959 Annual Report gave considerable emphasis to these figures and drew a conservative inference: "As the net income of operations other than those of the tank car divisions improves, their contribution to Union's over-all earnings should be significant."

[2] See Appendix Q.

With Mixed Feelings

Clifford Graves, at seventy-three, as honorary chairman viewed the new state of the company with mixed feelings of paternal pride and paternal concern. He himself, in the decade of his presidency and chairmanship, had paved the way for the big change. But many of the elements of that change had come with a swiftness and impact that he had not always approved.

He felt, too, as the year 1960 began, that the total economic situation was not promising. American industry had curtailed capital expenditures, especially for new plants. The seller's market had unmistakably ended a year earlier. There was over-capacity in many lines of heavy industry. The pinch was especially painful in plate fabrication and in steel production, areas in which UTC now had large investments. Hungry competition was cutting prices and narrowing profit margins in these fields to the point where ingenious calculation and good luck were both needed to bring a profit out of the average sale. There was far less business available than there had been a few years earlier, and much of what was available was not worth having. Competition was fierce, too, in the municipal and contractor's market where Smith & Loveless found its business, and in the consumer market on which Lindsay depended. Even the comparatively stable tank car and tank truck businesses were under pressure. The oil industry was in the doldrums, and there were more pipe lines to contend with than ever before.

Nevertheless, Graves recognized that some of the new administrative developments held promise for the future. The divisional chiefs were organizing and executing their programs with heightened efficiency. Advanced statistical methods, implemented by the headquarters staffs of UTC's financial and statistical departments, were beginning to produce substantial savings in operating costs. The tank car divisions especially were making progress. Their repair shops in the United States and Canada would soon be doing with 630 employees what had three or four years earlier required 900—and doing it better. With a total shop and office force of 750 the American tank car division alone was handling a $40,000,000 volume of business annually, and managing assets with a total book value of $170,000,000.

In other divisions statistical analysis showed that the sales force had been actively pursuing business which could not produce a profit; or had been basing estimates of cost on incomplete data. Sharp revisions in pricing policy followed, together with heightened selectivity and concentration in selling. The redirection of sales effort in Graver Tank and Graver Water Conditioning especially produced results which transformed the outlook for these divisions.

Moreover, the investment in research was beginning to pay off, as tank car engineers, working with Graver Tank specialists, pioneered the development of, and built for use, the world's first tank cars (and the largest vehicles of any kind) for the transportation of liquid oxygen; and as other divisions reported promising research gains.

An increased emphasis on sales also struck Graves as sound. In the new plan of organization, each individual chief was fully responsible for the performance of his division. As long as he produced satisfactory earnings within the framework of broad company policy he was not interfered with. But Locke urged that all of the divisional heads personally concern themselves with sales. "It is easy," he reminded them, "for an administrator to fall into the habit of letting the problems of budget, production, engineering, and personnel dominate his thinking at the expense of the sales operation.... In my opinion, the top man who immerses himself in administrative routine or technical matters is often unconsciously trying to get away from the thorny problems of organizational selling." Following this line of thought, he recommended measures in all divisions "to get at the guts of the sales problem"—measures such as improved sales personnel, closer study of buyer attitudes and promotional methods, and the provision of greater practical help for the sales force in every division.

On balance Graves considered the future hopeful. His own contribution, he felt, would in future be as a source of friendly and available counsel. When in April, 1960, he decided on his formal retirement, it was recognized by everyone in the company that its strongest link with the past was being severed.

A few days later another tenet of the old regime was broken. It had always been taken for granted that every vacant directorship would be filled from among the company's departmental heads. Out of this custom had come the traditional formality and cautious reserve of UTC's board meetings, and the tendency to leave important decisions to the chief executive officer. It was obvious that the judgment of a board composed solely of the company's operating executives might lack objectivity and scope of outlook. Locke strongly felt, and the board agreed, that UTC would gain by having a fair proportion of directors who were otherwise unconnected with the company, and who could bring tested judgment, an outside viewpoint, and experience of other industries to bear on the company's problems. The four new directors who came onto UTC's board in the summer of 1960 were the heads of some of the nation's most respected industrial, utility, and financial companies.[3] Their presence produced a swift and marked alteration of tone in board meetings, with deeper penetration into executive proposals than ever before.

World-wide

For UTC, 1960 showed substantial progress. Net income per share, at $2.20, was 18 per cent higher than in 1959.[4] Although in his 1960 Annual Report Locke again cautiously reminded readers that the unsettled condition of the national economy made predictions unsafe, it was unmistakable that UTC had made gains in more than dollars.

By persisting in the course it was following, Locke believed, UTC would in time be able to forget the anxieties and arduous struggle of the years just past, as a mother forgets the pangs of successful childbirth. But the time was not yet. The company faced problems many of which grew out of conditions far beyond its control.

One of the more important of these problems was the increasing competition of foreign producers in fields in which the United States had formerly held an advantage—especially in the manufacture of technical machinery and equipment, and in industrial construction. West Germany, England, France, Belgium, Sweden,

---

[3] See Appendix P.

[4] See Appendix Q, on the relation between UTC's earnings statements and its deprecation policy.

Japan—the list of formidable competitors grew steadily, taking advantage of the large gap in labor costs between their own countries and the United States. American industrial products and construction bids abroad were being undercut right and left by foreign concerns able to provide goods and services of comparable quality at much lower cost. Locke faced this problem both as president of UTC and as a member of a national Advisory Committee on Foreign Trade appointed by the Secretary of Commerce. His conclusion, stated in a published article, was that it was hazardous for American industry to delay even for a day in taking "the measures that will keep us fully competitive with the rest of the world."

What steps, specifically, could UTC take to strengthen its own competitive position in overseas markets? One need was to enlarge the company's avenues of distribution in other continents. During the summer of 1960, a chance arose to add materially to the potential of the company's operations abroad. The well-known and long-established import-export firm of Getz Bros. & Company, of San Francisco, was rumored to be available for purchase, primarily as a result of the recent death of its most important stockholder-executive. The Getz staff included engineers, chemists, and technicians, as well as commercial specialists, and as a result was able to deal in a wide range of imports and exports, such as machinery, construction materials, paper, foods, chemicals, drugs, and electronic equipment. Representing more than 200 United States and foreign manufacturers, in many instances the firm assumed total marketing responsibility for the products which it handled, and often participated as partner in foreign enterprises. Getz also acted as general agents for important steamship and airline companies, operated factories producing consumer goods in Japan and the Philippines, Hong-Kong and Mexico, and owned several brand names of considerable value in Far Eastern trade. Its 30 offices around the world were staffed largely by nationals of the host countries.

Locke felt that Getz's trained selling organization and knowledge of conditions in many parts of the world could aid in opening foreign markets for the patents, processes, and technical know-how of UTC's other divisions. At the same time, it seemed probable that with UTC's financial backing Getz would be in a position to begin a systematic expansion of its commercial activities.

In September, 1960, the deal was consummated. For $675,000 cash and 23,700 shares of UTC treasury stock Getz became a wholly-owned subsidiary of UTC. Steps followed promptly to relate its selling operation to that of other divisions.

One factor in the Getz purchase was Locke's conviction that the United States would soon have to take steps to increase its shrinking share in world trade. This became the theme of several talks that he made to business groups in 1961. His own favorite suggestion was that a program be launched to get 10,000 chief executives of American companies to go abroad, on the ground that firsthand exploration of overseas business opportunities was the best means of stimulating American concerns to lift their sights beyond the domestic market. The response to this proposal in the press, the business community, and among government officials revealed, he felt, a heartening awareness of the urgency of the problem.

The New England Conscience

It was not only in size and scope that the company had grown. Earlier discomfort generated by Locke's drive to get men to do the best work of which they were capable had given way to a strong sense of participation and pride throughout the organization. Instances multiplied in which UTC's name figured in the areas of public service and business leadership. On the theory that what was bad for the country was bad for business, Locke felt that on important national questions affecting the company's interest a passive role would be poor policy and a sign of weakness, that there was an obligation on businessmen to stand up and be counted at the crucial times.

A case in point arose in connection with a widely publicized contest between two large competing railroads, both of which were attempting to acquire a third line, smaller but strategically located in the same region. That the smaller line ought, for economic reasons, to be absorbed by one of the others seemed incontestable; the question was, which? Studying the facts, it struck Locke that if road A succeeded in making the acquisition, the effect would be to establish a virtual railroad monopoly in much of the region served; but that if road B won out, its enhanced strength would make not for monopoly, but rather for more equal competition between road A and itself.

UTC's experience left no doubt that railroad monopoly anywhere worked against the interest of shippers, and so against the company's interest. Beyond this, however, was a larger issue—the danger for the nation as a whole of permitting monopoly to undermine the competitive character of the economy. Perhaps more than anyone else, the head of a company with UTC's history was in a position to understand that danger.

In the instance of the railroad dispute, Locke felt impelled to speak out. But there were complications. Road A had in the past given some of its plate fabrication business to UTC's Graver Tank division. It was obvious that further contracts from this source might not be forthcoming if the road took umbrage at Locke's intervention.

In making his decision, he explained his reasoning to some of those around him. "As I see it, if business is to continue to be a healthy influence in the country, the managers of business must provide leadership and set a useful example in matters of principle, as well as of profit. There are times when there is an obligation to let the private belief become the public commitment.

"I am not of course suggesting the reckless sacrifice of business interests to theoretical positions. I may say that in this particular matter, Union, in my judgment, stands to gain much more than it risks, in the long run, from my participation; but that is not my main reason for participating. Let us get away from the notion that the necessities of business require the stifling of personal conviction. The more that business men prove that they are not perpetually condemned to conformist behavior based on fear or appetite, the stronger and better their influence will be on American life."

Volunteering to appear as a witness at the official hearing on the proposed merger, Locke emphatically urged a decision that would avoid monopoly and it seemed probable that his testimony and that of other witnesses would have influence on the government's eventual decision in the case.

A few weeks after the hearing, a high official of road A called at Locke's office. Barely able to maintain a gloss of politeness over his rancor, the railroad man made it clear that in view of Locke's stand, the Graver Tank division would not be invited to bid on the road's future construction projects.

Locke replied that, properly regarded, his views on monopoly were a matter quite distinct from the railroad's relations with Graver Tank. Regardless of the railroad's decision, he himself had no intention of altering the amount of freight business that road A was receiving from several UTC divisions. But in any event, he had carefully considered his course beforehand, he regarded it as sound, and would do the same thing again if the opportunity arose. The railroad man seemed nonplussed as he left, but no less exercised. A little later, however, the railroad evidently reconsidered its position, for Graver Tank was after all invited to bid on its plate fabrication work.

Analyzing this and other episodes in Locke's public record, one of his associates remarked, "I've heard a lot about the New England conscience. Now I see what it means. It means standing up for your convictions and sitting down with a profit."

Anvil or Hammer

The year 1961 was the seventieth since UTC's incorporation. The company had, in a sense, been born old, in that from the very first it had resisted novelty and change. Now, in its ripe age, it suddenly found itself moved by a spirit of zestful adventure. For the first time in its history the large majority of its ranking executives were comparatively young and highly energized men for whom constant improvement and progress were psychological necessities—who, while respecting tradition, refused to be bound by it. Those whose recollections of the business ran back to the old days felt that it had entered on a new life cycle, and that they were experiencing a rejuvenation, with all the high hopes, relentless ambitions, painful disappointments, and resilient recoveries of youth.

In all of its seventy years the company had never known adversity. The pampered youngest child of a rich family, it had traded as long as it could on family status and automatically modeled itself after the paternal image. Only within the past decade had it found a direction and goal of its own, and it had surprised itself by the discovery of its own latent powers.

The spring of 1961 brought evidence that the company's forward surge was still in progress. After prolonged negotiation, Locke was able to announce the entry of UTC into the business of liquid and dry bulk storage. This move was made possible by acquisition of a remarkable site for the construction of a huge storage terminal on Lake Calumet, the strategic point connecting the inland waterways of the Midwest with the Great Lakes and the St. Lawrence Seaway. A new division, Bulk Terminals Company, was established for the purpose.

Net income rose steadily throughout 1961 and produced total per share earnings of $2.30. When, late in the year, a new office building, the Union Tank Car Building, was completed in Chicago's Loop, the financial press saw symbolic significance in the event. So did UTC's own employees as for the first time they occupied offices planned for organizational and individual efficiency. But although the risks that UTC had taken in its rapid expansion were apparently turning out well, an air of caution toward the future continued to prevail. Men reminded each other that in a chancy world there could be no guarantees. No matter how efficient the internal operation, reasonably good conditions in the national economy as a whole would be required to enable the company to fulfill its potential of growth.

No one doubted, however, that the potential was there, and the will to translate it into reality. Locke, who in his university days had written a thesis on Goethe, summed up the prevailing viewpoint in the poet's aphorism: "You must either lose or conquer, suffer or triumph, be the anvil or the hammer." The company, which a few years earlier seemed to have settled down to life as an economic anvil, had suddenly elected to become a hammer, and the sparks were flying.

For anyone familiar with the UTC story, it was natural to wonder what John D. Rockefeller would have said if he could have foreseen the mid-twentieth-century flowering of the once little company which had been so vital to his achievement. His fancy, it seems reasonable to surmise, would have been tickled. He himself had always believed in seizing the moment and adapting swiftly to changed conditions. Bringing imagination, daring, and competence to bear on the economic life and chances of his period, he had constructed in a few years the most remarkable industrial apparatus which the world had seen up to that time. In the process, he had taken advantage of the inadequacy of the laws regulating business to create a monopoly, and had trampled on competitors and on public sensibility. Yet when the dust had settled and the companies which he created had attained high and respected places in the American society, it was seen that he had built an enduring economic foundation on which they could stand. That a century after he had founded his own business one of its least offspring should within a period of three years be transmuted into a many-faceted corporate enterprise operating on a global scale probably would not have struck him as surprising. He knew better than most the economic magic that can be wrought when leadership and opportunity luckily combine.

APPENDIX

TABLE OF CONTENTS

A.	Railroad Cooperation with UTL in 1887	328
B.	UTL Technological Progress in the Early 1900s	328
C.	Significance of the Per Diem Rental Charge	331
D.	UTC Pioneers in Fusion Welding	332
E.	Employee Retirement Plans (1903–1933)	334
F.	Controversy with Mexico	335
G.	The ICC Investigates "Switching"	339
H.	Rental Rate Policy After 1950	341
I.	The 1956 Whiting Strike	343
J.	Evolution of the Hot Dog	344
K.	The Round Shop and the Big Dome	352
L.	The Graver Story	354
M.	Establishing a Price for Phoenix–Graver	356
N.	Foreign Affiliates of UTC.	356
O.	UTC's 1959 Earnings	357
P.	UTC's Directors, Officers, and Divisions	357
Q.	UTC's Earnings and Depreciation Policy	359

APPENDIX A: RAILROAD COOPERATION
WITH UTL IN 1887

The following excerpt from the 1907 Report of the U.S. Commissioner of Corporations reveals how W. H. Tilford's California operation in 1888 was aided by the rate-making practices of some of the country's railroads.

"An especially noteworthy instance of railroad discrimination during this period was an arrangement between Standard and the Southern Pacific Railroad and other transcontinental roads, which provided that Western lines would temporarily reduce the rates to the Coast to allow the Standard to accumulate large stocks of oil there, and then would suddenly increase the rates upon request. . . . Testimony before the Industrial Commission included a large number of communications between . . . Standard and . . . the railroads, showing that this arrangement was clearly understood by both parties. The following telegram from J. C. Stubbs, general traffic manager of the Southern Pacific, to W. Sproule is self-explanatory:

"San Francisco, November 14, 1888
"W. Sproule, San Francisco:
"Say to Tilford that association will probably consent to following agreement: oil rate from Cleveland to be one dollar; at this rate he can stock up; after doing so he to notify Chm. Leeds, who, after giving necessary notice, will advance rate to one dollar and twenty-five cents and continue that rate until such time as Tilford notifies him of reduced stock, when he will again reduce it to one dollar to enable him to stock up.

J. C. Stubbs"

APPENDIX B: UTL TECHNOLOGICAL
PROGRESS IN THE EARLY 1900s

At the turn of the century Standard refiners and marketers were facing a troublesome problem—how to ship paraffin and asphalt in bulk. It was easy enough to pour these commodities, in melted form, into tank cars; but how to get them out again after they solidified? The problem, especially in cold weather, was so acute that the Standard companies

329

for some years shipped paraffin and asphalt in cans, which were loaded into boxcars and heated individually on arrival at their destination. The highly uneconomical nature of this method was naturally a source of irritation. The demand for asphalt was soaring with the sale of automobiles and the improvement of roads; while paraffin was in steady demand, both in the United States and abroad, for votive candles, paraffin lamps, and other uses. No technical difficulty could be allowed to stand long in the way of their shipment by tank car.

There is a tradition that Standard's master technician, Van Dyke, first thought of the obvious solution. Why not introduce a steam pipe into the tanks of cars to be used for paraffin or asphalt, and at their destination force a supply of live steam into the pipes, thus melting the solidified contents of the cars? To provide the necessary steam installations at depots was an easy matter, and the heater-pipe tank car quickly became a commonplace. Soon the single steam pipe in the tank was replaced by elaborate coils which assured rapid and uniform heating.

Another significant innovation brought progress in a field which had always been a source of trouble—the determination of the quantity of oil contained in a given tank. Since freight charges were based on these determinations, the methods used in arriving at them were of prime concern to railroads and refiners. Congress itself, at the time of the "blind-billing" inquiry of 1887, had looked askance at UTL's statements of tank capacity. The early method of calibrating tanks had been to "strap" them—that is, to take their external measurements and calculate the cubic capacity accordingly. Later on tank cars were gauged by filling them with water, the quantity of which was measured. Critics of Standard were still dissatisfied, however. They pointed out that some cars, the capacities of which had been determined by UTL, appeared to hold substantially more water when gauged with railroad-owned apparatus than when gauged by Standard.

Charges that Standard's competitors and at least some railroads were being victimized by UTL's gauging practices began to circulate, and got into the press in 1900. At this point the executive committee of Standard ordered an inquiry into the matter. The responsibility fell on UTL's Master Car Builder C. M. Bloxham. In 1901, he submitted impressive evidence that alleged errors in the gauging of the company's tank cars had not been deliberate and in fact might not be errors at all. The reported discrepancies were owing simply to the fact that the apparatus used in water gauging at different places had not itself been properly calibrated. What was taken as a gallon of water by one gauge was less than a gallon for another.

Bloxham proposed that all water-gauging apparatus within the related industries be brought into uniformity. For this purpose he designed a heavy copper measure containing exactly five gallons, and accurate to one part in 38,000. Let this measure, he said, be tested and sealed in the care of responsible government officials and used thereafter to standardize the water gauge in use.

Within two years this task was largely accomplished. But criticism, stilled for a time, was soon renewed. Now it was alleged that UTL's water-gauged capacities differed from capacities determined by "strapping" the cars—and that the latter method was the more dependable. The issue was considered of sufficient importance by Standard's chiefs so that it was assigned for study to two of Rockefeller's veteran assistants, Van Dyke and W. P. Cowan, who later became president of Standard Oil of Indiana. It did not take them long to reach the conclusion that methods used in calculating the capacity of tank cars from their external dimensions were generally unreliable, haphazard, and subject to distortion. "We desire to express the opinion that such methods are inherently too inaccurate to be worthy of consideration. . . ." Bloxham's views on calibration, they reported, were entirely sound. Water gauging with standardized apparatus was the solution of the problem.

With this blessing UTL felt safe in putting into effect a comprehensive new program for calibrating new cars as produced, and recalibrating any old ones to which suspicion attached. No serious criticism of the company on the score of its listed tank capacities was heard thereafter. Fifty years later methods of tank gauging used by the American Petroleum Institute on behalf of the oil industry were substantially the same as those developed by Bloxham.

APPENDIX C: SIGNIFICANCE OF THE PER DIEM RENTAL CHARGE

The idea of basing charges to customers on a per diem rental grew naturally out of UTC's operation as part of the Standard combine. In order to satisfy the transportation needs of the many Standard refiners without having to provide an excessive number of tank cars, the cars were shuttled back and forth among them. This was feasible as long as a given car carried only one substance or substances that did not require cleaning of the car after each trip, and as long as the substance carried did not require the tank to have a special interior lining or other special construction. Cars suitable for regular interchange among petroleum companies came to be known as "general-purpose" cars. If a refiner found that he needed fewer general-purpose cars today than he needed yesterday, he could release the surplus cars, which would then be put to work promptly for another refiner.

A constant check was kept on each general-purpose car, day by day, and rental charges were billed to each Standard refiner using that car only for the number of days in which it had actually been in his service.

After the "dissolution" of 1911 this per diem system remained a distinguishing feature of UTC's operation, and was a source of considerable competitive advantage. It made for a high degree of efficiency in the use of petroleum cars, aiding UTC to keep its investment in new cars to a minimum. Customers benefited from rental charges which were lower than they would have had to be if UTC's general-purpose cars had been assigned by the month to the service of individual refiners—as was done by other tank car lessors.

Since "special-purpose" cars for the transportation of liquid-petroleum gases, chemicals, and foodstuffs could not be so readily exchanged among customers, such cars were generally placed in a different category and were leased by the month, usually under long-term contracts. By the mid-twentieth century, with UTC's tank cars carrying a vastly increased number of liquid commodities, there was a strong upward trend in the size of the special-purpose fleet. In terms of revenue, this development much more than offset a gradual reduction of the number of per diem cars.

APPENDIX D: UTC PIONEERS IN FUSION WELDING

In 1931, when government specifications called for construction of tanks by the forge-welding process, UTC's engineers had begun to explore a relatively new technique, fusion welding, which was being used in some other industries. At their request a few fusion-welded tanks were tested by the AAR Tank Car Committee. The results were closely studied by Joseph J. Root, who was then UTC's chief technical expert, and who would soon be a director of the company. He came to the conclusion that the fusion-welded tanks were even sturdier than the forge-welded, and could be more efficiently manufactured. Some technical problems had to be faced, but these could be met. It was feared by some that fusion welding would set up high stresses in steel. Root believed that such stresses, if they occurred, could be dealt with by putting every tank made by the process into a stress-relieving furnace. It was further learned that inspection of the weld could efficiently be carried out by X ray to assure the tank's soundness.

Root was certain that the future of the pressure tank car lay with fusion welding. Following his lead, the company asked the AAR Tank Car Committee to approve fusion-welded tanks for use. With their assent the company could then seek approval from the Interstate Commerce Commission, which held final power over tank car specifications. Root had already made sure that high-grade fusion-welded tanks could be produced to UTC's specifications by at least one leading plate fabricator.

He found, however, that the waters were deeper than he had suspected. Other tank car manufacturers, whose car shops were set up for the forge-welding process, were less than happy at the suggested innovation. Their attitude was understandable enough. Forge-welded cars were giving good service; why, then, make large capital outlays for a new process, especially at a time when business was tottering and deficits appearing in the books?

The AAR, recognizing the difficulty, decided to make no decision of its own. Instead, it dumped the problem into the lap of the ICC. Following its usual procedure, the commission arranged a hearing in Washington. There A. E. Smith and Root presented the case for the fusion-welded tank. The commissioners, however, were unenthusiastic. Their decision came promptly: the new tank had not yet been sufficiently tested to justify ICC approval.

It was a situation that called for tenacity. The company promptly retorted with a request for permission to build 10 cars with fusion-welded tanks for experimental use. A long delay followed, and although at last a nod came from Washington, it was 1936 before the new cars could be constructed.

The subsequent tests were exhaustive and conclusive. Careful technical studies showed that the fusion-welded tank was as much stronger and safer than the forge-welded as welding in general was stronger and safer than riveting. Smith and Root felt that they had proved their case—a feeling intensified when one of the new cars was involved in a bad train wreck, and survived with no failure of the welded seams.

Relevant data were placed in the hands of the ICC and the AAR. Not until 1941, however, would the government hand down new specifications for construction of pressure tank cars, and allow the use of the fusion-welding process. To pass this milestone in the tank car's technical history required ten years from first to last. It would be another fifteen years, in the 1950s, before forge welding for pressure cars was officially declared obsolete. But if the mills of the gods were grinding slowly, the result at least was progress.

APPENDIX E: EMPLYOEE RETIREMENT PLANS (1903–1933)

As it stood in 1933, the Retirement Plan had evolved a considerable distance from the old Standard Oil pension policy of 1903, which UTL had adopted. Under the 1903 plan, retiring employees aged sixty-five who had been with the company for twenty-five years could receive an annuity equal to 50 per cent of annual pay in the ten years preceding retirement; but large discretion as to this payment and additional benefits was left in the hands of the board of directors. Amended in 1909 and again in 1919, the plan had come to provide for retirement of employees at age sixty. A minimum of twenty years of service with the company assured the retiring employee of an annuity equal to 2 per cent of his average annual pay during the five years preceding retirement, multiplied by the number of years of his service up to thirty-seven-and-a-half years. A long-time veteran of the company might thus hope for as much as seventy-five per cent of his former pay as an annuity. All costs of the Retirement Plan, from 1903 to 1933, had been borne directly by the company.

Further amendment of the plan, in 1933, again followed a plan which was then being adopted by many of the oil companies. The company now offered to employees of sixty-five years or over retirement benefits equal to only 1 per cent of the employee's average salary calculated over his entire term of service, multiplied by the total years of his service. The employee could, however, increase the amount of his future annuity by contributing up to 3 per cent of his salary to his retirement fund. In that event the company would contribute a sum which when added to the employee's contribution would purchase an additional 1 per cent of the employee's average salary for each year of his service with the company. To insure payment of such annuities regardless of economic conditions the company negotiated a contractual arrangement with the Equitable Life Assurance Society; while requirements under the 1919 plan were met by purchasing from Equitable, in a lump sum, insurance equal to the amount of accumulated employee retirements credits up to 1933.

Stockholders, asked to approve the 1933 "amendment" to the Retirement Plan, unhesitatingly agreed. The plan was hailed by Drake as the most advanced in the tank car industry. From an actuarial standpoint, it was an undoubted improvement. And Drake was highly pleased by the resulting economies. Most employees, however, were somewhat less enthusiastic about the new plan. An employee of thirty years' service, if he took full advantage of the arrangement, could retire with a pension of 2 per cent times 30, or 60 per cent of his average salary for the rest of his life, but he would have to be exceptionally thrifty to do it. For the most part only the highly-paid top executives were in a position to set aside the 3 per cent of earnings which would entitle them to the additional 1 per cent of average salary after retirement. The typical employee's retirement annuity was being cut to less than half—less, because even the 1 per cent contribution guaranteed by the company was based on his average salary for his entire period of service, instead of for the last five years of service. Many an employee, contemplating his chances of a serene old age, was deeply disturbed. The board of directors could still, at their discretion, ease the strain for retiring employees by making them consultants to the company for a time; but since this practice was confined almost entirely to the high executive level, it afforded little solace to junior executives and clerks. Given the economic climate of the early 1930s, however, the company had some reason to feel that the revised Retirement Plan was entirely fair and even generous to its employees.

In 1951 the Retirement Plan was integrated with the requirements of the Federal Social Security plan, revised in other respects, and supplemented by the company's Profit Sharing Plan.

APPENDIX F: CONTROVERSY WITH MEXICO

"MEXICO HOLDS UP TANK CARS FOR UNITED STATES"

"Embargo Believed Step Toward Enforcing Oil Wage Rate upon Foreign Companies"

"Confiscation Is Possible"

"Firms Say That Equipment Was Recently Recalled by Owners Because of Unsettled Conditions"

"Special Dispatch to the *New York Times*

by Frank L. Kluckhohn

"Mexico City, Dec. 28 [*1937*] . . . The Mexican Government today ordered the halting of more than 100 United States Oil tank cars before they cross the Mexican frontier. The government thus moved toward a showdown on the oil wage controversy with the United States and British petroleum companies with an invest-

ment of $450,000,000 in Mexico. . . . The Mexican National Railroad Administration [gave] orders on 107 tank cars rented from a United States company named Products Tank Line by the Standard Oil of New Jersey subsidiary Huasteca. . . .

"With government finances strained, [with] foreign oil companies paying in taxes more than 6 per cent of the total State as well as Federal income . . . the government is apparently seeking to avert a conflict capable of causing serious international difficulties by holding the tank cars or else is seeking to obtain a trump card for use if difficulties develop.

"Since the tank cars are United States owned, whereas the oil company subsidiaries function as Mexican companies, it is reported that the halting is capable of causing international difficulties. The oil companies asserted today that they had not ordered the tank cars back to the United States but that the owner-company was taking that step because of the danger of developments here."

With this report there began for UTC its first experience in international diplomacy. Hundreds of the company's cars, under the Products Tank Line stencil, had been allocated for service to and from Mexico since the 1920s. Although the total revenues involved were not very large and although mileage allowances due from Mexican railroads had not always been promptly collectable, UTC was glad to have income from whatever source and on whatever scale, especially during the worst of the depression years. By 1937 economic conditions in the United States had improved enough and UTC's income had risen enough so that loss of rentals from cars used in Mexico could be taken lightly; but the cars themselves were another matter. Even though they were for the most part old cars, the company could not permit their confiscation.

Some years earlier Douglas Campbell had sent one of his partners to open an office in Chicago, assuring on-the-spot legal counsel for UTC. This attorney, Arthur Bristol, was immediately called in by Graves for consultation. Their first decision was to wait to see what effect the protest then being made by American oil companies and the Department of State would have on the Mexican government. On March 18, 1938, the position became plain, as it was announced that the Mexican government had expropriated foreign oil properties. Bristol then wrote to the oil companies, American and Mexican, which had been served by UTC, and to the Mexican railroads involved, demanding that the cars be returned. He was promptly informed that this was impossible. Mexico had imposed an embargo forbidding tank cars to leave Mexico, loaded or empty.

A week passed; and then the Mexican government telegraphed Graves with a proposal. Would he permit Mexico to lease or buy the embargoed cars? Graves' decision to say "no" grew in part from rumors then current of impending war in Europe and his recollections of the tank car crisis of 1914. This was no time to sell even old tank cars for service outside the United States. But he was also irritated by the Mexican government's seemingly hostile attitude toward the American oil companies that had investments there, and it was his sense of solidarity with UTC's customers, as much as anything, that caused him to word his refusal in brusque, not to say harsh, terms. In essence his telegram said that UTC would not lease or sell the cars, and demanded their prompt return.

Douglas Campbell's New York office was more than a little agitated when a copy of Graves' telegram arrived. Whatever the company's rights in the matter, some of the partners felt, it would be wise to recognize that the Mexican government had power to do UTC severe damage. It was conveyed to Graves that his correspondence and contacts ought to be conciliatory and diplomatic in tone, especially since the assistance of the U.S. State Department had been invoked.

Graves never doubted that his action was tactically sound, but he accepted the rebuke with a grin and thereafter left the affair to law and diplomacy. Success, or what seemed to be success, followed. Before the year was out the State Department was informed that "all cars of Products Tank Line formerly in service in Mexico have now been received in this country."

With a Touch of Light Opera

The trouble, however, was just beginning. The Mexican government's action in holding and using 130 tank cars for a year without payment had deprived UTC of revenue to which the company was entitled, and Graves was determined to collect it. Campbell's associates recommended that the matter be placed in the hands of a Mexican law firm, the senior partners of which were Americans. This firm accepted the case and asked the Mexican Petroleum Administration, familiarly known as PeMex, for approximately $75,000 as proper compensation of UTC.

The first news from Mexico City was discouraging. "There is at present little hope of collecting money from the Oil Administration. . . . They are losing money rapidly." By this time, December, 1939, the European war had begun, and Mexico's oil exports had been cut away. However, an interesting suggestion was made to Arthur Bristol. A dredge, the *San Christobel,* and a tug, the *Bellano,* both the property of PeMex, were at that time on the way to Mobile, Alabama, for repairs. Might not a legal proceeding in Alabama against the PeMex result in a court order to attach these vessels and so stimulate the interest of the Mexicans in settling UTC's claim? The dredge and the tug together were worth about $300,000. Bristol did not delay an instant before engaging an Alabama law firm for the purpose. His reward, a few weeks later, was a telegram from Mobile: "Attachment levied on dredge and tug today."

Wheels promptly turned with a grating noise in Mexico City. High officials of the Mexican government were then seeking to find ways to ease the strain between their country and the United States. It was no time to exacerbate the feelings of American industry. Mexico was collecting a substantial tax revenue from the Association of American Railroads, representing United States lines which were providing train service in Mexican territory. Who knew what attitude might be taken toward payment of this tax by the Department of State if Mexico withheld moneys due to an American corporation? Why let large expectations be jeopardized by small parsimony? UTC's representatives in Mexico City were told that if the company would moderate its demand—surely $75,000 was excessive—something might be done.

This much gained, Graves was willing to cooperate. Certain technical counterclaims of the Mexican government had to be considered; if these could be dropped, UTC was prepared to accept $25,000 in full settlement of its demand.

But now the Mexican government had a new worry. Other American companies with claims against Mexico had observed UTC's maneuver and had followed suit, requesting the state of Alabama to attach the Mexican vessels until their demands were satisfied. Since legally only one attachment could be put on the vessels at a time, a line had formed behind UTC for this purpose.

The news from Alabama created consternation at PeMex, which badly needed the dredge. It would take some days to complete the repairs then being made in a Mobile shipyard. If UTC on settlement of its claim were to ask for the dismissal of its case before the vessels could sail, then all would be lost. Subsequent court actions would keep the dredge at Mobile indefinitely. There was only one hope— the cooperation of UTC.

A request went to Chicago: would the company agree to arrange matters so that its case would not be dismissed until repairs could be finished and a Mexican crew could reach Mobile? In that way, with precise timing, the dredge and tug might get out of Mobile harbor before any other attachment could be levied. It was evident to Graves that UTC could hope to collect its claim only by acceding; for why should Mexico pay any of the suing companies if it could not get its property back? Late in May, 1940, a hectic exchange of telegrams between Chicago, Mobile, and Mexico City saw the arrangement in effect. Just as UTC's agents in Mexico City were receiving a government check for $25,000, the *Bellano* chugged out of Mobile Harbor, the *San Christobel* in its wake. All Mexican counterclaims against UTC were dropped. It was an agreeable situation. There was no publicity. The face of the Mexican government had been saved. UTC's self-respect had been preserved. True, after the various attorneys' fees had been paid the company's net gain did not amount to much, but the moral victory was an unmistakable demonstration of the advantage of wearing the velvet glove of diplomacy—as long as there was a strong fist within.

APPENDIX G: THE ICC INVESTIGATES "SWITCHING"

In the middle 1940s a division of the Interstate Commerce Commission was engaged in a far-reaching investigation of the terminal services provided by railroads. Its attention had focused on a long-established custom under which railroads agreed to switch tank cars, without charge, from their tracks to tank car repair shops and back again. Although the distance involved for any individual car was short, when multiplied annually by tens of thousands of such movements the cost of switching was far from insignificant. As early as the 1870s John D. Rockefeller had recognized the importance of the point; it was largely as a result of his insistence that early Standard contracts with railroads had made them bear responsibility for switching costs.

The ICC investigators did not deny that the cost of switching tank cars should be defrayed by the railroads. Their contention was simply that the railroad should in turn be compensated by the shipper for such service. It seemed to them that this was not being done under the existing system, that freight rates for oil products had not been set high enough to cover the cost of switching.

There was more. The investigators thought that as matters stood the railroads, in absorbing the costs of switching, were being victimized twice over. It was alleged that they were paying a tank car mileage allowance that had been calculated on the assumption that the shipper was responsible for switching costs. The mileage allowance rate, as approved by the ICC, was high enough to permit tank car owners or lessees to reimburse the railroads for the cost of switching—so ran the argument.

If these allegations could be proved, the matter was serious. A railroad that paid the regular mileage allowance without charging shippers for switching service could then be held to have paid a rebate and would be in violation of the Interstate Commerce Act. Even if it escaped penalties for the past, it would have to charge shippers for switching service in the future—increasing the cost of the railroad transportation of oil products.

As a test case the ICC Division selected the services rendered by the Illinois Central Railroad in "switching empty tank cars to, from, and between shops, building, yard, and tracks of the Union Tank Car Company at North Baton Rouge, Louisiana, for repairs, storage, or cleaning, without compensation."

"We Request That the Full Commission Reconsider . . ."

Most railroads were as reluctant as the tank car companies and the shippers involved to see the existing practice changed. Any rise in their charges for oil freight would inevitably weaken their position relative to trucks, barges, and pipe lines. And aside from competitive considerations, if the ICC division's stand should be upheld there would have to be a costly readjustment in contractual relations and accounting practice among railroads, shippers, and tank car companies. When the matter came up for hearing, no one was surprised to find that the attorneys representing the Illinois Central stood in opposition to the ICC's ruling together with representatives of Douglas Campbell's firm, which represented UTC.

A brief submitted by the UTC in March, 1946, strongly denied that switching costs were included in the existing mileage allowance. It points out that switching "has universally been performed by all carriers at all points without charge. . . . Since private car companies had never been called on to pay such a charge, the charge could not have been included in any figures submitted to the ICC . . . when the amount of mileage allowance was considered. . . ." The railroad had elected "to perform the switching" instead of compensating the shipper for performing it. It followed, in UTC's view, that the railroad had in no way violated the law, and that the present arrangements for switching should not be interfered with.

Attorneys for the Illinois Central went even further in challenging the ICC division's stand by questioning "the commission's jurisdiction over these particular movements . . . because such movements are intrastate in character. We . . . doubt that any such moves could be found to be interstate. . . . Under what circumstances could any of these movements of a few feet to and from or within the repair shop be deemed interstate moves?" Further, said the Illinois Central, if railroads charged for switching services, they could expect shippers to demand an increased mileage allowance. The net result would not be greater profit for the railroad, but simply greater billing and accounting costs. The shipper and the tank car company, in the long run, would not be much affected. The railroads were "the ones and the only ones who stand to lose. . . . We request that the Full Commission reconsider the decision . . . and reverse it with the finding that present practices are lawful."

"Not Unlawful"

In April, 1947, the full commission of the ICC rendered a final verdict. Reversing the earlier decision, it confirmed the view of UTC and the Illinois Central that existing switching practice was "not unlawful." It is probable that few rulings in American jurisprudence have given so much satisfaction to all of the parties of interest. It had been a case in which technical interpretations of law threatened for a time to create a serious problem for railroads, tank car companies, and shippers alike.

Nevertheless, there was benefit in the ICC's clarification of the problem. One of the commissioners, in dissenting from the majority, correctly pointed out that under the ICC decision there was nothing to prevent the tank car company from having its Baton Rouge cars "switched" to its repair shops in New Jersey and returned to Baton Rouge without charge. It was a point which UTC's executives were quick to note. Graves had always taken the position that the strongest asset of the company in its relations with the government was its reputation for integrity among its customers, its suppliers, and the railroads. Its status could only be preserved by maintaining a strong ethical standard. There must be no instance in which UTC could be said to have abused its right to free switching service. At locations where switching distances from repair shops to refineries ran above normal, arrangements were promptly made to protect railroads against excessive switching costs.

APPENDIX H: RENTAL RATE
POLICY AFTER 1950

During the late 1940s Graves had actually reduced rates. In 1952, however, the railroads raised the mileage allowance from 2.2 to 3 cents per mile. With increased mileage being credited to shippers, and a consequent lowering of their net rental charges, Graves felt justified in seeking a higher return per leased car. He achieved this, initially, not by raising rates, but by obtaining the joint concurrence of all customers to a change in the formula by which rental charges were calculated.

By the middle 1950s, the inflationary trend that began with World War II had driven costs so far upward as to require reappraisal of the rate structure. In 1955, a small group of UTC executives led by Locke began to press for a direct increase in rental rates consistent with current costs. It was their view that in order to meet its full obligation to customers and stockholders alike UTC had to improve its comparatively low return on capital. To adhere any longer to the old rates would not in the end serve the interest of customers. On the contrary, such a policy could only tend to weaken the technical performance of the company, the efficiency of its fleet, and the soundness of its financial position.

There was full agreement among UTC's directors that the company needed an improved return. The problem was to determine an economically sound rate that could keep the company in a strong competitive position while offsetting its higher costs. Some differences arose, however, as to the degree of need and the timing of the increase. Locke thought speed was essential; Graves was inclined to wait.

In the upshot, the conclusive influence was exerted by the railroads. Beset themselves by high costs, they acted in 1956 as they had in several prior years, to increase their charges for repairs to the tank car companies. After that the proponents of a prompt rise in UTC's rental charges made rapid headway.

The rise in rentals decided on by UTC in 1956 was still substantially below that which many of its executives felt to be necessary and justified. It was, in fact, so moderate that it could not offset the still-mounting costs of tank car operation. By 1959 a further increase was being advocated.

Again cautionary voices were raised in UTC's board room. What would the customers say? After full debate the conclusion was reached that UTC's customers would understand from their own experience the pressure of rising costs on prices; and that there would be little demur to a revised schedule of rentals—especially since UTC's charges would stand the test of comparison with those of other tank car companies. As for competition from trucks, studies showed that car rental prices were generally a minor factor in a shipper's decision as to whether to ship by rail or by truck; the bulk of his costs were determined by freight rates.

Late in 1959 the board put into effect a revised schedule of prices.

It was a step that needed no apology. The increase in rates to the shipper had been more than offset by another increase in the mileage allowance paid by the railroads, this time to 4 cents per mile, so the net cost of tank cars for shippers was actually less than in the past. Even with the new schedule, UTC's return on its total investment in tank cars was only 6 per cent, at a time when even public utilities were allowed a 6½ per cent return.

But the significance of the price increase went far beyond the favorable effect on income. It betokened the increasing flexibility of the company in adapting to change in its economic environment.

APPENDIX I: THE 1956 WHITING STRIKE

The first hint of the strike was an election which resulted in affiliation of the shop union with a powerful CIO International Union, the Oil, Chemical, and Atomic Workers. This came at a time when a new contract was to be negotiated and when the car-building program was nearing its peak. The company refused to accept all of the demands of the new union, whereupon the local union leaders called the strike.

UTC from earliest days had evinced a paternalistic interest in the welfare of its individual employees. During Graves' presidential administration there had been more constructive thinking about employee security than ever before. In the late 1940s the company's group life and sickness insurance coverage had been extended to include the dependents of employees and to yield larger payments for hospitalization. In 1951, Graves approved an unusual, almost unique profit-sharing plan, under which a percentage of the company's profits were allocated to the purchase of stock to be held in trust for employees, with dividends paid to them quarterly. Other employee benefits had been similarly strengthened. Wage rates paid by the company were believed to be at least on a par with those of the rest of the industry, and superior to those of the railroads for equivalent classes of work.

With so much zeal on the part of management to protect the individual employee, a few of the older UTC executives were inclined to regard collective pressure on the company by a shop union almost as ingratitude. Others, however, recognized that the day of managerial paternalism was fast vanishing. The rapid expansion in the national economy of the labor unions and their increased political power had created a radically changed situation, in which labor-management differences were likely to be more sharply disputed than in the decade past.

The decision of the Whiting union to strike was not grounded in the wage question, for the company's proposed contract offered considerably increased rates of pay. The main point at stake was the length of the contract. The union insisted on a contract for one year only; UTC's management, on the other hand, felt that so short a contract would gravely interfere with production planning. When two efforts at conciliation by the National Labor Relations Board failed, it became apparent that a strike of considerable duration was to be expected.

Week after week, negotiation proved fruitless. Both sides, however, made strong efforts to maintain a calm tone in their relations. During the work stoppage management kept intact the fringe benefits of the striking union members, such as group insurance and hospitalization. After nearly three months, an effort to end the strike in the interest of the two affected Indiana communities was made by their mayors, acting in conjunction; and under these unusual auspices union and management resumed negotiation and reached agreement. The union's acceptance of a three-year contract was paralleled by management's acceptance of the union's position on some minor contractual points.

APPENDIX J: EVOLUTION OF THE HOT DOG

There is a definition of luck which denies that it is synonymous with chance—which asserts that the lucky or unlucky break is usually produced not by external chance alone, but by chance and human response in combination. During 1953–1954, a line of action within UTC coincided with an unpredictable circumstance in the Association of American Railroads. The company responded, and emerged with a revolutionary new tank car known as the Hot Dog.

Tank Bands and Original Sin

At this time UTC had begun to speed up its retirement of small cars while increasing the rate of construction of larger ones, for oil refiners were finding that one 12,000-gallon car was more efficient for most purposes than two 6,000-gallon cars. Progress had been made, too, toward the nearly total elimination of riveting in the building of new cars. Not only tanks but underframes could now efficiently be put together by fusion welding. Other tank car companies were ahead in this respect, but UTC was catching up. In 1953, Chief Engineer Clyde Folmsbee had designed a prototype of an all-welded underframe which withstood every test and was regarded as superior to anything previously produced in the industry. Thereafter, the question of building an all-welded tank car seemed to be one of cost only.

UTC's Mechanical Department, feeling that it was well abreast of its job, was not overjoyed when Locke suggested that further thought might well be given to a new design for the all-welded car to be. He had been analyzing tank car repair and maintenance costs, and had been struck by the fact that an important item in maintenance was the tank band—the circular steel straps which ran around the tank, hugging it to the underframe. To keep the tank bands tight was a never-ending and costly struggle in UTC's shops. When they remained loose for a considerable length of time, they created danger that the bouncing tank would buckle or even fracture at the points of support. Then, too, loose tank bands would scrape off the tank's paint, producing streaks of corrosion which were expensive to remedy.

Why not, therefore, think of producing a car without tank bands? Here Locke was met with the weary smiles of experience. In the view of most of UTC's technicians, tank-band trouble in tank cars was like original sin in man. It was simply a fact of life, not to be avoided. True, fifty years earlier Van Dyke had designed a car—the old V-car —without an underframe, and which dispensed with tank bands, but it had never been entirely satisfactory, for it tended to leak at the points where the saddle supports and running board supports were riveted to the tank.

But was it not possible to build an all-welded V-car that would eliminate rivets and leakage? Some in the Mechanical Department took a dim view of the idea, but Folmsbee thought it could be done. The next year, 1954, he came forward with a prototype of a modified V-car, in which a conventional all-welded tank and the welded "cradle" that supported it made a single unit anchored and keyed to the welded underframe. Requiring no tank bands, the new car gave promise of important savings in maintenance.

Wrong for Eighty Years

So far, this was normal technical progress, a commonplace in American business, but now chance, the unpredictable circumstance, intervened. The AAR had just built a new laboratory in Chicago, designed to test cars by methods never before used. The fact that UTC's new car and the testing laboratory were completed at almost the same time made the car the first to be tested by the new methods. First, the ability of the car to withstand shock was measured under the so-called impact test. Strain gauges, connected by wires to recording instruments, were fixed at points where the tank was welded to the cradle, and also to the heads of the tank. The car was then run at representative speeds to collide with another loaded tank car. The instruments showed the resulting stresses at every crucial point in the car's structure.

The first impact tests were run while the tank was empty—the usual practice. The new UTC car stood up superbly. The next test was to make sure that the tank, when loaded, would sustain additional stresses caused by the weight and surge of liquid within. This test would be run with the tank shell filled with water up to the top, simulating the conditions under which a loaded tank car generally moved. Gauges to measure stress were again put on the heads of the tank, and again it was subjected to heavy external impacts. The results continued to be excellent.

The last step in the test was to find out the effect of impacts when the tank was less than full. At this point, the play of chance reached its climax. Prior to the use of the new strain gauges, it had always been taken for granted that stress caused by the surge of liquid in a tank increased when some of the contents were removed. Now, for the first time, this assumption was about to be tested.

Twelve vertical inches of water were drawn out of the top of the tank, and the impacts resumed, as before. The readings of the strain gauges made the men present rub their eyes. They had expected the stresses on the heads of the tank to be greater than when it was full. Instead, they were less, by about 75 per cent.

Was it possible that for eighty years tank car engineers had been laboring under an erroneous belief about a basic technical factor in their business? More water was drawn off, the tests were run again—and the result was still more emphatic. There could be no doubt. Contrary to all expectation, a partly full tank meant smaller and not greater stresses on the tank heads. Subsequent investigation revealed the reason. When the tank was full, the liquid contents instantaneously transmitted almost the total shock from one end of the car to the other; but when the tank was less than full, and the liquid was allowed to move freely, it acted as a "dampener," absorbing a considerable part of the external impact on the car, and spreading it out over a longer period.

For years thereafter copies of reports describing this test were in demand all over the world, as technical institutions and industrialists realized that an old superstition of tank car construction had been finally laid to rest. The experience, as Locke remarked, was a fine example of serendipity, the art of making happy discoveries by accident.

No Dome?

Chance had done its part; but so far no benefit for the company, no luck, that is to say, had appeared, good or bad. It was on its way, however. Locke promptly discussed the unexpected result of the AAR test with Graves, who drew a striking inference: that the traditional dome with which all ordinary petroleum cars were equipped had never really been necessary. The reasoning here was plain enough. The old-time engineers, taking it for granted that tanks were subject to less stress when full, wanted them loaded to capacity; but since petroleum products tend to expand as a result of increased heat during normal travel, they had felt it necessary to provide space for expansion, and the dome was the result.

Now suddenly in 1954 it appeared that tank-head stress due to liquid surge did not increase but decreased when the tank was only partly full. What purpose, then, did the dome serve? None, said Graves.

It was in 1872 that the dome had been adopted as a standard feature of the tank car, when Joseph Potts of the old Empire Transportation Company decided to eliminate upright tanks of the Densmore type in favor of horizontal "boiler tanks." One disadvantage of the Densmore cars was the leakage of oil through the manhole of the tank when increase of temperature in transit caused expansion of the cargo. The first iron tanks built in the late 1860s were unsatisfactory for the same reason. When full, they tended to leak extensively. To correct this defect a small Pennsylvania firm of car builders conceived the idea of putting a "cupola" on the tank. The first cupolas were not large enough to provide fully for expansion and prevent leakage, but Potts called in an engineering consultant, who devised a dome similar in shape and dimensions to that subsequently used by car builders. At this point the domed car came into, and remained in, general use.

To Graves the domes had been an irritating fact of tank car operation for a long time, for they were expensive to build and even more expensive to maintain. UTC's engineers had never succeeded in designing a dome which they could be absolutely certain would remain free from corrosion over years of service.

Unless UTC's domes were frequently and laboriously cleaned they threatened to contaminate commodities carried in the tank. The problem was especially annoying to Graves because it had been overcome by a competitor. The American Car and Foundry Company had developed a widely advertised "flued dome," made of a single steel plate, and superior to UTC's dome in that it eliminated corroding crevices.

Long before the AAR tests of Folmsbee's new car, it had occurred
to Graves that the best way to offset UTC's disadvantage in dome
construction might be to eliminate the dome altogether. But when he
discussed the matter with UTC's engineers, who were then still cap-
tives of the old stress theory, they shook their heads. You had to have
domes on petroleum cars, they said. True, the pressure cars used to
carry liquefied petroleum gas had long been built without domes.
But LPG cars involved problems very different from those of petroleum transportation. In moving liquefied gases under pressure, the
domeless tank cars traveled only partially full, so as to provide ample
room for gas formation above the surface of the liquid and minimize
the danger of excessive pressures. This technique was made possible
by the comparatively light weight of the gas. But, said the engineers,
you could not ship partly full in an ordinary tank car, because the
surge of heavy liquids would create too much stress on the tank head.

This was the position when Graves heard the results of the AAR
tests, demonstrating that a tank could move with greater safety
partly empty than when full. His immediate response was to recognize that, contrary to the prevailing notion, it was feasible to ship
liquids in a domeless car, provided that space for expansion was left
above the liquid. The dome, no longer needed for safety, could be
eliminated in future tank car construction. Merely by not loading tank
cars to the full and by leaving room within the tank itself for expansion of the liquid contents, tank cars would serve the shipper's need
without the costly dome.

Why Wheels?

It occurred to Locke that if the industry could be wrong for generations on so fundamental a point as the theory of tank head stress,
then it was time to question many another concept of tank car construction. Would it not be worthwhile to approach tank car design
with an open-minded determination to build a better tank car, regardless of tradition? Executives of the Mechanical Department pointed
out in reply that to design was one thing, but to get approval was
another. Tank car specifications were established by the AAR and
the ICC. Those powerful agencies had definite reasons for wanting
tank cars made as they were being made. They would not permit
bizarre innovations.

Locke was not convinced. What would happen, he wondered, if
without disclosing his purpose he were to "borrow" a few selected
young engineers with unimpaired imaginations, and put them in a
separate office with instructions to devise a radically better tank car?
Freed from other responsibilities and the domination of the Old

Guard, and with Folmsbee in charge and available to them for counsel, they might achieve—who knew what?

In his first meeting with the chosen task force Locke gave them their directive. It was brief and pointed. They had carte blanche. They were at liberty to break any and every tradition of tank car design. Any idea that sounded halfway promising, no matter how fantastic, had to be given fair consideration. "Forget the present specifications," said Locke. "Imagine yourselves in a wonderful world where you didn't have to worry about the AAR and the ICC. Design a tank car as it would be in such a world. But be sure you have a good reason for everything you do. When you come to me with your design, I'm even going to ask you why you have to have wheels on the car."

In this spirit, the work was begun. Secrecy was the order of the day. It was obvious that since the idea of a new type of car had occurred to UTC, it might also have occurred to competitors. Therefore, the less said about it the better, even within the company. No one outside the task force, no matter how high his rank, was to see the work of the task force until it was finished.

Not long after its inception the project found a name when Locke was shown a sketch of a possible tank car, domeless, without tank bands or underframe, and with a long, perfectly cylindrical, sausage-like tank. "It looks," he said, "like a hot dog." As a code for written communications, Hot Dog or HD was sufficiently mystifying to the uninitiated, while for the task force it was a private joke and pass-word combined.

The zeal with which the engineers on the HD project plunged into their work suggested that whimsy, as an executive tool, has its values. The secrecy of the project was not violated. A few of the company's highest-ranking executives were aware of its general nature, but the curiosity of others was left unassuaged. When now and then a question was asked, it was answered frankly—up to a point. An experiment was under way—it might come to nothing; competitors must not hear about it; everyone, it was hoped, would understand.

Legal and Illegal Hot Dogs

Conservatives of the Mechanical Department did not conceal their disapproval of the Hot Dog when it came off the drawing boards and they were asked to build prototypes. Critics of the new car told Locke that no car with a big tank and without an underframe could be safe. It was the same argument that had agitated UTC in the days of the V-car. But Locke felt no qualms in accepting Folmsbee's calculations. These showed that, although in a conventional car the tank was merely a burden on the underframe, in the Hot Dog the tank worked as both a structure and a container, contributing to the strength of the car.

Another factor in the debate was the omission from the Hot Dog, as first designed, of the side running boards that from early days had been a feature of tank cars. Opponents pointed out that the ICC required every tank car to be equipped with side running boards. But surely, the Hot Doggers countered, the ICC was not necessarily forever bound to such a specification. Since the commission consisted of reasonable men, it seemed likely that if the side running board could be shown to be superfluous they would drop it. In any event, running boards could, if necessary, be provided for the Hot Dog by welding them to the sides of the tank. Unlike the old V-car, where riveted running-board supports had caused leakage from the tank, the Hot Dog could take the weight of welded running boards on its tank without undue strain. Not without reluctance, the Mechanical Department agreed to produce the two prototypes needed for testing.

By 1956 the AAR had devised a type of structural test more severe than anything previously seen, in which the underframe of the car was compressed at both ends simultaneously to determine its ability to withstand buckling. UTC was the first company to submit a car—the Hot Dog—to the AAR for this new compression test. Squeezed at both ends under enormous pressure, the car made an extraordinarily good showing, and after successful impact tests received the approval of the Tank Car Committee of the AAR.

As matters turned out, the domelessness of the new car created no obstacle with the AAR or ICC, in view of the recent discovery in tank-head stress dynamics. Nor was the lack of underframe a problem. The side running boards, however, were. One of the new cars had been built with side running boards to meet ICC specifications; this was known as "the legal Hot Dog" and was to be shown to customers. The second car, "the illegal Hot Dog," was made without running boards, for demonstration at Whiting to members of the ICC's Safety Bureau.

The debate over the running boards, which began in 1956, was a source of profound irritation to those in UTC who had backed the giant new car from its inception. Side running boards were as obsolescent, said the dogged Hot Doggers, as the dome. The company then proceeded to challenge the relevant ICC safety regulation—something that had never previously been done in tank car history. Pending an ICC decision, the new car would be provided with running boards, but it was expected that their elimination would soon be permitted.

On this point Locke and the other advocates of the new car were due for disappointment. Antediluvianism was the order of the day in more places than UTC's Mechanical Department. The Railway Labor Executives Association refused to be convinced that tank cars without side running boards were actually safer than the old-style cars. A protest filed by this association with the ICC plunged the matter into lengthy litigation, and blocked approval of the new design without running boards. For some time, at least, Hot Dogs produced by UTC would have to be equipped with what its designers felt was an anachronism, an excrescence, and an aesthetic flaw in the otherwise sleek and visually satisfying structure. In all other respects, the original design was kept intact.[1]

When UTC's executives were invited to view the first completed and fully-tested domeless, underframeless, tankbandless, general-purpose petroleum tank car, everyone was impressed, but not everyone was convinced. The out-of-pocket expense for construction of the first Hot Dog cars—leaving out engineering costs and tests—had been 50 per cent more than for any other prototype previously built by the company. Old-line executives seized on this fact. Where was the advantage of eliminating the dome and the underframe if costs of manufacture were to rise? Energetic arguments ensued within the company. Proponents of the Hot Dog pointed out that future cars built to the same model would cost much less. As for technical objections, the car had been fully approved except for the elimination of the side running boards.

The question as to whether the Hot Dog could earn a profit was soon answered. By 1959, opinion in UTC had become unanimously optimistic on the subject. By then it was clear that the HD not only paid its way but made for manufacturing efficiency and conferred prestige. No one any longer denied that the accidental discovery about tank-head stress in the AAR laboratory five years earlier had been lucky.

The company took advantage of the fact that in building the HD, the outside diameter of the tank could be standardized for a broad range of tank capacities. To produce a larger car it was necessary only to vary the length.

Four 21,700-gallon Hot Dog cars completed at Whiting in 1959 were for a short time the world's largest tank cars in railroad interchange service, but only for a short time. The record survived less than a year. In 1960, UTC constructed on orders from customers several cars of 30,000 gallons each—described as the largest and most efficient tank cars ever built.

[1] An ICC ruling in 1961 upheld UTC's position on the elimination of side running boards from the Hot Dog; but this ruling was subject to review by the courts.

The next year a new development made the 30,000 gallon Hot Dog virtually obsolete, when the company produced the so-called Compact-30, a car of equal capacity but considerably shorter. By enabling shippers to put a maximum number of giant cars at one time on their loading tracks, the Compact-30 made for still greater efficiency and economy.

APPENDIX K: THE ROUND SHOP AND THE BIG DOME

For years previous to 1956, it had been evident that facilities in certain of UTC repair shops needed improvement. Many of them were old, and while their equipment was kept up to date, their physical structure was far behind the march of industrial design. The big Whiting and Philadelphia plants had been enlarged to increase their car-building capacity, but other shops had not been much improved since their construction in the early decades of the century. Strong arguments could be made for eliminating some of them, while expanding others to serve larger geographical areas.

The matter became more urgent when word was received that a UTC shop which was located within the compound of a large oil refinery at Baton Rouge, Louisiana, would have to move, for the land on which it stood was needed for expansion of the refinery. Goaded by necessity, the company faced the problem of erecting a new shop. At once the question arose: What kind of shop?

There was evidence that tank car repair shops as a class stood as much in need of creative review as the technology of the tank car itself. The pattern of the existing shops had changed little since the days of John D. Rockefeller. The question was raised: Why not utilize the opportunity at Baton Rouge to build a shop which would make use of up-to-date concepts of industrial planning—which would yield higher efficiency and permit reduction of maintenance costs, while creating optimum working conditions?

As in the case of the Hot Dog, Locke assigned a selected engineering task force to the problem of the new shop. Soon he had in his hands a general description of a shop which was a radical departure from UTC's past experience. The company's old shops were all contructed on a linear principle. The tank cars needing work came in at one end of the repair tracks, which were covered in part by a long, rectangular shed; and they moved progressively down the line until, repairs completed, they were hauled away. The movement of the cars was thus controlled by the slowest car in the line, making for considerable time losses.

The proposed design for the new shop broke completely with this tradition. Calling for a circular shop, it opened the way for greater efficiency and economy than had ever been seen in tank car maintenance, by enabling the shop to handle each car individually; so that a slow car no longer held up the others. The floor plan of the new Baton Rouge shop resembled in some respects the round house used by railroads for engine maintenance. The car entered the gate on a given track, moved toward the center, was switched by means of a transfer table to another track, and was moved back and out of the gate, having been given a complete maintenance overhaul during its passage. A long tail attached to the circular floor provided a paint shed for the cars.

An important feature of the plan was that it provided for a greater number of highly equipped repair stations along the tracks than had previously been feasible. In the older shops it had always been necessary to bring men and materials to each car as it entered the shop. The result was a considerable amount of lost motion and time, as men raced around the shop looking for the equipment and materials, crisscrossing each other's paths. In the new shop the men could stay at the repair station with all tools and equipment at hand, and the car and the materials would be brought to them—with a significant saving in expense.

All the other UTC executives concerned agreed with Locke as to the desirability of a round shop. The problem of the exterior building, however, still had to be resolved, and it rapidly became crucial. Whatever structure was decided upon would have not only to provide shelter, but to make possible efficient lighting, heating, ventilation, and work flow. In the opinion of the designers, a shed such as covered other UTC shops was unthinkable. It would be as grotesque as putting medieval armor on a twentieth-century businessman. The numerous steel girders necessary to support such a structure on so large a scale would in themselves constitute a serious obstacle to the efficient movement of cars, materials, and men. And, as everyone agreed, "It would look like hell."

At this stage Locke learned from one of the young task force engineers that the eminent inventor, R. Buckminster Fuller, had recently patented a novel principle of architectural construction which employed interlocking metal triangles to form the skeleton of a dome. Made of hollow metal tubes, these triangles permitted much more equal distribution of stress and much greater economy in the use of material than could be obtained through other forms of construction. For the first time it was possible, utilizing Fuller's concept, to erect domes of very large size without interior supports.

Small "geodesic" domes, as Fuller called them, could already be seen on experimental radar stations. Others made of aluminum tubing covered by a plastic skin had been successfully tested by the United States armed forces for use as military shelters, and their lightness did not prevent them from being extraordinarily strong, weather-proof, and wind resistant.

Could a geodesic dome be built on the huge scale required to cover the heavy industrial operations of the Baton Rouge shop? The idea seemed worth exploring. Conferences between Fuller, Locke, and other UTC executives and engineers brought the possibility closer. It was decided that, for a dome of the size contemplated, the tri-angles should be formed from steel pipe rather than from aluminum; that the "skin" had best be steel sheet, and that it should be possible to erect the dome at moderate cost. After looking at models of the shop and dome, all of UTC's directors were taken with the originality and promise of the conception. For UTC to pioneer the industrial use of the geodesic principle—to house the world's finest car-repair shop in the world's largest dome—would be a unique achievement.

Plans to erect the Baton Rouge dome were completed with the help of UTC's engineers and special consultants. The shop's interior plan was modified somewhat to take full advantage of the spatial possibilities of the dome. All administrative, supervisory, and clerical functions were housed in a structure at the center of the round shop. Problems of lighting, heating, and ventilation gave way under the attack of some of the country's ablest specialists in these fields.

By common agreement, publicity was carefully avoided. When in 1956 land was purchased in a suitable location at Baton Rouge and work was begun, no one outside the company and its intimate ad-visers knew what was in the wind. The decision to build the dome was made in a spirit of high enthusiasm.

APPENDIX L: THE GRAVER STORY

In terms of prospects for growth, Graver could hardly be called the ideal acquisition. The long story of the company was peculiarly American in its sharp alternations of prosperity and depression. In 1857—two years before young John D. Rockefeller went into the produce business for himself—the young sons of a German immigrant in Allegheny City, Pennsylvania, joined their father in his trade, working iron plate into boilers and other industrial vessels. The nearby discovery of oil and consequent demand for storage tanks transformed their little back-yard establishment into a thriving small business. By 1872 the younger son, William Graver, then thirty years old, opened his own establishment. Success followed. The Standard Oil Company entrusted to him much of its storage-tank construction in the Pennsylvania oil fields, and there he prospered until 1883.

That year industrial depression brought a ruinous cessation of demand for oil tanks and forced him to begin again elsewhere. Chicago was his choice—a booming city at the crossroads of America. Operating at first on a small scale, he gradually built up his tank business again. In 1888, he set up a small plant in East Chicago; his sons joined him; and hard work and good products established their reputation. By 1915, when William Graver died, their achievement was solid.

World War I brought William Graver's sons a huge volume of business. What had been the small Graver Tank Works blossomed into the Graver Corporation, one of the country's larger manufacturers of plate structures of all kinds. The boom of the oil industry in the hectic 1920s pushed them still further upward on the industrial scale.

Then, like their father before them, the younger Gravers found themselves caught in an economic hurricane. Pressed for money in the early 1930s, they had to sell the business. The purchaser was the Phoenix Manufacturing Company of Joliet, Illinois, makers of a miscellany of steel products. A new company, the Graver Tank & Manufacturing Company, was formed as a wholly-owned subsidiary of Phoenix, and for most of a decade battled the depression.

World War II reestablished the company's prosperity, and Graver became a major producer of steel-plate construction for many war industries. The postwar period found the company with five plants, offices throughout the country, and four distinct divisions—steel and alloy plate fabrication; industrial construction; oil-field equipment, and equipment for the industrial treatment of water. By 1949, however, its business had begun to show signs of a down trend in crucial departments, and it eagerly welcomed the large tank orders placed by Graves in that year and subsequently.

The position of the Phoenix steel operation had also become somewhat dubious in the 1950s. Although unusual flexibility of operation gave Phoenix some advantages over larger steel manufacturers, it was handicapped by the fact that it did not produce the steel that it worked. Compelled to buy billets on the outside, generally from the large "integrated" steel companies with which it was competing, it was burdened with comparatively high costs for materials. The disadvantage was most acutely felt in periods of strong demand, for then other mills were reluctant to forego higher profits by selling steel in semiprocessed forms, such as billets.[1] But at other times, too, Phoenix's operations were on a precarious footing. Possibly the most reliable segment of its business in terms of profit was the manufacture of horseshoes, of which it was the world's largest producer, and for which, in the automotive age, there continued to be a surprising demand.

The Phoenix–Graver situation, taken as a whole in 1957, was such as to leave no doubt in the minds of UTC's management that in acquiring the company they were taking on serious problems.

APPENDIX M: ESTABLISHING A PRICE FOR PHOENIX–GRAVER

The report of a "purchase investigation," made by outside accountants and investment analysts, showed that the Phoenix-Graver companies together had a book value of $16,000,000, including inventories. In the view of UTC's management the company was justified in offering substantially less than book value. It was obvious that the earnings of Phoenix would be uncertain, and that Graver's business in the last analysis would rise and fall with the expenditures of industry as a whole for capital equipment. Much work would be needed to tighten the Phoenix–Graver organizational structure, revise their policies, and improve their administration. As UTC saw it, the inevitable problems to be faced had to be considered in the purchase price. A prolonged and hard negotiation followed between the managements of the two companies, each flanked by its banking advisers. Agreement was reached in the early summer of 1957. All of Phoenix–Graver's assets were exchanged for 441,252 shares of newly-issued UTC stock. Since, at the time of actual acquisition, on September 9, 1957, the price of UTC stock on the New York Exchange was 28½, the equivalent cash value was about $12,600,000.

APPENDIX N: UTC'S FOREIGN AFFILIATES

In 1959, UTC formed Graver International S.A., of Caracas, Venezuela. Subsequently the company established ties with a leading Scottish plate fabricator, Mechans, Ltd., of Glasgow, and Ateliers de

---

[1] In 1962, when Phoenix had proved a consistent profit-earner, the division solved its billet-supply problem through a long-term arrangement with a prominent steel company, on a sound economic basis.

Construction de Willebroek of Brussels, Belgium. The latter was soon linked with other Belgium metal fabrication shops under the name of Compagnie Graver. The purchase of substantial stock interests in Mechans and Willebroek testified to the importance attributed to such foreign alliances. During 1959 leading plate-fabrication concerns in France, West Germany, and the Union of South Africa were licensed to represent UCT in their respective areas. (See Appendix P.)

APPENDIX O: UTC'S 1959 EARNINGS

The disappointing earnings-per-share figure for 1959—$1.86—threatened for a time to be even more disappointing. Several unforeseen factors came to the company's assistance. A nationwide strike affecting the larger steel companies during much of 1959 unexpectedly benefited the earnings of Phoenix Manufacturing, which had remained in production throughout the strike. Refiners Transport and Terminal during the year added to its volume and profit by the purchase for cash of another trucking company. The sales-and-profit figures of the newly-acquired Lindsay and Smith & Loveless concerns for the entire year also helped to bolster UTC's 1959 earnings. Added to the solid excellence of the tank car business, these gains were enough to enable the company to exceed by a small margin its regular annual dividend of $1.60 on its 3,500,000 shares outstanding.

APPENDIX P: UTC DIRECTORS, OFFICERS, AND DIVISIONS
(January 1, 1962)

DIRECTORS

Bennett Archambault, Chairman of the Board and President, Stewart-Warner Corporation

William B. Browder, Secretary and General Counsel

Alfred E. Gebhardt, Vice-President

Donald C. Graves, Vice-President

Robert P. Gwinn, President and General Manager, Sunbeam Corporation.

W. V. Kahler, President, Illinois Bell Telephone Company

Edwin A. Locke, Jr., President

J. W. Van Gorkom, Executive Vice-President

Kenneth V. Zwiener, President, Harris Trust and Savings Bank

358   APPENDIX

OFFICERS

Edwin A. Locke, Jr., President
J. W. Van Gorkom, Executive Vice-President
Alfred E. Gebhardt, Vice-President
Donald C. Graves, Vice-President
William B. Browder, Secretary and General Counsel
Ray L. Holland, Controller
Thomas P. O'Boyle, Treasurer

DIVISIONS AND SUBSIDIARIES

Bulk Terminals Company
 F. Baird-Smith, President
Getz Bros. & Co.
 L. L. Goodman, Chairman
 C. B. Briggs, President
Graver Tank & Manufacturing Company
 W. C. Root, President
Graver Water Conditioning Company
 M. Lane, President
The Lindsay Company
 R. D. Tyler, President
Phoenix Manufacturing Company
 J. W. Gosselin, President
Products Tank Line of Canada, Ltd.[1]
 R. M. Melvin, Managing Director
Refiners Transport & Terminal Corporation
 F. Baird-Smith, President
 J. R. Kruizenga, Executive Vice-President
Smith & Loveless
 V. A. Smith, Managing Director
 C. Loveless, Managing Director
Tank Cars–U.S.
 A. E. Gebhardt, Vice-President
 D. C. Graves, Vice-President

OVERSEAS SUBSIDIARIES AND AFFILIATES

Compagnie Graver, S. A., Willebroek, Belgium
Graver International S.A., Caracas, Venezuela
Graver Tank (Australia) Pty. Ltd., Sydney, Australia
Mechans Limited, Glasgow, Scotland

[1] In 1962, the name of this division was changed to Procor, Ltd.

APPENDIX Q: UTC'S EARNINGS AND DEPRECIATION POLICY

In the 1950s, as a result of a change in depreciation policy, statements of earnings became even more conservative than in the past. Beginning in the late 1940s, the depreciation taken by UTC on its tank cars had been based on the original cost of the cars and the expectation of a thirty-five-year average life for them. Since then, however, the cost of replacing the old cars, as of most other manufactured products, had risen sharply, and the obsolescence factor had become higher than in the past. The government, recognizing the need of many businesses for a method of depreciation suited to the times, enacted a statute permitting the use of the so-called "double declining balance" method of depreciation. Under this method much more of the cost of a piece of equipment could be written off in the earlier years of its life than in the past. UTC hesitated at first to avail itself of this privilege, for some of its older executives insisted that the familiar "straight-line" method of calculating depreciation was better suited to the company's interests. Locke pressed hard for a modernization of UTC's depreciation practice, and finally carried his point. Among other effects, the double-declining balance method produced earnings lower than those calculated by the straight-line method.

BIBLIOGRAPHY

BOOKS

Adams, Henry. *The New York Gold Conspiracy.* In Adams' *Historical Essays,* Scribner's, N.Y., 1891

Allen, Frederick Lewis. *The American Procession.* Scribner's, N.Y., 1949

*————. *The Big Change.* Scribner's, N.Y., 1956

*Allen, Wm. Harvey. *John D. Rockefeller: Giant, Dwarf, Symbol.* Inst. for Public Service, N.Y., 1930

American Petroleum Institute. Dept. of Safety. *Review of Fatal Injuries in the Petroleum Industry, 1951–1955.* N.Y., 1956

————. *Petroleum Industry Hearings before the T.N.E.C.* N.Y., 1942

————. *Petroleum Facts & Figures.* N.Y., 1956

*Ames, John, McE. "On Car Shortages." *Report of National Pet. Assoc.* September, 1916

Arnold, Thurman. *The Folklore of Capitalism.* New Haven, 1937

Association of American Railroads. *Study of Trans.: Petroleum.* Wash., D.C., 1945

————. *Quiz on Railroads.* Wash., D.C., 1957

*Babcock, F. L. *The First Fifty.* The Story of Standard Oil of Indiana (1889–1939), S.O. Indiana, Chicago, 1939

Bain, Joseph S. *The Economics of the Pacific Coast Petroleum Industry.* 3 vols. Boston, 1949

Baker, George, and Gayton Germane. *Case Problems in Transportation Management.* McGraw-Hill, N.Y., 1957

Banks, Robert B. *Efficiency of Private vs. Public Oownership in the Railway Field.* (Research project, completed 1958. Northwestern University, Evanston, Ill.)

Beard, Charles A. *The Rise of American Civilization,* 2 vols. Macmillan, N.Y., 1927

Beaton, Kendall. *Enterprise in Oil.* Appleton, N.Y., 1957

(*, denotes references of especial value; **, major sources of data)

Bendix, Robert. *Work and Authority in Industry*. John Wiley & Sons, N.Y., 1956

*Bining, Arthur Cecil. *Rise of American Economic Life*. 3rd ed. Scribner's, N.Y., 1943

Bureau of the Census (with the Cooperation of the Social Science Research Council), *Historical Statistics of the United States*, from Colonial times to 1957, U.S. Department of Commerce, 1959

Campbell, R. A., J. F. Whiting and R. A. Kemp. *Aluminum Car Impact Tests*. Report of Am. Soc. of Mech. Engineers, N.Y., 1958

Cochran, Thomas and Wm. Miller. *The Age of Enterprise—A Social History of America*. Harper Bros., N.Y., 1942

———. *Railroad Leaders, 1845–1890*. Harper Bros., N.Y., 1953

Connelly, Walter L. *The Oil Business as I Saw It; Half a Century with Sinclair*. Univ. of Oklahoma, 1954

Cooper, Frank E. *The Lawyer and Administrative Agencies*. Prentice-Hall, N.J., 1957

*Coughlin, E. W. *Freight Car Distribution and Car Handling in the United States*. AAR, Wash., D.C., 1956

Crum, A. R. and A. S. Dungan. *Romance of American Petroleum*. Mc-Graw-Hill, N.Y., 1911

Dearing, Charles L. and Wilfred Owen. *National Transportation Policy*. Brookings Institute, Wash., D.C., 1949

*Defense Transport Administration. *The Tank Car Story*. Wash., D.C., 1951

**Derrick's Handbook of Petroleum. 2 vols. Oil City, Pa., 1898

*Dodd, S. C. T. *Argument Relative to Bills Pending in the New York Legislature*. Standard Oil Company, N.Y., 1888

———. *Combinations: Their Uses and Abuses*. Standard Oil Company, N.Y., 1888

Drayton, Charles D. *Transportation Under Two Masters*. Yale Univ. Press, New Haven, 1946

Epstein, Ralph. *General American Transport Corporation* (GATX). North River Press, 1948

*Farrington, S. Kip, Jr. *Railroads at War*. Coward McCann, Inc., N.Y., 1944

Federal Trade Commission. *The Petroleum Industry: Prices, Profits and Competition*. Document #61, Wash., D.C., 1928

———. *A List of 1,000 Large Manufacturing Companies, Their Subsidiaries and Affiliates*. Pub. 1951 (G.P.O., Wash. 25, D.C.)

Fine, Sidney. *Laissez-Faire and the General-Welfare State*. Univ. of Michigan Press, 1956

Frederick, John H. *Methods of Payment for the Use of Shipper-owned*

Tank Cars. Research project, 1958. (Courtesy of author, Univ. of Maryland, College Park, Maryland.)

General American Transport Corp. (author). *General American Tank Car Journeys.* Chicago, 1931

*Gibbs and Knowlton. *The Resurgent Years.* Harper Bros., N.Y., 1957

**Giddens, Paul. *Birth of the Oil Industry.* Macmillan, N.Y., 1938

**————. *The Early Days of Oil.* Macmillan, N.Y., 1940

————. *Beginnings of the Petroleum Industry.* The Commonwealth of Pennsylvania, Harrisburg, Pa., 1941

**————. *Standard Oil Company (Indiana)—Oil Pioneer of the Middle West.* Appleton, N.Y., 1955

*Graves, B. C. Address on Tank Cars (delivered before Convention of the American Petroleum Institute, Nov., 1950)

Hadley, Arthur. *Railroad Transportation.* Putnam, N.Y., 1900

*Hall, Ford P. *Government and Business.* Prentice-Hall, N.Y., 1949

**Hepburn Committee. *Report of Special Committee on Railroads. Hearings.* 5 vols. *New York State Assembly.* Albany, N.Y., 1879

**Hidy, Ralph and Muriel. *Pioneering in Big Business, 1822–1911.* Harper Bros., N.Y., 1955

*Huebner, Grover and Emory Johnson. *Railroad Freight Service.* Garden City Press, N.Y., 1926

Husband, Joseph. *The Story of the Pullman Car.* Macmillan, N.Y., 1916

**Interstate Commerce Commission. REPORTS:
    In the Matter of Private Cars. Vol. 50
    The El Dorado Case. Vol. 258
    The Baton Rouge Switching Case. Vol. 264 and Vol. 268
    The RT&T Application. MCC-F no. 1936
    Petroleum Rail Shippers v. Alton & Southern RR. Vol. 243

**————. HEARINGS:
    Switching Charges and Terminal Services. Ex parte 104
    On Refrigerator Cars. I&S, docket no. 4572

————. *A Brief History of the Separation of Railroad Operating Expenses between Freight and Passenger Services.* Statement #577. Wash., D.C., 1957

*————. *Transport Statistics in the United States.* Part 9: Private Car Lines. Wash., D.C., 1957

*————. *Railroad Petroleum Traffic, 1948, 1950, 1953.* Statement #565. Wash., D.C., 1956

*Ise, John. *The United States Oil Policy.* New Haven, Conn., 1926

Kemnitzer, W. J. *Rebirth of Monopoly: A Critical Analysis of Economic Conduct in the Petroleum Business.* Cambridge, Mass., 1938

*Kennedy, Miles C. and Burgess, George. *Centennial History of the Pennsylvania Railroad*. Phila., Pa., 1949

Landon, Charles E. *Transportation: Principles, Practices, Problems*. Wm. Sloane Assoc., N.Y., 1951

Lilienthal, David E. *Big Business*. Harper Bros., N.Y., 1953

**Loyd, Henry Demarest. *Wealth against Commonwealth*. Harper, N.Y., 1894

*Louisiana Supreme Court. REPORTS:
   UTC v. *Louisiana Oil Refining Corp*. 184 LA 121, 165 SO 638
   UTC v. *Day* (Sheriff, et al.). 101 SO 581

Locklin, D. Phillip. *Economics of Transportation*. 4th ed. Irwin, 1954
———. *Current Developments in Transportation Policy*. Univ. of Illinois, 1958

**Maclaurin, John J. *Sketches in Crude Oil*. Harrisburg, Pa., 1896. 3rd ed., 1902

*Master Car Builders' Association. *Car Encyclopedia*

Maurer, Herrymon. *Great Enterprise: The Growth and Behavior of the Big Corporation*. Macmillan, N.Y., 1955

*Maybee, Rolland H. *Railroad Competition and the Oil Trade: 1855–1873*. Mt. Pleasant, Mich., 1940

*Middleton, P. Harvey. *Transportation—Prewar and Postwar*. Railway Bussiness Assoc., Chicago, May, 1943
———. *Carrier Equality or Nationalization*. Speech delivered at the Harvard Business School, 1950
———. *Transport Coordination in the United States*. Railway Business Assoc., Chicago, 1946
———. *Railways and the Equipment and Supply Industry*. Railway Business Assoc., Chicago, 1941
*———. *The Oil Industry and Transportation*. Railway Business Assoc., Chicago, December, 1943

Missouri v. Johnson (U.S. v. S.O.C. 1908–1912). *Testimony of UTC Officials on Tank Car Business and Rates*. (St. Louis Federal Court Library)

Mohr, Anton. *The Oil War*. Macmillan, N.Y., 1926

*Montague, G. H. *The Rise and Supremacy of the Standard Oil Company*. Harper Bros., N.Y., 1904

Moody, John. *The Railroad Builders*. Chronicles of America (Ed. Allen Johnson). Vol. 38, N.Y., 1920

*Moody's: Investment Manual, Industrials, Transportation Manual . . . 1912–1958

Moore, A. L. *John D. Archbold and the Early Development of Standard Oil* (undated Ph.D. dissertation, Columbia University Library)

Musgrave, C. R. *Development of Transportation by the Petroleum Industry and Its Contribution to the National Welfare.* U.S. Chamber of Commerce, Wash., D.C., 1951

National Petroleum Council. *Petroleum Transportation.* Wash. 6, D.C., 1958

National Resources Planning Board. *Study of Transportation* (Ed. William Way, Jr.). Wash., D.C., 1943

**Nevins, Allen. *Study in Power.* 2 vols. Scribner's, N.Y., 1953

O'Connor, Harvey. *The Empire of Oil.* Monthly Review Press, 1955

**Oil City Derrick (Compiler). *United States Industrial Commission and Pure Oil Trust v. Standard Oil Company.* Oil City, Pa., 1899–1900

Oil and Gas Journal. *Fifty Years of Oil in the Southwest.* Tulsa, Okla., 1951

Oil Industry Information Committee. *Petroleum Industry Record: 1918–1948.* N.Y., 1949

O'Mahoney (Senator). Hearings—*U.S. Senate, Special Committee Investigation Petroleum Resources.* 79th Congress, 1st and 2nd Session (1945–1946). G.P.O. Wash., D.C.

Pogue, Joseph E. *Economics of the Petroleum Industry.* Chase National Bank, N.Y., 1939

Potts, Colonel Joseph D. *Brief History of Standard Oil.* Harrisburg, Pa., 1900

Ripley, William Z. *Trusts, Pools and Corporations.* Ginn & Co., N.Y., 1905

Robins, F. W. *The Story of the Lamp.* Oxford Univ. Press. London, 1939

*Rockefeller, John D. *Random Reminiscences of Men and Events.* Doubleday, Doran, N.Y., 1933

*Rose, Joseph R. *American Wartime Transportation.* Crowell, N.Y., 1953

Rostow, E. V. *A National Policy for the Oil Industry.* Yale Univ. Press, New Haven, Conn., 1948

Shippers Car Line. *The Trend toward Leasing of Tank Cars.* N.Y., 1957

**Smiley, A. W. *A Few Scraps, Oily and Otherwise,* Titusville, Pa., 1907

Spencer, Colonel Wm. M. *"X"—Symbol of Independence.* Newcomen Society, 1956

Standard Car Equipment Company. *All about Tank Cars.* Phila., Pa., 1929

Standard Oil Co. *An Inside View of Trusts.* N.Y., 1899

Standard Oil Co. *From the Directors of S.O.C. to Its Employees and Stockholders.* N.Y., 1907

Stocking, George Ward. *The Oil Industry and the Competitive System: A Study in Waste.* Houghton Mifflin, N.Y., 1925

*Supreme Court. REPORTS:
El Dorado v. GATX—60 S.Ct.325, 66 S.Ct.843, 306 US 422, 104 F 2d 903
Ellis v. ICC—237 US 444
Federal Trade Commission v. Sinclair—261 US 463
UTC v. Georgia—10 SE. 2d 778

**Tarbell, Ida Minerva. *History of the Standard Oil Company.* N.Y., 1904

*Taylor, Walter F. *History of the Standard Oil Company.* 1911 (unpublished)

Texas v. Security Oil Co., Navarro Refining Co., and The Union Tank Line Co. *Transcript of Trial Proceedings.* Dist. Court of Travis County, 1909

T.N.E.C. *Control of the Petroleum Industry by the Major Oil Companies.* 1941. G.P.O., Wash., D.C.

Tuttle, R. C. "Transportation of Petroleum." *Manufacturers' Record.* Sept., 1938

Tydeman, A. F. *Brief History of Tank Cars.* 1938 (unpublished)

**U.S. Bureau of Corporations. *Report on the Transportation of Petroleum.* Wash., D.C., 1907

**———. *Special Message of the Commissioner with Statement by Theodore Roosevelt.* Wash., D.C., 1908

**U.S. Commissioner of Corporations. *Report on the Transportation of Petroleum.* Wash., D.C., 1906

**U.S. Commissioner of Railroads. *Annual Reports to the Secretary of the Interior.* 23 vols. 1881–1903

**U.S. Congress. Committee on Manufactures. *House Investigation of Trusts.* Wash., D.C., 1888

U.S. Department of Commerce. *Growth Industries in Transportation Equipment.* G.P.O., Wash., D.C., 1957

**U.S. Department of Commerce and Labor. *Report.* Wash., D.C., 1906

U.S. Federal Trade Commission. *Report on Profits, Prices and Competition in the Petroleum Industry.* 70th Congress, Ist Session. Senate Document #61. 1927. G.P.O., Wash., D.C., 1928

**U.S. Industrial Commission. *Investigation and Report on Trusts and Industrial Combinations.* 19 vols. Wash., D.C., 1899–1901

*U.S. Petroleum Administration for War (PAW). *History of the PAW Service in Wartime.* G.P.O., Wash., D.C., 1946

U.S. Senate. Committee on Interstate and Foreign Commerce. *Problems of the Railroads*. Part 4: Testimony on Private Shippers. (370 pp.) G.P.O., Wash., D.C., 1958

°————. Committee on Small Business. *Trucking Mergers—Concentration and Small Business: An Analysis of the Interstate Commerce Policy*. June, 1957. Wash., D.C.

°United States v. Standard Oil Company. Cit. No. 5371. District of Missouri: *Exceptions to the Petition*. 1907

Way, William, Jr. *Elements of Freight Traffic*. Transportation Assoc. of America, Wash., D.C., 1956

Weld, L. D. H. *Private Freight Cars and American Railways*. Garden City, N.Y., 1908

Westmeyer, Russell E. *Economics of Transportation*. Prentice-Hall, N.Y., 1952

Whitney, Simon N. *Anti-Trust Policies*. 2 vols. Twentieth Century Fund. N.Y., 1958

Williams, Ernest W., Jr. *Regulation of Rail-Motor Rate Competition*.

————. and Fair. *Economics of Transportation*. Harper, N.Y., 1956

Wiprud, Arne C. *Justice in Transportation*. Cambridge, Mass., 1945

Wright, R. V. (ed.) *Car Builders Cyclopedia*. Simmons–Boardman, N.Y., 1922

PERIODICALS

°*Century Magazine*. "The Oil Tank Car." October, 1883

°————. "Oil Creek." E. V. Smally. July, 1883

Collier's. "Plenty of Oil—But How to Get It." by Harold L. Ickes. pp. 14–16. August 9, 1942

Fortune. "What Historians Teach about Business." by Dr. Edward Savath, May, 1954

Freight Traffic Report. (Fed. Coordinator of Trans.) Vol. II, pp. 91–93. Wash. G.P.O., 1943

The Lamp. "Recent Transport Problems." October, 1943

°*Massachusetts Magazine*. "Report on Pennsylvania." July, 1791

°*Meadville Daily Tribune*. "Account on Early Oil Traffic." May 12, 1888

National Petroleum News. "Analysis of Oil Control and Production under the NRA." C. B. Ames, 26: 24T, 25–26, November 14, 1934

————. "Oil Grows Independent of Rail Transportation." December 3, 1941, pp. 22–23

°*New York Daily Tribune*. "Dispatch from the Oil Regions." August 11, 1868

New York Times. "On the Mother Hubbard Case." December 18, 1946

***Oil and Gas Journal.* "Diamond Jubilee Issue." Tulsa, Okla., 1934

———. "On the Mother Hubbard Case." December, 1946, p. 140

*———. "Development of Tank Cars." August 23, 1934

*———. "Oil—No. 1 Transportation Job." H. N. Emerson. November 18, 1957

**Petroleum Industry Research Foundation.* 80 pp. Report on the Petroleum Industry and Trade. July, 1944

***Railroad Magazine.* "900,000 Barrels a Day." Freeman Hubbard. 34, #2, July, 1943

***Railway Age.* 5 articles on Private Car Lines. J. W. Midgley. September through December, 1902

Railway Age. "Are 'Trainload Lot' Rates Feasible?" Lloyd Wilson. 99, p. 307 (1935)

*———. Editorial on the railway mileage allowance agreement between railroad managers. October, 1894

———. "Outlook for the Oil Industry." June 9, 1952

Railway Freight Traffic. "Tank Cars Stage Comeback." A. G. Andersen. February, 1954

***Scientific American.* "A Week on Oil Creek." Charles Seeley. September 1, 1866

***Titusville Morning Herald.* "The White Pine Tank Car." August 22, 1934

Trains Magazine. "The Indisputable Tank Car." Stephen Bogart. October, 1948. Pp. 42–43

Transportation Association of America (Pamphlet). "Transportation Research: A survey of current and potential research projects." Chicago, 1958

*(The) *Warren Mail* (Editorial). June 13, 1863

**World Petroleum.* "Tank Car Movement of Oil Saved the Day for the Eastern Seaboard." April, 1943

INDEX

Acme Oil Company, 54
Advertising policy of UTC, 312–313
Advisory Committee on Foreign
  Trade, 321
Alleghany River, 6, 8, 42
Aluminum tank cars, 238–239
American Car and Foundry Com-
  pany, 194, 270–273, 347
American Petroleum Institute, 229,
  242, 244–245, 331
American Transfer Company, 44
Ames, John, 172–173
Anderson, A. B., 153
Andrew, Samuel, 11
Anglo-American Oil Company, 113
Annual Reports of UTC, 317, 320
Antitrust actions, 82, 107, 148–159
Archambault, Bennett, 357
Archbold, John D., 54–55, 84, 87,
  108, 111–112, 118–119, 124,
  128, 130, 135, 137, 139, 146,
  155
Arnold, Thurman, 259–260
Asphalt, shipping problems, 329–330
Association of American Railroads,
  191, 338, 348
  Tank Car Committee, 332–333,
    350
  testing laboratory, 345–346, 350
Association of independent oil com-
  panies, 209–210
Astor, John Jacob, 16
Atchison, Topeka and Santa Fé Rail-
  road, 126
Ateliers de Construction de Wille-
  broek of Brussels, Belgium, 357
Atlantic and Great Western Railroad,
  27, 35

Atlantic and Great Western Railroad,
  monopoly of freight into Cleveland, 19
  oil transportation by, 9–11
  tank cars, 13–14
Automobile industry, 128

Babcock, Paul, 84
Baird-Smith, F., 358
Baltimore and Ohio Railroad, 43–44,
  178
Baltimore refineries, 58
Barges used to transport oil, 7–9, 136,
  140
Barnsdall Oil Company, 229–230,
  273
Barrel shipments of oil, 7–9, 11–12,
  22
  box cars designed for, 51
  cost of labor, 52
  demand for, 7–9
  freight charges, 59, 77
  improved, 51–52
  limited profits of producers and
    refiners, 11
  railroads' discrimination against,
    114
  for refined products, 114
  theft and leakage, 7–8
  weight determination, 75
Barstow, F. Q., 84, 193
Barstow, William A., 193–196
Baton Rouge repair shop, 301–302,
  341
  dome-covered round shop, 352–
    354
Benét, Stephen Vincent, 3
Bibliography, 360–368

369

Big business, 29
  antagonism of public toward, 258
Big Inch, 245–246, 253–254
Black Friday, 18
"Black gold," 4–6
Blanchard, trustee of Tank Car Trust, 55
Bloxham, C. M., 129, 330–331
Board of Directors, 193–194, 220–221, 314
  admission of outsiders, 320
  1962, 357–358
Boston and Albany Railroad, 252
Bostwick, Jabez A., 31, 55
Boycotting by producers, 30–32
Boyle, Patrick, 118
Bradford oil field, 38, 45
Brewster, Benjamin, 71
Briggs, C. B., 358
Bristol, Arthur, 336–338
Browder, William B., 357–358
Brown, John, 4
Bryan, William Jennings, 98, 153
Buffalo refineries, 58
Bulk Terminals Company, 325, 358
Business, free-enterprise economy, 16–23
  post–Civil War, 16–23
  principles, 88

Calibrating tanks, 130n, 330–331
California, antitrust actions, 152
  discovery of oil, 62
  rebates, 124
  Standard's marketing strategy, 85–87
  tank car operations, 124–127, 141–144, 329
Campbell, Douglas, 165–166, 169–170, 174, 182, 257–259, 336–337, 340
Car Trust (see Tank Car Trust)
Carley, F. D., 69
Casing-head gas, 188
Cement, cars for shipping, 239
Central Refiners' Association, 35–36, 38
Chase National Bank of New York, 285–286
Chemical tank cars, 238–239, 275–281, 288–294, 304
  demand for, 293–294
  specifications, 277
Chicago, agitation against Standard, 100–101
  meat-packing houses, 54
  oil freight, 34
  UTC headquarters, 214–217, 325

Chicago, University of, 203
Chicago and Great Western Railroad, 101, 103
Chicago Tribune, 98, 150, 159
Civil War, 4
  business after, 16–23
Clark, Maurice, 10–11
  partnership with John D. Rockefeller, 3–4
Cleaning tank cars, 331
Cleveland, Grover, 71
Cleveland, Ohio, effect of Pennsylvania oil strike, 4
  monopoly of rail freight into, 19–20
  oil capital of the midwest, 10
  refineries, 10, 18–19, 24–36, 44
    acquired by Rockefeller, 25–26
    boycott by producers, 30–31
    expansion of, 24
    shipments to, 10, 19–20
Columbia Conduit Company, 44
Commissioner of Corporations, 148
  on railroad cooperation with UTL, 329
Committee on Manufactures, 80
"Compact-30" tank car, 352
Compagnie Graver, S.A., Willebroek, Belgium, 357
Competition, 197, 200, 234, 278, 300
  conspiracy between railroads and Standard, 70, 329
  during the depression, 235–237
  economic advantages held by Standard, 72
  from foreign producers, 320–322
  Pennsylvania oil fields, 5
  pipe lines and tank cars used to destroy, 124
  Standard's system of intelligence, 69
  Tidewater pipe line and, 57–58
CIO International Union, the Oil, Chemical and Atomic Workers, 343
Congressional investigations, 22
  tank car monopoly, 72–81
  Union Tank Car, 261–262
  (See also Government investigations)
Construction of tank cars, AAR testing laboratory, 345–346
  elimination of the dome, 347–348
  elimination of rivets and leakage, 345
  elimination of running boards, 350–351
  fusion welding, 232n, 332–333
  Hot Dog cars, 344–352

Construction of tank cars, specifications established by AAR and ICC, 348
tank bands, 344–345
tank-head stress, 348–349
Consumer markets, interest in, 316
Continental Trading Company, 205–206
Contracts with refineries, 164–166
Conwell, Russell, 28–29
Cooke, Jay, 17
Coolidge, Calvin, 204–205, 208, 223
Cost of new tank cars, 190, 278
Cottonseed oil carried in tank cars, 75
Cowan, W. P., 331
Coxey's army, 98
Crédit Mobilier, 30
Crude-oil transportation, 57–58
Cuban liberation, 111, 121
Cupolas on tank cars, 347
Customers, relations with, 166–168
outside, solicitation of, 207–209
Cutler, Bertram, 214–216

Darwin, Charles, 17
Data-processing machines, 296
Defense Transport Administration, 275–281
Densmore, Amos, 12–13
Depreciation policy, 213–214, 219–220
changes in rate, 265–266
"double declining balance" method, 359
earnings and, 359
life-expectancy figures for tank cars, 265
Necessity Certificates, 279
tax write-off, 279
Depression of the 1930s, 71
competition during, 235–237
employee relations, 237–238
financial policies of UTC, 227–232
Devereux, James H., 59
Dewey, Admiral, 121
Dismantling of tank cars, 264–265
Dissolution of New Jersey Standard, 155–159
effect on stock prices, 157–159
Distribution system of Standard, 106
Divisions of UTC, 358
Dodd, Samuel C. T., 26, 48, 57, 64–66, 83, 91–92, 106, 118, 131
Dome-covered repair shops, 301–303, 352–354
dome designed by R. Buckminster Fuller, 353–354

Domes on tank cars, 32–33, 347–348
Domestic marketing, 85–87
Domestic Trade Committee, 72
Drake, Edwin L., 4
Drake, Lauren J., 215–222, 227–232, 237n, 239, 255–256, 258, 260, 263–266, 276, 285, 290, 334
Drew, Daniel, 17
Dunne, Finley Peter, 110

Earnings of Union Tank Car, depreciation policy and, 359
statements, 1959–60, 314
Eastman, Joseph B., 243
Eisenhower, Dwight D., 280
Elkins Act, 152–153
Empire Transportation Company, 21, 32–33, 35
acquired by Standard, 43
deal with Pennsylvania Railroad, 37–44
dome cars originated by, 347
expansion of company, 37
Green Line cars, 77–78
(See also Green Line cars)
price war with Standard, 39–41
property and holdings, 37
serious competitor to Standard, 38
tank cars, 32–33, 347
Employee relations, 237–238, 296–298
fringe benefits, 343
morale, 296
Employee's Retirement Plans, 237n, 334–335
Equipment certificates, 55
issued by Tank Car Trust, 49–50
Equipment Trust Gold Notes, 190, 218
Equipment Trust Notes, 195, 228
Equitable Life Assurance Society, 334
Erie Canal used for oil shipments, 59
Erie Railroad, 17, 27, 39
control of oil shipments to Cleveland, 19, 58
freight rates, 40
oil freight traffic, 57
share in pipe line to Cleveland, 58
tank car problems, 47–49, 55
tank cars controlled by Rockefeller, 20, 22, 32
tank cars leased from Tank Car Trust, 50
Eustice, Russell, 227
Executive personnel, 63, 192–201, 285–294, 304, 310–312, 314, 324
recruiting program, 296

Exploration and discovery, Bradford
    oil field, 38
California, 62
Ohio, 62
Pennsylvania oil fields, 3–15
Texas, 62
Exports to Europe, 62–63, 179

Fall, Albert, 205
Federal Bureau of Investigation in-
    quiry, 267–268
Federal Circuit Court in St. Louis,
    157
Felton, Henry, 136–138, 151, 158,
    163–177, 192–193, 195, 200–
    205, 208, 210–217, 261, 312
    before ICC, 169–170, 182–183
    expansion of car fleet, 154
    named president of UTL, 136–138
    retirement, 217
    witness for Standard, 130–147, 155
Financial panics, 18
Financial scandals, 29–30
Fisk, Jim, 10, 17–18
Flagler, Henry M., 18–20, 29, 36, 40,
    65, 81, 119, 155
Folmsbee, Clyde, 278, 345, 349–350
Forecasts of tank car requirements,
    276
Foreign affiliates of UTC, 356–358
Foreign trade, 150, 314–315
    competition from foreign produc-
        ers, 320–322
    need for American know-how, 315–
        316
    opportunities, 321–322
Free-enterprise economy, 16–23
Freight charges paid by Standard, 44
Freight rates, after World War I, 188
    blind billing, 77–79
    effect on profits, 24–25
    Felton and, 136–137
    Garfield investigation, 140–147
    rebates paid by roads, 25
    (See also Rebates)
    trainload discounts, 234–235
    used to pressure rivals, 26–27
    World War I, 180
Frenzied Finance (Lawson), 133
Frick, Henry C., 134
Fringe benefits for employees, 343
Fuel oils, 5
Fuel shortage of 1947–48, 266–267
Fuller, Chief Justice, 106–107
Fuller, R. Buckminster, 353–354
Fusion welding of tank cars, 232n,
    332–333

Galéna Signal Oil Company, 72, 103,
    215
Garfield, J. R., 135–136, 152
    hearings conducted before, 139–
        147
    report of, 144–148
Gases, pressure tank cars for, 190,
    267–269, 273, 348
Gasoline, 128
Gauging practices, 130n, 330–331
Gebhardt, Alfred E., 357–358
General American Transportation
    Corporation (GAT), 130, 164
    182–184, 194, 197, 203, 206–
    207, 232, 270, 280
    number of cars, 228, 230
    symbol on cars, 130
General-purpose tank cars, 331–332
German-American Transportation
    Company, 130
Gesner, Abraham, 5
Getz Bros. & Company, San Fran-
    cisco, 321–322, 358
Goodman, L. L., 358
Goodwin, Edward N., 182–184, 213–
    214, 259–260
Gosselin, E. N., 273–274, 305–307,
    358
Gould, Jay, 10, 17–18, 27, 30
Government investigations, campaign
    to dissolve Standard Trust, 80–
    82, 148–159
    freight rebates, 72–74
    Garfield hearings, 139–147
    by the Industrial Commission,
        110–122
    ownership of tank cars, 53–55
    Rockefeller before, 22
    tank car monopoly, 53–55, 67
    (See also Interstate Commerce
        Commission)
Government regulation, of private car
    lines, 168–170
    of railroads, 178–190
    Standard's attitude toward, 87–88
    (See also Interstate Commerce
        Commission)
Grangers, populist movement, 71
Graver, William, 355
Graver Corporation, 355
Graver International, S.A., 356–358
Graver Tank & Manufacturing Com-
    pany, 273, 319, 324, 355,
    358
    acquired by UTC, 305–307, 354–
        356
    foreign expansion, 314–315, 358
    Lang Company acquired, 309

Graver Water Conditioning division, 316, 319, 348
Graves, B. Clifford, 174–177, 184, 196–198, 200–201, 206–210, 216–218, 220–221, 228–239, 245–247, 255, 258, 261, 263–274, 278–279, 285–289, 300, 305, 318–319, 337–339, 343, 347–348
  becomes president, 266
  chairman of the board, 295
  entry into trucking business, 255–262
  on rental rates, 341–342
  retirement, 311, 319
  tank car operations in World War II, 240–243
Graves, Donald C., 357–358
Great Britain's need for oil in World War II, 241–244
Great Lakes oil shipments, 59, 325
Great Northern Railroad, 86
Green Line cars, 43, 50, 60, 72, 77–78, 81, 113
Gwinn, Robert P., 357

Hanna, Mark, 108, 110, 122
Harding, Warren G., 208
Hardy, Charles, 271–273
Harkness, H. V., 19
Harley, Henry, 12–14, 20
Harley, John, 195n
Harrison, F. M., 176, 196
Hayes, Charles, 125–126
Hayes, Rutherford B., 42
Hearst newspapers, 121
Heater-pipe tank cars, 130n, 330
Hepburn, Alonzo Barton, 53–55
Hepburn Act, 134–135, 146–148, 169
  attempts to amend, 180, 187
Hepburn Committee, 39, 53–55, 67
History of the Standard Oil Company (Tarbell), 133–134
Holland, Ray L., 358
Hot Dog tank car, 299–301, 304, 306, 344–352
  advertisements on, 301
  capacity, 351–352
  "Compact-30," 352
  cost of, 351
  criticism of, 349–350
  elimination of running boards, 350–351
  tests, 345–346
Howe, E. W., 106
Howe, Julia Ward, 16
Hudson River terminal, 31

Ickes, Harold L., 241–245, 252
Illinois Central Railroad, 340–341
Illuminating oils, 5, 103
Imperial Oil Company of Canada, 281
Independent refineries, 35–36, 44
  Central Association dominated, 35–36
  demand government seizure of private car lines, 172
  effect of tank car squeeze on, 45–61
  forced to use barrels, 51–52
  Standard's relations with, 71
Industrial Commission hearings, 112–114
  confusing testimony, 112–114
  investigation of Standard Oil, 110–122
  membership of, 111
Interstate Commerce Act of 1887, 72–73
Interstate Commerce Commission, 74, 77, 81, 87, 124, 133
  appeals concerning trainload discounts, 234–235
  application to expand trucking business, 257–262
  Baton Rouge switching cases, 339–341
  decision on running boards, 350–351
  government control of railroads, 179–190
  investigation of private car lines, 169
  investigations of Standard Oil, 110, 148
  investigation of "switching," 339–341
  investigation of tank car business, 180–184
  on mileage allowances, 186
  power to regulate pipe lines, 145–146
  powers extended, 134
  probe of UTL, 97–100
  report (1918), 184–188
  reports on Standard, 148
  Safety Bureau, 350
  seeks authority over tank cars, 141–147
  tank car specifications established by, 333, 348
Investigations (see Government investigations)

Jardine, W. M., 199
Jewett, Hugh, 48–49, 51, 57–58

Johnson, Joseph French, 151
Joliet, Ill., 307

Kahler, W. V., 357
Kellogg, Frank B., 156
Kerosene, 5, 249
   lamps and stoves, 19, 63, 154
   West Coast market, 86
Korean War, 275–281
Kruizenga, J. R., 358
Kyle, Senator, 111

Labor relations, 71, 98, 296, 304
   1956 Whiting Strike, 343–344
   Pittsburgh riot of 1877, 41–42
La Follette, Robert M., 134–135
Lake Shore Railroad, 20, 34–35, 59–60
Landis, Kenesaw Mountain, 149–150
Landis decision, 150–154
Lane, M., 358
Lang Company, 309–310
Lawson, Thomas, 133
Leakage of tank cars, 344–345
Lee, Ivy, 30
Lima (Ohio) project, 195
Lime, cars for shipping, 239
Lindsay Company, St. Paul, Minn., 316, 357–358
Liquid petroleum gas cars (LPG), 190, 267–269, 273, 348
Litigation, fought by Standard, 151
   Federal courts, 155–159
   Ohio courts, 108–110
   Supreme Court, 158–159
   Texas, 107
   (See also Interstate Commerce Commission)
Lloyd, Henry Demarest, 98, 133
Lobbying, 92
Locke, Edwin A., Jr., 285–290, 304–326, 342, 350–351, 357
   chemical cars, interest in, 288–290
   decision to build dome-covered shop, 352–354
   development of "Hot Dog," 299–301
   elected president, 295–303
   emphasis on use of language, 298–299
   expansion of company, 307–311, 314–316
   New England conscience, 322–324
   personality, 296–298, 322
   selected by Graves, 285–288
Louisiana, antitrust actions, 152
Louisville refinery, 73

Loveless, C., 358
Lubricating oils, 19, 62, 72, 86, 103

McAdoo, William, 179–180, 187–188
McClure's magazine, 133
McCutcheon, John T., 159
McGee, James, 83–84
McGee, Walter, 84
McKinley, President William, 110, 123, 134
Manhattan Oil Company, 113
Market prices of oil, 4–5, 14, 150
Markets for oil, expansion of, 62
Master Car Builders' Association, 173–174
Mayer, of General American Transportation, 182–184
Mechans, Ltd., of Glasgow, 356, 358
Mexico, controversy with, 335
Midgley, J. W., 131
Midgley affair, 130–132, 181
Milburn, John C., 156
Mileage allowance, 97, 101–102
   changes after 1950, 341–343
   for empty cars, 74–75, 101–102
   ICC investigation, 170, 186, 339–341
   Midgley on, 132
   Page's testimony, 119–121
   rate allowed, 186
   World War II, 249
Mileage Equalization Rule, 104, 249
Mississippi River, 200
Mississippi Valley market, 85
Missouri, antitrust actions, 149–150, 152, 165
   Standard Oil companies in, 154
Missouri Pacific Railroad, 249
Missouri Valley market, 85
Monnett, Frank, 108–111, 122
Monopolies, 17, 44
   in American transportation, 135
   Congressional investigations, 72–81
   growth of, 17, 44, 71
   Standard charged with, 123
Moody's Industrials, 221
Morgan, J. P., 152
Motor tank trucks, 199–200
   (See also Trucking of oil)
Muckraking, 133–134

Naphtha, transportation of, 188
Napoleon Bonaparte, 3
National Industrial Recovery Act, 233
National Labor Relations Board, 344
National Petroleum Association, 172
National Transit, 68, 76, 82

Natural gas pipe line, 34
Necessity Certificates, 279
Nelson, Donald, 286
New Haven Railroad, 115–116
New Jersey, laws of incorporation, 83, 92
New York Central Railroad, 27, 35, 40, 43
  rebates paid Standard, 34
  relations with Standard, 102
  tank cars, leased from Tank Car Trust, 50–51
  ownership of, 55
  shortage of, 55
New York City, corruption in, 30
  refineries, 58
New York State Legislature, 20, 39
  probe of Standard, 53–55, 67, 92, 152
  (See also Hepburn Committee)
New York Stock Exchange, 189, 290
New York Times, 151
New York Tribune, 106
New York University, 151
New York World, 106, 151
1929 stock market crash, 222–223
Norris City, Illinois, 253
North American Review, 80

O'Boyle, Thomas P., 358
O'Day, Daniel, 68, 72, 76–77
Office of Defense Transportation (ODT), 243
  emergency program during World War II, 246–249
  trucks given monopoly over shorthauls, 255–256
Ohio, court action against Standard, 82–83, 87, 91–92, 108–111
Oil business, 5
  in 1880s, 62
  growth after World War I, 189–191
Oil City, 7–9, 31
Oil Creek, 6–9
Oil Creek Railroad, 9–11, 20
Oil Tank Car Trust, 49
  (See also Tank Car Trust)
Oklahoma oil fields, 169
Olean, New York, 140
Overseas subsidiaries and affiliates of Union Tank Car, 358

Pacific Coast Oil, 125
Page, Howard, 73–75, 81, 83–85, 95–97, 100–104, 127–130, 261
  before Industrial Commission, 106–122

Page, Howard, defense before investigative bodies, 133
  negotiations with railroads, 74–77
  retirement, 130–131, 136
Paraffin shipping problems, 128, 329–330
Payne, Oliver, 59, 78–79
Pearl Harbor, 244
Pennsylvania-Empire deal, 37–44
  price war, 39–41
Pennsylvania oil fields, 3–15, 64
  Bradford, 38
  economic tyranny, 14–16
Pennsylvania Railroad, 19–20, 27, 178
  backed Empire Company against Standard Oil, 37–44
  cooperation with Standard, 69–70, 102
  mob riots in Pittsburgh, 41–42
  oil freight, 43, 57–58
  pipe line built along tracks, 58
  shortage of tank cars for independents, 47
  Standard loans money to, 43
  tank cars, 35
    leased from Tank Car Trust, 50
    "90 per cent deal," 47
Pennsylvania State Legislature, 27, 29–30
  influenced by Standard, 53–54
  investigation of Standard's monopoly of tank cars, 48
  on pipe lines as common carriers, 76–77
  shortage of tank cars, 46–47
Pension policies, 334–335
Per diem rental charges, 165–166, 331–332
Petro-chemical products, 293
Philadelphia, oil business center, 64
  refineries, 39, 57
  Union Tank Car repair shop, 352
Philadelphia and Erie Railroad, 20–21
Philadelphia and Reading Railroad, 57, 70, 81
Phillips, Thomas W., 111, 124
Phoenix Manufacturing Company, Joliet, Ill., 306–309, 355–356, 358
  earnings in 1959, 357
  purchase by UTC, 354–356
Pierce, H. C., 107
Pipe lines, 21–22
  Big Inch, 245–246, 253–254
  built along Pennsylvania tracks, 58
  as common carriers, 76–77

Pipe lines, competition from, 234
  crude oil shipments, 57–58
  first built by Samuel Van Syckel, 11–12
  Harley's, 12, 20
  ICC power to regulate, 145–146
  interstate subsidiaries, 146
  natural gas, 34
  product, 198–199
  reaction of teamsters to, 11–12
  Standard's network, 44, 58, 72
    breaking up, 198
  Tidewater, 47–48, 63–69
    advantage to Standard's competitors, 57–58
Pithole, Penna., 5, 21
Pittsburgh refineries, 7–9, 40, 58
  riot of 1877, 41–42
  steamboat tow to, 8–9
Pond freshets used for transporting oil, 6–7, 10
Populist movements, 71
Potts, Joseph, 20–21, 37–44, 347
  Pennsylvania-Empire deal, 37–44
Pratt, C. M., 123, 146
Press, attitude toward Standard Oil, 110, 123, 146, 153
Pressure tank cars, 188, 190, 267, 273, 276
  forge-welded, 332–333
  fusion-welded, 332–333
Price of petroleum, 4–5
  effect of railroads and refineries on, 14
  price wars, 52–53
    between Empire and Standard, 39–41
Procan, 304
  (See also Products Tank Line of Canada)
Procor, Ltd., 358n
Producers, association formed by, 15, 30, 48
  at mercy of railroads and refineries, 14–15
Producers Union, 30, 48
  boycott by, 29–31
  protested shortage of storage tanks, 45–46
  tank car squeeze and, 45–61
Production, Bradford wells, 45
  Pennsylvania oil fields, 7
Products Tank Line, 210, 229, 236
Products Tank Line of Canada, 304, 358
Profit-sharing plans, 204, 335, 343
Profits, 14, 63, 150, 278
  Standard Oil, 99–100

Profits, Standard Oil of New Jersey, 151–152
  Union Tank Line, 97, 99, 100, 102
Public agitation against Standard, 29–30, 70–72, 106–122, 258
  decrease in, 121–122
Public opinion, polls, 258
  power of outraged, 29–30
  reaction to Landis decision, 152–154
Public relations, 70–72
  not understood by Rockefeller, 29, 56–57
Pulitzer, Joseph, 106
Pullman cars, 144–145
Purchasing Department, UTC, 297–298
Pure Oil Company of Pennsylvania, 108–109, 111, 133, 230

Railroads, agreements with Standard, 34–35
  alliances with refineries, 14
  bankruptcy, 168
  concessions to Standard Oil, 34–35, 70, 112, 124
  cooperation with UTL in 1887, 329
  decision regarding tank cars, 32–34
  effect of pipe lines on, 57–58
  effect of rate war, 41–44
  effect on price of oil, 9–11, 14, 24–25
  free-enterprise economy and, 16–23
  government regulation, 169, 178–190, 240–254
    (See also Interstate Commerce Commission)
  merger opposed by Locke, 322–324
  mileage allowance (see Mileage allowance)
  negotiations by Page with, 73–77
  Pennsylvania-Empire deal, 37–44
  rebates (see Rebates)
  Standard apportions business among, 43
  tank cars (see Tank cars)
  Transportation Act, 188
  World War I, 178–190
  World War II, 240–254
Railroads' War Board, 178
Railway Age, 103, 131
Railway Labor Executives Association, 351
Railway Question, The (Stickney), 101–102

Rebate system, 24–36, 73–74, 113
  average figure, 73–74
  legislative investigations, 53–57,
    72–74
  paid by Pennsylvania Railroad, 37,
    63
  paid in California, 124
  paid to Standard, 26–27, 43–44,
    72–74
  on refined products, 72
  secret, 115
  South Improvement Company and,
    27–36
Recession of 1957, 308
Recording movement of tank cars,
  96–97, 174–175, 195, 251
Red Fox, steamboat, 8–9
Reeser, Edwin B., 229, 273
Refineries, 128
  alliances with railroads, 14, 35–36
  Cleveland, 10, 18–19, 24–36, 44
  early beginnings, 5–15
  European, 63
  independent (*see* Independent re-
    fineries)
  Philadelphia, 39, 57
  Pittsburgh, 7–9, 40–58
  relationship between UTL and,
    163–166
  Whiting, Ind., 101–272
Refiners' Transport and Terminal
  Corporation, 265–272, 304, 357–
  358
Refrigerator cars, 130, 145
Rental charges for tank cars, 171,
  278–279
  during the depression, 237–238
  monthly, 332
  per diem, 165–166, 331–332
  policy after 1950, 341–343
Reorganization of UTC, 295–303,
  313
Repair of cars during World War II,
  251–252
Repair shops, 296, 318
  dome-covered round shop, 301–
    303, 352–354
  geodesic dome, 354
  paint shed, 353
  publicity value, 303
Replacement of old cars, 264
Research and development programs,
  313, 319
Restraint of trade, conspiracy in, 80,
  112, 123, 156
Retirement of small tank cars, 344
Rice, George, 68–69, 77, 94, 97, 108,
  111, 124

Roberts, Owen, 261
Rochester, New York, 140
Rockefeller, Frank, 56–57
Rockefeller, John D., 118, 135, 150,
  152, 165, 202, 325–326, 354
  attitude toward public relations,
    29, 56–57, 68
  before Congressional committees,
    81, 155
  before Ohio courts, 108
  brought out Clark, 11
  business optimism, 24–25
  Cleveland refineries, 10, 18–19
  control of transportation facilities,
    22–23, 32, 44
  effect of legal actions on, 83
  enters oil business, 10–11
  financial manipulations, 66
  financial statements, 159
  gains control of tank cars, 20–22,
    26, 32
  liquidation of Standard Trust, 93–
    94
  management skill, 11, 31, 36
  nationwide alliance of refineries,
    35–36
  participation in South Improve-
    ment Company, 27–29
  philanthropies of, 119
  power possessed by, 36
  president of Standard of New Jer-
    sey, 119
  quotations, 90, 110
Rockefeller, John D., Jr., 203, 205–
  206
Rockefeller, William, 19, 36, 119
Rockefeller, Andrews and Flagler
  (RAF), 18–19
  addition of Harkness money, 19,
    25
Rockefeller family, 203, 214
Rockefeller Foundation, 193–194,
  203, 214, 290–292
Rogers, Henry H., 67, 84, 119, 146
Roller-shade tabulations, 96, 195
Roosevelt, Franklin D., 233, 241,
  243, 286
Roosevelt, Theodore, 29, 121, 123,
  134–135, 144–145, 148
  determination to dissolve trusts,
    152, 169
Root, Joseph J., 332–333
Root, W. C., 358
Roper, Elmo, 258

St. Lawrence Seaway, 325
St. Louis Federal Circuit Court, 157
Salaries of executives, 95–96

Schoonmaker, Judge, 99
Scofield, Shurmer and Teagle, 56–57, 81
Scott, Thomas A., 19–20, 27, 37, 40–43, 57
    losses suffered in Pittsburgh rioting, 42–43
    South Improvement Company, 27–36
Securities and Exchange Commission, 289, 292
Seniority system, 296, 311
Sheridan, Penna., 129
Sherman Anti-Trust Act, 80, 87, 92, 112, 122, 155, 233
Shippers' Car Line Company, 197, 270–271
Shock Oil Company, 208–209
Sicardi, E. C., 174–176, 192–193, 196–197, 199–202, 206, 208, 211–217
Sinclair Oil Company, 208, 230–232
Skelly Oil Company, 230
Smith, A. E., 207, 218, 221, 230, 263, 333
Smith, Henry Knox, 145, 148–149, 150
Smith, Ray, 272
Smith, V. A., 358
Smith & Loveless, Inc., 316, 318, 357–358
Snubbers installed on cars, 253–254
Social Security, 335
South Improvement Company, 27–32, 43
    collapse of, 34, 68
Southern Pacific Railroad, 86–87, 124–127, 141–143
    deal with Union Tank Line, 329
Spanish-American War, 111, 121
Sparling Tank & Manufacturing Co., Ltd., 310
Special-purpose tank cars, 332
Specifications for tank cars, 190–191
    set by AAR and ICC, 300, 332–333, 348
Sproule, W., 329
Standard Oil Company, 355
    business principles, 88, 103–105
    capitalization, 25
    competition, 57
    (See also Competition)
    conspiracy between railroads and, 34–35, 70, 77–78, 112, 124
    corporate structure, 108
    dividends, 54
    economic advancement, 106
    efficiency of, 63

Standard Oil Company, Empire Transportation acquired by, 43
    executive team, 63–64
    Garfield investigation, 139–147
    government campaign against, 53–57, 77, 111, 148–159
    investigation of tank car shortages, 53–57
    loan to Pennsylvania Railroad, 43
    management policies, 63–64, 69, 88, 103–106
    marketing methods, 51
    monopolistic power, 156
    pipe line system, 34, 124
    price cutting, 39–41, 52–53
    profits, 99–100
    properties and holdings, 35
    public agitation against, 29–30, 70–72, 106–122, 258
    railroads, concessions by, 34–35, 70, 77–78, 112, 124
    reaction to government regulations, 87–88
    rebates paid to, 26–27, 43
    (See also Rebates)
    salaries of executives, 95–96
    system of intelligence, 69
    tank cars, leased from Union Tank Line, 83
        monopoly of, 46–47, 67, 124
    shipping methods, 51–52
    Tidewater pipe line acquired by, 63–64
    transportation advantage, 156
    Trust (see Standard Oil Trust)
    United Pipeline Company, 44–45
    Waters-Pierce Co. and, 107
Standard Oil Company of Indiana, 84–85, 96, 101, 124, 179, 202–207
    holdings of Rockefeller family, 203
    Landis decision, 149–150, 153
    stock prices, 159
    struggle for control, 220–221
    threat to break with UTC, 202–210
Standard Oil Company of Iowa, 85
Standard Oil Company of New Jersey, 83–84
    becomes holding company, 119
    capitalization, 94
    charter, 83, 92–93, 118–119
    component companies, 93, 95
    control over oil business, 122, 148, 156
    dissolution, 155–159
        effect on stock prices, 157–159
    Federal action against (1907), 155–157

Standard Oil Company of New
  Jersey, Felton made head of
  UTL, 136
government campaign to dissolve,
  148–159
net worth, 122
position of world leadership, 156
profit making, 151–152
UTL stock held by, 154
Standard Oil Company of New York,
  65, 67, 176, 196
Standard Oil Company of Ohio, 195
agreements with railroads, 34–35
boycott by producers' association,
  30–31
contempt proceedings, 118
court action against, 108–110, 122
divested of Union Tank Line, 83
expansion, 34–35, 62
founding of, 25–26
identification of tank cars, 60
monopoly charges, 82–83
pressure on competitors, 26
properties and holdings, 62
purchase of Star properties, 34, 37
smaller companies purchased by,
  25
in South Improvement Company,
  27–32
Standard Oil Trust, 49
attacks on, 80–83
charges of monopoly, 91–92
Congressional investigations, 80–
  85
control of the combine, 65
dissolution of, 92–93, 108–110,
  118–119, 155–157
Executive Committee, 95
home office, 94
Liquidating Trustees, 93–94
pipe line policy, 75–76
public suspicion increased, 67
reasons for forming, 64–67
state tax laws and, 64–66
Standard Steel Car Co., 194
Star Tank Line, 21–22, 33–34
purchased by Standard, 34, 37
State Legislatures, influence of
  Standard on, 53–55
litigation to break power of Standard, 146–147
shortages of tank cars reported to,
  46–47
Statistical methods, 318
Stewart, Col. Robert, 202–207, 211,
  215
Stickney, A. B., 101, 103, 131
Stock market, 17

Stock-purchase plans, 200–201
Stocks, common and preferred, 218–
  223
after dissolution of New Jersey
  Standard, 158–159
Union Tank Car Company, 158,
  189–190, 200, 274, 280
first public offering, 289
price (1959), 317
split, 291–292
used to acquire other companies,
  305
Stone, Chief Justice Harlan, 261
Storage tanks, 12, 45
Storage terminals, 325
Strikes, 71, 343–344, 357
Stubbs, J. C., 329
Subsidiaries of Union Tank Car, 358
Supreme Court appeals, 106–107,
  157, 260–261
Surplus tank cars, purchase of, 267–
  268
Surplus Property Administration,
  268
Symbol trains, World War II, 250–
  251

Taft, William Howard, 153, 157
Tank bands, 344–345
Tank Car Stabilization Committee,
  233
Tank Car Trust, 49–53
controlled by Standard, 56
legislative investigations, 53–55
method of financing, 49–50
method of operation, 50
mileage allowance, 50
Tank cars, assembly of, 272–274
calibrating, 130n, 330–331
capacities, 120
competition from Tidewater pipe
  line, 57–58
complexity of railroad rates, 56–
  57
Congressional investigations of
  monopolistic practices, 72–81
controlled by Rockefeller, 32
cost of, 173, 190, 278
depreciation allowance, 219–220
  (See also Depreciation policies)
design of, 127–129
development of, 12
dismantling of, 264–265
dome cars, 32–33, 347–348
Empire Transportation Company,
  21, 43, 60
  (See also Green Line cars)

Tank cars, empty mileage allowances, 74–75, 101–102
freight charges, 77–79
(See also Freight rates)
fusion-welded, 232n, 267
general-purpose, 331–332
gondola, 86–87
government regulation, 168–180
great squeeze, 45–61
heated, 130n, 330
Hot Dog, 299–301
(See also Hot Dog tank cars)
identification of, 60–61, 78
instrument of power, 34, 85
invention of, 12–13
leakage, 127–128
legislative investigations, 47–48, 53–55
life-expectancy figures, 265
LPG, 267–269, 273, 348
lumber carried on return trip, 86
mileage allowance, 55, 74–75
(See also Mileage allowances)
Mileage Equalization Rule, 104
number of, 25, 52, 189–190, 197, 222, 240, 263–264
Oil Tank Car Trust, 49
ownership of, 33, 55–56, 113
investigations of, 53–55
pressure cars, 188, 190, 267, 273, 276
privately owned, 33
RAF gains control of, 20–21
recording movement of, 96–97, 174–175, 195, 251
repainting of, 77–78
Rockefeller control of, 20–21, 26, 44
safer, need for, 129
shipping rates, 33
shortages of, 45–61
independents' use of barrels, 51–52
legislative investigations, 46–48, 53–57
Tank Car Trust, 53
size of, 300
special-purpose, 332
specifications, 173–174, 190–191
set by government, 332–333
Standard's monopoly of, 81, 112
Star Tank Line, 21–22
steel, 128–129
Tank Car Trust, 49–53
technological progress in design, 190–191
Union Tank Line (see Union Tank Line)

Tank cars, V-cars, 129, 155, 264, 345, 349
weight determination, 75, 113, 120
on oil products, 120
World War II, 240–254
X-cars, 130, 155
Z-cars, 264
Tank Cars–U.S., 358
Tank-head stress, 348–349, 350, 351
Tank trucks, 199–200
Tank wagons, 113, 199
Tanker fleets, 63
World War II, 244
Tarbell, Franklin, 133
Tarbell, Ida M., 133–134
Taxes and taxation, 16, 278
depreciation rate, 213–214
fast write-off, 279
Teamsters' objections to pipe line, 12
Teapot Dome Scandal, 204–206, 211, 221
Technical innovations, 299–301
Hot Dog car, 299–301
Texas, antitrust actions, 149
court action against Waters-Pierce Company, 107
inquisitory probes, 111
oil fields, 62, 169
Standard Oil Companies in, 154
Texas Oil Company, 209
Tidewater pipe line, 47–48, 63–64
advantage for independents, 57–58
common carrier, 47
Tilford, Wesley Hunt, 31, 34, 62, 72, 73, 75, 83, 84, 96, 101, 119, 124, 128, 131, 136–137, 146, 202, 312, 315
California tank car operations, 124–127, 142–143, 329
developed California market, 85–87
head of UTL, 84–85
resignation from UTL, 138
Titusville, drilling of first well, 4–5
Trade association of independent oil companies, 209
Training programs, UTC, 296
Transportation of oil, barges towed by steamboats, 8
controlled by Standard, 47
Pennsylvania oil fields, 6–15
pond freshets used for, 6–7
railroads enter the picture, 8–11
Rockefeller concentrated on tank cars, 22–23, 31–32, 44
by scows and flatboats, 6–9

Transportation of oil, by trucks, 234, 255–263, 342
  by water, 6–9, 140, 198–200, 234
  World War II, 240–254
Transportation Act, 188
Trucking industry, competition from, 234, 342
  monopoly on short hauls, 255–256
  threat to tank lines, 199–200
  UTC entry into, 255–263
  use in World War II, 244–245
Truman, Harry S., 286–287
Trust baiting, 123
Trusts, American sugar, 11
  dissolution of, 92
  status of, 49
  (See also Monopolies; Standard Oil Trust)
Turner, E. S., 256–257
Turpentine carried in tank cars, 75
Tweed, Boss, 30
26 Broadway, New York City, 119, 145, 163
Tycoons, 17, 27
Tyler, R. D., 358

Union Pacific Railroad, 86
Union Tank Car Company, acquisitions of 1957–58, 304–311
  Annual Reports, 317, 320
  board of directors, 193–194
  1962, 357–358
  Bulk Terminals Company, 325–326
  capital expenditures, 317
  captive of car builders, 270–272
  car records, 195
  competition, 278
  costs, 278
  decision to build and store cars, 194–195
  depreciation policy, earnings and, 359
  divisions and subsidiaries, 358
  during the depression, 227–232, 233–239
  earnings, 274, 308, 317
    depreciation policy and, 359
    1959, 357
    statements, 1959–60, 314
  entry into trucking business, 255–262
  Equipment Trust Notes, 195
  executive personnel, 192–201
  expansion policy, 280, 285–294
  fighting spirit, 239
  financial policies, 218–220, 285–294, 305

Union Tank Car Company, during the depression, 227–232
  purchase of company stock, 231–232
  financing new equipment, 190
  foreign affiliates, 356–358
  foreign trade, 314–315
  future outlook, 199–200, 262, 319
  Getz Bros. acquired by, 321–322, 358
  headquarters transferred to Chicago, 214–217
  Imperial Oil Company acquired, 281
  improvements in car construction, 190–191
  indebtedness, 305, 317
  Lang Company acquired, 309
  Lindsay Company acquired, 316
  Mechanical Department, 349–351
  name changed from Union Tank Line, 188–189
  net income, 279–280, 295, 314
    1959, 316–317
    1960, 320
  new office building in Chicago, 325
  number of cars, 189–190, 197, 222, 263–264
    to meet peak demands, 264
  officers of company, 357–358
  operating costs, 318
  oversupply of cars, 194–195
  Phoenix-Graver acquired, 305–307, 354–356
    establishing price for, 356
  pioneer in fusion welding, 232n, 332–333
  post–World War I, 194–195
  Products Tank Line subsidiary of, 210
  rate of growth, 197
  Refiners' Transport and Terminal Corporation acquired, 256–262
  revenue, 295
  size of fleet, 189–190, 197, 222, 263–265, 280
  Smith & Loveless acquired, 316
  solicitation of outside business, 207–209
  Sparling Tank Manufacturing Co. acquired, 310
  stock, 189–190, 193, 218–220, 221–223, 231, 280, 305
    public offering, 289
    split, 291–292
  stock-purchase plans, 200–201

Union Tank Car Company, taxes, 278
technical innovations, 299–301
Union Tank Line, 34, 60, 72, 78, 81, 91–105
accounting methods, 186
acquisition of companies, 228–230, 313
action of midwestern railroads against, 100–103
antitrust action by Texas, 149
capitalization, 122, 154
car records, 96–97, 174–175
Car Service, 96–97
chartered in New Jersey, 83–85
complexities of business, 144
construction program, 129–130, 163–164, 270–272
contract with refineries, 164–166
depreciation allowances, 99–100, 121, 137
description of, 95–97
dissolution of New Jersey Standard, 158
earnings, 188–189
elimination of profits from statement, 99–100
employees, 168
executive group, 174
expansion of fleet, 154–155
financial policy, 99–100, 137, 188–189
freight charges, 97
function of, 163
government investigations, 95, 97–99, 137, 141
Industrial Commission, 110–122
government regulation, 168–170
ICC seeks authority over, 141
lease agreement with Southern Pacific Railroad, 124–127
method of operation, 144
mileage allowance, 97, 101–102, 119–121
for empty cars, 101
(See also Mileage allowance)
Mileage Equalization Rule, 104
name changed to Union Tank Car Company, 188–189
(See also Union Tank Car Company)
need for new leadership, 135–138
number of cars owned, 112–113, 154–155, 163–164, 172
owned by Standard Oil of Ohio, 83
Page in charge, 127–129
per diem rental, 165–166

Union Tank Line, power exercised by, 97
profits, 97, 116–117, 121, 137, 189
investigations of, 143
recapitalization, 154
relations, customer, 166–167
with railroads, 100–105, 329
with refineries, 163–165
rental rates and loading charges, 171, 188
repair facilities, 97
salaries of executives, 117
stock, 158, 189–190
stockholders, 117
subsidiary of Standard of New Jersey, 83, 119, 142
symbol UTLX on railroad cars, 60–61, 78
tank cars (see Tank cars)
technological progress, 329–330
trucking subsidiary, 245–246
Waters-Pierce use of tank cars to pressure customers, 107
weight determination of oil products, 120
in World War I, 171–172
government control, 179–190
United Pipeline Company, 44, 45
United States, Commissioner of Corporations, 148, 329
Defense Transport Administration, 275–281
Department of Commerce and Labor, 135
Internal Revenue Bureau, 213–214
depreciation rate, 265–266
Office of Defense Transportation (ODT), 243
emergency program in World War II, 246–249
trucks given monopoly on short-hauls, 255–256
Supreme Court, 106–107, 157, 260–261
United States Industrial Alcohol Co., 176, 196
United States Steel Company, 152

V-cars, 129, 155, 264, 345, 349
Vanderbilt, Cornelius, 17, 27, 40
Vanderbilt, William, 35, 52–53, 55–57
Vandergrift, "Captain" Jacob Jay, 8–9, 21, 34
bulk boats built by, 8–9

Van Dyke, John W., 128–130, 155, 190, 330–331, 345
Van Dyke anchor, 130, 190
Van Gorkom, J. W., 357–358
Van Syckel, Samuel, 11–12

War Production Board, 286, 289
Ward, Artemus, 25
Water, industrial treatment of, 315–316, 355
"Water-compelled rates," 136, 140
Waters-Pierce Company, 149, 156
   court action against, 107, 122
Waterway transportation of oil, 6–9, 140, 198–200
   competition from, 234
Watson, Peter, 34
Wealth Against Commonwealth (Lloyd), 98, 133
Weight determination of tank cars, 75, 113, 120
Welding of tank cars, 232n, 332–333
West Coast markets, 85–87, 124–127

White, Chief Justice, 157
Whiting (Ind.) refinery, 101, 272
Whiting (Ind.) repair shops, 296, 350, 352
Wilson, Woodrow, 168, 179, 187
Wood River (Ill.) repair shop, 302–303
World War I, effect on private car lines, 170–171
   government control of railroads, 178–190
World War II tank car operations, 240–254
   ODT emergency program, 246–248
   all-out effort, 249–251
   equipment, 248–249
   leakage problems, 251–252
   repairs, 251–252

X-cars, 130, 155

Z-cars, 264
Zwiener, Kenneth V., 357

ABOUT THE AUTHOR

Albert Z. Carr's previous historical books include *Juggernaut*, a study of dictatorship, and *The Coming of War*, which deals with events of early American history. An economic consultant for a number of corporations, he served during World War II as assistant to the Chairman of the War Production Board, and subsequently as a member of the White House staff under Presidents Roosevelt and Truman. In these capacities, he was a member of missions to England, China, Japan, and other countries. Later, as a director of the Inter-Allied Reparation Agency, he worked on the postwar problem of German reparations. He also served as a consultant to President Truman during his celebrated 1948 campaign for reelection.

Leading magazines to which he has contributed articles include *Harper's, Life, Reader's Digest*, and *The New York Times Magazine;* and he has published numerous short stories under the name of A. H. Z. Carr, several of which have been made into motion pictures.

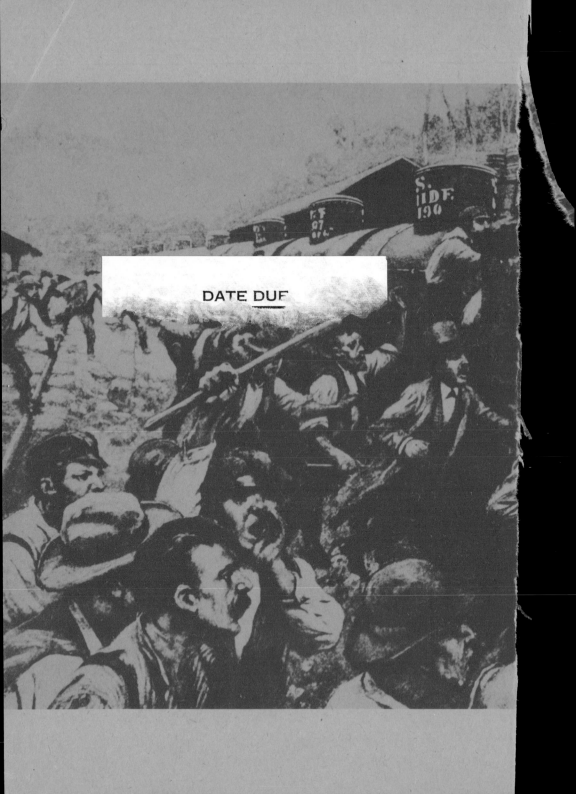
DATE DUE